Data Privacy Program Guide

How to Build a Privacy Program that Inspires Trust

David Goodman, Justine Phillips, Matt Stamper

Copyright © 2022 CISO DRG

Data Privacy Program Handbook
How to Build a Privacy Program that Inspires Trust

ALL RIGHTS RESERVED

No part of this book may be reproduced, stored in a retrieval system, or transmitted in any form, or by any means whether by electronic, mechanical, photocopy, recording or otherwise, without the prior written permission of the copyright owner except in the case of a brief quotation embodied in a critical review and certain other noncommercial uses permitted by copyright law. For all other uses, requests for permission may be sent to the publisher, "Attention: Permissions Coordinator," at the address below:

>CISO DRG Publishing
>P.O. Box 928115
>San Diego, CA 92192-8115
><www.CISODRG.com>
>info@cisodrg.com
>ISBN 978-1-955976-11-4

DISCLAIMER: The contents of this book and any additional comments are for informational purposes only and are not intended to be a substitute for professional advice. Your reliance on any information provided by the publisher, its affiliates, content providers, members, employees, or comment contributors is solely at your own risk. This publication is sold with the understanding that the publisher is not engaged in rendering professional services. If advice or other expert assistance is required, the services of a competent professional person should be sought.

To contact the authors, write the publisher at the address provided above, "Attention: Author Services."

>Edited by Bill Bonney
>Artwork by Gwendolyn Peres
>Copyediting by Nadine Bonney
>Production by Last Mile Publishing

Acknowledgments

Privacy as a profession is relatively new, and indeed, as we hope we convey in this book, there's vital work to be done as privacy leaders develop and oversee their organization's privacy programs. While many organizations are just now starting their privacy journey, the community of privacy professionals is highly collaborative and willing to share insights and best practices. In this spirit, the authors would like to extend their gratitude to their colleagues throughout the privacy profession. Our collective insights—granted from highly disparate perspectives—have benefited from the discussions, writings, and conferences that now more commonly speak to privacy as a unique corporate function. There is a willingness within this privacy community to lend a hand and share insights on particularly challenging privacy matters. We are indebted to our community.

Thank you to Mathew Chacko, Dr. Jörg Hladjk, Morgan Gower, Riccardo Mascucci, Marines Mercado, Toni Millican, Federico Mirri, Sandy Moul, Neha Parekh, Rebeca Perez-Serrano, Rebecca Perry, Mark Schultz, Rob Sloan, Chelsea Staskiewcz, and Hiroyuki Tanaka for your time to review and provide thoughtful feedback.

David, Justine, and Matt would also like to thank their spouses and families for their support and patience throughout the process of bringing this book to fruition. Books are never written in isolation and require dedicated time to distill thoughts into a coherent set of ideas. This requires time—time that would otherwise be spent with families and friends. Again, we are so thankful for their support and patience throughout this process. Our thanks also extend to Bill, Nadine, Chris, and Wendy, who helped bring this book to life with thoughtful stewardship, edits, and nudging.

Preface

David Goodman, Justine Phillips, and Matt Stamper have very different backgrounds but have each built very successful careers in and around the data privacy space. David's interest in privacy began early in his career when he was involved in developing and promoting directory services, realizing first-hand how closely enmeshed identity is with security and privacy/data protection concerns. Justine has focused her career on data privacy because, in her mind, privacy is the new human rights frontier. Matt was drawn to privacy because he believes that to really know a business, you must understand privacy and how that organization uses personal data.

This book came together through eighteen months of weekly Zoom meetings. And while many were driven into Zoom purgatory because of the raging pandemic that gripped the world between 2020 and 2022, our embrace of Zoom was a delight as it allowed Matt and Justine to collaborate with David (a resident of Scotland) who had a front row seat to the emergence of European Union (EU) privacy thinking and subsequent regulations, including the very influential General Data Protection Regulation (GDPR). Eighteen months was about twice as long as we expected the project to take, but events have conspired to place a greater burden on privacy and cybersecurity experts than ever before, causing team members to drop everything and help clients battle the latest breach. You benefit from this because the advice we provide in this book is truly battle-tested.

There is no better way to blend our varied perspectives than to use the tri-perspective technique that Matt helped pioneer along with Bill Bonney and Gary Hayslip, the three amigos that authored the CISO Desk Reference Guide and now publish the CISO DRG catalog. David, Justine, and Matt care deeply about our chosen field and our collective mission. We hope that providing our three perspectives over the following pages will provide you with helpful insights that you will find useful in your role as a privacy professional.

At the time of publication, two emerging developments in the U.S. may significantly impact the privacy space. The first development is the decision by the U.S. Supreme Court in the case of *Dobbs vs. Jackson Women's Health Org* that vacates the landmark *Roe v. Wade* decision from 1973, which holds that the federal government may not interfere or restrict a woman's right to choose to have an abortion. As Justine discusses in her essay for Chapter 1, "Why Privacy Matters to You," the court recognized a broad constitutional right of privacy with this decision. Unfortunately, we don't know at this time what the eventual impact will be on the real or inferred privacy protections illuminated by the *Roe v. Wade* decision.

The second development is that the U.S. Congress is considering the *American Data Privacy and Protection Act* (ADPPA) with bipartisan and bicameral support. ADPPA is a federal privacy bill that could elevate a multitude of privacy protections to a national level in the U.S., with the potential for both new requirements and requirements that could supersede various state protections. This potential bill, and others that didn't make it to this stage, have identified and, in many cases, fleshed out various provisions that may make it into a final bill if one does emerge. That being the case, we will try to address some of these issues in the appropriate chapters, understanding that nothing is set, and much could change.

One practical lesson from these developments is that privacy professionals must remain current. We've referenced many sources throughout this book, but one we would like to call out as especially useful to keep yourself current is the International Association of Privacy Professionals (IAPP – https://iapp.org). If you are not a member, consider it. If you are a member, we encourage you to take advantage of the education programs they provide.

Table of Contents

Preface i
Introduction iii
    How to Use this Book iv
In Pursuit of Privacy 1
    Why Privacy Matters 3
        Introduction 3
        Why Privacy Matters to Me ~ David 6
        Why Privacy Matters to You ~ Justine 13
        Why Privacy Matters to Us ~ Matt 23
        Key Insights and Recommended Next Steps 29
    Whole of Enterprise View 31
        Introduction 31
        Whole of Enterprise View ~ David 34
        Enterprise Risk Management ~ Justine 41
        Whole of Enterprise Impact ~ Matt 54
        Key Insights and Recommended Next Steps 64
Preparing the Program 67
    A Strong Foundation 69
    The Role of the Privacy Leader 71
        Introduction 71
        The Role of the DPO/CPO ~ David 73
        The Role of the Privacy Professional ~ Justine 79
        The Evolving and Expanding Role of the Chief Privacy Officer ~ Matt 84
        Key Insights and Recommended Next Steps 92
    Elements of a Privacy Program 95
        Introduction 95
        The Practical Details of Implementing a Privacy Program ~ David 97
        The Privacy Professional's Role in Building a Privacy Program ~ Justine 106
        How Privacy Programs Come Together ~ Matt 121

Key Insights and Recommended Next Steps	137
Privacy Technology	**139**
Introduction	139
Privacy and Technology – Justine	141
Protect and Preserve – David	150
Two Sides of the Privacy Technology Coin – Matt	158
Key Insights and Recommended Next Steps	167
Privacy Lifecycle	**169**
Introduction	169
Privacy Lifecycle—Driven by Context – David	171
Data Lifecycle – Justine	176
Privacy Lifecycle—A Helpful Construct – Matt	182
Key Insights and Recommended Next Steps	199
Global Privacy Regulations	**201**
Introduction	201
Global Privacy Regulations – David	203
How Global Privacy Regulations Come to Be – Justine	210
Clearing Up the Confusion about Global Privacy Regulations – Matt	219
Key Insights and Recommended Next Steps	228
Privacy by Design	**229**
Introduction	229
Privacy by Design – David, Justine, and Matt	231
How to Operationalize PbD	245

Risk Assessments 247

Shining a Light on Risk	249
Data Classification and Discovery	251
Introduction	251
Data Classification and Discovery—Essential to Data Governance – David	253
Data Classification—Name It to Tame It – Justine	258
Data Classification – Matt	268
Key Insights and Recommended Next Steps	276
Vendor Risk Management	279

Introduction 279
Vendor Risk Management—Protect Your Reputation - David 281
Vendor Risk Management—Shared Risk, Shared Accountability - Justine 285
Managing Vendor Risk - Matt 293
Key Insights and Recommended Next Steps 301

Reasonable Security 303
Introduction 303
Reasonable Security—Not Just the Minimum Required - David 305
Reasonable Security—What the Courts and Regulators Say - Justine 312
A Holistic Approach to Reasonable Security - Matt 326
Key Insights and Recommended Next Steps 341
Appendix to Chapter 11 – Security Question Checklists .. 342

Making It Happen 351
Prepare to Respond 353
Data Breach Response 355
Introduction 355
Breach Response - David 357
Preparing for Breach Response - Justine 364
Mitigating the Risks of Data Breaches - Matt 376
Key Insights and Recommended Next Steps 387

Handling Data Subject Requests 389
Introduction 389
Handling Data Subject Requests - David 391
Data Subject Access Requests - Matt 397
Privacy Rights Requests - Justine 405
Key Insights and Recommended Next Steps 425

Conclusion 427
Appendix to Data Program Privacy Guide 429
Disambiguation Guide 431
The GDPR and Its Terminology 437

Glossary of Terms and Acronyms 441
 Terms 441
  Acronyms 462
Security Policy – Bill Bonney 469
Index 477
 About the Authors 485

Introduction

The order of the essays within each chapter follows the arc of the authors' differing backgrounds and perspectives. David Goodman's essays lead off most chapters and provide a high-level view reflecting his background as a consultant and analyst in the areas of identity, cybersecurity, and privacy. For those who want to understand why we're covering a particular topic and how it might affect your firm, David's essays provide the perfect grounding. Justine Phillips' essays usually come next, and her perspective from her privacy practice at DLA Piper provides context that only someone guiding clients through the legal aspects of data breach preparedness and response can bring. Her review of regulations from a lawyer's perspective and her practical advice for preparing for and handling data breaches and privacy rights requests are invaluable. Finally, Matt Stamper's essays finish most chapters. His experience as a cybersecurity and privacy leader, analyst, and practitioner provides the deep technical context to help privacy professionals deep dive as needed. Taken together, the three perspectives provide unmatched insights for assessing or building your data privacy program.

It may be tempting as you start to get familiar with the writers' styles to skip ahead and read the next essay by your favorite author. We caution you to resist that as much as you can. Readers have shared that triangulating the essay topics from three perspectives, sometimes closely aligned, and sometimes highlighting very different points, is invaluable.

This is an action-oriented book. There are over 100 key points and recommended next steps. While there is no requirement to follow every recommendation at the end of every chapter, if you are wondering "now what," we've got you covered. There is nothing passive about data privacy. It is a full-contact team sport.

We've tried to limit the jargon as much as possible, but we recognize that any technical field will have jargon and technical concepts that are literally impossible to avoid if we do justice to the topic. We also recognize that this is an evolving field and that our viewpoints are in some cases quite different. We have therefore provided a glossary that will both define the technical terms we use in the book and provide a disambiguation reference to clear up any confusion we may cause in how we use various emerging terms.

How to Use this Book

We have organized the book into four sections. We start in Section One by making the case for privacy. Why privacy should matter to every citizen of the digital world, and why protecting every consumer or data subject's data is a whole of enterprise affair.

In Section Two we map out all the functions that make up the privacy ecosystem and provide the context you need to build and manage your privacy program. After defining the role of the privacy professional, we go deep into the privacy program, with chapters on the elements of the program, the role of technology, the privacy lifecycle, and global privacy regulations. We conclude Section Two with a consolidated piece on Privacy by Design.

In Section Three we address three fundamental risk assessments. We start with classifying the data you hold, then we dive into vendor risk management and finally, we look at the security program charged with protecting the data entrusted to you with an eye toward creating a defensible approach to "reasonable security."

After risk assessments, we transition in Section Four to what we call "Making It Happen." How your organization responds to data breaches and handles data subject access requests will determine the standing you maintain with regulators and the courts; and, more importantly, the trust you endow in your brand. Simply put, will your customers continue to trust you with their data and continue to do business with you?

Each chapter consists of five parts. First, there is an introduction that sets up the topic for that chapter. Then each of the three authors provides their unique perspective on the subject. Each chapter concludes with key insights and next steps.

We've tried to create a progressive set of steps you can take to build your program such that steps we recommend in Chapter 8, for example, regarding a RACI matrix, builds on that concept initially defined in Chapter 4. And in Chapter 3, we suggested you use the list of functional leads you identified in Chapter 2 to understand how data is collected and used.

Finally, the regulations governing data privacy and the privacy-enhancing technologies we recommended in this book continue to evolve. We've made every effort to provide the most current guidance, and to give you the tools to stay current, we've provided links and references in well over one hundred footnotes. We encourage you to bookmark the links relevant to you and consult these references as you keep your privacy program and your privacy expertise current. And now a note of caution. While we often cite case law for illustrative purposes, this book should not be considered an exhaustive treatment of any regulation nor a research tool for preparing legal guidance. The information we share in this book is intended to help you optimize the role of your data privacy program to inspire trust. It is impossible in one book to provide a complete data privacy legal reference and attempting to do so would obscure our mission.

Section 1

In Pursuit of Privacy

Chapter 1

Why Privacy Matters

Introduction

In the first section, "The Pursuit of Privacy," we examine why we value privacy as individuals and the value of a privacy program to your company. Although this book primarily focuses on building and managing privacy programs, we believe it is essential to make the case that a privacy program has value for companies because privacy has value to us as individuals.

As you read this first chapter, "Why Privacy Matters," we'd like you to be thinking about four concepts. The first is the rights that society has decided to bestow on individuals. These rights have evolved over millennia, starting with rights to protect one's physical well-being, property, and reputation from harms visited on them by their fellows. Over time, new constitutions eventually extended these rights to protect against harm that governments might visit upon their citizens. So, for example, instead of being protected only from assault and theft, people gained protections against searches, seizures, and improper imprisonment. Eventually, legislatures and courts extended these rights to individual autonomy. Now that we are firmly in the digital age, the rights of autonomy and protections against thefts and seizures are being extended into the digital realm.

The second concept we'd like you to think about is scale. The impact of scale often makes simple systems and simple problems very complex. For example, protecting oneself from harm that a single person might do might be challenging. Protecting oneself from harm that a mob could do is significantly more complex. Likewise, safeguarding sensitive information regarding one matter poses a very different set of challenges than safeguarding sensitive information regarding millions of individuals. This is made even more challenging when applying dozens of sometimes conflicting rules for safeguarding said information.

The third concept to consider is anonymity. Ask yourself what we gain with anonymity and what we give up for it. One thing we gain with anonymity is freedom from certain harms. People who value their privacy would consider being tracked without consent a harm. Two things we give up with anonymity is getting to know and getting to develop an understanding of the people remaining anonymous. And that brings us to the final concept, trust.

It is interesting to think about trust in value terms. How much would I value having you trust me? How much do I value trusting you? What does it cost me to establish your trust in me? What attributes do I require to place trust in you? How would you demonstrate those attributes in a way that is acceptable to me? Does each of us value that trust equally?

What follows are three essays that approach the question of why privacy matters from three different viewpoints.

David starts by bringing us along for a personal and professional journey. Anyone who grew up in a smaller community than they live in now will recognize the differing attitudes about privacy. It is instructive to see how David ties the commercial realm into his journey and then helps us explore the question of whether privacy should matter. His essay is "Why Privacy Matters to Me."

Justine unfolds for us some of the governmental privacy protections being established as a reaction to harms and potential harms, to address citizens' desires for greater protections, and to repair the erosion of trust between the public, governments, and corporations. She also helps us understand how the regulations are constructed to restore balance between the competing rights of different parties. Her essay is "Why Privacy Matters to You."

Matt examines the ways in which the consumer's rights of privacy are being tested by technology and the insatiable appetite that corporate interests and governments have for data about consumers and citizens; their buying habits, their movements and actions, their associations, both casual and commercial, and how the lack of understanding of the capabilities being brought to bear in the effort leaves people vulnerable. His essay is "Why Privacy Matters to Us."

Why Privacy Matters to Me ~ David

David Goodman

In the 1990s, I worked in the hot new areas of directory services, directory applications, and security starting at a university in London. Then, moving through a start-up in the U.S. to Lotus Development and its acquisition by IBM, I was back to a start-up in Europe. During that time, concepts around privacy were pretty hazy. The privacy laws that existed in most countries were of varying degrees of stringency and irregularly policed, except in extreme circumstances. The first European directive on data protection was published in 1995, when very few had any real idea of what the consequences might be twenty years later. After all, it was only a directive—not a regulation—which effectively meant that the Member States of the European Union were not strongly motivated to enforce it, through either a lack of a sense of urgency, trusted mandate, or budget. At that time, there was little personal data of any consequence available online. Still, corporations were far more concerned about letting information about their employees or their customer lists fall into the hands of potential competitors than they were about protecting any nebulous and ill-defined privacy rights.

By the turn of the millennium, corporate interest in directory services and associated applications had morphed into the broader concepts associated with identity management, such as the applications that could provision and deprovision employees and assign their roles and access rights. Consequently, IT departments started to be asked to investigate how corporate data information systems could be leveraged to manage access to company resources that were increasingly becoming accessible through published APIs. However, there was a conspicuous lack of awareness of any consequence of developing employee and later customer profiles—the much-sought-after holy grail was single sign-on.

During the course of the 2000s, I listened diligently to the emerging debates on privacy in the context of identity management and the nascent ideas around user-centric personal data management. Remarkably, at a time when Mark Zuckerberg was still trying to get a date at Harvard, one of the ideas that gained currency was whether privacy was even an issue. Even more remarkable, that notion has not completely gone away—in many situations the expediency of freely using personal data for business purposes still prevails—although it is now more easily contested in law.

Away From It All

After a lifetime of city living, one day seventeen years ago our family decided to up sticks and go and live on an island off the west coast of Scotland. We were drawn not only to the rugged brooding atmosphere of the mountains and the sea, but to the strong sense of community in a landscape that was otherwise deserted of human inhabitation.[1]

Formerly known as the Ardvasar Hotel, Isle of Skye, Scotland

The village we lived in had at best 100 inhabitants, as well as a pub, a village hall, and a shop, which was more than all the other hamlets

---

[1] Due to the Highland clearances, which decimated scores of villages when whole families made the treacherous journey to the New World in the 18th and 19th centuries to escape hardship and grinding poverty, the population in 1820 was almost double what it is today.

within a twenty-mile radius. Grainy photographs of the village from the 1890s do not look substantially different from ones taken today—not much changes in remote communities, except for the people and technology.

Now The Inn @ Aird a' Bhasair, nothing much has really changed in this Highland village over generations. Everyone still knows everyone else and their business.

Although I was connected through the internet to the wider corporate world of IT in North America, Europe, and beyond, my wife worked locally and the children went to the local schools—we were an integral part of a community where no-one locks their doors at night. During the course of any particular day, I would be confident of knowing everyone I met—they all knew me—we all knew each other. We shared varying degrees of trust, depending on where we were and what we were doing. My appearance and my age (with greater or lesser degrees of accuracy), where I lived, who my family were, who my friends were, and how I earned a living were common knowledge. I worked on the assumption that everyone in the village knew me and my business, even in some cases before I did. If I were to know something confidential about a person, I would take the trouble to ask their consent before sharing with anyone else—apart from being altruistic I would trust that person to apply the same principle with respect to me.

The trust that exists in the community is established on an unspoken, delicate balance that occasionally gets disrupted, but is by and large self-correcting. If questioned, most villagers would politely smile at the idea of having to protect their privacy from their neighbors: in a transparent society the risk assessment considerations associated with questions of privacy are considerably less than in a non-trusted environment. Being "public" is challenging at first, but, under the right circumstances, can ultimately be rewarding.

Crucially, small, isolated communities are circles of trust that instinctively seek to protect their ecosystems from harm.

A World Apart

In the city, we keep our doors locked. We may not know who our neighbors or our neighbors' neighbors are. On the internet, as the famous New Yorker cartoon illustrated,[2] nobody knows who we are—and we don't even have neighbors. The experience of open trust in a non-digital community could not be more diametrically different to that which has emerged globally in the last ten years, with almost universal access to the internet, on one or generally multiple devices, in most regions of the world. Even with the bare minimum of involvement in social media, there is a mountain of information about me available online. This information is enough to compile a highly detailed profile or dossier that would probably reveal aspects of my lifestyle preferences and behaviors—and history—that I might scarcely be conscious of myself. Individual pieces of that profile or digital identity might not be significant or of much interest and hold little intrinsic value. But, in a particular context or in combination with other pieces of my digital identity, a collection of specific data attributes and claims about me could be used by a bad actor, invariably anonymous, to cause me great financial or reputational harm. Even with the best of intentions, those organizations storing

---

[2] Peter Steiner's "On the internet no-one knows you're a dog" p.61, The New Yorker, July 5, 1993.

vast amounts of data might not have adequate protections in place to prevent sophisticated hackers and criminal organizations from getting access to everything there is to know about me or my company. The lack of protection is a global daily reality, both for individuals and corporations. Even before the internet, large corporations were not trustworthy data environments, and the internet has made them more vulnerable than ever.

Who Cares?

To the conundrum I raised earlier—does privacy, in fact, matter? Do individuals understand the ramifications of the experts' privacy concerns, particularly if there are no perceptible harms arising from sharing the details of their lives online? Corporations, seeking to understand how best to navigate the gulf between privacy regulations and many customers' apparent lack of privacy concerns, are understandably befuddled by this privacy paradox.

As one such individual, if I have nothing to hide, which I would like to believe I don't, why should I care, for example, if someone deduces how much I earned last year? Everyone has their tax record published in Scandinavia, and Scandic societies seem to manage just fine. As Amazon knows exactly what I have bought over the last five years including where I've casually browsed, it has a fairly intimate knowledge of my interests and needs. Generally, I am not remotely concerned that I am providing these insights into my purchasing habits. In fact, I am quite likely to consider Amazon, offering me all manner of recommendations, a benefit given how well it appears to know me. If asked whether they like having product recommendations rather than seeing them as being intrusive, the answer for most people, most of the time, would be a simple "yes—bring it on." It's as if your closest, best friend is looking over your shoulder—or simply another voice inside your head—advising you at every step of the way. What's not to like?

Ironically, many people, who are comfortable with ignoring or overlooking, when shown, what unseen things companies they transact with might be doing with their data, would just as easily express strong opinions in support of privacy protection principles.

The further irony is that individuals are consumed with a similar privacy paradox that is similar to one that afflicts the businesses they interact with.

Things

For many years, our relationship with the online world has been through a limited number of devices—a computer, a tablet, a smartphone—often with the keyboard as the primary interface. But that is already changing and will continue to evolve as we develop a more pervasive approach to people and "things," from device sensors to smart fridges to home control systems to autonomous automobiles—the list is potentially endless.

Many of us are already living in emerging smart cities. In this futuristic online world, there will be far more things than people that will know who we are and what we're doing at any time of the day or night. As they become increasingly internet-enabled, even our own homes will take on a variety of new non-human identities that will want to know something about us, our families, and our collective and individual lifestyles. These internet-enabled things could have the capacity to share elements of that information—what time we eat, go to bed, use the bathroom—with other things in the house and even beyond. The not-insignificant concern that the security of such things is not as standardized, regulated, or, speaking plainly, secure as we would like is not without foundation. Needless to say, these things and objects that make our lives more comfortable and convenient are not likely to be beholden to any privacy programs. It's particularly alarming personally to imagine what might happen in our homes, but the same transformation of "ordinary objects" into communication devices also applies to our offices and factories.

If we are, in effect, inviting into our homes and workplaces inanimate objects with the potential to store and disseminate personal data, somehow, we have to figure out how to establish trust relationships with them, and any associated unseen 'animate' controllers.

Privacy and Security

Ultimately, despite the plethora of new privacy and data protection regulations, there is still a lot of work to be done to re-calibrate identity and trust between people—and things. We must remove the current ambiguities and anomalies regarding what is private and invest in parallel efforts to shore up cybersecurity and minimize cyberattacks. The corporate world has to find the equivalents in the digital sphere to the trust, unspoken balances, and corrective actions that exist in small trust-based communities.

Come the day when we've got it all sorted, privacy concerns might no longer be an issue. Until then, privacy really does matter.

Why Privacy Matters to You ~ Justine

The Root of Privacy

Justine Phillips

I have always loved language, and throughout my career as a California attorney specializing in data, I have learned the importance of being precise with my use of words. Indeed, certain legal outcomes rest solely on the meaning of a single word in a contract or law. We freely use words we are taught by society that have some ascribed meaning—essentially a code that signals to other humans a particular feeling, action, or thought. I often look to the origins of words to explore and help tell a story about what specific words are intended to convey over time. Let us begin by talking about privacy.

Precise definitions of words help us decode their meaning and what they convey. For example, today, the English word *private* has several different meanings (synonyms include separated, apart, alone, and secluded) and is used both as an adjective and a noun. It can be traced back to its Latin roots, as a noun, *privus,* meaning "single, individual," thence a verb, *privare,* "to bereave or deprive," from which the past participle provides an adjective, *privatus,* meaning "withdrawn from public life," and hence its usage in late Middle English denoting "a person not acting in an official capacity," e.g., *in a private capacity*. Although the corresponding concept of *privacy,* "a state in which one is not observed or disturbed by other people," has been used in English for several centuries, its popular usage steadily grew during the second half of the 20th century. And since then, our understanding of *privacy* has rapidly evolved as an expression of how humans seek to withdraw from the public eye.

Privacy advocates have historically believed that the digital age presents an existential threat to individual privacy. The internet's interconnectedness with all things is at odds with the notion of being separate, apart, or secluded. Those beliefs ultimately led to various state laws and the creation of an inalienable right to privacy in certain state constitutions. The founding fathers of California's constitutional right to privacy (George Moscone and Kenneth Cory) argued that including privacy within the constitution was necessary to our freedom and independence. In other words, privacy matters because humans want the right to be left alone, including the data elements that identify them as individuals.

This section explains how privacy laws and regulations came about and why those frameworks define what is (and is not) private information.

What Are You Trying to Keep Private?

Why privacy matters depends on what you are trying to keep private. Individuals may want to safeguard their personal information so it does not get into the hands of somebody who will steal their identity.

Businesses may want to keep their trade secrets and confidential information private from their competitors. Governments try to safeguard classified data from nation-state adversaries. One common thread that weaves through all theories is that unintended disclosure of private information creates discomfort, risk, and liability.

The Privacy Revolution: Discomfort Perpetuates Change

During the 1970s in America, privacy was primarily regarded as a right to keep government out of an individual's private life. The United States Constitution's fourth Amendment protects Americans against "unreasonable search and seizure." As telecommunications emerged, the fourth amendment was applied to virtual searches and seizures like wiretapping and intercepting radio transmissions.

Public trust in the government was eroding, and invasive government surveillance dominated news headlines. In 1970, a former Army intelligence officer testified before Congress that the Army had conducted massive spying operations targeting protesters and political organizations and was even constructing a database to distribute this data across the intelligence community.[3] The Pentagon Papers were released in June 1971, and the New York Times reported military electronic snooping on private radio transmissions during the Republican National Convention.[4] In 1972, the Washington Post tied the Nixon administration to the bugging of phone lines at the Watergate Hotel.[5] The privacy movement was not limited to media outlets.

In 1973, the Supreme Court of the United States issued its landmark decision in *Roe v. Wade*, holding that the federal government may not interfere or restrict a woman's right to choose to have an abortion. There was nothing more fundamentally private than a woman's right in her own body to choose to be separate or secluded from the government in her decision to make choices about her own body. In its ruling, the court recognized for the first time that the constitutional right of privacy "is broad enough to encompass a woman's decision whether or not to terminate her pregnancy." (*Roe v. Wade* (1973))[6]

The scandals involving government spying and surveillance technologies coupled with a threat to individual freedom from government interference with one's body precipitated a turning point in privacy law. The people sought autonomy and separateness from government intrusion.

---

[3] *Ex-Officer Says Army Spies on Civilian Activists*, NY Times (Jan. 16, 1970) https://www.nytimes.com/1970/01/16/archives/exofficer-says-army-spies-on-civilian-activists-1000.html.

[4] Seymour M. Hersh, *Files Disclose More Army Snooping Under Johnson*, NY Times (Sept. 1, 1972) https://www.nytimes.com/1972/09/01/archives/files-disclose-more-army-snooping-under-johnson.html.

[5] See Carl Bernstein & Bob Woodward, *FBI Finds Nixon Aides Sabotaged Democrats*, The Wash. Post (Oct. 10, 1972) https://www.washingtonpost.com/politics/fbi-finds-nixon-aides-sabotaged-democrats/2012/06/06/gJQAoHIJJV_story.html.

[6] At the time of publication, the Supreme Court of the United States is considering *Dobbs vs. Jackson Women's Health Org.*, a case that may overturn *Roe v. Wade* which could impact whether the federal constitution offers privacy protections.

Birth of a Constitutional Right to Privacy

California is the birthplace of consumer privacy in the United States.[7] Although privacy is inferred in certain parts of the United States Constitution, it does not include an express right to privacy. Most Americans believe privacy matters and that privacy is a fundamental human right; however, only 11 states[8] expressly provide a constitutional right of privacy. California was the first. Behind every great law is a great story.

Moscone and Cory co-authored Proposition 7, a ballot initiative on the November 1972 ballot that proposed to amend the California Constitution to include "privacy" as an inalienable right listed in Article 1, Section 1 of the California Constitution. If you ever attended the RSA Conference at the Moscone Center, it was named after George Moscone—a trail-blazing lawyer who later became the mayor of San Francisco.

Before his assassination alongside Harvey Milk in 1978,[9] Moscone's proposal and the passage of Proposition 7 created a legal and enforceable right of privacy for every Californian that would have resounding implications for privacy laws worldwide.

---

[7] Privacy transcends all cultures and countries, but for purposes of my chapters, I write from the perspective of a privacy and cyber lawyer geographically situated in California. Although my chapters focus on American privacy laws and rights, they include offerings and lessons for global privacy programs.

[8] As of 2021, eleven states have explicit provisions relating to a right to privacy in their constitutions: Alaska, Arizona, California, Florida, Hawaii, Illinois, Louisiana, Montana, New Hampshire, South Carolina, and Washington. Additionally, Michigan and Missouri constitutions provide explicit protection from unreasonable searches and seizures of electronic communications or data. Privacy Protections in State Constitutions (ncsl.org).

[9] See *40 Years After The Assassination Of Harvey Milk, LGBTQ Candidates Find Success*, NPR (Nov. 27, 2018). https://www.npr.org/2018/11/27/670657965/40-years-after-the-assassination-of-harvey-milk-lgbt-candidates-find-success.

Why Privacy Matters 17

George Moscone in Columbus Day(?) Parade - Gary Stevens

Moscone and Cory prophetically articulated the dangers of data loss if we did not constitutionally recognize a fundamental and innate right to privacy:

> Each time we apply for a credit card or a life insurance policy, file a tax return, interview for a job, or get a drivers' license, a dossier is opened, and an informational profile is sketched. Modern technology is capable of monitoring, centralizing and computerizing this information which eliminates any possibility of individual privacy.[10]

This new right of privacy, when applied by courts, prevented the LAPD from placing officers disguised as students in classrooms at UCLA to eavesdrop on conversations.[11] The right has also founded the basis of consumer protection as we know it in the United States.

---

[10] Kenneth Cory & George Moscone, Argument in Favor of Proposition 11, 1972 California Ballot Pamphlet pp. 26–28.
[11] 13 Cal. 3d 757, 775 (1975) ("Several important points emerge from this election brochure 'argument,' a statement which represents, in essence, the only 'legislative history' of the constitutional amendment available to us. First, the

In large part, privacy mattered enough to Moscone and Cory to create a vehicle that allowed voters to amend the constitution because technology created more opportunities for personal information to get into the "wrong" hands. Nearly 50 years ago, Moscone and Cory cited the very issues that we deal with today:

- "government snooping" and the secret gathering of personal information;

- the overbroad collection and retention of unnecessary personal information by government and business interests;

- the improper use of information properly obtained for a specific purpose, for example, the use of it for another purpose or the disclosure of it to some third party; and,

- the lack of a reasonable check on the accuracy of existing records.

Reactive and Evolving Privacy Laws

When a community concludes that privacy matters, they enact laws to protect individual privacy interests. When California residents voted to adopt an inalienable constitutional right of privacy, it set the expectation that privacy is as fundamental and necessary to freedom as life, liberty, security, and happiness. Over time, the right to privacy has expanded to increase digital transparency about data collection efforts like "shining the light" on mandatory online privacy policies and requiring consumer notices of data breaches (2003), as well as public disclosures in some jurisdictions for companies that experience data breaches.

Privacy laws have exploded over the last several years, especially in California. Given that California was at the forefront of the internet's early adoption, it is not surprising that California was at the vanguard for laws that created a safeguard for misuse of online data. It is no coincidence that this explosion has taken place amidst the

statement identifies the principal 'mischiefs' at which the amendment is directed").

controversy involving artificial intelligence, data scraping, data analytics, and online behavior analysis. There is often fear in the unknown, and data collection/use/sharing practices were enigmatic for many years. In the last ten years, headlines have been riddled with stories of data breaches, sharing and analytics of data to influence human behavior, and increased discomfort and distrust around privacy. Laws and regulations, by their nature, are reactive. As the veil was pulled back on privacy and security practices, California responded with reactive and sweeping laws.

- In 2003, California began requiring businesses and government agencies to notify California residents when they experience a breach of residents' personal information.

- In 2008, California added medical and health insurance language to the breach notification law's definition of personal information in light of increased medical identity theft and its health consequences for California residents.

- Since 2012, businesses and government agencies have been required to notify the Attorney General of breaches affecting more than 500 California residents.

- In 2013, the law was amended to include a username or email address, in combination with a password or security question and answer, due to criminal organizations hacking more online accounts. For example, right before this amendment, Yahoo suffered a breach of billions of usernames and passwords but was not legally required to give notice.

- In 2015, data from automated license plate reader systems were added to the definition because of the sensitive location information associated with that data.

- In 2018, the California Consumer Privacy Act (CCPA) was quickly passed into law after the Cambridge Analytica scandal opened the public's eyes to the types of data analytics being conducted, which arguably influenced the 2016 presidential election.

- In 2020, California residents again voted on a Proposition addressing privacy rights and passed the California Privacy Rights Act (CPRA) after the original authors of CCPA believed legislative amendments had weakened CCPA.

Privacy Is a Balancing Act

Although privacy matters, the right is not absolute. Like many legal tests, privacy is a balancing act. For example, as the U.S. Supreme Court articulated in *Roe v. Wade*, "The right of personal privacy includes the abortion decision, but this right is not unqualified and must be considered against important state interests in regulation" (*Roe v. Wade* (1973)).

Envision Lady Justice blindly balancing her scales of justice. As compelling needs to access private information increase, privacy protections and rights decrease. When compelling needs go down, privacy protections and rights go back up. This teetering and balancing is a dynamic and fluid analysis that is constantly changing based on the totality of circumstances. In litigation, parties must disclose private and sometimes privileged information if a legitimate and compelling need overrides the right to privacy. For example, medical records are considered among an individual's most sacred and private data. Yet if an individual sues a person or business and alleges physical or mental injuries/damages, then medical records relevant to those claims may be discoverable, and the defendant(s) can subpoena the records from plaintiff's doctors and healthcare providers. Similarly, testing urine, blood, or hair for evidence of drug use is not permitted under normal circumstances. However, a person on probation has decreased privacy rights due to the state's compelling interest in validating compliance with the conditions of the person's probation in order to reduce recidivism.

The 2020 global pandemic exemplified the rise and fall of individuals' right to privacy in their own bodies. Given the existential threat to human safety presented by the coronavirus, businesses' interest in worker and public safety reached an all-time high. As a result, some government agencies, like the Equal Employment Opportunity Commission (EEOC), which interpret federal laws and protect employees' rights to privacy, issued guidance that temporarily relaxed their guidelines on employee privacy to allow businesses to maintain a safe work environment during the pandemic.

Federal laws in the United States generally prohibit employers from compelling workers to submit to medical examinations that are not "job-related and consistent with business necessity" 29 CFR § 1630.14(c). For example, temperature checks are considered a medical test, and employers are typically not allowed to monitor and collect such data. However, in 2020, the EEOC and state regulators declared that employers may lawfully test employees for COVID-19 infections via temperature checks, health screenings, or COVID-19 tests to determine whether the employee presented a direct threat to workplace safety. At the same time, the EEOC forbade the administration of COVID-19 antibody tests. The Commission stated that the antibody test is not "job-related and consistent with business necessity." Foremost, antibody tests provide little value to employers to determine whether their employees pose an actual threat to the workplace. Second, COVID-19 antibody tests are more invasive because they require blood samples. Third, they are not always reliable and consistent. In light of these facts, the EEOC permitted employers to test an employee for an active infection but prohibited employers from testing for previous infections.

COVID-19 testing illustrates the fine line between businesses' compelling need to maintain safe workplaces and employees' privacy rights that ought to be protected by federal and state laws. This "scales of justice" approach to privacy is consistent with the original intent to include a constitutional right of privacy under California law: "the amendment does not purport to prohibit all incursion into individual privacy but rather that any such intervention must be justified by a compelling interest."[12]

---

[12] *White v. Davis*, 13 Cal. 3d 757, 775 (1975). California Supreme Court's first decision interpreting Proposition 11, where the court applied a compelling interest test to a privacy violation by law enforcement surveillance on university campuses.

Why Privacy Matters to You

Privacy is the new human rights frontier—which attracts many of us to this industry. Privacy professionals face tremendous challenges in creating new boundaries for businesses. Often with little budget, scarce resources, and small teams, privacy professionals must navigate exponential growth in data, complex legal obligations, and tremendous supply chain risk. You may feel like Sisyphus pushing your rock up the mountain, only to have it roll down so you can push it back up again. The threshold question for the individual managing privacy issues is why privacy matters to you. Your answer to that question will help build the foundation for your privacy program. Perhaps, more importantly, the answer will keep you grounded in times when you may feel separate, apart, and secluded.

Why Privacy Matters to Us ~ Matt

Matt Stamper

Few topics have become so integral to our society and our organizations as privacy. Seemingly overnight, the topic of privacy has risen to be a concern for executive leadership teams and boards of directors alike. Of course, the ascent of privacy's importance has not been overnight. Media focuses attention on organizations such as Facebook (now Meta). Governments have enacted comprehensive privacy regulations, including the European Union's (EU's) General Data Protection Regulation (GDPR). These developments, along with the pervasive use of new technology that enables facial recognition and the re-identification of de-identified personal data using machine learning algorithms highlight the many reasons why the topic of privacy warrants our attention. This focus bridges our professional and personal lives. Personally, our data is a currency traded in both legitimate and nefarious circles for the benefit of others. Professionally, our jobs require that we understand the multitudinous areas where privacy practices impact our organizations (the topic of our next chapter). As individuals, we either benefit from or are the victim of the privacy programs and practices of the organizations with whom we interact. The importance of this dual context cannot be overstated.

Privacy matters. Privacy impacts our daily lives in ways we may not see overtly. Still, privacy plays a pervasive role in all aspects of our lives and society, both professionally and personally. Notably, privacy is foundational to engendering trust. Without the confidence that our personal lives and the personal data about our lives are kept confidential when we want them to remain confidential, how we interact with one another, and the economic impact of these interactions is shaken. Stephen Knack, who served as a senior economist at the World Bank before his untimely death, highlighted how integral trust is to our economies. Knack famously noted that "If you take a broad enough definition of trust, then it would explain basically all the difference between the per capita income of the United States and Somalia."[13] Trust underpins our modern economy and our modern society. This trust, however, is being assaulted. Daily, we hear of another data breach or organizations using the data we entrusted with them in ways we did not authorize nor anticipate.

The role of privacy in our economic life is changing dramatically. With most of us having a pervasive digital presence, our ability to maintain private personal lives is questionable.[14] In the U.S. and elsewhere, personal data is frequently treated as a commodity to be monetized and freely traded rather than protected and used according to the individual's preferences. The landmark California Consumer Privacy Act (CCPA) now requires that organizations that collect personal data on California residents indicate the types of data collected, its sources, and whether it is sold or shared with third parties. Like the GDPR, the CCPA establishes notable privacy rights for consumers. This is a positive first step to reclaiming the right to privacy over our personal data. But we still face many obstacles in keeping our personal data private or used only according to our stated preferences.[15]

The lines between public and "private" spaces are blurring. Not long ago, concerns related to privacy at home were minimal, primarily focused on shredding those documents we didn't want dumpster divers to find, adding our names to do not call lists, and opting out

---

[13] Stephen Knack's quote appears in a previous article in Forbes (https://www.forbes.com/2006/09/22/trust-economy-markets-tech_cx_th_06trust_0925harford.html#6e80823e2e13). His writings on trust economics are worth a read for those interested in how trust drives economic growth.

[14] Think about all the devices that have access to your personal data, "smart" TVs, mobile phones, appliances, the social media platforms we use—Instagram, Tik Tok, WeChat, and the like—to the global positioning system (GPS) coordinates that are frequently embedded in the pictures we take with our smartphones.

[15] When there were efforts to allow internet service providers (ISPs) to sell browsing history, I was interviewed by a national newspaper doing a story on how virtual private networks (VPNs) could be used to "ensure" privacy. I remembered thinking to myself that if privacy was contingent upon my mom learning how to use a VPN, privacy is doomed.

of junk mail. Today, our homes are filled with devices that listen to our conversations, waiting for a query to interject and offer assistance. We certainly welcome the convenience that these voice-activated tools offer ("Alexa," "OK Google," and "Hey Siri"). However, we may not be fully aware of how these smart devices and smart speakers encroach upon and listen to private conversations. The case with Samsung's SmartTV highlights this well.[16] I'm bringing in these personal examples to highlight an important dynamic that is shared with cybersecurity. Security awareness training at work has become more effective when the impacts of security issues and data breaches can be related to corporate context and at a personal level. We're the victims as much as the company that had its security controls bypassed. So too are the privacy impacts with consumer-oriented services and technology. Take pause and consider "why privacy matters" for not only your organization, but also for how it impacts your personal life and the lives of your family, friends, and colleagues.

Our privacy in public spaces is also under assault. The reality is that our ability to absent ourselves from public scrutiny and minimize our digital footprint requires significant effort. Public spaces, including restaurants, parks, venues such as stadiums, and city streets, are filled with webcams and other devices to monitor activity. These cameras have proven remarkably useful in solving crimes, including the notable instance of the Tsarnaev brothers, who were quickly identified using an amalgam of video clips around the site of the Boston Marathon bombings. Those same cameras also capture intimate moments of ordinary individuals walking down the street with friends. Daily we see crime videos, fights on campuses, and rude behavior captured on mobile phones and uploaded to popular sites such as YouTube. Open-Source Intelligence (OSINT) expert Michael Bazzell's most recent book—*Extreme Privacy: What it Takes to Disappear*—comes in at over 550 pages. Keeping private is not for the faint of heart.

---

[16] Here's an interesting recap:
https://money.cnn.com/2015/02/09/technology/security/samsung-smart-tv-privacy/index.html.

Law enforcement and intelligence agencies' extensive use of surveillance techniques cuts both ways. Individuals who serve in law enforcement are frequently "doxed." Indeed, a good friend of mine who works in law enforcement is concerned that his personal, private information (including his unlisted phone number, address, and details about his family) will be exposed, placing them at risk. The same OSINT techniques that Bazzell writes about and that are used to find domestic violence offenders, human traffickers, terrorists, and criminals are frequently reversed and used on law enforcement and innocent victims, frequently to deadly effect. Victims of domestic violence who are trying to build new lives and escape their perpetrators are frequently discovered after the posting of some seemingly innocent picture to a social media site by a friend who does not recognize that the photo's embedded metadata contains the GPS coordinates where the victim can be discovered. Anyone who works for a battered women's shelter trying to help the victims of domestic violence knows that privacy can be a life and death matter.

Social media and privacy are antithetical. Users unknowingly abandon their privacy in the daily flurry of social media posts, not recognizing the long-term consequences of photos shared with friends. These posts can have a legacy they may not anticipate. There are also generational aspects as to how we view privacy. Although we're wary of generalizations, younger generations do seem to act as if privacy is a given while it clearly is not. Older generations often act as if privacy is not possible when some privacy clearly is, if one if willing to put in the work. Though we can't lay all societal grievances with social media at privacy's door, sexting, body shaming, and cyber-bullying are all examples of social media abuse made far worse by the simple sleuthing that makes it easy to tie an online profile to a real-world person.

Technology's impact on privacy cannot be overstated. The Chinese government's use of high-fidelity facial recognition software is employed to identify and target protestors in Hong Kong and other locations throughout mainland China. In Zhejiang province, facial recognition software is used to track the behavior and attendance of students in high school.[17] Concerns with how facial recognition software could be used led Washington State to enact SB 6280, which is the first legislation aimed at controlling and regulating facial recognition applications. Concerns have also been raised by the inherent biases introduced into the algorithms employed by facial recognition applications.

Illinois' Biometric Information Protection Act (BIPA) highlights the dynamics of using biometric information to support authentication mechanisms for various transactions. The Act importantly highlights that 'biometrics are unlike other unique identifiers.'[18] I can change my password— I cannot realistically change my fingerprint or retina. If these biometric identifiers are compromised, the victim doesn't have any recourse and is subject to heightened risks of identity theft.

Other widely available technologies also have the effect of exposing personal data in ways we may not fully anticipate as consumers. Searches in Google lead to highly targeted ads across multiple platforms and other websites. It never ceases to amaze me that a quick search in Google results in ads seen on LinkedIn and other websites. From cookies to site preferences to devices that know our locations, we are always exposed. Our privacy is never really protected unless we take overt, proactive measures to minimize our digital footprint.

Even when we take active measures to control how our personal data is being used, machine learning algorithms can readily de-anonymize personal data to the extent that the individual is identifiable. The re-identification of personal data is a core concern of the GDPR and one of the reasons data scientists have developed measures to determine the likelihood of re-identifying personal data with approaches such as k-anonymity.[19]

---

[17] The Technology That's Turning Heads, Sintia Radu, US News & World Report, available here: https://www.usnews.com/news/best-countries/articles/2019-07-26/growing-number-of-countries-employing-facial-recognition-technology.

[18] Biometric Information Privacy Act 740 Section 5 (c): https://www.ilga.gov/legislation/ilcs/ilcs3.asp?ActID=3004&ChapterID=57.

[19] Latanya Sweeney. 2002. k-anonymity: a model for protecting privacy. Int. J. Uncertain. Fuzziness Knowl. Based Syst. 10, 5.

We are only now beginning to see the unintended consequences of an always-on, connected life. We feel a certain creepiness when we start to discover that items we thought were private, are just a few clicks away with a search engine. In the classic *Schneier on Security*, Bruce Schneier notes, "If we ignore the problem and leave it to the 'market,' we'll all find that we have almost no privacy left." How our organizations balance the needs to protect the personal data they collect, provide tailored services, and comply with myriad privacy regulations requires a concerted, whole of enterprise view of privacy. This context is necessary to ensure that the privacy programs we implement for our organizations reflect the data subject's or consumer's preferences and consent while not stymieing growth and innovation. How we manage these potentially competing priorities is ultimately how our privacy programs will be judged. The personal impacts to our privacy conveyed in this chapter are there to highlight that our privacy programs are not just corporate affairs—they have real consequences to the individuals who interact with our organizations. As privacy leaders, it's incumbent on us to keep these dynamics front and center.

Organizations that lean into the expanding debate on privacy and work to deliver services in a manner consistent with the consumer's preferences engender trust. As Stephen Knack's research notes, the value of this trust cannot be underestimated. Avoiding the proverbial "unfair and deceptive trade practices" builds trust. Engaging the consumer or data subject and empowering and informing them to take meaningful actions consistent with their privacy rights are at the heart of privacy programs that build enterprise value.

Key Insights and Recommended Next Steps

Key Insights

- There are many online consumers that form, in numerical terms, a much larger community than even the largest cities. Ironically, because of advances in communications technology, we have far less anonymity online than living in New York, Tokyo, or Berlin before the digital age began.
- Trust is the foundation of commerce and community. Privacy is foundational for trust and autonomy.
- Without strong mechanisms to support privacy, trust erodes, and commerce, community, and autonomy suffer.
- Although we started conceiving of online privacy protections in the 1970s, even by the 1990s privacy regulations were still not well-formed. It is no wonder, because we did not yet know what was waiting for us as we moved our lives online.
- The advances in regulations to protect privacy over the last two decades stem from the dual recognition that (1) substantial harm is being done to consumers because of the unchecked collection and exploitation of data about them and (2) consumers (or citizens, residents, people) should have certain rights of autonomy over data about them.

Recommended Next Steps

- Develop empathy for your customer. Create a profile of your average customer based on what you know about them via the data you collect, and list the privacy concerns this customer might have. Would you feel comfortable with how your organization uses this data if it were collected about you?
- Establish for yourself, as a privacy leader, a set of principles that address protecting your company from running afoul of privacy regulations and advocating for your customers' privacy rights. Do these principles engender trust?

Chapter 2

Whole of Enterprise View

Introduction

The volume of information flow is another way of looking at scale. When we were building the first connected systems, we described "internet scale" as the ability to process transactions at a rate of two or more orders of magnitude greater than unconnected systems could handle. That means 100, 1,000, or 10,000 times the number of transactions. But that's when we had only millions of systems connected. We now have tens of billions of systems connected. Transactions for a single household come from TVs, phones, tablets, PCs, smart speakers, and other devices. These transactions create history. We don't just record the purchase amount and payment method used, but also device information, location, buyer, item purchased, and all the defining attributes of these pieces of data.

The temptation to mine this data for descriptive and predictive patterns has proved irresistible. But purchases are not the only transactions that take place. People have conversations online, search for information, and browse news sources. People also use social media. Sometimes to do all the transactions we just listed, and sometimes to create new content, some benign, indeed, banal. And some controversial. And still, there is more. People move about. People are in different places as they generate the data that forms their history. The location of each transaction becomes another defining attribute, and we've mined that too; movement itself becomes data.

Historically, data mining was done mostly without consent because consent was not required. Few merchants sought consent from the data subject. Few marketers sought consent from governing bodies. Few data processors sought the consent of the information collectors to use the data differently than was initially contracted. Yet these activities took place, and in most places, still do.

In Chapter 1 we discuss the privacy paradox, which refers to people who said they cared how data about them was used but acquiesced to various types of mistreatments when presented with a convenience or a discount. We also recount some examples of government surveillance that, once uncovered, left us chilled and motivated to effect change. Add to that what has been collected and mined from the transactions listed above, and it's no wonder that legislatures and government agencies are putting in place much more robust regulations to address online privacy. In fact, new regulations are so robust that they require the whole enterprise to address them appropriately.

In "Whole of Enterprise," we make the case that the privacy program is the province of the entire organization—a whole of enterprise affair.

David will start by extending the discussion about trust in his essay "Whole of Enterprise View." The new legislative measures are focused on re-establishing the trust that has been lost because corporations have not always properly managed the data they've collected. However, it will take the whole enterprise to rebuild that trust, regardless of whether it was broken because data was used differently than the subject understood or carelessly handled.

Justine then focuses on the risks that organizations assume when they collect and process consumer data in her essay "Enterprise Risk Management." She looks at the types of risks organizations deal with and how several regulatory bodies get involved in assessing and policing how companies address the risks. She concludes by showing examples of how to identify these risks, how to quantify the risks, and finally, how to manage the risks.

Then Matt, in his essay "Whole of Enterprise Impact," takes us on a tour through an organization and examines each department with two different lenses that show how their activities can expose the organization to privacy risks. The first lens looks at the ingestion, classification, storage, and manipulation of personal data, and the second lens is the processing of privacy-related data. While these are by no means the only way privacy risks manifest, these are handy lenses for demonstrating that the whole enterprise is part of your privacy ecosystem.

Whole of Enterprise View ~ David

For corporations large and small, privacy is not only about ensuring "just enough" compliance with the relevant privacy regulations; it's just as much about showing respect for customer and employee data and establishing relationships built on mutual trust. This trust can only be achieved when the whole enterprise, from top to bottom, is engaged in transforming old business models and re-orienting attitudes to capturing, storing, and managing personal data. Taking this approach is not without cost, but the benefits massively outweigh the disruption.

Trust Lost

The new legislative measures appearing in multiple jurisdictions are already having a significant impact on businesses that hold data about their customers—and increasingly, their employees too. The fines and the public shaming for non-compliance or breach are not, as perhaps first thought, red tape for red tape purposes, nor business costs with no commercial objective. On the contrary, one of the key underlying objectives of much of the new legislation is to increase customer trust in digital services and thus accelerate technology adoption with all its associated efficiency savings and economic upsides. It is also a mechanism for harmonizing data management laws for businesses, simultaneously reducing potential legal costs and facilitating greater customer engagement opportunities.

In the not-too-distant past, public shaming was considered a very effective motivator for corporations to get their house in order. "Staying out of the headline news" and avoiding the PR nightmare of having to restore belief in hard-fought brand recognition should have prevented many of the disasters that occurred. But, as with other types of recurring disaster scenarios, businesses survived to tell the tale after a brief and painful stutter. The resultant "data breach fatigue" has not diminished the damage potential and the loss of customer confidence. Still, both tend to be seen as temporary inconveniences for a dedicated team of staffers to clean up. Based on the reasonable assumption that a major corporation will recover and "do the right thing" whatever that might be, many customers are more than likely to stick with the devil they know rather than go to the trouble of searching out alternatives. Even though this, perhaps cynical, perspective might encourage some companies to do the very minimum in terms of privacy protection, it would be a high-risk strategy—the tide of public opinion could so easily turn again.

Customer trust is usually taken to be a function of marketing or sales, or even of the IT department if digital trust is seen through the lens of data security. Although ironically, it would be unusual to find qualified or quantified criteria for customer trust in any corporate job description. And how often do human resources departments assume that employees show up every day believing the company they work for is beyond reproach. Unfortunately, this inattention leads to the situation whereby customer data is inadequately protected and used or shared inappropriately for purposes other than those that the individual originally understood or agreed to.

The Verizon 2021 Data Breach Investigations Report[20] suggests that insiders are responsible for around 22% of security incidents, and it would appear that between 2018 and 2020, the frequency of incidents involving insider threats increased by 47%.[21] The worst insider threats come from those employees with malicious or mischievous intent.

According to Herbert Stapleton, deputy assistant director in the FBI's Cyber Division, "Most internal actors are motivated by greed—they're trying to cash in on the data they steal. A much smaller percentage are in it for the laughs. Fewer still are holding a grudge against their employer. And finally, we get to those who are doing this to start a competing business or benefit their next employer."[22]

---

[20] Verizon 2021 Breach Report available here: https://enterprise.verizon.com/resources/reports/2021/2021-data-breach-investigations-report.pdf.

[21] Insider Threat Statistics You Should Know: Updated 2022 By Maddie Rosenthal, https://www.tessian.com/blog/insider-threat-statistics/.

[22] Data Breach Report Emphasizes Cybersecurity's Human Element

This observation speaks to what is largely, but not entirely, a culture problem. Some behaviors can be addressed by training and education to reinforce better attitudes towards the company; whereas more malevolent, ingrained behaviors may be harder to detect and require "informed" vigilance by line managers, fellow colleagues and the HR department. On the other hand, a common cause of data loss is accidental, often due, for example, to employee carelessness in managing sensitive data or simply sending wrongly addressed emails—problems that can partly be tackled with better security awareness training.

Trust in digital services, particularly those provided by governments, decreases year on year. According to one 2021 report, the "informed public" surveyed trusted three out of four institutions, whereas the "mass population" surveyed trusted none—a trust gap that increased from the previous year. Consumers who consider their data misused when it transpires that information shared was used for undisclosed purposes, such as being sold to third parties, could simply turn around and say, "I don't trust you anymore."[23]

Privacy legislation is a re-balancing of rights and powers between individuals and data processing organizations. If a company abuses or misuses trust in the way that it processes consumer data, then consumers and other data subjects have new rights. They can sue or even seek class-action lawsuits. Companies that don't respond rapidly will find themselves left behind by competitors who do; or hit with fines or lawsuits large enough to destroy their business (although some companies robust enough to absorb hefty fines see that as the cost of doing business). Reluctant personal data sharers,[24] who ideally would prefer not to share their personal details but feel compelled to

---

By Drew Robb https://www.shrm.org/resourcesandtools/hr-topics/technology/pages/data-breach-report-emphasizes-cybersecurity-human-element.aspx.

[23] The 2021 Edelman Trust Barometer https://www.edelman.com/sites/g/files/aatuss191/files/2021-03/2021%20Edelman%20Trust%20Barometer.pdf.

[24] A term first used in the MEF's Global Consumer Trust Report 2016 http://www.mobileecosystemforum.com/wp-content/uploads/2016/01/CTR16_Executive_Summary.pdf.

do so to gain access to a service or product, are potential prospects for companies that decide to embrace the intent of privacy legislation as a business opportunity.

It's a challenge for any business to keep up with new jurisdiction-specific legislation even if they recognize what is potentially at stake. However, every business can grasp the importance of having a set of guiding principles, and this is just a new set to comprehend and inculcate into the company culture. The management of the privacy challenge belongs to the whole enterprise: it starts with the executive leadership, embracing, in turn, the CISO and the DPO, as well as marketing, sales, and IT.

How customer data is managed can either contribute business benefits, or, if not dealt with properly, can be a toxic issue that requires expensive attention to remedy. Effective leadership maximizes the former and minimizes the latter.

The Privacy Principles

Consumers want to assert their privacy rights but are prepared to choose convenience over validated, trustworthy service. The "privacy paradox" occurs when the reluctant personal data sharers say that they care deeply about who has their data and what they are doing with it, but rarely if ever bother to read a company's privacy policy or take the time to understand what they're giving away in return for accessing an online service.[25] But, as a result of media reports on data breaches and increasing insights into the consequences of privacy or data loss, consumers are often more conservative than they ought to be about online transactions. Digital business is undoubtedly growing, but there is untapped growth potential in a trustworthy digital engagement model. More commerce could be done or done more cost-effectively if people had more trust in how their data is being used—or perhaps were simply more reliably informed.

---

[25] The term was first coined in this context by Susan Barnes and has been the subject of numerous academic articles since. Barnes, S. B. (2006). A privacy paradox: Social networking in the United States. *First Monday, 11*(9). http://dx.doi.org/10.5210/fm.v11i9.1394.

Privacy in a digital context is hard to define. Additionally, what is considered private by one person may not be by another. Culture, nationhood, upbringing, religion, morals, ethics, education, age, and more alter every person's response to what may be considered private and vary depending on context.

Socially, trust is a confident expectation that sharing data will not lead to the exploitation of vulnerabilities. A digital business relationship is that and more: the exchange of personal data is a value proposition that should be fair and equitable.

Making companies accountable to their customers and employees for the use, care, and protection of their personal data is a major focus of the new legislation. In addition, the rights individuals have over the access to and use of their personal data serve to demonstrate how a re-balancing of empowerment between businesses and their customers is taking place.

Most of these rights place a burden on the business to administer, but negligence is seen to be impactful. Customers can demand to have their personal data removed from your systems and take their identity profile, future transactions, and preferences to a competitor. A lot more control is in consumers' hands, and businesses need to sustain customer trust to continue to gain the value of their data. Privacy-compliant competitors ensure prospects are aware of these rights in a sales or marketing process, leaving those who don't keep up with an inability to compete effectively.

However, it would be naïve to assume that the privacy landscape is a level playing field. Although large businesses will always attract more attention after a data breach than small companies, at least they stand much less risk of being put out of business altogether. The extreme example is that of monopolies such as Facebook (now Meta), Amazon, Google, et al., which can abuse privacy, knowingly or otherwise, in ways that smaller companies really can't and seemingly only have to worry about being caught out by the regulators.

Trust Regained

The new personal data-related trends that have emerged in parallel with the work of legislators have shifted the focus from the protection of personal data to a person-centric model with individuals having rights over their data and its myriad uses.

Although it may appear contradictory (because it is!), while the law would not recognize ownership rights over personal data, the concept of the individual owning any data that pertains to them is at the center of the new legislation and associated vendor trends. So much so that businesses are well-advised to consider themselves mere temporary custodians of customer personal information, privileged with the rights granted to them by customers to process that information for their companies' profit.

This central concept undermines historical business models for the traditional internet giants—a strategic opportunity that some at least recognize and are taking steps to compromise their highly profitable ways of working. Traditional business models, unfettered by the concepts of personal rights, have created the current climate of growing customer distrust. However, there is an opportunity for forward-looking companies to adopt a different attitude to privacy regulations and take to market a privacy-respectful business model. At the very least, most multinational corporations are mindful of the pitfalls associated with the cross-border transfer of data, made even more complicated with data storage in the cloud.

The world of privacy has already intruded into our lives and, despite the complex and forbidding task of compliance, the guiding principles behind all the rules and regulations are basic common sense. The steps that need to be taken in your business to align with them are relatively simple to understand and not as onerous as might be thought to implement. Customer and employee privacy and personal data security have become a business necessity and no longer a nice to have.

Making changes in attitudes to business processes provides an excellent opportunity to get closer to all the individuals in your ecosphere and to assuage their concerns about how you handle their personal data. Moreover, if you successfully manage that trust relationship, customers and employees will want to stay with you and perhaps recommend your business to others. All of this adds up to a significant competitive advantage, with the bonus that you will not fall foul of the regulatory enforcement agencies and run the risk of incurring a crippling fine if you apply the principles of privacy by design.

The sweeping changes in attitudes to privacy and providing adequate protection for customer and employee data are no longer solely the domain of sales and marketing, who traditionally have managed customer relationships, or the IT department to install the latest data security patches, or human resources. Key to making this work for dynamic, forward-thinking companies is having the right kind of leadership that can adapt company culture, mindset, and processes to the spirit rather than the letter of the new laws. The CEO and senior executives must ensure that the right message permeates across the workforce, from top to bottom. In a nutshell, that message is— ensure that you have the consent of your customers and employees to use their personal data and make it clear what it is going to be used for.

Nevertheless, it is important not to lose sight of the truism that 'consent' does not equal 'privacy'. Privacy is a right, whereas data is to be protected and consent is a transaction that encompasses a wide set of fundamental responsibilities purpose, ranging from transparency and control to ethics and information provision at the right moment in the correct amount to the right person or third-party organization.

The message also needs to impart that these interactions are not hypothetical or nice-to-have: the consequences for not respecting individuals' privacy, however they perceive it, could be catastrophic financially and damaging to the company brand.

That's another reason why privacy matters.

Enterprise Risk Management ~ Justine

Understanding and Explaining Risk

To me, enterprise risk generally means the risk borne by the company as a whole. This means managing that risk must also be the responsibility of all humans within the enterprise. A critical role of executives—including privacy professionals—is reasonably calculating and predicting risk, then explaining it simply to others. First, let's get some terminology out of the way to break down our understanding of risk.

Risk is a situation involving exposure to danger. Risk tolerance or risk appetite are terms that indicate how much or how little risk an individual or business is willing to accept. The most successful risk managers appreciate and factor in the risk tolerance of key stakeholders throughout the enterprise. Contrast that to a risk manager who only considers their own risk appetite in making decisions—such practices are often misaligned with the organization and other leaders and can lead to legal liability.

A risk matrix is an index or spectrum that visualizes risk by categorizing the probability of something occurring with the severity of potential harm. For example, an unlikely privacy risk with negligible or marginal harm is a lower priority on the risk matrix. It is still a risk, but the enterprise may be willing to accept it. On the other hand, a catastrophic event that is likely to occur (e.g., data breach) is classified as an "extreme" risk and will likely be of the highest priority to executives. This level of risk will likely result in the organization avoiding the activity altogether or trying to mitigate or reduce the privacy risk. The far ends of the spectrum are easier to manage. The recommendations are more explicit than the middle parts of the spectrum, which can be more complicated to explain and manage because the ambiguity makes the decision less obvious and clear-cut.

It is helpful to use a risk matrix adopted enterprise-wide and incorporated into policies like Incident Response, Business Continuity, and Disaster Response. Colors (red, orange, yellow, green) work well because our brains associate these colors with risk categories. Referring to these categories routinely also helps sensitize other stakeholders to how privacy risk translates into enterprise risk.

	Severity				
	4	3	2	1	
	High (16)	High (12)	Serious (8)	Medium (4)	4
	High (12)	Serious (9)	Serious (6)	Medium (3)	3
	Serious (8)	Serious (6)	Medium (4)	Low (2)	2
	Medium (4)	Medium (3)	Low (2)	Low (1)	1

Figure 2.1 4X4 Risk Matrix

One of the ways a matrix like this helps is by introducing neutral language to describe risks of varying probability and severity. For example, it may not be intuitive to all personnel that a high probability of occurrence might elevate even a moderately severe issue or that a high severity issue of low probability needs management attention. But by using the risk matrix and showing that a probability of 2 and severity of 4 yields the same risk score as a probability of 4 and severity of 2, we can avoid the oversight that sometimes occurs when considering only probability or severity.

ISO 31000 RISK MANAGEMENT

Since 1946, the International Organization for Standardization (ISO) has provided generally accepted global standards on various topics impacting technology and manufacturing, including privacy, security, and risk. ISO was named after the Greek term *isos*, which means "equal." Based out of Switzerland, ISO is an independent, non-governmental organization that convenes global experts to share knowledge and develop international standards and concepts.

In addition, ISO sets out a risk management standard. A helpful visual in ISO 31000 explains how to approach risk management. Starting at the top of the core processes, we first describe the risk being evaluated (context), define which business processes are affected (scope), and the conditions necessary to trigger the risk (criteria). Then we perform a risk assessment, which includes identification, analysis, and evaluation. The assessment output will consist of such values as the probability of occurrence and the severity of the impact if the risk is triggered. These values feed directly into the risk matrix described above. The risk treatment describes the changes that can be made to business processes (including systems and business logic) to address the risk. Finally, the surrounding chevrons speak to the ongoing meta processes used to keep stakeholders informed about new risks we uncover and how we manage our existing risks.

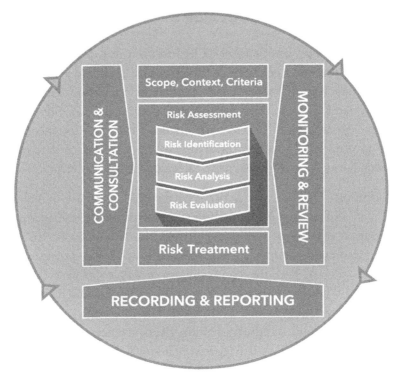

Figure 2.2 Risk Management Processes, ISO 31000

Identifying Privacy Risk—I Know It When I See It

Identifying risk before it arises requires sleuthing, knowledge about laws and regulations, and analytical reasoning. The best privacy professionals are naturally curious, great listeners, and ask many questions. Therefore, I recommend that you first gather and organize information about the data elements collected, such as: how, why, when, where it will be stored, who it will be shared with, and its purpose. Then, work collaboratively to identify what laws or regulations are implicated by the data type or jurisdictions involved. Next, analyze what risks are inherently present and explain the risk in simple terms using the risk matrix. And finally, propose a solution to manage the risk (avoid, accept, mitigate, transfer) and make a recommendation.

Privacy risk continues to evolve as the laws change, new technologies are introduced, and new uses of data and partnerships emerge.

Certain technologies, like endpoint threat detection, can help monitor, identify, and triage risk. Auditors and consultants can also help determine risk. In addition, information sharing and hearing stories about other businesses can help identify risk.

Understanding the Reactive Brain and Proactive Brain

Identifying risk can be a nerve-wracking experience that sends adrenaline and cortisol pumping through the human body and the amygdala firing on all cylinders. The amygdala (derived from the Greek word for almond because of its shape) is the reactive, instinctual part of our brains that kept us alive when we were living in the wild. We will refer to this part of our brain function as the "reactive brain." When activated, the reactive brain tells our body through stress hormones that we are in danger and responds with the fight, flight, or freeze defense mechanisms. The prefrontal cortex is the new brain responsible for our executive functions, cognitive abilities and, most notably, the ability to analyze complex scenarios and make analytical decisions. We shall call this part of our brain function the "proactive brain"—when activated, it breaks down a situation and makes reasoned, analytical decisions. When making decisions about enterprise risk, we aspire to use the proactive brain.

When a serious, scary, or challenging event occurs, like a ransomware attack, the reactive brain takes over to ensure the enterprise is kept alive. This is a normal and natural response to the situation. Stress hormones like cortisol and adrenaline can keep you up for hours fighting to establish containment of the event. Yet, when making important executive decisions in the middle of the crisis, you want to move out of the reactive brain and into the proactive brain.

The first step in transitioning from the reactive to proactive brain function is to (1) take a long deep breath in through your nose for four seconds to fill up your lungs completely, (2) hold your breath for four seconds, and (3) slowly exhale for four seconds. Repeat this three times. This type of breathing expands the diaphragm, which triggers the parasympathetic nervous system and signals the reactive brain to stop the release of adrenaline and cortisol.

The second step is giving the threat or risk a name. For example, in a ransomware attack, name the actual risk: an encryption event with potential data breach. This will allow the proactive brain to think ahead and anticipate your next move. The incident response plan or ransomware playbook may also include a checklist that names the steps you need to quickly navigate. During crisis events, some leaders can effectively access both the reactive and proactive brains so that they work together to resolve the risk.

Types of Risk

Privacy risk may be legal, regulatory, brand or reputational, or financial. Identifying the types of risk helps drive compliance and change. Your message may change depending on the audience. If you are briefing the CFO, they likely will focus on financial loss. The General Counsel may care most about legal and regulatory risk. The Chief Marketing Officer may be most interested in the brand or reputational loss. Although different stakeholders have different interests, expertise, and motivators, the role of the privacy professional is to orchestrate the entire production. Below are common types of privacy risks.

Legal. Litigation (civil or criminal) is the most common legal privacy risk. In the United States, cases can be filed in federal or state court. If there is a mandatory arbitration agreement, the case may be subject to arbitration. Typically, individuals file privacy claims in state court. If personal information is compromised, individuals have a right to receive notice of the breach. California is currently the only state that provides a private right of action for individuals if their private information is compromised.[26] If data was not reasonably secured, statutory damages may be awarded in an amount between $100 and $750, per consumer per incident. Reasonable minds will differ as to what it means to "reasonably secure" data. See Chapter 11 for a closer look at reasonable security. Other states have now proposed similar legislation. Class action lawsuits can be filed for privacy violations

---

[26] At the time of publication, the U.S. Congress is considering, with bipartisan and bicameral support, the *American Data Privacy and Protection Act*, a federal privacy bill that includes a private right of action.

even if the state does not provide a private right of action. Legal risk can also arise for contractual violations between parties.

Regulatory. Regulatory risks include regulatory proceedings, fines, penalties, and investigations. Certain federal and state laws require notice to regulators if certain privacy violations occur. HIPAA requires notice to the Department of Health and Human Services' Office of Civil Rights (OCR-HHS) if patient health information is compromised. Pursuant Executive Order 14028, federal government contractors have a 72-hour reporting obligation to DHS-CISA if their systems are compromised.[27] The SEC is promulgating new disclosure regulations that will regulate how and when businesses must give notice if they experience a cyber event.[28] In late 2021, the FTC published new privacy safeguard rules.[29] States also have similar laws and agencies that require reporting. For example, in Massachusetts and New York, only one individual impacted will trigger reporting obligations to the state. However, in California, the Attorney General must only be notified if 500+ California residents' personal information is compromised. That notice is then publicly posted on the Attorney General's website.[30] The Attorney General is currently responsible for enforcing the California Consumer Privacy Act. Soon the California Privacy Protection Agency will enforce the California Privacy Rights Act (CPRA). The FTC and SEC also investigate privacy and security violations. The Payment Card Industry (PCI) Council can also investigate.

Brand/Reputational. Brand or reputational loss includes losing consumers' trust, confidence, and business. Privacy events can erode consumer trust and can have lasting impacts. Surveys of large breaches identify that the number one risk post-event is damage to

---

[27] Executive Order on Improving the Nation's Cybersecurity (14028) https://www.cisa.gov/executive-order-improving-nations-cybersecurity.
[28] Cybersecurity Risk Management, Strategy, Governance, and Incident Disclosure, https://www.sec.gov/rules/proposed/2022/33-11038.pdf.
[29] 16 CFR Part 314: Standards for Safeguarding Customer Information (Final Rule), https://www.ftc.gov/legal-library/browse/federal-register-notices/16-cfr-part-314-standards-safeguarding-customer-information-final-rule.
[30] The breach list is located here: https://oag.ca.gov/privacy/databreach/list.

reputation/brand.[31] The reputational risk may deter consumers from entrusting their data (or purchases) to the breached business. Lost trust and confidence can also impact share prices and market value following an attack.

Financial. Financial risks include loss of income or revenue, penalties, fines, and sanctions. Risk can have both financial and legal implications. Establishing the financial loss is an attempt to quantify the harm. For example, the maximum sanction under HIPAA for a breach is $250,000. Or, in jurisdictions (like California) that provide for statutory damages, multiply the number of consumers by the amount of the statutory fine ($100-750 per person) or penalty ($2,500-7,500 per violation of the law) to quantify potential financial risk.

Regulators Mount Up

On May 12, 2021, President Biden issued an Executive Order to activate regulatory agencies to pursue privacy and security attacks against U.S. businesses. The agencies included the Cybersecurity and Infrastructure Agency of the Department of Homeland Security (DHS-CISA), the Federal Trade Commission (FTC), the Securities and Exchange Commission (SEC), and the Federal Bureau of Investigation (FBI). The most active regulatory agency on privacy and cyber in the United States is the FTC. The FTC protects consumers against unfair, deceptive, or fraudulent practices through investigations and enforcement of federal laws. In recent years, the FTC has sanctioned companies for failing to uphold promises made to the public about "reasonable security" in online privacy policies. Companies that attest in consumer-facing policies that they "reasonably secure" data and then later are the victim of an attack may be subject to an FTC investigation and sanctions.

The FTC has recently introduced a new penalty for businesses that fail to comply with privacy laws: algorithmic destruction. For

---

[31] *Global Risk Management Survey*, AON (2019) https://www.aon.com/getmedia/8d5ad510-1ae5-4d2b-a3d0-e241181da882/2019-Aon-Global-Risk-Management-Survey-Report.aspx.

example, in its complaint against Weight Watchers (now known as WW International), the FTC alleges the business marketed a weight loss app for use by children and then collected their personal information without parental permission in violation of COPPA.[32] In a March 4, 2022 settlement order, the FTC ordered WWI to delete personal information collected from children under 13, destroy any algorithms derived from the data, and pay a $1.5 million penalty.[33] This algorithmic destruction penalty has many businesses evaluating the types of data used to create AI models and the privacy practices related to consumer data collection.

KISS Method

Making things appear simple is incredibly complex. The Keep It Super Simple ("KISS") method[34] is a helpful tool to gather basic facts. The KISS results will then inform a more profound analysis (if necessary) to fully appreciate and evaluate risk. KISS is essential because it requires the proactive brain to articulate fundamentals about the nature of risk so that anybody can understand, especially key stakeholders and management.

Identify the five Ws: who, what, where, when, and why. Get comprehensively curious about the risk. "Who" is impacted by the privacy risk, or "Who" created the risk? "What" people, processes, or technologies are involved? "Where" did the risk arise physically, or "Where" do the individuals impacted reside for purposes of applicable laws? "When" did the risk start, and when did it end? "Why" identifies the reason for taking or the cause of the privacy risk.

---

[32] Complaint for Permanent Injunction, Civil Penalties, and Other Equitable Relief, United States of America, Plaintiff, v. Kurbo, Inc., a corporation, and WW International, Inc., a corporation, Defendants https://www.ftc.gov/system/files/ftc_gov/pdf/filed_complaint.pdf.

[33] Stipulated Order for Permanent Injunction, Civil Penalty Judgment, and other relief. United States of America, Plaintiff, v. Kurbo, Inc., a corporation, and WW International, Inc., a corporation, Defendants https://www.ftc.gov/system/files/ftc_gov/pdf/wwkurbostipulatedorder.pdf.

[34] You may have heard of this referred to as Keep It Simple, Stupid, or a variation of that. I prefer not to invoke stupidity into the phrase as it is counter-productive when instructing others to follow a path of simplicity.

KISS method analyses can be performed preemptively to help prepare for privacy risks or diagnostically to help is understand how we can improve our processes.

In February 2021, the California Department of Motor Vehicles (DMV) suffered a data breach after its vendor, Automatic Funds Transfer Services (AFTS), was hit by a ransomware attack.[35] Over 38 million California vehicle registration records were exposed, including names, addresses, license plate numbers, and vehicle identification numbers (VINs). A post-event KISS Method analysis looks like this:

Who: California residents
What: Personal Information accessed by an unauthorized user
When: February 2021
Where: A vendor ransomware attack
Why: TBD

A KISS Method analysis conducted before the event took place may look like this:

Who: Vendor is Automatic Funds Transfer Services (AFTS)
What: Vendor hosts DMV data and processes California residents' sensitive personal information
When: Ongoing data transfers according to contract
Where: Vendor is located in Seattle, Washington
Why: Vendor is verifying consumers' addresses

By performing a KISS analysis before events occur, i.e., when you are considering an opportunity, you may anticipate and possibly mitigate potential risks. A post-event KISS analysis can also provide valuable data that may inform a KISS analysis you conduct prior to a future opportunity.

---

[35] Visit the California DMV portal for the breach disclosure: https://www.dmv.ca.gov/portal/security-breach-at-address-verification-company-may-compromise-dmv-information/.

Privacy Risk Assessment

A privacy risk assessment must address all types of risk: legal, regulatory, brand/reputational, business/operational, and financial risk. Privacy risk assessments will commonly identify how the risk may arise, the laws that govern, and the regulatory and legal consequences of a breach. They will also determine whether a private right of action exists, the likelihood of harm, worst-case and best-case scenario in terms of loss or harm, technological controls, and risk resolution. Impact on the business is also critical. Try to articulate and document the costs and benefits of the technology or acts that create the risk. For example, marketing may identify an attractive digital marketing campaign that utilizes third-party analytics to market to customers. The privacy risk assessment is a 360-degree look at the risk that the business can use to make informed decisions. In our digital marketing risk assessment, we could analyze:

- what laws may restrict this activity
- whether opt-in or opt-out mechanisms are required
- the cost and benefit of the campaign
- whether there are ways to reduce the risk by data minimization, geo-filtering certain jurisdictions or tokenizing the personal information.

A thorough risk assessment doesn't just identify the risk, it strategically and pragmatically documents how to treat the risk.

Risk Treatment—The Big 4

We identify the risk by gathering facts through risk assessments like Records of Processing Activity (ROPAs), Data Protection Impact Assessments (DPIAs), Data Transfer Impact Assessments (DTIAs) or vendor management surveys. Once we understand the risk, there are four primary ways to treat the risk: (1) avoidance; (2) acceptance; (3) mitigation, or (4) transference.

Avoidance means just that. It can be *complete* or *partial* avoidance. Once you identify and assess the risk, if there are no ways to sufficiently reduce or transfer the risk, you avoid the act to avoid the harm. For example, complete risk avoidance is not pursuing the aforementioned marketing campaign. Partial risk avoidance could be pursuing the marketing campaign but not marketing to California residents because the laws may create more risk than you are willing to accept. Or pursuing the campaign but not collecting certain data elements within the campaign or not sharing data back with third parties.

Acceptance means you understand the risk exists and choose to accept it. Accepting risk can also be *complete* or *partial*. This approach acknowledges that there is a likelihood that the privacy risk may materialize. Nearly all organizations and people accept residual risk every day. In terms of our marketing campaign example, after fully understanding the legal risks created by the digital marketing campaign, you may choose to accept the risk and pursue the campaign for all jurisdictions.

Mitigation is the act of reducing privacy risk in either *severity* or *frequency*. For example, aggregating or de-identifying data limits the applicability of most laws that protect personal information. Encryption or multi-factor authentication will reduce risk in security because they offer safe harbors under laws and can thwart threat actors from accessing protected data. Data minimization principles lessen the amount and types of data to reduce the level/severity of the risk. Most privacy professionals spend a good chunk of their day finding ways to creatively mitigate or reduce privacy risk. One way to reduce or minimize risk in our digital marketing campaign example is to enable a cookie preference center that allows individuals to disable targeted marketing cookies on your website. Empowering the consumer to control their experience is then explained in a cookie banner and the privacy policy and will reduce privacy risk. Laws like CCPA or GDPR may require this right to opt-out (or opt-in), but regulators in many jurisdictions are not there yet.

Transfer. Risk transference is shifting or sharing risk with another party. Pragmatically, the party that can control that risk is the one that should carry the risk. But frequently, risk transference is limited by terms that limit liability. The classic examples of risk transference are (1) the purchase of cyber insurance that provides coverage if there is data loss and (2) the inclusion of indemnity provisions in vendor contracts. Outsourcing IT or InfoSec are also methods of risk transference. In our digital marketing campaign example, you may hire a third-party marketing company to conduct the campaign. In the service agreement, you may transfer the privacy risk to the marketing company by requiring them to comply with the privacy and security laws of all jurisdictions where the campaign will be active, enable required cookie settings, process consumer requests, and indemnify your business if there are any privacy claims related to their marketing activity.

People, Process and Technology

Enterprise risk management is not just about the humans doing their part to manage the risk—the machines and processes must also do their part. Admittedly, the machines and processes will depend on the humans to ensure they are aligned. Consider all the ways you can harmonize people, processes, and technology around enterprise risk to mitigate privacy and cyber risk further.

Whole of Enterprise Impact ~ Matt

It is easy to think of privacy as the exclusive domain of the legal department, where legal staff draft standard privacy policies that are added to the corporate website accompanied by the now obligatory cookie notices. The whole process appears removed from other corporate functions and organizational context. The reality, however, is that privacy has pervasive impacts across the organization. Indeed, privacy has a whole of enterprise impact for most companies. Organizations that assume privacy is just a policy and a few website settings will invariably discover that this overly narrow focus introduces a level of risk clearly unanticipated by executive stakeholders, who may be caught flat-footed when privacy risks are realized.

Let's consider how pervasive the impacts of privacy can be within a typical organization. There are certain functions where privacy's effects are more evident than others. We will start with these more direct functions and move into more subtle areas where privacy's impacts may not be so clear but are certainly still significant if not managed well.

Human Resources (HR)

The HR department is clearly a high-impact function given the direct employee data that staff in these departments collect, process, and have access to, as well as the personal data of employees' spouses and children. In addition, HR staff, or outsourced professional employer organizations (PEOs), have details on salaries and benefits and significant employee-specific data, including age, sensitive employee files containing disciplinary and performance reviews, and special accommodations, among other data sets. For obvious reasons, this information should be kept confidential, and its access limited to only those with a legitimate need to know. HR systems and workstations and the applications used to support the function should be segmented from other organizational functions to ensure this confidentiality. Specifically, this implies that file shares, networks, and access to HR applications should be adequately segmented and access controlled and monitored for unauthorized access. These basic security measures become part of the firm's "reasonable" security practices and should be validated by the organization's CISO or security leader.

HR also plays the central coordinating role in corporate training. HR departments must ensure that requisite security awareness and privacy training is provided to employees and contractors alike. This training must be tracked and evaluated for effectiveness.

Finance and Accounting

The accounting department also has access to sensitive employee data, though granted not to the same extent as staff working in human resources. Certain members of the accounting department (and by extension the finance department) have access to the general ledger entries associated with payroll. Depending upon the specific applications employed by the organization, most payroll data is not necessarily conveyed as individual line items. Still, disaggregated payroll data is available to certain finance and accounting team members. There is a similar dynamic concerning options, bonuses, and other incentive payments. While what employees earn is certainly "financial data" from an accounting perspective, salary and benefits detail are some of the most sensitive data most organizations process, notably from the employees' perspective. Non-routine, payroll, and benefits information may also be considered material, non-public information (MNPI) under certain circumstances (notably around executive compensation and bonuses). Like other forms of employee data, this information requires appropriate protections, including access controls and ideally encryption of this data at rest and in transit.

Sales and Marketing

The sales and marketing departments have access to the business contact information of clients and vendors alike for organizations operating in a business to business (B2B) model and to consumer data for those focused on business to consumer (B2C) markets. The sales and marketing functions require extra attention from a privacy perspective. As we will highlight throughout this book, good privacy practices may conflict with other organizational priorities. A core tenant of privacy governance is to collect the minimum information necessary to fulfill the stated purpose of the given process or transaction. Further, unless there is a contractual or regulatory reason to the contrary, this information should not be retained longer than is required to meet the stated purpose of the transaction. Marketing activities, notably those focused on consumer markets, are notorious for collecting as much information as possible through as many channels as possible to develop a consumer profile (essentially a dossier).[36]

The privacy risks associated with overly aggressive data collection practices within sales and marketing departments cannot be overstated. Accordingly, regulatory action should be anticipated when personal information is used in a manner that differs from the stated purpose and notice provided to the consumer or data subject. Indeed, in the U.S., the FTC is charged with protecting consumers from what is noted in Section 5 of the Federal Trade Commission Act as "unfair and deceptive trade practices."

The dilemma this presents is especially challenging. Marketing departments have amassed an impressive array of data collection techniques to process and correlate personal data. However, just because a capability exists does not mean that it should be employed. Organizations collecting information inconsistent with the stated purpose for its collection face significant regulatory risk—a topic

---

[36] As consumers, we see the effects of rampant data collection about our preferences, most notably as we browse the internet. Our Google searches lead to highly targeted ads on social media sites like Facebook (Meta) and LinkedIn, among other social media sites. This is not coincidental. Indeed, massive collection of our personal data occurs as we interact with any number of devices or applications that connect to the internet. Ever wonder why applications downloaded from Apple's App Store or Google's Play request access to your contacts, files, and pictures? This information is used not only to support the application – clearly, applications like Uber and Lyft need your location to deliver their service – but also to profile your connected and online behavior for targeted advertising and messages. Netflix's 2020 documentary *The Social Dilemma* offers a fascinating view into how social media platforms have been designed to profile nearly all aspects of our lives. This is a topic we will be addressing throughout this book.

addressed later in this book. Personal information that is collected and stored without a legitimate purpose also represents an "unfunded" liability in the case of a data breach (e.g., breach notification, credit monitoring, and remediation expenses) or whistleblower action at one extreme and more general ongoing storage and IT costs at the other. There are also potential regulatory challenges if that personal data was collected inconsistent with or in violation of privacy regulations.

There is a perfect storm brewing between the disciplines of marketing and privacy. Marketing teams have never had more tools and capabilities at their disposal to collect, analyze, and process personal data from consumers to develop high-fidelity profiles. Conversely and globally, we are witnessing the golden era of privacy regulations. Whether it is the European Union's General Data Protection Regulation, the California Consumer Privacy Act, Canada's Personal Information Protection and Electronic Documents Act (PIPEDA), India's Personal Data Protection Bill (PDPB), Japan's Act on the Protection of Personal Information (APPI), or the numerous sector-specific and state breach notification laws in the U.S., privacy regulations governing the use and disclosure of data are near-ubiquitous. When marketing teams are "unaware" of these regulations, the risks for regulatory action are high.[37] Regulatory action caused by management's negligence may also result in shareholder action or litigation with investors.

Application Development (AppDev) and Product Management

Application development represents another function that may have significant privacy considerations. We have all heard of cases where development environments were compromised only to find out that the development data was actual production data containing sensitive personal information. As we will discuss in Chapters 5 and 6, there are techniques including pseudonymization, tokenization,

---

[37] You can find detail related to FTC enforcement actions here: https://www.ftc.gov/enforcement/cases-proceedings, and details related to GDPR enforcement actions here: https://gdpr.eu/category/news-updates.

and format-preserving encryption that can take sensitive data and make it available for development environments without jeopardizing the actual production data that is uniquely identifiable. Like marketing teams, development teams may also be unaware of privacy requirements and implement tools and capabilities into applications that have important privacy implications. These might include tracking beacons, location data, and other "cool" data sets, without realizing the requirements for informed consent from the end-users of these applications. This speaks to the security and privacy training noted above. Minimally, organizations would be well served to train development teams on core privacy by design and privacy by default principles (the topic of Chapter 8).

We are seeing improvements with websites and web applications that empower consumers to have a more informed perspective of how applications behave when they enable specific preferences. Still, the default settings may not be consistent with privacy regulations (e.g., asking the data subject or consumer to opt-out of sharing sensitive personal information or their location versus opting in prior to the collection of this data). Developers may use application programming interfaces (APIs) and other methods to move personal data from one application to another. These, too, should be evaluated for their privacy impact. Like sales and marketing, application development and product management are functions that are clearly in-scope from a privacy perspective.

Infrastructure and Operations (I&O)

IT teams also have an important role to play with respect to privacy governance. Overseeing infrastructure and operations typically comes with a level of access to organizational systems that other teams may not have. These elevated privileges or administrative rights to applications and systems indicate that many staff within IT will have access to sensitive information stored in corporate file shares, cloud services, or on-premises applications. Third-party applications, frequently delivered in a software-as-a-service (SaaS) model, may not have the same exposure as internally managed applications. However, these applications should also be inventoried and evaluated for privacy implications. IT teams also have access to log data that provides insights into employee behavior (e.g., system login data, proximity cards for facility access). The degree of employee "monitoring" that is acceptable is also relative and should be reviewed both in terms of the organization's acceptable use policy (AUP) and applicable regulations. The level of employee monitoring and what is permissible under the regulations varies notably. Employees in the U.S. generally have limited expectations of privacy in the workplace, whereas expectations for workforce privacy are notably higher in Europe. Privacy leaders need to understand what is or is not occurring for employee monitoring and validate this based on jurisdictional context. These are perfect scenarios for conducting privacy impact assessments (PIAs) or in the context of GDPR, data protection impact assessments (DPIAs) based on the level of risk and degree of proportionality associated with these monitoring activities.

Security

In a similar vein as that of the IT team, the security team may have tools and capabilities to monitor employee behavior. User entity and behavior analytics (UEBA) tools, which look at logs and other sources of online behavior, can be used to monitor employee activities. Similarly, data loss prevention (DLP) applications are frequently used to detect access to sensitive data and preclude it from being inappropriately shared or stolen. Endpoint detection and response (EDR) applications also collect information that inventory applications, processes, and files on employee laptops and workstations. These applications frequently capture detail about which websites employees visit, the most frequently used applications, and the type of data they access as part of these security tools' efforts to preclude malware or ransomware from impacting the device. Mobile device management (MDM) applications enable IT and security teams to remotely wipe devices that may have been lost or stolen or when an employee is no longer associated with the organization.

Because of the nature of their work for the organization, I&O, IT, and security teams collectively may have access to highly sensitive personal data, notably around monitoring employee behavior and unfettered admin access to sensitive personal data found in numerous systems and applications. These teams, however, may not be versed in the regulatory context of their efforts. Regulations and corporate norms regarding employee behavior monitoring vary notably. As a gross generalization, the expectations for privacy in the U.S. workplace are somewhat limited. Acceptable Use Policies in the U.S. generally note that email, system use, and websites visited will be monitored as part of the employee/employer relationship. Monitoring employee behavior in a GDPR context is more nuanced than the blanket "we monitor everything" clauses seen in many U.S. AUPs. Security and I&O leaders are advised to seek out support from their counsel proactively regarding what cannot be monitored within the organization and to ensure that access, based on admin rights, to sensitive personal data is logged and timely reviewed.

Customer Care

As noted earlier, there's been an explosion of new privacy regulations introduced globally. Many of these regulations create specific privacy rights for consumers. These consumer rights include, for example, the right to access their data, data portability, the right to be forgotten, the right to know what data is collected about the consumer, and whether that data is being sold to third parties. Throughout this book, we will address these privacy rights, so these rights are noted as just high-level background here. What's important is that customer care teams are aware of how they should respond to consumer or data subject requests. They must understand how to validate the consumer's identity, especially in the context of the request, and whether the request can be processed (not all requests to be forgotten can or should be processed). They must also know how to ensure that disclosures are handled correctly. Unfortunately, customer care teams are frequently left out of the planning sessions to address privacy rights. As a result, they are left to wonder how client, consumer, or data subject requests should be addressed appropriately. With many regulations, including the CCPA and the GDPR, requiring timely responses, these teams must be well trained to handle many consumer or data subject request scenarios. It is incumbent upon customer care leaders to proactively work with their privacy counterparts in legal and other departments to ensure that their teams are adequately informed and trained on how to address privacy rights appropriately.

Legal

An organization's internal legal team or external counsel are frequently at the forefront of privacy actions for the organization. As noted at the beginning of this chapter, the legal team is drafting privacy policies, reviewing contracts for privacy and security considerations, keeping abreast of fast-moving privacy regulations, and ensuring that the organization's risk exposure to privacy matters is managed proactively. The legal function's role in privacy is omnipresent. Unfortunately, legal departments may be isolated from the ground truth of organizational practices, unaware of specific organizational capabilities and competencies related to security and privacy objectives. This risk cannot be overstated and requires that the legal team be especially cognizant of any gap between regulatory requirements and functional capability. To that end, legal teams should collaborate closely with the data protection officer (DPO) or chief privacy officer (CPO), if they are not one and the same, as appropriate. Equally important, the legal team should engage the chief information officer (CIO) and chief information security officer (CISO) to review data classification, data retention, and data security expectations and practices. Misunderstandings between these stakeholders can be significant and costly. For example, CIOs may invoke data retention periods that don't align with contractual or regulatory obligations because they simply do not have adequate storage. Bluntly, the legal team addressing privacy needs to be engaged with the business, getting to know the organization's key stakeholders to validate requisite or mandated privacy practices.

Equally challenging is that certain data protection requirements may not be adequately implemented because of incorrect data classification. Declare war on ambiguity and ensure that the security, IT, and legal teams are aligned on requirements. These stakeholders have a symbiotic relationship. Each requires appropriate resources and capabilities to ensure that privacy and security practices are adequately aligned to organizational risk tolerances, regulatory requirements, and contractual obligations. Don't overlook the dividends of a simple brown bag lunch session with these stakeholders.

Internal Audit (IA)

Larger organizations may have an internal audit (IA) function that primarily reviews financial and accounting activities for appropriate internal controls. The organization may also call upon the IA team to conduct audits related to privacy controls and specific security functions. While IA teams have historically focused on financial and accounting oversight, given the pervasive digital nature of most organizations, their engagement in privacy oversight should be anticipated to increase over time. Minimally, IA teams can be trained on good privacy practices and complement existing privacy functions within a firm, helping to validate that requisite privacy controls are designed and operating effectively.

Executive Leadership Team (ELT)

Ultimately, the organization's leadership role cannot be overstated. The executive leadership team plays a critical role in privacy governance. ELTs set the tone at the top for the organization. When executive leaders take a dismissive attitude toward privacy requirements, it permeates the organization. Resources may not be adequately aligned to required privacy and security functions, exposing the organization to regulatory and litigation risk. Checkbox compliance is generally insufficient to address the nuance that privacy controls require. Executive leadership teams that proactively embrace good privacy practices—ensuring that the privacy program is well-resourced and contextualized to the organization's strategy—create a positive tone at the top. This tone encourages stakeholders, business partners, and business teams to take privacy seriously. Indeed, how organizations manage privacy is often a harbinger of how the organization manages enterprise risk. Good enterprise risk management (ERM) programs look holistically across the organization—assessing risk and impact to operations, finances, reputation, compliance, and safety. When privacy practices are part of this broader ERM effort, there's greater organizational alignment and visibility of different forms of risk. Executive leaders need to convey to the organization that privacy matters, that privacy is a core organizational function, and that the privacy program is inextricably linked to the organization's broader strategy and initiatives.

As we have seen, privacy has pervasive impacts on the organization, and, in light of this dynamic, organizations should establish a comprehensive privacy program. Privacy programs that are narrowly focused and under-resourced present risk to the organization. In the next chapter, we'll discuss the elements of a privacy program and how the privacy lifecycle plays a vital role in the program's design and operations.

Key Insights and Recommended Next Steps

Key Insights

- The loss of trust has both direct and indirect consequences. When given a choice, consumers may opt not to use an untrustworthy service and be slower to consume new offerings. Trust underpins enterprise value.
- New privacy regulations are driven by a desire to define and secure consumer rights in the digital age. Implementing the programs necessary to ensure compliance and therefore deliver existing and newly defined rights also begins rebuilding the lost trust. As a result, the consumer benefits from better privacy, and companies benefit from the potential for increased consumption.
- In addition to being a whole of enterprise endeavor, privacy risk must be elevated as a critical risk consideration for organizations that capture or process personal information.
- It is challenging for any business to keep up with the speed with which these changes are being called for without a set of principles that can drive company culture and behavior.
- To deal with the risks generated by security events that threaten personal data, privacy professionals should integrate their privacy program with their organization's enterprise risk management framework.
- Every core function of the enterprise has some role in safeguarding personal data.
- The cumulative weight of the risks and the impact on the organization to mitigate these risks and respond to threats requires a comprehensive privacy program driven by a proactive tone at the top.

Recommended Next Steps

- Develop an inventory of the data elements collected by each department and apply the KISS approach to each data set. This won't be the final risk assessment but can identify initial focus areas.
- Review how your principles would apply to each function that handles private data and begin to socialize the principles with their leadership.
- If you have not already integrated your privacy function with the organization's ERM function, reach out to the leader of the ERM function and begin a dialog.

Section 2

Preparing the Program

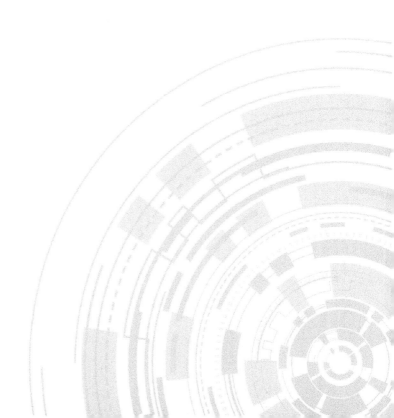

A Strong Foundation

In Section Two, "Preparing the Program," we're going to unpack six essential considerations for you to keep in mind as you construct or evaluate your privacy program. In Chapter 3, "The Role of the DPO/CPO," we start with the role of the privacy leader in your organization, often referred to as the Chief Privacy Officer. Then each author outlines what constitutes the critical elements of a privacy program to them in Chapter 4, "Elements of a Privacy Program." In Chapter 5, "Privacy Technology," we dive into the role technology plays, both in creating the data we need to protect and then offering that very protection. The last three chapters in this section cover the data privacy lifecycle (Chapter 6), global privacy regulations (Chapter 7), and the key concepts of Privacy by Design (PbD) (Chapter 8).

As you are touring the world in Chapter 7, keep in mind that while enforcement capabilities may seem variable as the different regulatory authorities build up their administrative régimes, your goals are to create a program that protects citizens' data privacy rights and prepare to meet your compliance requirements. Justine offers valuable advice regarding how to prioritize the efforts in your program.

In this section, you will see how David's, Justine's, and Matt's different backgrounds inform their unique views of how to approach building a privacy program. Every company is different, shaped by the mores of its people and the norms and regulations of the industry in which they compete. The ability to mix and match approaches and learn from the experiences of three thought leaders will help you build a program that is best suited to your company's needs.

Chapter 3

The Role of the Privacy Leader

Introduction

In Chapter 2, "Whole of Enterprise View," we put forth the case that given the risk being assumed, the myriad ways that personal data flows into an organization, and the opportunity afforded by increased intimacy with customers and partners that a robust privacy program provides, you should enlist the whole enterprise in creating good privacy outcomes. In Chapter 3, "The Role of the Privacy Leader," we will reverse the lens and describe the critical aspects of the roles and the vital attributes of privacy leaders.

The temptation is to assume that technical skills or legal knowledge are paramount. However, you'll see that leadership, empathy, and relationship building are critical if the privacy leader is also to be a change leader. Whichever title your organization uses to refer to the privacy leader's role, it is a challenging job requiring a combination of technical skills, regulatory knowledge, leadership, influencing, empathy, and professional courage.

We said in the book's introduction that our varied perspectives and the evolving nature of the field create ambiguity in the terminology we use. One area where this is most apparent is in the way we refer to privacy leaders, especially by title. While "Chief Privacy Officer," or CPO, is perhaps the most straightforward of the roles we describe, this should not be confused with a role like Chief Executive Officer or Chief Financial Officer, which usually come with executive leadership responsibilities and fiduciary duties to shareholders. When HIPAA applies, it is like the Chief Information Security Officer (CISO) who is increasingly carrying freight for regulatory bodies that are requiring some organizations to designate a high-level executive who has a defined oversight role and unfettered access to the board.

Absent HIPAA, the Chief Privacy Officer is akin to a Chief Information Officer, meaning the focal point in the organization for a particular organizational capability. They simultaneously bring a disciplined expertise and act as a nexus within the organization.

The Data Protection Officer, by contrast, does have title and duty defined by statute, as David and Matt will explain in more detail in their essays, and the GDPR sets out in a way that also empowers the DPO to serve an authority external to the organization's management team. In this case, the duty is to the data subject and not the board.

And finally, we also use the terms privacy professional and privacy leader. By privacy professional we mean a person learned (often with certification) in the field, who keeps up with best practices and regulatory pronouncements and helps the organization pilot the privacy program. When we refer to a privacy leader, we refer to a subset of privacy professionals who typically lead the privacy function within an organization.

In "The Role of the DPO/CPO," David draws on his love of music and likens the privacy leader's role to providing rhythm or cohesion for the entire organization. He then makes the point that although explicitly defined by regulators, this role can be so much more. Continuing his theme of engendering trust, he argues that the privacy leader's role should go beyond merely obeying a statute and actively seek to create trust.

As Justine explains, the essential attribute needed by privacy leaders is their emotional intelligence (EQ). In her essay, "The Role of the Privacy Professional," Justine breaks down the five key elements of emotional intelligence: awareness, management and regulation, motivation, empathy, and proactively managing relationships.

Matt points out in his essay, "The Evolving and Expanding Role of the Chief Privacy Officer," that the privacy leader is first a privacy advocate, focused on building and maintaining the trust of the individuals whose data the company collects, uses, and therefore must protect. To succeed, the privacy leader needs to work closely with departments across the organization.

The Role of the DPO/CPO ~ David

If this book pivots around a single set of personas or rather roles more than any others, it is that of the Data Protection Officer (DPO) or in some cases the Chief Privacy Officer (CPO), with a respectful glance at the evolving role of the Chief Information Security Officer (CISO).

If you were to compare your company's privacy program to the Rolling Stones—a bit of a stretch admittedly—then the DPO/CPO could be likened to Keith Richards, the band's rhythm guitarist. As well as co-writing the songs, Richards provides the tempo for the bass and drums as well as the melody for Mick Jagger, the lead singer. Remove Richards from the picture, and the band wouldn't get beyond the first few bars. If you are not familiar with the Rolling Stones, you could apply a similar metaphor to the conductor of a symphony orchestra. The DPO or CPO establishes the privacy tempo for the rest of the company, from the senior executives to the IT department, to follow and adhere to.

In Europe, although some organizations may voluntarily appoint a DPO, other organizations that collect, store, or process large amounts of personal data about EU citizens, whether employees, individuals outside the organization—or both—subject to certain criteria, may be mandated under Article 37 of the GDPR to appoint a DPO.[38]

DPOs must be:

> … appointed for all public authorities, and where the core activities of the controller or the processor involve 'regular and systematic monitoring of data subjects on a large scale' or where the entity conducts large-scale processing of 'special categories of personal data.'

Although data protection and privacy regulations differ in other jurisdictions, the responsibilities associated with the DPO that are

---

[38] The Article 29 Data Protection Working Party together with the EDPB published a comprehensive set of guidelines on DPO including a FAQ in the Annex: Guidelines on Data Protection Officers ('DPOs') WP 243 rev.01, https://ec.europa.eu/newsroom/article29/items/612048.

outlined in the GDPR can be seen as a template for the role elsewhere.

The DPO is an enterprise privacy leader responsible for overseeing data protection strategy and implementation to ensure compliance with the requirements of GDPR and other applicable data protection regulations.

DPOs are responsible for ensuring that company employees are trained on important compliance requirements, that there are staff trained in data processing, and that regular security audits are conducted. In addition, DPOs serve as the point of contact between the company and any supervisory authorities that oversee activities related to data.

The DPO's tasks are delineated in Article 39 of the GDPR to include:

- Informing and advising the controller or processor and its employees of their obligations to comply with the GDPR and other data protection laws.

- Monitoring compliance with the GDPR and other data protection laws, including managing internal data protection activities, training data processing staff, and conducting internal audits.

- Advising about data protection impact assessments when required under Article 35, which defines the processing of DPIAs.

- Working and cooperating with the controller's or processor's designated supervisory authority and serving as the contact point for the supervisory authority on issues relating to the processing of personal data.

These responsibilities mirror those of privacy professionals elsewhere around the globe and signal a growth spurt for the profession. However, evidence suggests that many firms will outsource DPO responsibilities to specialized agencies or consultancies. For example, a company with multiple subsidiaries (a "group of undertakings"[39]) may appoint a single DPO who should be "easily accessible from each establishment." The GDPR also allows the DPO functions to be performed by either an employee of the controller or processor or by a third-party service provider, creating opportunities for consulting firms, and other agencies to offer outsourced DPO services.

Under the GDPR, DPOs have many rights in addition to their responsibilities. They may insist upon company resources to fulfill their job functions and for their own ongoing training. They must have access to the company's data processing personnel and operations, significant independence in the performance of their roles, and a direct reporting line "to the highest management level" of the company. DPOs are expressly granted significant independence in their job functions and may perform other tasks and duties provided they do not create conflicts of interest. Chief amongst them is a DPO's freedom to have unquestioned access to any hidden corner of the organization. If for a large corporation that is an overreaching ambition for one person to carry out, then others should be delegated to ensure the responsibility is achieved. Job security is another perk; the GDPR expressly prevents dismissal or penalty of the DPO for the performance of their tasks and places no limitation on the length of this tenure.

In short, although it's an aspect of the role of the CPO to protect corporate interests, the DPO has the authority to drive positive outcomes for the business by shaping the relationship between the

---

[39] See GDPR Recital 37: "A group of undertakings should cover a controlling undertaking and its controlled undertakings, whereby the controlling undertaking should be the undertaking which can exert a dominant influence over the other undertakings by virtue, for example, of ownership, financial participation or the rules which govern it or the power to have personal data protection rules implemented. An undertaking which controls the processing of personal data in undertakings affiliated to it should be regarded, together with those undertakings, as a group of undertakings."

company, its employees, and its customers in the context of personal data management.

The Conundrum

Of all the requirements and expectations, the most demanding challenge facing DPOs is the balancing act between protecting corporate interests and customer (regulatory) rights. Through a corporate lens, the balance may go one way, but don't be in doubt that, at least according to the GDPR, the interests of customers/consumer/data subjects come first – as it should be! It's not surprising that many (but by no means all) DPOs have a legal background, ideally with a privacy and technology focus. It makes sense for companies that may face severe penalties for data mismanagement violations: a lawyer may be better equipped to protect and defend the company in such cases than a professional who is not educated in the law. Unfortunately, prioritizing a company's interests over consumer rights is an approach that is, sooner or later, going to come unstuck. As the introduction to this article demonstrates, the pendulum has swung very much in favor of citizens' rights. The only corporate strategy that resonates today engages with the core privacy principles underpinning the GDPR that can both respect consumer rights and provide a competitive advantage.

Some companies have a further conundrum, managing relationships in both a B2B and B2C context. For example, many companies have other companies as their customers but may also be serving consumers, or patients in a healthcare environment, on behalf of the third-party company. In other words, they would be both data controllers and data processors.

There is no reason why any company cannot be both a controller and a processor of personal data, providing processing services to other controllers, but at the same time being a controller for other (personal) data. Confusing? It doesn't have to be as long as you bear in mind that a data controller determines the purposes and the means by which personal data is processed, and a data processor processes personal data only on behalf of the controller.

Irrespective of whether your company is acting as a controller or a processor—and particularly if both—it is critical that your systems and procedures distinguish between the two different roles. Especially if some of the data is the same, your systems must be able to apply the appropriate different processes and measures to each.

The key is to build a long-term trust relationship with customers (and consumer) that is predicated on keeping them informed through transparency and ongoing dialogue.

Project Fear

But if you think that the role of the DPO is a fearsome function associated with raising the company drawbridge against the "gotchas" of the GDPR, it doesn't have to be. Although many may perceive the job as a dull administrator or a bureaucratic policeman, it doesn't take a great leap of faith to realize that it can be so much more than that. Really! More than most other desirable skills, an ability to communicate well at all levels within an organization and instill trust with partners and customers is essential.

Building better customer relationships is the cornerstone of every successful business. One of the key players in achieving that is the person who controls the levers at the company-customer interface. That is, the DPO. DPOs have the authority to drive positive outcomes for the business by creating trusted relationships with clients, protecting their consumer rights, and enabling them to partner in the management of their personal data. In other words, the DPO has a really important role in the company, one that adds value and avoids penalties.

At first sight, achieving and maintaining compliance with the GDPR—or any other data protection regulation—appears to be a daunting prospect. As we have shown, the way to overcome these concerns is to turn the new regulatory landscape into a competitive business advantage by engaging positively with customers to create a win-win scenario.

Above all, though, the primary responsibility of the DPO is to protect the data subject rights first before looking after corporate interests.

The Role of the Privacy Professional ~ Justine

Know and Slow Your Role

Before understanding your "role" within your organization, let us first look to the meaning of "role." Role can mean a part played by a person in life or a part or character one takes. Other phrases that depend on the role include "role model" and "role reversal." Discovering the privacy part, character, or function that you have in your organization will depend on several factors like corporate structure, industry, leadership, budget, and many other factors not always under your control. Nevertheless, clearly articulating and documenting your role, whether in a job description or job functions, will help others in the organization understand and respect the role of the privacy professional.

What's In a Name

There are many types of privacy professionals. However, some roles are required by laws like the GDPR (Data Protection Officer) or HIPAA (Chief Privacy Officer or privacy official). Certain jobs may require certifications like CIPP or CIPM. Looking across LinkedIn and the various job posts available, there are many names ascribed to individuals that perform privacy functions within an organization:

General Leadership Positions	Privacy Focused Roles
Chief Information Officer (CIO)	Chief Privacy Officer (CPO)
Chief of Cybersecurity and Privacy	Privacy Program Manager
Director of Compliance & Privacy	Privacy Risk Manager
	Privacy Attorney
Data Focused Roles	Privacy Manager
Data Protection Officer (DPO)	Privacy Engineer
Information Protection Officer	Privacy Policy Manager
Data Misuse Manager	Privacy Incident Manager
Data Privacy Specialist	Privacy Product Strategist
Data Privacy Analyst	Privacy Operations Manager
Data Protection Counsel	Privacy & Compliance Manager
	Privacy & Data Specialist

Figure 3.1 Sample Data and Privacy Titles[40]

Each of these roles requires the privacy professional to manage and govern privacy risk effectively. In addition, the roles require an understanding of applicable privacy laws, compliance regulations, the organization's risk appetite, reputational interests, and the ability to balance cost vs. convenience. For purposes of this chapter, I will broadly refer to individuals that inhabit these roles as "privacy professionals."

The Most Important Quality

"Emotional intelligence" (or what I call "enterprise intelligence") (EQ) is the single most important quality a privacy professional can possess. Cognitive intelligence (IQ) is only one element of an individual's professional success and may be less critical than EQ in a privacy role. Psychologist Dan Goleman first explained the concept of emotional intelligence in 1995 in his highly acclaimed book *Emotional Intelligence: Why It Can Matter More than IQ*. Unlike IQ, Goleman believes individuals can learn emotional competencies and

---

[40] I identify *Data Protection Officer* as a data focused role and it should be noted that this role comes with specific duties for organizations that control or process data subject to the protections provided by the GDPR.

improve their abilities in this area, rather than them being fixed at birth. At a high level, the basic EQ framework as it applies to privacy includes:

(1)   **Awareness.** EQ requires situational and self-awareness. The privacy professional is frequently responsible for making the organization aware of its data collection and use practices, which requires gathering facts about how it collects, uses, stores, shares, and disposes of data. Awareness requires intentional and mindful planning by the privacy professional. The privacy professional should develop a privacy plan that increases awareness (individual and collective) and embraces a culture of curiosity and discovery, and solicits feedback from other stakeholders to get their perspectives about privacy and related processes. Documenting those efforts and incorporating multiple perspectives (e.g., consumer, business, employee, legal, financial, reputational) allows the privacy professional to develop 360-degree situational awareness. Making the enterprise self-aware of its privacy risk and responsibilities is a significant duty of the privacy professional.

(2)   **Management and Regulation.** Self-management is a critical skill, particularly when confronted with challenging situations like data loss, lack of responsiveness, cyberattacks, and demanding business units. Regulating the enterprise around privacy is also essential. EQ management and regulation use some of the same skills discussed in Chapter 2 (reactive vs. proactive brain function) that make space for reasoned and documented decision making. Develop coherent policies, protocols, and standards to become the rules that regulate the enterprise. Following, auditing, and enforcing the policies is how we manage the enterprise. The serenity prayer is the privacy professional's compass: "To accept the things I cannot change, courage to change the things I can, and wisdom to know the difference."

(3)   **Motivation.** Motivation is a feeling that rises inside and inspires us to take action and get things done. Money can motivate you to come to work, but internal or intrinsic motivation is something you sense in yourself as doing something that matters. Some privacy professionals have described their role and work as

purposeful because they believe privacy is a fundamental human right, and they are doing their part to safeguard those rights. This perspective can sustain privacy professionals through challenging times because they are motivated by an altruistic purpose. However, the consumer protection perspective must be aligned with the interests of the enterprise and what motivates it. For example, the risk of privacy class action lawsuits, regulatory investigations, shareholder distributions, reduced profitability, and fear of cyberattacks are essential motivators that can help the privacy professional drive change. The most sustaining motivators in life come from a place of love, not fear. When I am afraid of something, I tend to avoid it. When I love something, I nurture it.

(4) **Empathy.** Empathy is the ability to know or sense what somebody else is feeling. Some understand this to be an intuitive skill to perceive another's thoughts or beliefs. This skill is vital to be able to deeply understand the concerns of colleagues, leadership, customers, and consumers. For example, employees may be concerned about their privacy rights as their COVID-19 vaccination data is requested and collected by their employer. Customers could feel that the business is not transparent about its privacy practices. Colleagues may perceive the privacy professional as an obstacle to their innovation and creativity. The ability to step into the shoes of others and understand what they may feel as a result of a particular data collection practice will allow the privacy professional to preemptively address the concern or feeling. The ability to anticipate risk and empathize with others forges real privacy change. For example, if you ask for an increased budget to adopt new privacy technology, you might recognize and acknowledge the CFO's feelings about not increasing funding (without personalizing them). This empathic skill will allow you to build a specific case for the CFO describing how the new technology will ultimately save the business time and money because you will not have to hire another person to collect and enter consumer requests manually. Before others can understand your position and perspective around privacy, you must first understand their position and perspective.

(5) **Putting EQ Into Action.** The final piece of the EQ framework is putting it all together to manage relationships

productively. Putting EQ into action requires exercise and testing. For example, after releasing a new privacy policy, protocol, or training, take a colleague to lunch to hear their thoughts and feedback—bonus points if the person is willing to be candid and may not be a privacy fan. Ask questions and be an avid listener. Did their feedback make you aware of something you did not already know? Or did you find yourself trying to explain your perspective? Does the input tell you anything about how you regulate or manage the enterprise and whether changes may be required? Or do you feel like the policies, protocols, and training were perfect, and it was just the individual that did not understand? Were you an active listener to the feedback and able to understand their position and perspective? Or did you find yourself defensive about your policies, protocols, and training? "Privacy with a purpose" can transcend just doing what the job requires. It helps develop meaningful relationships with others and allows you to grow by seeing the world from another perspective.

The Evolving and Expanding Role of the Chief Privacy Officer ~ Matt

The privacy leader's role within the organization is evolving. The importance of privacy practices has clearly become front-and-center for organizations that collect, process and store personal data. In addition, myriad new privacy regulations require that the privacy leader assume a more expansive and organizationally informed role.[41] To put it bluntly, the privacy leader's role—including reporting relationships—within the organization must move beyond the legal context of privacy practices. It must begin to encompass a broader operational understanding of processing activities within the organization and the security over privacy functions, including vendor and third-party risk management. Finally, and critically, it must advocate good privacy practices that engender trust.

Let's visit some of the critical competencies and functions associated with the privacy leader's role within the organization. First and foremost, the privacy leader must assume a lead advocate role within the organization. Specifically, the privacy leader should be the principal advocate for the privacy rights associated with the organization's employees and the consumers or data subjects who use the organization's goods and services. In this context, the privacy leader should be at the forefront, validating that the organization's processing activities are consistent with the applicable regulations and that these activities engender consumer trust. Stated differently, the advocacy of privacy practices that are respectful of the data subject's or consumer's preferences should translate into a higher trust of the organization from that individual.

---

[41] Section 4 and specifically Articles 37 through 39 of the GDPR outline the specific GDPR context of the Data Protection Officer (DPO). This role is distinct from how I'm referencing the privacy leader's role in this chapter. The DPO role, in the context of the GDPR, must be independent and accessible and attend to data subjects and the exercising of their privacy rights. The DPO is charged to monitor compliance with the GDPR and liaise with data protection authorities. Effectively the DPO serves as an independent subject matter expert on the GDPR for the respective controller or data processor.

In marketing circles, where the value of the brand and its reputation are integral, organizations frequently use the Net Promoter Score® (NPS). The NPS offers a simple measurement of whether an organization's customers would promote that organization's goods and services to others.[42] The NPS is a measurement of trust. Organizations with high NPS scores are perceived to deliver on their promises. Organizations that proactively communicate what information they collect, how they will use it, whether it will be sold or shared, and, most importantly, the data subject's rights over their information will likely engender trust. The value of the organization's brand and reputation will increase. The privacy leader is central to these trust-enhancing functions. Being an ever-present advocate for the consumer and data subject will help grow enterprise value, while also reducing the exposure to regulatory risk when processing activities are "unfair and deceptive," and not consistent with good privacy practices. In this context, skilled privacy leaders are essential to organizational strategy and initiatives where personal data is in scope. Privacy leaders advocate the respectful and transparent processing of this data consistent with regulatory obligations, and the explicit validation of whether contemplated activities engender trust and reflect the data subject's explicit consent.

Privacy leaders must know the business. If the privacy leader's time is primarily spent behind a desk addressing legal elements of the privacy program, value is lost. Instead, learn the business by proactively engaging with other stakeholders throughout the organization. Key stakeholders to engage should include customer care and contact centers, human resources, sales and marketing, procurement and vendor management, and importantly, IT and security teams. The objective is to understand how the required privacy practices impact these departments or functions and compile a list of issues that may warrant a proverbial double-click to understand current practices and incorporate them into the privacy risk register. The value of the context and insights gained from each

---

[42] To learn more about NPS scores, visit the following: https://www.netpromoter.com/know/.

department cannot be overstated. Here are some high-level topics that apply to the respective departments.

Customer Care and Contact Centers Understand how these departments interact with consumers and data subjects. Determine if the information they collect, process, and retain is consistent with the applicable privacy notice or policy. Spend time with the front-line teams that interact with consumers. Do not limit your conversations to the department leaders. Validate if the contact and care teams are adequately trained to handle data subject access requests (DSARs) and review how these teams authenticate the data subject's identity based on the context of the DSAR. Review common scenarios such as requests to have information corrected or updated, have their information shared with another entity or with the data subject directly, and how requests to have the individual's information purged from the organization are handled. We address privacy rights requests and DSAR scenarios at length in Chapter 13. Ensure that the customer care and contact center staff know when privacy rights are absolute and must be fulfilled and when the request should be denied based on contractual or regulatory context. Use these insights to facilitate future training and see whether the systems, tools, and applications used by these functions are adequate for their purpose. Take this context and review it with both the IT and security leaders of the organization.

Human Resources (HR) Privacy rights and privacy expectations vary dramatically based on jurisdiction. Collaborate with the HR leader to review department-specific privacy practices. Review the system of record for various employee data processing activities such as payroll and benefits administration. Determine, along with IT and security, if and how employee behavior within the workplace is monitored and whether such monitoring practices are consistent with the organization's culture and regulatory obligations. Include in your review notifications to employees about which workplace activities are being monitored. To state the obvious, expectations related to privacy in the workplace differ notably. Privacy leaders who oversee international organizations should understand what's applicable in different locations. For example, different rules apply in Germany, Brazil, and the United States. Of particular note are those situations where work councils and employer associations that may govern privacy practices in the workplace. Spend time with the HR team to understand the nature and extent of the privacy training provided. Some organizations may have mandatory training requirements, such as those associated with the U.S. HIPAA-HITECH regulation. Work with HR to ensure that this training is sufficient for these regulatory requirements.

Sales and Marketing Sales and marketing are distinct corporate functions that are frequently grouped together, but they have their own unique nuance and potential privacy issues. If the same leader manages both, your collaboration will be streamlined. Otherwise, spend time with each leader and their respective teams. Especially with respect to marketing activities, validate what type of information is collected about data subjects and consumers and the sources of this data. Determine whether it is shared or sold to third parties, and if the marketing team uses its own tools to address "opt-out" or "unsubscribe" requests from data subjects. Ensure that any collection activities are consistent with the stated privacy notice.

Do not underestimate the sophistication of marketing technology. Given expansive definitions of personal data, be sure to review which information is collected by media, applications, technology, and venue. For example, IP addresses, cookies, and other digital content can be considered personal data depending on jurisdiction. Privacy leaders will want to ensure that this context is well understood and captured—ideally with a privacy impact assessment. The GDPR defines the term as a data *protection* impact assessment (as outlined in Article 35) and it is used in a more structured and defined manner than general PIAs to address processing activities that are 'likely to result in a high risk to the rights and freedoms of natural persons.' The assessment evaluates privacy and governance practices, including how personal data is protected. Sales teams may be ill-equipped to address privacy and data governance issues. Spend time with both sales and marketing teams to explain how the respectful and consistent use of personal data, with explicit consent, engenders trust and supports the brand. In your collaborations with both sales and marketing, be aware of the tell-tale signs of personal data being used for derivative purposes—purposes that were not part of any privacy notice or description of processing activities. A typical example would be salespeople obtaining attendee lists from events to message individuals directly without their prior consent.

Procurement and Vendor Management The privacy leader will want to have an accurate, complete, and up-to-date inventory of vendors and suppliers who could impact privacy practices for the organization. These could be processors and sub-processors to technology providers who perform algorithmic analyses of personal data. Think expansively—it's surprising how and where personal data is shared.

As you collaborate with procurement and vendor management colleagues, be aware that departments frequently procure services and technologies outside of vendor management and the formal procurement process. Validate the nature and extent of any risk assessments performed during the onboarding and vetting process for services and technologies that are material from a privacy perspective. Determine if the risk assessments are still valid or if newer assessments and analyses should be performed. Be skeptical about the results of SOC 2 and similar audits and certifications. While these may offer "reasonable" assurance, don't overly rely on the findings for inherently high-risk vendors. If a vendor processes sensitive personal data on behalf of the organization, collaborate with the CISO and the security team to dig deep into the vendor's or data processor's privacy and security practices. Ask if the procurement and vendor management teams have identified risks about which they'd like to have more detail or a deeper review, but simply lack adequate time and resources to perform the assessment. Capture this detail in your privacy risk register.

Legal Counsel Frequently, the privacy leader already comes from a legal background. If that's not the case, the privacy leader would be well-served to spend time with the organization's counsel to review regulatory requirements and contractual obligations that the organization has that are germane to its privacy practices and its privacy program. Further, validate key topics such as data retention requirements, data security requirements (e.g., where an organization may be required to encrypt certain data elements), and data breach obligations should a data breach occur. The organization's counsel will likely have substantial input if not the definitive definition of personal data (ideally, these definitions are consistent with regulatory definitions such as that found in Article 4 of the GDPR). Counsel will also have an important role in defining permissible terms in data processing agreements and providing context on what level of privacy risk should be acceptable to the firm.

Information Technology (IT) and Infrastructure and Operations (I&O) The IT and I&O teams, typically led by the organization's Chief Information Officer (CIO), along with the security team, will have important context for the privacy leader to evaluate. Identify the systems used by the organization that collect, process, store, or share personal data and the backup and data protection mechanisms for these systems. The privacy leader should coordinate with the IT & I&O teams to review data flows, validate data retention periods, and understand how access to these environments is logically and physically controlled and logged. These teams will also have insights on third-party infrastructure as a service (IaaS) vendor that are employed by the organization. The nature and extent of IaaS services should be thoroughly vetted with these teams to determine any jurisdictional issues associated with where personal data is stored. The privacy leader will also want to capture detail on core SaaS applications overseen by IT. Generally, validate these findings with lines of business and functional areas for additional insight. Frequently, SaaS applications are procured directly by lines of business with little or no IT or procurement review.

Security Similar to the collaboration and validation associated with IT and I&O teams, the privacy leader will need to collaborate closely with the Chief Information Security Officer (CISO) to ensure the use of requisite data security protections throughout the personal data lifecycle. Areas that warrant attention include cryptographic services to secure personal data, approaches to pseudonymization and tokenization of personal data, and general access controls for systems that process and store personal data. As the adage goes, you can have security without privacy, but you cannot have privacy without security. Therefore, the CISO and privacy leader must work hand-in-glove to identify risks to personal data across the organization and ensure that these identified risks are captured in the risk register to support risk treatment and remediation that has the visibility of other members of the ELT.

Executive Leadership The executive leadership team and board ultimately set the tone at the top for the organization and guide organizational strategy and initiatives. Moreover, the ELT, ideally properly informed of risk considerations, should determine organizational risk tolerances. The privacy leader should ensure that the topic of privacy is captured for the strategy of in-scope initiatives—notably those that are consumer-oriented—and validate the privacy-related risks of these initiatives. Where and to whom the privacy leader reports are also integral. Privacy leaders who do not have visibility with the ELT may not be able to address privacy risks and practices adequately. Ideally, the privacy leader is a member of the ELT—either as general counsel or directly reporting to the CEO.

Beyond these critical organizational relationships, the privacy leader serves as the titular head of the organization's privacy program. This includes the development of privacy policies (in conjunction with legal counsel if separate from the privacy leader), privacy practices related to DSARs, and vendor oversight. It also includes the procedures that convert policies to actual functions. To be effective, the privacy leader should report privacy program status to the ELT at least quarterly or, more appropriately, should be a member of the ELT directly. The privacy leader may also need to develop a budget to support these activities, including applications to process DSARs, third-party assessments, and any applicable audits. Consider establishing an organization-specific privacy calendar that notes the cadences and participants for specific privacy functions. Items on the calendar should include privacy-centric training for employees, when to conduct data protection (privacy) impact assessments, maintenance and periodic reviews of the privacy risk register, and other privacy-specific assessments. It's critical that the risks that have been identified through the collaborative efforts noted above be appropriately documented, prioritized, and managed through risk treatment and remediation. These activities be reviewed collaboratively with organizational stakeholders.

The insights garnered through this process will help the privacy leader to truly know the organization and its core functions. This "know-the-business" aspect of the role must be a top priority of any privacy leader.

Key Insights and Recommended Next Steps

Key Insights

- While privacy is a whole of enterprise endeavor, the privacy leader is the individual who focuses the effort and acts as the primary subject matter expert.
- Section 4 Article 37 through 39 outline the unique requirements of a DPO in the context of the GDPR - recognizing that for some organizations they may use the term interchangeably with that of a CPO. In the context of GDPR, it's essential to recognize the unique obligations of the DPO role as defined.
- Regulatory bodies have tasked the privacy leader with explicit mandatory functions and endowed them with specific rights to protect the position from undue influence so they can act as advocates for the rights of consumers or data subjects.
- Technical skills are essential, but more important are the soft skills, highlighted by high emotional intelligence (EQ), influence, and leadership.
- The privacy leader plays a critical role in engendering consumer trust in your company.
- The privacy leader must spend time with each of the functions that participate in the privacy ecosystem and learn how private data is collected and used and their key contributions to the enterprise.

Recommended Next Steps

- Take a personal inventory of the skills highlighted in Chapter 3 and develop an action plan to close the identified gaps.
- Draft and use a risk register to keep track of identified privacy risks. Use the risk register to validate understandings of material risks with other organizational stakeholders.
- Schedule time with the leadership function you identified in Chapter 2 and begin to develop an understanding of the contributions to the organization and the personal data they collect and use. Read ahead to Chapter 4 before sitting down in person so you have a full understanding of what you want to achieve with each conversation.

Chapter 4

Elements of a Privacy Program

Introduction

The "corporate purpose," wrote Ted Levitt, "rather than making money, it is to create and keep a customer." He made this statement in his seminal 1983 book, *The Marketing Imagination*. In this book he also introduced the "total product concept," positing that a product is more than the end-product we think we are buying but instead consists of all the components that come together to create that product.

The total product concept was a groundbreaking idea, later built upon by marketing legends such as Regis McKenna, who rebranded this idea the "whole product" and added the notion of the "compelling reason to buy," and Tom Peters, who wrote a whitepaper called *The Eye of the Beholder*. In it he distinguished between the producing company, which saw the product in terms of reliability and features, and the consumer, who instead saw the support provided for the product and the reputation of the company. Peters went on, "Successful companies are those that come the closest to seeing the world as their customers do. Really understanding what your customer values offers opportunities for you to improve customer service and satisfaction, or even to create whole new markets."

In Chapter 3, "The Role of the Privacy Leader," we showed how the role of the privacy leader, however it is titled, can be much more than a regulator's mandate. We demonstrated the value of EQ to be successful in the role and gave a breakdown of all the functions that make up the data ecosystem and what you need to examine with the folks who lead those functions to understand how data that must remain private flows into and through the organization. In Chapter

4, "Elements of a Privacy Program," we will begin to unpack the components of the whole privacy program.

In "The Practical Details of Implementing a Privacy Program," David points out that the success or failure of any organization is predicated on building and managing trust. You could say that in the eye of the consumer, reputation is trust. David then explores the practical elements of implementing a privacy program, such as scoping risk, accounting for legislative impact, and preparing the organization for the problems that will inevitably occur while doing our best to protect precious data and comply with our obligations.

Justine likens the role of the privacy professional to that of a gardener, contributing not just the seed, soil, and water but the passion and advocacy necessary for the garden to flourish. In her essay, "The Privacy Professional's Role in Building a Privacy Program," Justine shows how people, processes, and technology combine with a multi-disciplinary approach to create an entire ecosystem that drives value and reduces risk.

Matt believes strongly in the value of a charter, and in his essay, "How Privacy Programs Come Together," explains how to construct a charter that will serve as the backbone for your privacy program. Matt, Justine, and David espouse several shared beliefs. Two of these are that good privacy practices engender trust in clients, partners, and employees and the acts of building and maintaining the privacy program allow the privacy professional and the whole organization to have a better understanding of the customer's needs and even how the company functions.

The Practical Details of Implementing a Privacy Program ~ David

As we have already seen, privacy is not a concern of one department over another—it stretches across executives, marketing, sales, IT, and HR. Moreover, a privacy program isn't just about seeking compliance with the GDPR, CCPA, or the legislation relevant to your jurisdiction: it embraces elements of law, technology, education, awareness, and procurement.

Overall, without a pervasive alignment of privacy-aware culture across the corporation, however large or small, the program will be flawed, with the associated risks of fines, brand damage, and loss of reputation and confidence with everyone the business touches.

Before we look at the practical details of implementing the all-important program, let's remember that the most essential aspect of making your company privacy-aware is understanding its purpose. In other words, why privacy matters to your company, its employees, business partners, and customers.

Regardless of the rules enshrined in legislation, the success or failure of any organization is predicated on building and managing trust. Indeed, many people have become inured to the daily reports of security breaches involving the handling of personal and commercial data—what we might call privacy fatigue. However, no one should be in any doubt that employees, customers, suppliers, and partners will be wary of transacting with any organization that cannot demonstrate that they have in place measures to protect the data that they are responsible for collecting, storing, and managing, and for mitigating the risks of having personal or commercial data compromised.

There are important considerations to be factored in based on industry type, company size, and other variables that will determine many of the practical aspects of setting up and running a privacy program. Not every company has infinite resources or the infrastructure to support a fully-fledged privacy program—and yet have as great a need as the largest corporation. And even then, challenges anticipated as only applying to small and medium-sized enterprises (SMEs) are frequently found with large firms.

No company can guarantee that they won't be impacted by a cyberattack from hackers or criminals seeking to steal sensitive data or cause damage to make ransom demands. Equally as dangerous from a reputational and financial perspective is the loss of sensitive data due to human error—whether losing or misplacing a flash drive or device in a public place, or inadvertently or deliberately letting sensitive data fall into the hands of unauthorized third parties.

Even the largest corporation would struggle to prevent any of the above. But at the very least, the risks—and the consequences—can be reduced.

Getting Started

There are several ways any company can understand and then approach the privacy program they are about to embark on but primarily, they are either from the perspective of the data subjects (i.e., the employees, suppliers, customers, et al.) or from the standpoint of the company itself. The two are inextricably linked through the set of procedures that will assess and ultimately manage risk. Risk regarding the damage that an individual person or, in the case of suppliers, a third-party company may have to endure. Or risk to your company in terms of reputation loss or pecuniary fines, not to mention system repairs after a data breach.

Generally, medium to large size corporations have more resources than the average small or micro-business. Although in some respects, as we observed in the previous chapter, the situation is complicated by the plethora of departments and subsidiary companies that to all intents and purposes act independently of each other. Focusing the privacy program on specific "islands" that are more willing to participate than others will not get the job done. It is vital for success to get all the key stakeholders, starting at the CxO level, to understand and approve what is being undertaken from the get-go. It's unlikely that senior executives will get directly involved unless called upon. Still, they must buy into and propagate the message and the change in culture, the details of which the rest of the company will deep dive into.

Does your company have a data protection officer (DPO)? If so, all well and good. However, if not, whether or not they are given the title of DPO, someone has to be appointed to orchestrate and choreograph the program's implementation.

Scoping the Risk

The risk to scope pivots around the possibility of problems arising from processing personal or sensitive company data and their impact should problems occur.

These risks include issues such as technical measures that lack appropriate safeguards, social media attacks, mobile malware, third-party access, negligence resulting from improper configuration, outdated security software, social engineering, and lack of encryption for emails or data storage. The quantification of the vulnerabilities will be unique to your organization and its risk management policies. The use of methodologies based on FAIR (Factor Analysis of Information Risk) is one well-established approach you can take.

In that context, it has become increasingly clear to many companies that compliance with regulations alone is not enough, not least because privacy-related risk is as much a business issue as it is one of technology. The specter of financial and reputational loss are two major factors that influence decision-making, as is the need to protect the company while successfully running the business.

One aspect of risk assessment that falls into the category of "realpolitik" is how to respond when asked, "How much privacy is 'enough'?" which may come on the coattails of "How much is this all going to cost?" A privacy program is effectively an insurance policy both for your company and your customers, and, like any insurance salesperson, you will have to juggle the numbers. When you are asked to compromise with influential naysayers or those who impose an unrealistic or excessively challenging financial ceiling on the program, you must be ready to let them know, giving them chapter and verse, the level of exposure the company will be subject to. In other words, make it at least a shared responsibility. If, or sadly and more likely, when there is a data breach, the consequent inquiry and investigation may well come back to one of those early conversations.

Elsewhere in this book, we categorize the types of risks a company may be exposed to in more detail. Broadly speaking, they can be broken down into internal and external threats and further qualified according to whether the intent behind each type of threat is malicious or mischievous or caused through negligence or carelessness. For each scenario, a thorough analysis by your security experts will determine the appropriate responses, how they should be provided, and how they should be incorporated into the privacy program.

The Legislation

It's important to know who is setting the rules that will underpin your program. For most companies (but not all), geography will determine that.

Although there is a tendency to focus on the EU and the US when it comes to privacy legislation, globally, approximately 140 countries have privacy laws; and, for example, in the Asia Pacific (APAC) region, privacy is highly regulated in Australia, Hong Kong, Japan, Malaysia, and Singapore.

Until recently, unlike many other jurisdictions, the United States did not have the prospect of a single law that would cover all aspects of privacy for all types of data across all 50 states of the Union. Increasingly, individual states had been stepping up to the plate with their own set of similar but individual comprehensive privacy laws. Still, the more established legislation is determined by a specific industry or application vertical—or both. The mix of legislation can be overwhelming as it pertains to healthcare (HIPPA), finance (FCRA, FTC, GLBA), education (FERPA), communications (ECPA), protecting children (COPPA), and even rental records (VPPA).

It definitely gets more complicated for companies that operate in more than one jurisdiction or, more specifically, hold information about data subjects who reside in multiple jurisdictions.

The most important criteria for assessing the extent to which your privacy program should be cognizant of any piece of legislation require going back to the basics of why privacy matters: understanding the spirit and the driving principles behind the work of the legislators and what they were trying to achieve. Of course, compliance is important, but principles are a lot easier to communicate to your entire workforce.

However, all that could change with the proposal for a unifying federal data privacy act, first introduced in June 2022 by the U.S. Congress, and cited as the American Data Privacy and Protection Act (ADPPA) . The ADPPA draft highlights the urgency for protecting consumer data privacy across the United States. However, as of the time of writing, there is still a long way to go to get a comprehensive agreement on its final shape and scope.

Privacy Impact Assessment

Once you've established in principle that your company will proceed with a privacy program, the next thing to do is to establish the scope of the task which will impact the effort required and the cost budget. First, begin with a privacy impact assessment (PIA).[43] A PIA is a review of your company's data assets that will demand the engagement of department heads, system administrators, and a wide range of employees to analyze cross-platform and inter-departmental applications, storage systems, information/data flows, and the content on company websites and across social media accounts.

---

[43] A PIA and a DPIA (Data Protection Impact Assessment) are separate processes. A PIA helps establish a privacy program by analyzing how an organization collects, uses, shares, and maintains personally identifiable information. In a GDPR context, the DPIA replaced the PIA and is used to identify, mitigate, and minimize risk. Compare this with a ROPA, a 'record of processing activities' which is an ongoing maintenance activity and a requirement under Article 30 of the GDPR.

The person best qualified to lead the PIA is the DPO. In the absence of a DPO, a compliance officer or a representative group of senior executives should step in.

It will be vital to determine which processes and procedures are in place for the individuals and applications with access to inputting and maintaining personal data entering the system. One of the outcomes of the risk assessment exercise will be to tighten policies around the rationale both for collecting data and where it is stored—whether in the cloud or on individuals' devices—and for how long. In large companies, the responsibility for getting these processes straightened out will require a diverse team comprising departmental decision-makers, IT, system architects, and legal working together despite the potential for competing priorities among these groups.

Carrying out this assessment for the first time will be an exacting task, but it will reap benefits when you return to the exercise on a regular, annual, or bi-annual basis.

Be Prepared

As is evidenced daily by organizations globally, the likelihood of a data breach is a question of when not if. Although it may never happen, it's still a reasonably sound—verging on essential—premise to work from.

It is unrealistic to have 100% security on- or off-premises; in today's environment, particularly with the unprecedented growth in home-working due to COVID-19 restrictions, the enterprise perimeter that used to be a fortress wall is no longer what it was, if it exists at all. Bring your own device, identity, key, or network policies have ceased to be the exceptions to the rule that they used to be just a few years ago. In addition, protecting enterprise resources when employees are working at home in a family environment, with their company computer system potentially exposed to family members oblivious to the consequences of a few errant keystrokes, is challenging, to say the least.

If a data loss occurs—it's not inevitable, but there are no guarantees—it is critical to have a plan in place for handling what happens next. Several key things are:

- **Detect any breach as quickly as possible.** The symptoms of a breach may be detected by anyone, anywhere across the whole organization. Therefore, all employees and in-house contractors need to know what to look for, what types of "abnormal behavior" to recognize, however seemingly trivial, and how to report what they've come across. These reporting lines should be short and involve only people who need to know—ideally the CISO/DPO and the assigned cybersecurity experts—to ensure that the next stage of the process happens as quickly as possible.

- **Assess the source of the reported anomaly.** This requires intense exploratory activity by the cybersecurity team. Once they have initially identified the probable source and provenance of the reported anomaly, they can ascertain the scale and scope of the damage so far.

- **Understand the nature of the attack or breach event.** The cybersecurity team's report to the CISO should include the recommended steps to limit or restrict any further damage. The recommendations may include drastic measures such as switching off crucial parts of the IT infrastructure that would normally be vital for running the business.

- **Communicate the news to internal stakeholders.** As the above steps are underway, senior members of the leadership team must communicate the news of what has happened and what steps are being taken, initially with those who are directly impacted. For example, it may be necessary to tell certain groups of employees not to send any more company emails until further notice.

- **Communicate with all relevant external stakeholders.** The leadership team should interact with the impacted third parties and all the relevant external stakeholders and other interested parties at various points in the process. This may include the media and the statutory authorities responsible for privacy and data protection in the jurisdiction(s) relevant to your company. As more information becomes available about the source, impact, and response to the data breach, when and how to formulate the drip-feed of communications will involve serious judgment calls. This will involve the whole leadership team. The news and how and when the news is delivered will affect all aspects of the business.

We have more—much more—on data breaches and how to respond in Chapter 12.

Transparency Is Key

Keeping abreast of privacy and data protection regulation is highly demanding. There is a lot to keep track of, including the European GDPR and ePrivacy regulation, California's CCPA, the United States' HIPAA, COPTA, and FACTA, the Canadian PIPEDA and Privacy Act, and all the other emerging legislation worldwide, particularly in APAC. And, as if this was not enough, the recently heralded draft of ADPPA provides even more material to speculate on. The challenge does mean that companies must pay far greater attention to how they implement privacy and data protection safeguards than ever before. The chances are that the effort, and likewise the cost, will be greater than expected, and it shouldn't come as a surprise, if and when someone questions the validity of the privacy program undertaken. The chances are they will have underestimated the scale and extent of the disruptive and transformative change to business models and practices that a full-scale privacy program entails.

In other words, transparency is key: it is vitally important to stay visible to the senior executive team and other strategic stakeholders—including, whenever and wherever appropriate, your customers and employees whose data you are safeguarding—and keep them constantly aware of what you must do, what gaps have subsequently been identified, and the cost of the program. Looking beyond managing stakeholder expectations, for your privacy program to be successful, everyone must be on board and prepared to be actively engaged. The program's key messages will need to be repeated and reinforced through every line of business.

Given the option, no one likes to have to pay for insurance. But today, not having a privacy program is not an option. So, if or when the investment in the privacy program is questioned or criticized, a reference to the headlines on the latest corporate data breach should provide the necessary corrective.

The Privacy Professional's Role in Building a Privacy Program ~ Justine

Privacy professionals are the cartographers of the privacy program—they envision, create, build, implement, and oversee the entire program. To do so, they must first develop a common language that is used and understood enterprise wide. Ludwig Wittgenstein, a German philosopher, wisely observed: "The limits of language are the limits of my world."

Proactive vs. Reactive

In privacy (much like life), we can only control two things: (1) how we prepare for what might happen ("proactive") and (2) how we respond to what just happened ("reactive"). A privacy program is a proactive and documented initiative to govern data privacy. Governance includes complying with law and regulations but also extends to identifying, understanding, and mapping privacy risk, shifting, transferring, and reducing that risk, creating policies, training humans, and managing third parties. A sane privacy professional controls the things she can, accepts or avoids the things she cannot, and possesses the wisdom to know the difference. This chapter explains the key components of building a successful privacy program.

Cultivating Your Privacy Garden

People, process, and technology are the proverbial "three legs of the stool" required to build a privacy program. A more purposeful analogy is the privacy garden—planting seeds and growing sustainable roots to nourish the privacy garden. Using analogies can help non-privacy professionals understand privacy in a relatable way.

The People. Think of the people as your fellow gardeners: humans that identify, create, and solve privacy risks. It is possible to build a garden all on your own—but it will be small and difficult to nourish the entire enterprise. Therefore, it is essential to rally privacy people to help support and implement the privacy program. People may be employees or third parties who provide services like contractors, consultants, and vendors. Employees create both the most significant vulnerability and best defense for privacy risk. Therefore, privacy programs must educate and empower people to understand consumer rights, privacy policies, processes, and technology. Examples include regular training on privacy and security, non-disclosure and confidentiality agreements, acknowledgment of policies that protect privacy, privacy hotlines, and a culture of respecting and understanding privacy and security.

"The People" should also include the consumers that your business serves. They are the ones that entrust their data to your organization and are often the benefactors who enjoy the harvest your garden produces (or the spoils from a virus that eliminates your crop). You may call these customers, users, members, data subjects, or something else. Notably, consumer rights create the risk businesses are trying to manage. The key to a successful privacy program is considering how these humans may react to or receive initiatives that may impact their privacy. Humans have individual preferences—so give them choices. Humans do not like to be surprised—so make the disclosures in consumer-facing policies clear and easy to understand. Humans like to be part of something greater than themselves—so empower consumers to feel connected to your business through their data.

The Processes. Processes are the procedures and practices, informed by policies, standards, guidelines, and protocols, that operationalize the privacy program and create a roadmap for compliance. Legal teams, consultants, Human Resources, IT, and Information Security professionals spend an exorbitant amount of time on processes. Sometimes I am asked for a "cyber policy," and I think it is like asking for the secret to happiness. If only it were that easy to address in a single document. Instead, "policies" are the individual instruments being played that make up an orchestra of cyber processes.

Think of "policies" as the container or box for your garden: these are the rules that generally define the basic purpose and framework for the privacy program.[44] Not all writings that describe privacy practices and rules are policies. The language we use is essential. Policies are documents that create an authority within the company that must be followed by all employees and are often included in an employee handbook and signed with other onboarding documents. Policies are agreements between the business and employees that state the rules the employees are expected to follow. If employees break the rules, it creates risk, and they can be disciplined up to and including termination. Policies may be revisited annually and often do not change unless a law requires further revisions. Some organizations require board or executive approval to change policies, which can be a lengthy process. You can create a policy on policies (I am not joking—it is a real thing) to clearly articulate what to call written documents, who must approve them, the frequency of their review, and who owns them. Policies may also be signed by third-party vendors that access systems and technologies. The vendor agreement may impose such obligations on the third-party employees.

The next layer of processes is the standards, guidelines, procedures, and protocols ("process documents"): the soil or dirt filling the garden box. These process documents are intended to be practical and fluid, frequently change as needed, not require board approval or oversight, not require employees to counter-sign, and be specific to the business unit. Not all process documents may be available or applicable to all employees. Availability may be role-based. For example, a patch management procedure may only apply to employees in Information Technology and Information Security that may have a role related to keeping software patches up to date. Yet, an information security policy or acceptable use policy (AUP) may require all employees to comply with specific rules like password management and data loss prevention. The IT standards then explain practical and straightforward guidance, so an employee doesn't have "password" as their password or forward a confidential record to their home email address. Password management guidelines may change based on the technology utilized.

---

[44] See the Appendix for a reprint of the essay from the CISO Desk Reference Guide defining the hierarchy of policies, procedures, standards, and guidelines.

The final layer for processes is the "practices," like the act of planting the privacy seeds in the garden. Be thoughtful of the seeds you plant and where you place your attention. Practices are the humans putting the processes into action through daily compliance, auditing, testing, training, and exercises. Without practices, the garden would just be a box filled with soil.

There are some key factors to consider when deciding whether to adopt policies vs. a process document. First, identify whether the rule applies to all employees or if an employee can be disciplined for breaking the rule outlined in the document. If the answer is yes to either question, a policy may be better. Second, if the rule directs an individual to perform a task or function that may be part of their specific job duty, it is better to articulate those expectations in a process document. Third, if the rule calls out any specific technology or may need to be modified on a more frequent basis, then a process document is the more appropriate program document.

The Technologies. Technologies are the hardware and software that host data and systems to operate businesses. Think of these as the tools you need to plant, cultivate, and harvest your privacy garden. They are the irrigation systems that keep our businesses running and nourished. Gone are the days when understanding "computers" is for IT and Information Security professionals. You don't need a professional gardener to turn on the automated sprinkler system and pull the weeds; however, the experts should still do the heavy lifting with technologies like fixing broken sprinkler heads. We live in a time where it is imperative that all employees know how to use technologies properly and water the garden. Nearly all jobs require some basic competence in technology. The hardware and software are the vehicles that carry the data.

Although we focused this section on the people, process, and technology within your own organization, your privacy garden is interdependent on your vendors' privacy gardens. Vendors are comprised of their own people, processes, and technologies, and these third parties are an integral part of the privacy ecosystem to operate your business. Think of this as a nearby garden—if a virus spreads in their garden, it will impact yours too. The vendor's people, processes, and technologies also matter. See Chapter 10, "Vendor Risk Management," for a deeper discussion on managing vendors.

Creating Space for a Privacy Program

Corporate Social Responsibility and Privacy

Consumers and investors are increasingly focused on socially responsible businesses because it bolsters a company's image and brand and proliferates consumer trust. Corporate social responsibility programs (CSR) are purpose-driven initiatives that consider how business decisions impact more than just financial gains/losses. CSR programs factor in the social impact to employees, the public, stakeholders, and the natural world by empowering employees to leverage the corporate resources at their disposal to do good. According to the Harvard Business Review[45] CSR programs can boost employee morale and lead to greater productivity. In addition, CSR policies and programs can be integrated into privacy programs and provide board and executive buy-in to support privacy programs.

Increasingly, strong CSRs can *be* the brand—like Patagonia. On its website, Patagonia states: "Everything we make has an impact on people and the planet."[46] Their environmental and social responsibility program is public-facing and demonstrates the careful decisions in sourcing and manufacturing their clothes to minimize the impact of our planet as a whole, including economic, environmental, and social factors. In return, consumers trust that buying Patagonia products has a positive impact on the planet—essentially, the corporate values align with consumer values. Businesses can take this model and apply it to privacy for their business. If privacy is a fundamental human right, then privacy programs naturally integrate with CSR programs and initiatives to empower the business and its employees to do good. Abide by the

---

[45] 15 Eye-Opening Corporate Social Responsibility Statistics
https://online.hbs.edu/blog/post/corporate-social-responsibility-statistics.

[46] Patagonia's website can he found here: https://www.patagonia.com/our-footprint/.

philosophy that "anything you do, is everything you do." Those core values then become part of the brand and cultivate consumer trust.

Manifest Your Mantra

Our family has a mantra: *Be Smart, Be Kind, Be Grateful.* It is what we say to our kids when they step out of the car for school. It is a simple reminder to act by our core family values throughout their day. Privacy mantras ("Privacy Charters" or "Privacy Missions") are essential guides and reminders for an organization. Manifesting a mantra is not a game of solitaire. It is a collaborative process shaped during meetings with other key stakeholders. Some businesses have simple privacy mantras like "Customers First," which shapes their policies, training, and response in a cyber event. Others opt for a longer privacy mantra: "The responsible use and protection of data to respect individual privacy, ensure the confidentiality, integrity, and availability of information resources, and comply fully with all laws and government regulations." When developing a privacy mantra for your business, keep it simple. Think big picture and long term. Think about how your mantra might waterfall into policies and training. Engage marketing and bounce the ideas off them.

Consumer Protection

Most privacy laws are consumer protection laws—laws that restrict or prohibit businesses from engaging in a particular activity that is misleading, unfair, or deceptive. Many laws now require companies to provide transparency into data collection practices and give consumers the right to request access, modify, or delete their personal information. Consumers typically do not have individual bargaining power to negotiate terms with businesses in the digital age. To install an application, users must accept the terms that are presented. The challenge for companies is complying with various laws. Privacy laws offer protection to residents of a particular jurisdiction. For example, a business operating in California that sells products or services to consumers in 50 different jurisdictions must comply with the laws of all 50 jurisdictions.

Waking Up the Organization to Privacy

The Secret to Happiness

Privacy programs include public disclosures about privacy practices. Tremendous risk exists if the business misrepresents its actual privacy practices. Mahatma Gandhi opined that the secret to happiness is when what you think, say, and do are in harmony. In other words, when the outer self and your actions are consistent with the inner self. This wisdom is most helpful when applied to privacy disclosures. If a business believes they collect, maintain, use, or share data in one way and disclose such practices to consumers in a privacy policy, but in reality those statements are inaccurate or untrue, then businesses face tremendous regulatory and legal risk for deceptive, fraudulent, and misleading information. One example is how businesses describe their security practices or make assurances about safeguarding data in their privacy policies. Following a data breach, the plaintiff's attorneys often copy and paste those representations in the complaint to form the basis for a fraudulent or deceptive practices argument. They contend that if they had secured the data, it would not have been compromised. These blanket assertions are often tenuous, but the burden will be on the business in litigation to demonstrate and prove that their security practices were reasonable and consistent with the representations in their privacy policy.

Data Mapping

Maya Angelou believed that "if we know better, we do better." If we know what data our organization maintains, we can better meet our legal obligations. Knowing what data your organization collects and where it is stored are critical for two reasons: (1) disclosure obligations—a business cannot explain its practices as required by various laws and regulations if it doesn't know them; and (2) security obligations—a business cannot secure data if it does not know where it lives and who has access.

Data mapping is the process of documenting a comprehensive inventory of data. Streamline and organize the process by developing assessments, questionnaires, or live interviews to allow key stakeholders to provide accurate feedback and information about data collection/use/practices. Once you know how data flows in and out of the organization, prepare a visual diagram to help navigate other tasks. Data flow visualization can help convey important information to other stakeholders in a way that Excel spreadsheets cannot.

Data Mapping: Identifying and Classifying What the Business Is Trying to Keep Private

Data mapping is the process of getting to know your data: how it is collected, stored, accessed, secured, shared, and ultimately destroyed. The data mapping assessment or questionnaire is the tool that contains the questions to gain a deeper understanding of your data. Some laws and regulations like GDPR and CCPA proscribe what questions must be asked to inform data subjects or consumers about data collection practices. For example, that you must understand the data elements collected, the purpose for their collection, how the business uses the data, who the data is shared with, whether the data is sold, and the length of time before it is destroyed.

Although some company data belongs to consumers (personal information) or is public facing (website, marketing campaigns), most company data is private (such as trade secrets, emails, HR data, finances). Don't forget to identify the 3 Rs: data that makes you rich (trade secrets, inventions, financials, business information), could ruin you (reputational damage, violating the law, sensitive data that triggers breach obligations), or is required to be maintained by laws or regulators (employee data, financial information, compliance). After we identify and classify data, we can conduct a cost-benefit analysis to determine the risk and value of the data, which will then inform how many resources should be dedicated to keeping it private.

For years, the idea that possession was nine-tenths of the law echoed through privacy laws. Many breach statutes apply to businesses that "own or license" data. The fact that a company had a consumer's personal information suggested ownership rights to the data. And businesses acted accordingly by analyzing data, using it for targeted marketing and understanding consumer preferences. Those behaviors were the natural consequence of possessing big data and were not regulated forcefully until laws like GDPR and CCPA returned the rights to personal information to individuals. As a result, many businesses now have data at the election and control of the consumer.

Data Topography—Charting Your Course

Data maps start by identifying the brightest stars in your enterprise, like your customer database or invaluable intellectual property. After identification and classification, move on to specifying all the locations or assets where data resides. Information assets and data are often widely distributed and may reside on your servers, in the cloud, with vendors, on employees' mobile devices, and beyond. Data maps do not have to be fancy; instead, make them functional. Create the data map in a Word chart, Excel file, Visio, or Adobe Illustrator. Use a program that is easy to modify so the map can evolve with additional information as you learn more about your data. Only after we identify, locate, and classify the data can we reasonably secure it. Just as ancient astronomy evolved, so too will your understanding of your data and its illustrations.

A Privacy Program Requires Privacy Leadership

Who Are You?

Another critical component to effective enterprise management is knowing who you are, your role, and your language. Enterprises or businesses are comprised of individuals with various and unique talents, skillsets, and responsibilities or functions. Who we are within our company is only one manifestation of who we really are. It is important to understand our values, ethics, preferences, and motivators, but that is the topic of a different type of book. This section requires you to understand your organizational role or the role you seek to have. For example, a Chief Information Officer may be responsible for managing and implementing information and computer technologies and speak about binary operating systems and algorithms.

Chief Financial Officers are responsible for financials and accounting and speak in the language of dollars and cents and Generally Accepted Accounting Principles. Human Resources Officers are responsible for managing workplace issues and speak a language that fosters workforce engagement and culture. It can feel like the Tower of Babel when you bring so many different stakeholders to the table. Attempts to communicate are obfuscated by different languages used by different stakeholders. Personal information holds a different sentiment and meaning to various people in an organization. The stakeholders need a common language around cyber and privacy to manage the enterprise. A data dictionary or privacy glossary can help make policies consistent and reduce confusion among critical stakeholders.

Privacy Wheel—Be the Hub

Lying at the core of all privacy programs is a privacy leader. This person rays out in all directions of the enterprise, like spokes from the hub of a wheel or rays of sunshine beaming from the sun. The privacy leader thinks about privacy and security both horizontally and vertically. As discussed in Chapter 6, "Privacy Lifecycle," the pattern of privacy is cyclical. Understanding enterprise risk is also circular. The privacy leader is open and receptive to learning from all points of view. The privacy leader understands and steadily processes business needs, technical capabilities and limitations, consumer rights, emerging laws and trends, engineering needs, employee rights, finances and budgets, exposures, and timing. Each organization has a unique purpose and personality that informs how enterprise management is structured. Privacy leaders earn the trust of decision-makers they report up to, the subordinates they manage, and peers they support. Effective leaders are emotionally intelligent, are better listeners, and often gain the trust of other employees. Asking great questions and being a good listener are natural skills for the privacy leader.

Create a Privacy Family Tree

Create a chart or "family tree" that visualizes the organizational structure and identifies the various business units and how they relate to each other. Biomimicry looks at the natural world to inspire new ideas, patterns, or ways of describing. Think of the business units as branches—although they may grow in different directions, they connect to the same root. This family tree is a valuable roadmap for enterprise management. All business units have some interest and responsibility in managing privacy. Finance must protect and safeguard financial controls and financial data. Human Resources must protect and safeguard employee and benefits data. Engineering must protect and safeguard intellectual property and source code. And privacy must protect all types of private data, especially consumer data. Yet having the various business units work in silos towards their respective interests and goals without considering privacy risk will ultimately increase costs and risk. Pulling threads of commonality throughout the enterprise is critical. Also, helping business units understand other business units' privacy needs and concerns allows for a great understanding of enterprise management to help leaders make better decisions.

Vendor Management

Increasingly, privacy laws like HIPAA, CCPA, and GDPR include flow-down provisions that require businesses to understand and manage how third parties use, share, and secure the business' data. Vendor management is critically important because so much data is hosted in the cloud. Even if a business shifts the responsibility for hosting data to a third party, it remains accountable and liable to the consumer for safeguarding such data.

Identify third parties, independent contractors, and vendors who receive business data and conduct vendor inquiries and diligence about using, sharing, and securing the data. CCPA requires specific language in third-party agreements to qualify as a service provider (service providers are given some safe harbors for CCPA violations). To the extent third parties receive sensitive data like social security numbers, driver's license numbers, financial information, or health information, ensure that they have implemented strong security and data governance practices to protect the data. Applicant data contains a treasure trove of sensitive data, and notice is required if that data is breached—even if the breach occurs on your vendor's website and not your own systems.

Fundamentals Of a Thoughtful Privacy Program

Data Minimization Principles

As discussed in more depth in Chapter 8, "Privacy by Design," privacy-centric organizations reduce the amount of data collected to the minimum data required to achieve their objective. Data minimization principles can apply to collecting data (collecting less information or fewer data elements), keeping data for a short time, establishing processes for destroying legacy data or automating destruction, or de-identifying data to minimize the risk and application of privacy laws. To effectively implement data minimization principles, people must be trained, processes must be created and enforced, and technologies must automate and be trained.

Update Consumer-Facing Disclosures

Dust off existing privacy policies and include disclosures about categories and types of information collected and the purpose for its collection. Whether in employee handbooks, stand-alone disclosures, onboarding documents, or online privacy policies, businesses should update their disclosures to ensure they provide all the necessary information required by CCPA and other relevant privacy laws.

Data Destruction

As further discussed in Chapter 6, data has a lifecycle. Data destruction processes help businesses identify data types and mandate their destruction pursuant to a schedule or an individual requesting deletion. Frequently, the schedule follows legal obligations to retain data for a certain period. After the period passes, businesses destroy the data. Deletion requests trigger obligations on the business to establish workflows to locate and delete certain types of personal information. Increasingly, businesses archive or maintain data long after it has value to the organization. This type of data hoarding creates unnecessary risk with little to no probative value. It can be difficult to shift the culture from data hoarding to a healthier relationship with data retention, but it is a necessary component to managing data.

Internal Processes to Maintain Privacy

Businesses must also implement internal policies and protocols (collectively, "processes") to operationalize and fulfill promises made to consumers in external policies. Below are examples of internal processes that regulate employee conduct to keep company and consumer data and systems private. Note that the EU Acceptable Use Policy listed in figure 4.2 signals a U.S. company with consumers residing in the EU should have a policy or policies regarding acceptable use that may differ substantially from the acceptable use policies pertaining to their U.S. consumers.

Incident Response and Crisis Management Policies	
Name	**Description**
Incident Response Plan	How the company will manage an incident and remediate the impact to operations
Crisis Management and Communication Plan	How the organization will prepare for/respond to/recover from a crisis (includes disaster recovery plan)

Figure 4.1 Incident Response and Crisis Management Policies

Employee Behavior and Communications Policies

Name	Description
Acceptable Use Policy	How assets can be used (can include computer usage agreement)
Access Control Policy	How information is accessed
Bring Your Own Device Policy	How employees can use personal devices for work purposes
Email/Communication Policy	How employees can use the organization's email and communications system(s)
Employee Privacy Notices	Outlines company's privacy policies and employee data collection, use, and disclosure practices
EU Acceptable Use Policy	How assets can be used (applies to employees in EU)
Insider Trading and Security Transactions Policy	How to comply with insider trading laws
Social Media Policy	How social media can be used
Corporate Communications Policy	Governs external communications with outside parties for all brands

Figure 4.2 Employee Behavior and Communications Policies

Information Systems and Data Use and Protection Policies

Name	Description
Change Management Policy	How changes are made to systems
Contract Management Policy	How and when contracts will be managed or reviewed and who is responsible for managing
Customer-Facing Privacy Policy	Outlines company's privacy policies and data collection, use, and disclosure practices
Data Classification Policy	How data is classified
Data Destruction Security Policy	How to securely destroy data
Data Retention Policy	Where and for how long data is stored
Data Use Guidelines	How personal data can be used
Encryption Policy	How data is encrypted
Firewall Policy	How to name and configure firewalls
Multi-factor Authentication Policy	How to protect networks with multi-factor authentication
Network Security Policy	How network systems are secured
Physical Access Policy	How physical access is obtained and granted
Remote Access Policy	How employees are to use electronic devices not owned by the employer for work purposes
Termination of Access Policy	How employees are removed from systems when employment is terminated
Sarbanes-Oxley Compliance Plan	How to comply with SOX requirements (including audits, data classification, data protection, security controls, and management of electronic records)
Security Awareness Policy	How security awareness is carried out (i.e., training, simulations)
Vendor Data Use Guidelines	How vendors can use the organization's data
Vendor Management Policy	How to manage and properly vet vendors

Figure 4.3 Information Systems and Data Use and Protection Policies

How Privacy Programs Come Together ~ Matt

Privacy programs are multi-faceted, and as we saw in Chapter 2, privacy has a whole-of-enterprise or whole-of-organization impact. In this chapter, I'll contextualize how privacy programs come together, some of the key participants in overseeing the program, the benefits of maintaining privacy programs, how the privacy lifecycle impacts the program, and the risks organizations confront while managing privacy functions.

Before delving into the requisite components of a privacy program, I want to jump on a soapbox and share a couple of thoughts. There are two categories of organizations: those that embrace privacy and view their privacy program and practices as integral to the organization's strategy, and those that view privacy as a checkbox obligation—something that must be done versus something that should be done and embraced.

Organizations that embrace privacy and instill good privacy governance throughout the organization will likely engender trust with consumers, clients, and employees alike. Those organizations that are focused on doing the bare minimum to simply "comply" or "avoid" privacy obligations do so at their own risk. The latter face increased likelihood of regulatory action and risk seeing their enterprise value diminished as consumers, clients, and, indeed, employees exercise their choice and pursue other options that are more respectful of privacy governance practices. Accordingly, building a strong privacy program should not be an obligation but rather an opportunity to align data governance and privacy management practices with organizational strategy.

One last point from the soapbox is that privacy governance represents an efficient way to really understand the organization. Organizations run on data and information. Knowing what type of data is collected, notably from individuals, how it is used, where it is shared, and how it is stored and protected, provides important insights into the organization's inner workings. As we'll discuss elsewhere in this book, one of the more powerful tools to understand these inner workings is a data flow diagram that visually conveys how information—in this case personal data—comes into the organization, how it is used internally, and if and where it is shared. The insights garnered from understanding data flows are second to none. DFDs are underpinned by first reviewing and validating the underlying legitimacy and purpose of the contemplated processing activities. You are effectively asking whether there is a legitimate and defensible rationale for processing personal data. It may be instructive in this context to create a narrative or a description of processing activities (akin to the 'record of processing activities' found in Article 30 of the GDPR coupled with the details of a PIA. Linking these data flows to business processes and how the organization derives value is key for developing your privacy program and risk management and establishing good governance.

A Programmatic Approach to Building Your Privacy Program

Let's begin with a programmatic approach to building your privacy program. I'll describe below the critical considerations, factors, and tools that should be contemplated as part of the security program. The nine elements of the program I'll discuss are:

Figure 4.4 Privacy Program Elements

Admittedly, there is some overlap between these nine elements. Regardless, the key takeaway is that privacy programs should have a solid foundation based on respect for the individual's rights over how their personal data is used and the broader governance expectations for the organization and its privacy program.

There are elements of a privacy program that are already in place for most organizations. However, they may not be tied together coherently or comprehensively. Any well-governed privacy program aims to have a consistent view of privacy practices and privacy obligations where privacy functions are documented and understood by core organizational stakeholders. This starts with the tone at the top. Of all the elements integral to a comprehensive privacy program, few are more important than the tone at the top of the organization. If you build your program and the executive leadership team has not fully embraced privacy governance as integral to the organization's strategy, your efforts will be more challenging. It will be incumbent upon you to help executive management learn to value privacy functions and show how privacy governance builds trust and enterprise value. A vital tool to start the process is to establish a privacy charter.

Program Charter

Charters help define organizational roles and responsibilities, accountability for crucial outcomes, resourcing, how to arbitrate internal conflicts, and broader expectations for the subject at hand. Therefore, the privacy leader should establish an agreed-to privacy charter that authorizes and sanctions the privacy program and outlines the expectations for the privacy leader's function, required resources, and the roles of other departments and staff that interact with the privacy program.

Charters are powerful tools. A privacy charter effectively sanctions the privacy program and establishes an appropriate tone at the top vis-à-vis the program. Charters should be executed by the senior-most executive within the organization, generally the managing director or CEO. Privacy charters are not privacy policies. Instead, charters are internally focused and help establish roles and responsibilities for privacy governance across the organization. As we saw in Chapter 2, privacy has pervasive impacts, and many organizational functions play an essential role in privacy governance.

These stakeholders should be invited to participate and collaborate in privacy governance, including highlighting risk considerations and risk treatment. Keep your risk register handy to document and track identified privacy risks.

Charters should not be lengthy—anything over five pages is too long—and should be reviewed and updated annually for any material changes in the organization, its privacy program, and new risks that may have surfaced. Charters should unambiguously convey the organization's commitment to privacy governance. The commitment should respect the data subject's or consumer's rights over how their information is collected, processed, and shared. It should outline the scope of the privacy program (e.g., the organizational functions that are part of the process). Additionally, it should establish privacy-by-design principles (more on this in Chapter 8), acknowledge regulatory and contractual obligations, and guide risk treatment decisions when privacy risks surface. Finally, the charter plays a critical role in anticipating organizational conflict related to privacy practices. As noted in Chapter 2, sales and marketing teams may have distinct perspectives regarding the collection and use of personal data that differ dramatically from those of the legal and privacy teams. These differing perspectives need to be arbitrated within the organization. The charter establishes guidance for this treatment. Establishing a privacy charter should be a high-priority task in building out a successful privacy program.

Program Scope and Boundaries

Ambiguity is a corporate sin. Ensure that the privacy program has a well-defined and agreed-to scope and that the departmental boundaries between stakeholders are well defined. Cases in point could be in data classification, data retention, and data governance practices. Ideally, the privacy program charter should indicate who defines data retention practices and data classification functions, and how to protect personal data. Ensure that stakeholders agree to these expectations and functions.

Defining the scope and boundaries of the privacy program are also vital. Any department or corporate function that collects, processes, shares, has access to, or retains and stores personal data is in scope. While the privacy program may be overseen by a Chief Privacy Officer, each department should have a designated point of contact to proactively collaborate with the head of the privacy program on privacy matters. This collaboration is foundational to any successful privacy program. Stakeholders need to be transparent in documenting privacy risks, privacy practices, and governance decisions. The notion of a boundary—differing responsibilities and accountabilities for organizational functions—is especially salient. Data flow diagrams are critical to understanding how personal information moves within and outside of the organization. Boundaries allow us to validate understandings, risk treatment practices, data classifications, and business processes that use personal data. The privacy program should clearly define organizational functions, departments, business processes, and associated trust boundaries to ensure that privacy matters are not inadvertently overlooked.

Program Participants

One of the more powerful tools to clarify roles and responsibilities within the privacy program is a responsible, accountable, consulted, and informed (RACI) matrix. The head of the privacy program should use a RACI matrix to define who the participants and stakeholders are within the privacy program and, consistent with the privacy program's charter, clearly indicate each participant's specific function within the program and throughout the privacy lifecycle. RACI matrices can be highly detailed or high-level depending upon the maturity of the organization's privacy program. Minimally, a RACI matrix should capture critical elements of the privacy lifecycle and include expectations for various organizational functions, including human resources (HR), sales and marketing, legal, IT, security, and customer care as the cases may be. RACI matrices will take time to develop and should be re-validated each year to capture and reflect any organizational changes.

Phase / Role	Privacy Leader	Legal	HR	Sales	Marketing	IT	Security	Executive Leadership
Legitimate Purpose								
Notice								
Consent								
Classification								
Collection								
Protection								
Use								
Sharing								
Retention / Archiving								
Destruction								

Key: R-Responsible | A-Accountable | C-Consulted | I-Informed

Figure 4.5 Sample RACI Matrix

- **R**esponsible – The department or function that performs a given function.

- **A**ccountable – The department or function that owns the outcome and is held to account for the results. There is only one accountable party when the RACI matrix is focused on named individuals.

- **C**onsulted – The departments or individuals who are consulted for their subject matter expertise or insights on a given privacy topic.

- **I**nformed – The departments or individuals who are made aware of the status of given privacy functions or activities.

Governance Model

Ensure that the privacy charter also incorporates the key elements of the governance model. To this end, the privacy governance model should include expectations for ethical behavior, vision and strategy for the privacy program, the role for policy and procedure, expectations for specific privacy controls, metrics, reporting relationships, training expectations, and communication and escalation expectations, among other context details for the privacy program.

Privacy governance further requires that the organization establish an appropriate governance model. Governance is an amalgam of disparate factors, including risk tolerances, risk management, resources, training and awareness, required skills and competencies, metrics, accountability, reporting relationships, monitoring, and disclosures.

Figure 4.6 Privacy Governance Model

Your privacy program should capture each of these essential topics. The privacy charter helps to clarify many of these, but you should unpack each element of governance in detail as you document the broader privacy program expectations. Good governance leads to predictable outcomes, well-managed risks, and organizational alignment. A key element of organizational alignment is the documentation of authorizations and accountabilities. The RACI matrix clearly helps in this regard.

Authorizations and Accountabilities

The privacy charter should overtly address specific authorizations and program accountabilities conveyed to the privacy leader. Many accountabilities will be the charge of the privacy leader, and if the privacy leader also functions as counsel, this would include privacy notices and policies.

Privacy leaders need to validate authorizations and accountabilities in addition to having them documented in a RACI matrix. This validation requires proactive engagement. Privacy leaders are well served by directly reviewing specific privacy functions and risk scenarios with their colleagues across the organization. Several cases will highlight the importance of this proactive approach. For example, for organizations with a business-to-consumer (B2C) business model, the customer care department is on the frontline regarding consumer interaction, fielding service calls and other inquiries. The CPO should spend time with these customer care teams and their leaders to validate their understanding of data subject access requests and how the consumer's identity is authenticated or verified. Similarly, collection practices should be reviewed and documented with sales and marketing teams.

As this organizational context is established, the privacy leader must establish consensus on authorized activities and who is ultimately accountable for privacy risk management decisions. Risk management decisions should rarely occur in a vacuum, and risk factors should be clearly documented, triaged, and evaluated in a consistent and formalized manner. These authorizations and validations of organizational accountability are at the heart of good governance.

Privacy by Design (PbD) Principles

The privacy program should be founded on core **privacy by design** principles. Notably, this includes data minimization, purpose specification, respect for data subjects and consumers, default settings that support privacy (e.g., opt in), among other foundational expectations related to transparency and secure processing practices. We'll address privacy by design in more depth in Chapter 8, but I think this context here is warranted when thinking about your overall privacy program.

Privacy by design principles are part of a broader "shift left" focus found in many disciplines. Implementing good privacy controls earlier in a process is a sound governance practice. Privacy by design will effectively reduce risks for the organization. Key elements of privacy by design include:

- **principles such as opt-in versus opt-out functionality** – effectively not collecting personal information without the overt, explicit consent of the data subject or consumer

- **data minimization** – only collecting those data elements that are explicitly required for the documented processing activities

- **defined data retention** – only retaining data for the minimum period required to complete the processing activities unless longer periods are mandated by regulations or required contractually

- **data protection and data anonymizing capabilities** – including encryption, tokenization, and pseudonymization of sensitive data elements, privacy by default in application and system settings, transparency over processing activities

- **and the proactive, informed, and engaged participation of the consumer or data subject.**

Privacy by design requires proactive measures throughout the privacy lifecycle with a series of binary decisions. Effectively, at each stage of the privacy lifecycle (see the graphic below), the core question is whether the functions and activities are respectful of the consumer's or data subject's interests. Article 25 of the GDPR, 'Data protection by design and by default,' offers guidance on many of these principles. Where activities diverge from these interests, there is essentially "drift" from privacy by design principles.

Privacy Lifecycle Key Phases

The program should also reflect the dynamic nature of the privacy lifecycle and reflect best practices through each phase—be it notice, consent, classification, collection, protection, use, sharing, retention, and ultimate destruction or deletion of personal data.

Privacy practices have a defined lifecycle.

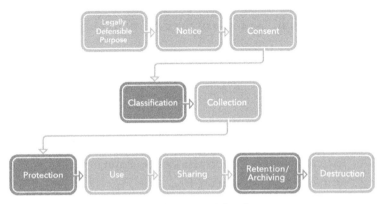

Figure 4.7 Privacy Lifecycle

Your privacy program should be aligned to each phase of this privacy lifecycle. The privacy lifecycle is the topic of Chapter 6, and Chapter 8 will address privacy by design best practices in further detail. Certain phases, notably classification and retention objectives require pre-planning and validation.

Metrics and Reporting

The privacy program's charter will also identify the metrics associated with the privacy program. These could include response times to DSARs, privacy incidents, and the like. Validate the metrics with other organizational stakeholders as part of broader reporting expectations for the privacy leader.

Your program should be measurable, and metrics are an integral part of ensuring that the executive leadership team understands the health of the privacy program. Work with your colleagues to establish a minimum set of metrics to evaluate the program's overall status. Of course, these metrics will vary from one organization to another. Still, they could include fundamental topics such as the number of vendors assessed for privacy risks, the response timing on DSARs, and the status and coverage of PIAs and/or DPIAs for departments within the organization. It's important to note that DPIAs in the context of the GDPR have explicit requirements as outlined in Article 35 (e.g., assessing the risks associated with the technologies employed as part of the processing activities, evaluation of the data subject's rights in the context of the contemplated processing activities including issues related to proportionality, measures employed to reduce identified risks, among other factors).

Your privacy program will evolve with greater contextualized detail on the nature and extent of the data that's collected, the level of detail to describe processing activities, and refinement of your privacy metrics. In Chapter 5, we will discuss the importance of technology to your privacy program.

Some foundational metrics to consider include the following:

- Percentage of employees who have received privacy training
- Percentage of vendors who process or store personal data that have had a PIA and/or DPIA performed within the last year
- Average time to response to DSARs
- Percentage of identified privacy risks that have been formally triaged with an agreed-to risk treatment plan
- Percentage of systems and applications that process personal data that have been reviewed from a security perspective

Documentation and Procedures

Several core documents and procedures are integral to the privacy program, including the organization's privacy notice and policies, data flow diagrams, PIAs and/or DPIAs, risk registers, and control matrices. To support the program, the privacy leader should maintain an inventory of the program's core documentation, its status (e.g., reviewed and approved for use), and how frequently these documents and the procedures they contemplate should be re-evaluated and updated. At a minimum, templates for data flow diagrams, a privacy risk register, and assessment tools (e.g., the PIA and/or DPIA) should be at the ready.

The documentation and policies noted here provide important context to your privacy program. Solid documentation underpins governance. Validate expectations, configurations, settings, roles and responsibilities, and other pertinent variables. Ensure that these core documents do not exist in a vacuum. Review them, ideally with a defined cadence, with colleagues throughout the organization. Most critical are the inputs and validations of the legal, security, and IT teams related to privacy program functions regarding data classification, data protection, and data retention.

Other, more tactical elements to your privacy program include core documentation and policy. Essential privacy program documentation includes the following:

Data Classification – The legal department should validate the organization's data classification scheme if it is not drafted directly by the legal team. Important definitions that should guide data classification activities include:

- personal data (PD) (ideally leveraging the definition from Article 4 of the GDPR)
- personal information (PI)
- personally identifiable information (PII)
- sensitive personal information (SPI)
- protected health information (PHI)

In addition, data classifications should be ubiquitously understood throughout the organization and by all stakeholders in the privacy program. Moreover, certain data and information may also be subject to legal (litigation) holds that will necessitate special protection and retention obligations. Lastly, there are categories of personal data within these classifications that may require additional treatment notably around PHI and SPI.

Data Retention – Like data classification, data retention schedules should be tied to regulatory requirements, contractual obligations, or data governance principles, including the data subject's expectations for how long their information should be retained based on the context of the processing activities. Retention periods should be explicitly documented and validated with counterparts in IT. Anticipate challenges with resources. Retaining large data sets, notably security logs associated with PHI required by HIPAA, can be costly. In many cases, retention practices are governed more by expediency than regulatory requirements or contractual obligations.

Elements of a Privacy Program 133

This approach presents a real risk for the organization. Where there is a disconnect between what is required versus actual practice, this fact pattern should be added to a privacy risk register for executive input.

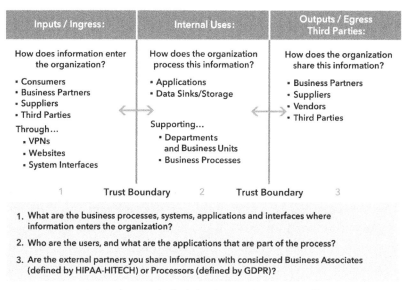

Figure 4.8 Sample (high-level) Data Flow Diagram[47]

Data Flow Diagrams (DFDs) – Data flow diagrams should be established for all material processes where PD, PI, PII, SPI, or PHI are in scope. While there is a certain elegance to refined DFDs, do not let the pursuit of perfection impede the pragmatic. I often tell CISOs and CIOs that a blank piece of paper with two lines to create three columns is more than sufficient.

The left column highlights sources of personal data (and all variants). The middle column is how the information is used internally (e.g., business processes, departments, applications, data sinks, and the like). Finally, the right column indicates where personal data is shared. Over time, these data flow diagrams can be refined to show trust boundaries, interfaces, and more specific detail.

---

[47] This table is reproduced from Chapter 8 of the *CISO Desk Reference Guide, Volume 1, 2nd Edition,* CISO DRG Publishing – Bonney, Hayslip & Stamper.

Data Mapping and Descriptions of Processing Activities – As Article 30 of the GDPR requires, a description of processing activities is required for entities subject to the GDPR and a valuable best practice even for those organizations not subject to GDPR compliance. Data mapping and descriptions of processing activities function as a narrative, highlighting which data elements are collected, the justification for their collection, how they are used, requisite security considerations, and contextual details related to the processing activities. DFDs can be used to help validate understandings, risks, and other nuanced context to the processing environment. This documentation should be referenced and updated frequently and helps inform privacy impact assessments.

Privacy Impact Assessments or Data Protection Impact Assessments – PIAs and DPIAs are foundational documents to your privacy program. Like other forms of risk assessments, PIAs and DPIAs outline the impacts to the organization and the data subject or consumer if their personal information is not governed correctly or adequately protected. PIAs and DPIAs should be re-assessed annually (or when there have been material changes to the operating environment) for high-risk processing activities or those functions that are deemed to be material from a privacy perspective where materiality could be defined based on the number of records processed or the sensitivity of the data elements processed or a combination of the two.

Data Protection Requirements – Standards related to data protection should be documented and validated with key organizational stakeholders, including the CIO and CISO. Ideally, there should be written expectations about how certain data elements should be protected based on their classification. These objectives should extend to how personal data and sensitive information are protected when shared with third parties, as would be the case with PHI shared with business associates in the context of HIPAA or from a controller to a data processor in the context of GDPR. In addition, as part of the broader security program, data protection requirements should address incident response and disclosure obligations.

Privacy Policy – Consumer privacy policies or, more appropriately, privacy notices are foundational to any privacy program. Privacy policies outline the data subject's or consumer's rights over their information. This includes how the consumer or data subject can exercise their privacy rights, identify which information is collected, whether it is shared or sold to third parties, and how the data collected is used, among many other variables. While legal counsel generally drafts privacy notices, the privacy practices they contemplate should be validated and reviewed with in-scope departments or line-of-business functions, most notably sales and marketing and the HR department.

Acceptable Use Policy – AUPs outline organizational expectations about the use of company assets. One such company asset is information. AUPs reinforce expectations about the confidentiality of information and, in many cases, the expectations for privacy in the workplace. As noted elsewhere, expectations for privacy in the workplace vary dramatically from one jurisdiction to another. Privacy leaders should validate that the contemplated activities within the AUP align to actual practices, and counsel has reviewed these.

Privacy Calendar – Good governance does not happen at a single point in time and frequently involves activities that recur at different times throughout the year. Just as our colleagues in finance and accounting have calendared activities for monthly financial closes and quarterly earnings, your privacy program should have a detailed calendar of activities. Establish a privacy calendar that contemplates updating privacy impact assessments, reviews of processing activities, mandated disclosures, and reporting and metrics. Ensure that the time requirements for each identified function are adequately captured. There is nothing worse than having a two-week item appear with a 15-minute notification on your calendar. Plan these activities accordingly.

Board Presentation Deck – Privacy programs don't occur in a vacuum. There are generally expectations to provide status updates on the program to the executive leadership team or the board of directors. The privacy leader should use the established metrics and other critical variables associated with the program to inform these stakeholders. Having a pre-defined deck to convey this status will be invaluable. While privacy may be the privacy leader's primary professional interest, privacy may not hold the attention of the executive leadership team and the board for too long. Keep the deck concise. If your presentation takes more than 20 minutes, consider culling slides that can be conveyed as appendices. Be prepared to deliver your key message in 10 minutes or less if necessary.

As we have seen, privacy programs are much more than a privacy policy or notice on an organization's website. Privacy programs now have a whole-of-enterprise impact that requires collaboration, governance, and thoughtful administration.

Key Insights and Recommended Next Steps

Key Insights

- It bears repeating that regardless of the rules enshrined in legislation, the success or failure of any organization is predicated on building and managing trust.
- It is often said you can have security without privacy, but you cannot have privacy without security. And while it is true that there are many technical aspects of your privacy program that require mastery, it all starts with the passion of the privacy leaders and must spread through the organization. You must understand your *raison d' être*.
- Foundation is key: mantra, charter, policy, RACI, process, education, notice, and tools. You must have a thorough understanding of the privacy ecosystem.
- Repetition doesn't spoil the prayer; the privacy leader must spend time with each of the functions that participate in the privacy ecosystem and learn how private data is collected and used and their key contributions to the enterprise. Revisit periodically or when there are significant changes.

Recommended Next Steps

- Engage with your key stakeholders to craft your privacy mantra. Give yourself the luxury of knowing that refinements to your program's documentation and practices take time. Iterative, incremental progress will result in substantive improvements to the privacy program over time.
- Keep your risk register handy and updated based on interactions with other organizational stakeholders. Spend the time necessary to validate understandings, perspectives, and key risks that surface through these interactions.
- Use data flow diagrams to help visualize how personal data is collected, used, and shared. Over time, these diagrams will become more refined and detailed.
- With a full understanding now of what you want to achieve with each conversation, conduct interviews with your stakeholders to begin crafting a privacy charter and inventory the data flows and data handling practices of each group.

Chapter 5

Privacy Technology

Introduction

Hari Seldon was a fictional character created by Isaac Asimov in his Foundation Series. The premise of the series is that Seldon, a mathematician, develops a theory of psychohistory that enables him to predict the future of large populations using statistical laws of mass action. Applying these theories leads him to discover that…well, no sense in spoiling the plot. But while this complex algorithm allows accurate predictions of the actions of large populations, it does not extend to the prediction of individual behaviors. Asimov was a brilliant writer and foresaw the emergence of behavioral analytics in the 1940s, at about the same time we first started to use commercial computers. But he did not anticipate the full power of big data; or what would happen if we used computers to perform the psychohistory calculations.

In Chapter 5, "Privacy Technology," we provide some historical context about the creation and use of data and the capture and exploitation of big data sets. We've repeatedly made the point that data is the detritus of everyday life and how we use that data, or don't use that data, is a debate we must have. Remember, talking in Chapter 1 about the recommendation engines that run on data about you, David said, "It's as if your closest, best friend is looking over your shoulder." So yes, the owner of the recommendation engine can make more money by making good recommendations, but they are also making good recommendations.

However, we also said in Chapter 1 that tracking someone who does not wish it violates their privacy and might constitute harm done to them. Further, indefinitely storing large caches of personal data creates a liability for the data controller. Here in Chapter 5, we explore both sides of the privacy technology coin. How data collection and exploitation create problems for us, and how we can address these problems with privacy-enhancing technologies.

In her essay, "Privacy and Technology," Justine starts with a high-level review of the evolution of data and technology. As she approaches modern times, the potential harm and liability begin to accelerate, demonstrating our dilemma. She concludes with wise words about the value of strong contractual protections.

In "Protect and Preserve," David uses a charming analogy to explain the layered defenses that companies use to protect their valuable data. He also shows how the technology landscape has changed, how that has affected our defenses, and how new technologies can shift the balance back in our favor.

Matt is passionate about making sure that technology users are well-informed about the parts of their lives that are harvested as data. Matt explains how pervasive data capture is in his essay, "Two Sides of the Privacy Technology Coin." He makes the point that if we're not careful, our every move is tracked. To conclude his essay, he unpacks seven essential processes that companies should employ to uphold their end of the data protection bargain.

Privacy and Technology ~ Justine

The First Evidence Humans Created Data

Humans lived on Earth for millions of years before creating data. The documentation of humans existing and attempting to communicate across time and space (a.k.a. data) came nearly 2.5 million years after humans began to inhabit the Earth! One of the earliest discoveries of data is a stencil of a hand in red ochre paint left by a Neanderthal in lime caves in Portugal. Archeologists believe "the hand" reaches back 65,000 years. The oldest human petroglyphs (rock engravings) discovered in Indonesian caves are thought to have been created 45,000 years ago. The data depict animals that looked like boars and may have been left to warn future generations. It was not until 40,000 years later—a mere 5,400 years ago—in Mesopotamia (now modern-day Iraq) that humans began writing codes on clay tablets. It seems appropriate that the earliest evidence of humans writing was code—a binary system of symbols to represent a specific command.

The First Coder Was a Princess of the Moon Gods

The earliest evidence of data written as codes was approximately 2285-2250 BCE. The author was a princess and priestess of the moon gods in Mesopotamia named Enheduanna (which translates to Ornament of Heaven). Enheduanna holds the distinction of being the first known author and poet in humankind. A couple of thousand years later, in 375 BCE, Plato and Aristotle explored the great questions about justice and ethics, writing their theories on papyrus or leather. Paper was invented in 105 CE in China but did not become globally used until over a thousand years later, around 1200. Paper was used predominantly to create data until likely the 1900s. Data has come a long way in the last 40 years as we enter the digital age. The first computer was created in 1943, and the first home computer was created in 1976. However, it was not until the 1980s that home computers became popular and accessible to humans.

My First Computer Was an Apple II

When I was five years old, my parents bought my three older brothers and me an Apple II computer. It had 4KB RAM and an external floppy disk drive for playing simple Olympic games with pixelated stick figure avatars. That computer sparked my interest in technology and eventually my passion for cyber law. My three brothers are all IT/cyber professionals—likely because my parents were early adopters and believers in computers. In the early 1980s, word processing software such as Word and Word Perfect began to replace typewriters. In 1989, the world wide web was born primarily so scientists and universities could share data. By the 1990s, applications began to transform how businesses communicated, and the race was on to create more and more data. With the exponential growth of data, humans need technologies to collect, use, process, and manage it.

Big Data

IBM recently posted that 90% of the data in today's world was created in the last two years. When we wrote this book, some staggering statistics described the copious amounts of data created each day.[48]

By the time this book is printed, these numbers will have grown.

- 1.7 MB of data is created every second by every person.
- 2.5 quintillion bytes of data are produced by humans daily.
- 463 exabytes of data will be generated each day by humans by 2025.
- Every day, 306.4 billion emails are sent, and 500 million Tweets are made.

---

[48] How Much Data Is Created Every Day in 2022? [You'll be shocked!] (techjury.net) https://techjury.net/blog/how-much-data-is-created-every-day/#gref.

Data storage expressed numerically:

Unit	Value	Size
bit (b)	0 or 1	1/8 of a byte
byte (B)	8 bits	1 byte
kilobyte (KB)	1000^1 bytes	1,000 bytes
megabyte (MB)	1000^2 bytes	1,000,000 bytes
gigabyte (GB)	1000^3 bytes	1,000,000,000 bytes
tera byte (TB)	1000^4 bytes	1,000,000,000,000 bytes
petabyte (PB)	1000^5 bytes	1,000,000,000,000,000 bytes
exabyte (EB)	1000^6 bytes	1,000,000,000,00010001000 bytes
zettabyte (ZB)	1000^7 bytes	1,000,000,000,000,000,000,000 bytes
yottabyte (YB)	1000^8 bytes	1,000,000,000,000,000,000,000,000 bytes

Figure 5.1 Data Size Chart

Devices that never before connected to the internet, such as cars, refrigerators, watches, and doorbells, now possess internet connection capabilities. These internet-connected devices are referred to as the "Internet of Things," and they are producing data at unprecedented rates. Software developers who used to license software to their clients now host data and offer Software as a Service (SaaS). Service providers, like accountants and lawyers, that used to receive data from their clients now host and create data on their clients' behalf. The speed at which data is produced, shared, and entrusted to others increases exponentially every day. Managing the new applications, systems, vendors, and risks is a full-time job for many businesses. There is also the time-consuming task of managing legacy data. Companies collecting, processing, storing, and using this data must comply with quickly evolving laws to keep pace with the data explosion. With the exabytes of data being created, it is critical to utilize privacy technology to manage the data, even for smaller companies.

Privacy Technology

Privacy professionals and IT functions often evaluate how enterprise technologies impact privacy. The first step is assessing the privacy risk that is created by using the technology. A privacy impact assessment gathers data points that will help identify the risk. Additional questions to include in the assessment are how the technology can be customized or modified to reduce privacy risk. For example, are there settings that can be enabled to require MFA? Can you restrict or reduce the type of data elements collected? Will the technology allow users to opt-out of certain features? Increasingly, technology companies are offering privacy enhancements, add-ons, or features to help businesses comply with privacy obligations owed to consumers.

Automation is another way to leverage and utilize technology. Settings that control how long to keep data before it overwrites is a form of automating data retention. Each application that is in use must be examined to enable settings and automation to manage the volume of data. Comprehensive privacy laws require that businesses only keep data as long as "reasonable" or "necessary." What is reasonable or necessary to a business may differ from consumer expectations. This difference in expectation is why it is increasingly important to communicate in privacy policies/notices/statements the purpose for collecting data and the length of time it is maintained.

Technology Required for Global Enterprise Management

As technology and laws quickly evolve, a segment of the industry is specifically dedicated to providing software that helps businesses comply with privacy requirements through automation or streamlining the process. Privacy technologies designed to help businesses comply with certain aspects of privacy obligations are essential to scale privacy programs. For example, a business that receives five privacy rights requests a month may manage those requests manually. However, a business that receives 500 privacy rights requests per month may need to automate the process or risk the consequences of non-compliance.

Some of the fastest-growing technology companies in the world are privacy-focused. And for good reason. Data and legal obligations are growing at a pace that humans cannot manage. An aspect that compounds the challenge is that privacy rights are different depending on where the consumer and/or data resides. Soon, businesses will be unable to comply with consumer privacy laws without utilizing technology. For example, certain companies subject to the California Consumer Privacy Act must provide notices and forms on their website to allow consumers to exercise their privacy rights.

Head in the Clouds

Starting in the late 1990s and exploding into the millennium, we began migrating data from servers stored onsite at the business in a secure closet, server room, or building ("on-prem") to a virtual "cloud-based" host ("off-prem"). Cloud data is stored, hosted, and distributed by a third-party vendor on their servers. This combined offering of software coupled with data storage is called Software as a Service—or SaaS. The individual user or business can access the "cloud data" from any device or remote location. Unfortunately, in recent years, cyberattacks on cloud-based SaaS providers and vulnerabilities in trusted software have forced us to take our head out of the clouds.

The problem with cloud-based technology is also the solution: recognizing and accepting our interdependence and connectedness to our vendor ecosystem and SaaS providers. Once we recognize and understand this risk, we can begin managing it. Sometimes, cloud-hosted options are safer than storing data on-prem. For example, Amazon Web Services (AWS) employs a small army of skilled cyber professionals, far more than any business can afford to employ. However, the power to negotiate with prominent vendors like AWS is de minimis. An enormously important part of any privacy professional's job is managing cloud risk. With third-party vendors, the dance to shift/share risk begins and ends with the contract.

Contractual Risk Shifting/Sharing for Privacy Technology

Privacy technology agreements are primarily memorialized in various types of agreements, all of which require careful review and revisions by legal:

- **Software Licensing Agreement (SLA).** An SLA memorializes an arrangement where a business licenses software from a vendor to run the software and store any data on their own systems. SLAs are not typically robust in privacy or security provisions because the vendor does not have access to the data. For example, the SLAs will cover pricing, details about the license, the agreement related to patches and updates, and damages for downtime. However, recent vulnerabilities in software that create privacy or cyber risk weigh in favor of including some form of risk shifting language.

- **Master Services Agreement (MSA).** An MSA is a comprehensive agreement between two parties that attempts to set forth the terms and mutual understanding between the parties. As the title indicates, the agreement will usually involve some form of service and technology. MSAs are frequently negotiated and revised by legal counsel. Privacy or security exhibits are often addended to the MSA to set forth specific privacy and security provisions. In addition, a Scope of Work (SOW) may accompany an MSA to describe specific work or projects that the provider is engaged to perform and includes the estimated fees/costs for that particular SOW.

- **Software as a Service Agreement (SaaS Agreement).** A SaaS agreement is like an MSA. It memorializes an arrangement where the vendor provides software through a web or application service and is responsible for hosting the data generated from those services. SaaS agreements typically have in-depth provisions related to privacy and security requirements and obligations between the parties. See Chapter 10, "Vendor Risk Management," for additional details about the provisions to include in a SaaS agreement.

- **Terms of Use.** A vendor typically offers terms that provide a standardized type of software service that is non-negotiable. However, agreement to the terms is required before the software can be used.

Keep in mind that GDPR Article 28 requires that controllers only use processors that comply with the GDPR and validate that standard contractual language is used when it is provided by the Commission. This is especially germane for international data transfers.

The official marriage between privacy and technology is memorialized in a contract that symbolizes a meeting of minds. A contract is a legal vehicle to shift or share risk onto the party in the best position to control and manage the risk. For example, a SaaS vendor is responsible for maintaining and securing a database filled with valuable consumer data. If the vendor experiences a data breach, then the contract may require the vendor to pay for the cost of an investigation, consumer notice, notice to regulators, and any damages experienced by the customer for the vendor's data loss.

Privacy Is a Feeling

Privacy is a feeling. It cannot be reduced to binary code. That said, certain technologies that offer enhanced privacy settings may improve how a consumer feels about privacy. Giving consumers control to enable their privacy settings also fosters privacy trust.

Some technologies thrive because they create a feeling or sense of privacy. For example, ephemeral messaging platforms appeal to users because they think the data created does not last in perpetuity. However, the reality is that all data that is put in the "public domain" or online can be captured, archived, and scraped, even if the creator does not intend for it to last in perpetuity. When a consumer's expectation of privacy is breached, the natural consequence is that they will stop using the product or service. For example, businesses like Facebook have met public scrutiny in the wake of scandals such as the one associated with Cambridge Analytica.

According to a 60 Minutes report,[49] Dr. Kogan a data scientist and research associate at the University of Cambridge, developed a psychological questionnaire that allowed Cambridge Analytica to collect personal details of 80 million Facebook users.

The questionnaire was marketed on Facebook as a happiness survey. Facebook did not host the survey or data, rather the user took the survey on a platform hosted by a company called Qualtrics, which provides a platform for online surveys. The happiness survey consisted of dozens of questions often used by psychology researchers to assess personality, such as whether the respondent prefers to be alone, tries to lead others, and loves large parties (the answer choices range from "disagree strongly" to "agree strongly"). The questionnaire took about 10 to 20 minutes to complete.

Lawsuits filed against Facebook after the scandal alleged that the Facebook offering harvested the respondent's profile data and data from the profiles of all the respondents' Facebook friends. Their names, birth dates, and location data, as well as lists of every Facebook page they had ever liked, were downloaded. All this data was collected without any notice, knowledge, or express consent, before respondents completed the first survey question.

Cambridge Analytica then used the Facebook data to build tools that it claimed could identify voters' personalities in elections and influence their behavior. The scandal impacted the personal information of more than 80 million individuals. Cambridge Analytica claims this "psychographic modeling technique" contributed to the outcome of the 2016 U.S. Presidential election of Donald Trump and the referendum on Brexit in the United Kingdom.

The scandal exposed Facebook practices that were grossly misaligned with Facebook users' expectations. Many Facebook users had a "feeling" of privacy in the content they created even though that

---

[49] Aleksandr Kogan: The Link Between Cambridge Analytica and Facebook, September 2, 2018. Leslie Stahl reports. For details see: https://www.cbsnews.com/video/aleksandr-kogan-the-link-between-cambridge-analytica-and-facebook-1/.

content could be accessed by their Facebook friends and sometimes by the public. The Facebook scandal news broke in May 2018. In response, three short weeks later, the California legislature passed the California Consumer Privacy Act.

Protect and Preserve ~ David

Until relatively recently, companies could comfortably reassure themselves that the protection provided by the firewall kept their assets safe from cyberattacks and other unwanted forms of intrusion. And that what existed within the enterprise firewall—from customer data to personnel records stored in commercial software products or makeshift databases—stayed within the organization. What has changed since those halcyon days of innocence? These changes appear to fit into a progressive chain of events:

- The enterprise perimeter has been disappearing for years for many reasons, including the perceived value in making enterprise applications available to suppliers, partners, and customers.

- The overall blending of private and professional lives has meant more employees homeworking, dramatically increased as a result of the COVID-19 pandemic, and seeking to bring their own devices, keys, and networks.

- The scale and impact of major data breaches have grown significantly over the last 10 to 15 years and have been relentlessly reported in the media—and social media—giving a vast audience a heightened awareness of cyber threats and a realization of the consequences of identity theft and data exploitation.

- This, in turn, has led to a growing awareness of the increased monetization potential of data, both legitimate and nefarious; and,

- In parallel, there has been a marked improvement in data protection and privacy legislation but less improvement (so far) in the policing of those regulations.

There is plenty that a company can—and must—do to mitigate the changing landscape through the privacy program in terms of re-assessing processes, procedures, and business culture. But as the majority of data management, processing, and storage is dependent on the various combinations of hardware and software, what are vendors doing to help?

Making It Difficult

In essence, the goal of all the various existing approaches to data protection and privacy, including the associated technologies, is to protect and preserve the integrity of a data subject's personal or sensitive data and reputation; and in so doing, to ensure a data controller's compliance with the GDPR or whichever legislation is appropriate for the domain in which the data is stored and managed.

And therein lies a conundrum: in presenting the role of this data in operating the business to management, you are expected to serve two sets of constituents—managers and data subjects—and to protect them from two widely different sets of threats, liability, and exploitation. Needless to say, getting the balance right is crucial!

If that wasn't challenging enough, the plethora of terminology associated with addressing these concerns is mind-numbing and not for the faint-hearted or at least anyone without a technical aptitude for cybersecurity or computing in general.

As we've said before, it's vitally important to be realistic about the job at hand: work on the assumption that your organization will be under attack—or rather *is already* under attack—and your task is to make it as difficult as possible for attackers to get what they are looking for or, as is often the case, what they happen to find.

Consider the data under your stewardship to be like the Crown Jewels in the Tower of London. How do you prevent them from being stolen or damaged?

Henry VII at the Tower of London, 1485-1509—fit for purpose to safeguard your crown jewel? (from a manuscript of Poems of Charles, Duke of Orleans)

(1) Firstly, you would fill the surrounding moat, raise the drawbridge, and post sentinels on the castle walls to guard against any ingenious intruders. If the moat is deep and wide and the drawbridge strong, that should keep most, but not all, attackers at bay.

(2) Assuming some will get through, next you want to be certain that the guards watching every entrance into the Tower are alert and have an up-to-the-minute, authoritative list of those to whom they are allowed to permit entry and can recognize them.

(3) Attackers are wily and will have found ways to penetrate the locked or guarded rooms of the Tower. It's now become a matter of carrying out a series of precautions to limit damage. This could be by:

- splitting the jewels up so that they're not easy to reassemble;

- creating several look-alike copies of the jewels;

- ensuring the jewels are under lock and key and that the distribution of the keys is restricted;

- hiding the real jewels in a place that very few people know about;

- burying the jewels in an undistinguished covering that would make them unrecognizable even close up; and,

- making sure those overseeing access can communicate with each other rapidly and securely at any sign of an attack.

None of the above are mutually exclusive: it's vital to ensure that you have done everything in your power to protect what you have.

It may be a stretch to think of the data assets you own or are responsible for as a set of Crown Jewels. Still, whatever vertical you operate in, your organization contributes to and is a beneficiary of a data-driven economy. Its value is almost incalculable.

In estimating that value, it's also important to weigh the positive value of doing good with the data against the potential harm inflicted on the data subject should the data be inappropriately handled or accessed. We only get a true sense of this value coin if we keep the two sides in mind as safeguards are being designed.

Although any analogy can creak at the edges, the basic principle of the techniques outlined above applies more or less to the job at hand—enabling your privacy program.

Privacy by Any and All Means Necessary

The concept of privacy by design, or better still privacy by default, applies equally to the manufacturers of privacy-enhanced products and to the application of privacy principles by a DPO. Another label that has gained considerable currency over the last several years, particularly with software developers, is "privacy-preserving"—and it's worth starting the deep dive right there. While we're at, we'll take a look at "privacy-enabled" and "privacy-enhancing" technologies. These are all methods of protecting data, using techniques to minimize the possession of personal data without losing the functionality of an information system.

Before we start, let's break down the key objectives of a privacy program into three bite-sized pieces, which are:

- Traffic policing
- Identity stripping
- Scuttling and hiding

Traffic Policing

Implement controls to prevent unauthorized access to personal data, whether of employees or customers, and irrespective of whether the access is likely to be legitimate or potentially nefarious.

Various approaches should be taken to manage controlling access, all of which are complementary:

- **Intrusion detection systems** complement firewalls and are designed to detect all types of malicious network traffic and computer usage that cannot otherwise be detected. They capture all network traffic flows and examine the contents of each packet for malicious traffic or policy violations.

- **Separation (or segregation) of duties** involves splitting a policing task into two or more parts so that more than one person, department, or function is required to complete it. This improves oversight, which increases the likelihood of catching errors and helps prevent fraud or theft.

- The principle of **least privilege** means any person or function should only be given the minimum set of privileges necessary to access the information and resources required to carry out the appointed policing task.

- **"Need to know"** indicates that a person has a legitimate reason to access sensitive information, possibly only for a limited period. Least privilege can then be implemented to limit that access and limit what the user can do with the information recovered.

Identity Stripping

Identity stripping essentially de-sensitizes the information itself by either hiding or removing key pieces of the data while not invalidating the usefulness of the data for statistical or analytical purposes. Anonymization and pseudonymization are de-identification techniques used to replace an individual's identity or the identifying data elements with an artificial identifier. This prevents malicious actors from getting hold of the most sensitive information without having to compromise data integrity for the purposes of data analysis.

Examples include:

- **Communication anonymizers** hide real online identity attributes such as email or IP addresses and replace them with non-traceable or disposable tokens that can be applied to any variety of communication channels.

- **Shared non-attributable online accounts** are created by one individual and then shared with others, using data that does not contain any personal data about any real person.

- **Masking or obfuscation** practices refer to the process of obscuring a data profile by inserting misleading information, thereby hiding sensitive data. If done carefully, this can befuddle an attacker into not recognizing real from bogus data.

Scuttling and Hiding

Scuttling and hiding are used to ensure that, even if unauthorized actors get their hands on potentially sensitive data, they cannot do anything further with it. Or putting it another way, only those with appropriate access rights can perform operations on the data, and only those operations that they are entitled to do. These are two broad-brush approaches that can be adopted to make it hard to do anything with the data (scuttling) and make it difficult to find (hiding).

Examples include various forms of encryption:

- **Enhanced privacy ID** is a digital signature algorithm supporting anonymity. Traditional digital signature algorithms consist of a unique public key (for verification) and a unique private key (for signing). Enhanced privacy provides a single public verification key associated with many unique private signature keys.

- **Homomorphic encryption** allows computation on ciphertexts with the benefit that encrypted data can be acted upon without first decrypting the data.

- **Zero-knowledge proof** lets one entity prove to another that they know a particular value without transmitting the information itself. **Non-interactive zero-knowledge proof** is a zero-knowledge proof that does not require the participating entities to interact.

- **Secure multi-party computation** is a cryptographic protocol that distributes a computation across multiple parties and no individual party can see any other parties' data.

- **Format-preserving encryption** refers to encrypting so that the output (the ciphertext) is in the same format as the input (the plaintext).

- **Blinding** is a cryptographic technique by which an agent can provide a service to a client in an encoded form without knowing either the real input or the real output.

- **Differential privacy** makes it possible for technology companies to collect and share aggregate information about user habits while maintaining the privacy of individual users.

In later chapters we will re-visit the approaches and technologies described here and put them into context.[50] But for now, rest assured there is plenty of support out there to help you keep your own crown jewels safe.

---

[50] It should also be emphasized that this list is not exhaustive and newer technologies are constantly being advanced, such as synthetic data, federated learning, and confidential computing.

Two Sides of the Privacy Technology Coin ~ Matt

There was a time when private lives were precisely that, private. Our friendships, interests, and social interactions were not the fodder of social media. Our homes were largely devoid of "smart" devices listening to our conversations and gathering data on our behavior. Before the modern internet, that pre-connected world certainly had important privacy challenges but nothing to the magnitude we are witnessing today. Technology and privacy make for strange bedfellows.

Technology moves fast. With the advent of the internet of things (IoT) and the interconnection of devices across all realms of our daily lives, our ability to have a private space is challenged as never before. Our homes previously offered some semblance of a private space. We now confront various smart devices (be they speakers, thermostats, sensors, or TVs) that continuously wait for cues to interact or "surveil" our actions. Indeed, our ability to have a genuinely private space requires us to go off-grid and unplug from the connected fabric of omnipresent devices we use in our daily lives.

We rarely pause to recognize just how much personal information these devices and their services collect. These applications know our preferences, physical location, purchasing history, health factors, and at what temperature we like to keep our homes and cars. Essentially, these devices know the ins and outs of our daily lives. They are also configured to make this ubiquitous capture of personal data by default and design. Be it personally or professionally, technology's impact on privacy cannot be overstated.

The pace of change is daunting. I remember giving a talk at a regional cloud conference in 2012 in which I was offering perspectives on data governance and how the growth of data is fundamentally changing enterprise architecture. I noted that when "human" data becomes part of the enterprise, all bets are off. My insights were inspired by hearing Eric Topol, a renowned cardiologist, lecture about several innovative uses of wireless technology in medicine. He highlighted how diagnostic capabilities could be brought to the patient's home, and the analysis of medical data necessary for patient exams could be transmitted back to the doctor's office or the hospital via wireless transmission.

At the time, this approach was innovative. Today it is commonplace to see "telemedicine" in action. We can purchase handheld electrocardiogram (EKG) devices on Amazon for less than $100. We also see continuous glucose monitors that send glucose levels to smart watches and phones. Of note is this notion of "continuous," ongoing streams of medical data sent to various sources for analysis and processing. We cannot underestimate the scale of this data.

Our ability to collect, process, store, and archive data for subsequent use has been enabled by technology, not just with cheaper and faster storage arrays but networks with seemingly infinite carrying capacity. We have gone from the days of 56K fractional T1 circuits to near-ubiquitous broadband to our homes with connection speeds measured in 100s of megabits per second if not gigabit levels. Indeed, 5G wireless (and subsequent generations of wireless technologies) only further this trend to ubiquitous, high-speed networks. This trend will create new and innovative business models—many of which will have significant impacts on how we collect, transmit, process, and store personal data.

I bring up this technological context to note that we are witnessing a vital confluence of dynamics that make our efforts with privacy all the more critical. Technological change and the capacity to monitor and collect personal data is running headfirst into a wall of privacy regulations empowering individuals with codified rights as to how their information can and will be used. The result is that data subjects and consumers have more control over how and where they decide to provide their information. As we will see, privacy regulations are about notice, consent, and choice. Too often, collection practices, enabled by technology, frequently collide with the spirit of the regulations.

The days of sanctuary from digital surveillance are long gone. As Shoshana Zuboff notes in her amazing book, *The Age of Surveillance Capitalism: The Fight for a Human Future at the New Frontier of*

Power, our lives are the raw material of a new economy. The goal is to monitor our actions and predict and change our future behavior. Predicting and changing an individual's future behavior requires a near-perfect dossier. The dossier must be of such high fidelity that its creation can only be built using *continuous* access to personal data about this individual. Such personal data is derived from browsers and websites, smartphones, GPS coordinates, smart TVs, smart speakers, sensors, biometric data, and many other sources. Many of these data sources are derived from the combination of the digital and physical worlds.

Indeed, the extent of surveillance—not only the concerns about government access to personal data noted in the Schrems II decision[51] that invalidated Privacy Shield[52]—has led some to develop strategies of "extreme" privacy. Michael Bazzell's *Extreme Privacy: What it Takes to Disappear* highlights the steps required to disconnect from an overly connected world.[53] Bazzell's book comes in at over 500 pages—this speaks volumes about what's required to protect privacy in today's interconnected, digital world.

Privacy and technology topics are expansive and cannot be adequately captured in a single chapter. What I would like to offer, however, is some high-level context of this dynamic and a discussion of the technical implications for managing a privacy program. I'd also like to highlight some areas where how we design and use technology will be especially salient for your privacy program. Technology is a double-edged sword. Near-infinite technologies can gather personal

---

[51] The CJEU judgment in the Schrems II case (European Parliament) https://www.europarl.europa.eu/RegData/etudes/ATAG/2020/652073/EPRS_ATA(2020)652073_EN.pdf.

[52] The EU-US Privacy Shield was a framework for regulating transatlantic exchanges of personal data for commercial purposes between the European Union and the United States. It replaced the International Safe Harbor Privacy Principles which were declared invalid in 2015. Please see this document for further information: https://www.privacyshield.gov/eu-us-framework.

[53] As an aside, I purchased a copy of *Extreme Privacy* for a friend who works in law enforcement. His concerns with doxing and the safety of his family were such that he needed to find ways to hide his personal information from the public. Doxing has become a real concern for not only those in law enforcement but also politicians and celebrities alike.

data about individuals—too frequently without informed consent. However, some technologies can enhance or support privacy objectives. We will focus on the latter here—those applications that have been created to help manage privacy programs and support privacy rights. Zuboff's book offers an in-depth treatise for those readers looking to understand how personal data is collected at scale in our modern societies and how our personal data is used much like oil and coal were during the industrial revolution to fuel new economic models.

As discussed in Chapter 8, privacy by design principles are integral to integrating technology into our privacy programs, the products and services we develop, and how we use technology in our personal lives. Privacy leaders need to understand technology. We do not need to be software developers, cybersecurity experts, data scientists, or experts in the vast array of technologies that can impact privacy for our companies and, importantly, our personal lives. Still, we do need to understand the mechanics and context of technology. Context counts.

Your organization runs on information. Many companies derive economic value from consumers' personal data. Therefore, it is incumbent upon privacy leaders to understand the core technologies and applications of the firm. In the *CISO Desk Reference Guide*,[54] I noted the value of business impact assessments to clearly document core business processes, the applications used by these processes, and the underlying dependencies on technologies, service providers, and staff. Privacy leaders need to understand the same. Know the data flows. Understand how information comes into the organization, its sources, and details (e.g., the data elements). Identify how information and personal data are used internally within the organization, including which departments, applications, and staff have access to this personal data. This organizational context should inform your evaluation of your organization's use of technology.

---

[54] *CISO Desk Reference Guide, Volume 1, 2nd Edition*, CISO DRG Publishing – Bonney, Hayslip & Stamper.

Privacy regulations require that organizations develop data governance practices that classify the data that is collected, validate and track the status of consent from the individual, track where and how that personal data is used within the organization, how it is protected, where it is stored, how it is shared with third parties, and ultimately, its deletion or destruction. While it is easy to highlight various elements of data governance, implementing data governance is a complicated affair.

The challenge of data governance is the product of multiple factors, including organizational complexity. Personal data enters the organization from various sources including sales and marketing efforts, consumer-focused websites, applications, third parties, HR functions, and a multitudinous suite of technologies employed by the organization—be they websites, mobile devices, or sensors, among others. This creates governance challenges as privacy leaders will need to interface with colleagues and counterparts in departments including human resources, sales and marketing, IT, vendor management and procurement, and research and development. In short, managing a privacy program that successfully navigates these data governance challenges requires tooling to help document and automate essential privacy functions, including data discovery, data classification, and appropriate responses to data subject access requests. For most organizations, manually addressing these functions simply does not scale, nor does it work.

As privacy programs have expanded in scope and grown in maturity, a new class of privacy management applications has been developed to bring order to the chaos of enterprise data governance and privacy program management. These applications help privacy practitioners or other line-of-business personnel who address privacy functions to fulfill critical privacy tasks more predictably and reliably, such as the following:

Data classification. While data classification should be overseen from a legal perspective (e.g., classifying personal data, sensitive personal data, protected health information, and the like based on legal or contractual definitions), use applications to help label data in its structured and unstructured forms. Accurate data classification is integral to data governance and privacy. Once appropriately classified, different data sets can be governed in accordance with that classification, allowing for distinct practices vis-à-vis retention periods and data protections tied to that specific classification.

Data discovery. Data sprawl is real. Data is shared, copied, transferred, altered, backed up, and essentially let free within most organizations. The result is that few organizations truly know what personal data they have, where it resides, how they manage it, and where and how personal data has left the proverbial four walls and been shared with other entities. Privacy management tools should help facilitate the process of data discovery. You need to find classes of data in both structured (e.g., in applications and databases) and unstructured (e.g., emails, images, files on laptops, and data lakes) formats across the organization. Like classification, data discovery is a foundational component to data governance and privacy management practices.

Data mapping. Data moves. Personal data is apt to move between systems, departments, and organizations. Understanding and documenting data flows requires data mapping capabilities within privacy programs. Data mapping will allow you to accurately show where and how personal data enters the organization, how it is used internally (e.g., the departments, applications, and IT infrastructure), and importantly, where this personal data is shared with third parties.

Mature data mapping identifies legal obligations that may arise when personal data is shared with third parties or crosses international borders. Accurate and complete data mapping is foundational to respond to data subject access requests, notably those requests from data subjects asking for their personal data to be deleted. If the organization cannot accurately and timely identify where these data elements are located, fulfilling requests may be challenging, exposing the organization to compliance risks. Privacy leaders must be prepared to address scenarios where personal data is processed in a manner inconsistent with the privacy notice or in violation of regulations.

Data subject access requests. As discussed in Chapter 13, data subject access requests present important considerations from a workflow perspective, namely, how is the data subject's identity verified, is the request valid and permissible, and how are these requests tracked and documented through fulfillment? Privacy practitioners who attempt to manage DSARs on a manual basis with tools like spreadsheets will quickly realize that more programmatic capabilities are in order. As an important aside, DSARs impact multiple organizational functions, including marketing, sales, IT, and customer care.

Data inventories. The volume of data elements and specific consumer or data subject records that an organization controls and processes is especially salient in the context of applicability to privacy regulations that have defined thresholds that determine if or when the regulation applies to that entity. These vary in context and include requiring mandated breach disclosures when personal data has been exposed. As a case in point in the U.S., data breaches that involve protected health information (PHI) must be reported to the Office of Civil Rights within the Department of Health and Human Services.

The scope of regulations may also be predicated on the total number of records an organization has under its control (as another case in point, the California Privacy Rights Act (CPRA) applies to organizations with personal information of more than 100,000 California residents). Organizations need to know the nature and extent of the various forms of personal data that they either control or process. To achieve this requires accurate, timely, and complete detail on data inventories. To provide a centralized view of all records by type, privacy management programs may need access to underlying databases and the applications they rely on. This integration will likely require application programming interfaces (APIs) between the privacy management application and the system of record where personal data is processed and stored.

As part of the data inventorying process, privacy practitioners should also validate if the applications can track which records have been accessed (either legitimately or in the context of a breach investigation). As noted above, most data breach disclosures have specific record thresholds. Technically corroborating which records have been accessed using DLP tools or log analysis can help limit disclosures in certain circumstances. We discuss "reasonable" security requirements in Chapter 11. With no knowledge of where and how many data subject records exist, the organization should consider this gap an unfunded liability.

Data protection impact assessments (aka PIAs). Privacy practices have pervasive impacts across the organization, spanning IT, security, legal, HR, sales, and marketing. How these practices are administered can either engender trust and reduce risk or create the opposite effect and place the organization in the crosshairs of regulators while risking reputational damage if the organization's privacy and security practices are inadequate.

As described and required in Articles 30 and 35 of the GDPR, entities need to document processing activities and perform data protection impact assessments (DPIAs). This can help leadership validate risk tolerances, risks to the data subject or consumer, regulatory requirements, and risk treatment recommendations and effectively shine a light on the organization's current privacy practices. DPIAs, like business impact assessments (BIAs), provide foundational insight and offer higher fidelity context to inform privacy decisions when they capture the insights and risk factors identified by multiple stakeholders across the entity. Privacy management applications typically have pre-defined DPIA templates and survey tools that facilitate the collection and documentation of the state of privacy for the organization.

Privacy risk registers. As privacy leaders develop a more detailed understanding of their organization's privacy practices, they will undoubtedly identify challenging issues that require attention and remediation. Having a central repository for these privacy risks is necessary to ensure broader organizational context, prioritization of risk treatment, and assignment of accountability for identified risks. In addition, every risk should have an accountable risk owner. Ideally, this individual also owns the business consequences if a privacy risk is realized.

Privacy risk registers bring structure to privacy risk management and offer a centralized view into the organization's risk management functions. As with DPIA functionality, privacy management applications typically offer a means to capture identified risk and manage that risk (be it to avoid, mitigate, transfer, or accept) through its lifecycle. However, unlike DSARs that benefit from more sophisticated tooling, privacy risk registers can be handled manually via a spreadsheet. Whether part of a comprehensive privacy management application or a stand-alone spreadsheet, privacy risk registers are a critical tool for privacy leaders to employ.

Technology changes rapidly, and privacy leaders need to embrace the nature and extent of their organization's use of technology and how it impacts privacy practices across the firm while also leveraging applications that can help manage privacy functions. Absent a strategy to identify the linkages between technology and privacy, privacy leaders will be blindsided and ill-equipped to manage privacy risks for their firm.

I want to offer a final cautionary note regarding technology. There is an adage that the world runs on software. About that, there's little debate. However, complicated mathematical models—algorithms—that drive and support business decisions underpin many of the applications that run our economy. Privacy leaders will need to understand how algorithms impact their organization and which algorithms influence decisions made related to personal data. As more and more software is abstracted to APIs and algorithms, we run the risk of being ultimately too distant from the technologies we're purported to govern.

Key Insights and Recommended Next Steps

Key Insights

- With the emergence of internet commerce and data generated by connected devices, we are rapidly collecting vast sums of data that could threaten consumer privacy.
- The advent of cloud-based computing and more distributed technical supply chains is spurring companies to focus more on contract language and service agreements to better connect execution, accountability, and liability.
- It is essential to deploy a layered security approach and augment the layers with privacy-enhancing technologies.
- It is wise to instill the discipline within your company of maintaining private data only while it is necessary and stripping away identifying data elements to derive knock-on values from the data with less risk.
- The widescale adoption of smart devices and social media has created a personal data generation engine that takes diligence to keep from running over individuals.
- We can restore balance by implementing privacy management applications that help reduce risk and increase privacy protections.

Recommended Next Steps

- Partner with your procurement and vendor management teams to review the contract language governing your relationships with third parties and enhance as needed.
- Work with your IT organization to fully understand your deployment of privacy management applications and ensure you have adequate coverage for the essential functions.
- Collaborate with your security team to understand which privacy-enhancing technologies your company employs and how they are used.
- Understand the pace of technological change and the impacts to your organization recognizing the special role of APIs and algorithms.
- Automate those privacy functions that are especially error-prone if managed manually.

Chapter 6

Privacy Lifecycle

Introduction

For most of recorded history, we've focused on preserving data. Before the digital age, data was fragile. Parchment, pulp, and linen are flammable, subject to the elements, and for several species of insect, delicious. To protect data, we built libraries, made copies, and when dealing with particularly sensitive or delicate content (physically and by subject matter) we restricted access. Other than the frequent politically and religiously motivated disputes about the value or provenance of the scrolls, books, and documents that we've felt compelled to save, we've always been disposed to collect, not to destroy. Frankly, through calamity and carelessness, destruction took care of itself. Anyone who has ever attempted to research a family tree or consult an old survey map to justify a property claim can attest to just how unreliable record-keeping has been.

Our track record for preserving data does not inspire confidence. But here we are in the digital age, and we have the opportunity to start anew, turn over a new leaf (pun intended), and get the governance right. But while improving our preservation game, we must now learn to embrace the destruction of some data as required and desired. Ironically, we must now avoid the temptation to hoard data, especially personal data.

Chapter 6, "Privacy Lifecycle," narrows the focus on data governance from a broad program-wide view to directly governing the data. To begin, each author addresses fundamental concepts, including the reasons to collect personal data, under what terms we may use it, and for how long. From there, Matt, David, and Justine provide their unique perspectives on the elements of data governance using the lifecycle construct.

In "Privacy Lifecycle—Driven by Context," David reminds us that context is everything. Knowing why we need the data we're wishing to collect drives informed consent and forms the guardrails we place on the processes we execute at each stage of the privacy lifecycle. He points out that continual reassessment is integral to keeping lifecycle activities in the proper context.

In her essay, "Data Lifecycle," Justine starts by emphasizing the time value of data. As data ages, its value to the organization changes. Building on the theme of transformation as a part of any lifecycle, Justine illustrates how organizations can use data-transforming technologies to reduce the liability of holding personal data and increase the value of aging data.

Matt's essay, "Privacy Lifecycle—A Helpful Construct," expands the lifecycle to include several pre-ingestion stages. Matt does a deep dive into each stage, showing how each relates to good governance and maps back to the applicable data privacy regulations. While Matt focuses mainly on the GDPR, CCPA/CPRA, and HIPAA, these serve as excellent proxies for and super-sets of data privacy regulations.

Privacy Lifecycle—Driven by Context ~ David

Next, we deep dive into the whole soup to nuts, cradle to grave, life of data from the perspective of preserving the privacy of the data subjects. But before we go there, we must be clear about what we're referring to and our terms of reference. From a privacy perspective, there are essentially two ways of looking at the lifecycle of data in a company's possession.

(1) The lifecycle of the retained data is predicated on several different criteria associated with the rationale for its collection in the first place; primarily:

- the consent of the data subject to whom the personal data relates or to whom it is relevant to process a set of data attributes, subject to a clear definition of purpose with a well-accepted set of 'rules';[55]

- the reason or rationale and purpose for requesting the personal data and for holding it; and,

- the length of time it was stated to the data subject that the personal data would be held for each defined, specific purpose.

It would be relatively easy for a company to get their customers to agree to use elements of their data for an immediate purpose, such as completing an online transaction or registering for an event that would take a matter of minutes. However, without fully understanding what a company intends to use their personal data for and how that data will be managed subsequently, it's difficult for a customer to know what to agree to, particularly if the company doesn't bother to ask the relevant questions.

Hence, it's essential for customers to have clarity on the duration of the agreement, whether it's:

---

[55] For example, the right to revocation or the expiration of a shorter retention period through the early achievement of stated purpose.

- five minutes for the purposes of a transaction, a day, or a week in order to verify aspects of the data; or

- a year because it's the beginning of a relationship such as a loyalty card or a cinema subscription that both parties agree to and anything less than twelve months doesn't make sense.

What the customer—and the company, but for different reasons—should avoid is having an indeterminant arrangement whereby, after the initial consent is given, the company is under no obligation to delete the data from its records.

(2) The reason why the caveat above also applies to the company in question can be seen in the second aspect of data lifecycle management: the lifecycle of the privacy protection mechanisms themselves, which should form the cornerstone of an organization's privacy management practices and controls.

Where do we begin? Needless to say, given the caveats and considerations discussed above, there are several different angles for evaluating how privacy should be approached. Most of them are joined at the hip with the lifecycle of the data assets you are seeking to protect—or rather the individuals to whom those data assets relate. From the moment a piece of data is collected or generated, the privacy-related responsibilities begin in terms of:

- **Collection and notice:** who can access the data, or more to the point, who has the right to access it;

- **De-identification:** whether (and to what extent) the data will be encrypted or anonymized, which can make it more difficult for unauthorized persons to identify or access sensitive data;

- **Processing:** what the personal data will be used for, as agreed with the data owner, and, essentially, aligned with everyone who has access to the data;

- **Storage:** how and where the data is stored in terms of location (on-prem or in the cloud) and whether (and to what extent) the data is encrypted. It's also vital to consider whether the data is going to be backed up or replicated and how the transmission is to be adequately protected;

- **Sharing:** who, if anyone, the data is going to be shared with, either internally or externally with third parties. Again, the organization's privacy policy should ensure that the rules concerning data sharing are in line with what is agreed with the data owner at the point of data collection; and finally,

- **Destruction:** when to delete the data. Think of the data asset as a perishable food item with a "use by" date.

To this last point, there are two aspects that are important to look into:

- **Data Quality.** Beyond that "use by" date, if your personal data asset has a potential variable component (e.g., postal address), when that component changes, the data asset gets stale and becomes the data equivalent of a health hazard: storing and re-using inaccurate data is a potentially costly liability. With a moldy piece of cheese, it doesn't matter how well it's stored; it will eventually develop a fungal growth. Your data asset can be kept fresh, but it requires regular iterations with the data owner, which becomes a considerable management overhead. If the intention or the agreement is to store data, this needs to be clear.

- **Long-Term Access.** It should have been made clear to the data owner how long you required the data. Hence, the "use by" date should be aligned with what the data owner understands to be the case. Your privacy policy should ensure that the data owner is asked to agree or consent to how long you are entitled to keep hold of this data asset—and ideally to be informed when it is deleted. Multiple regulations, such as HIPAA, have requirements that mandate retention periods.

The data lifecycle is littered with privacy banana skins waiting to trip you up and cause untold harm to your finances and reputation.

Given the growing number of jurisdictions worldwide which are developing privacy regulations that are far stricter and more consumer-friendly than ever before, collecting, storing, and re-using data has become a potentially risky occupation. Collecting data is a form of investment that you are obliged to protect.

To ensure that you fully understand the consequences of the data privacy compliance you are committed to undertaking, running alongside your company's privacy policy, you should also:

- Undertake a complete **risk assessment** and report, which is effectively a data privacy impact assessment;
- Execute and plan a **risk mitigation** analysis and collect documentary evidence;
- Complete and certify a **checklist** to confirm the risk mitigation exercise; and,
- Conduct and publish regular **audits** based on the risk profiles identified.

It is self-evident that these "regular" audits should be carried out as a regular maintenance exercise. The same can also be said for the other three tasks, say once a year. What is less obvious are the criteria for carrying out a risk assessment more often than that and what should trigger an unscheduled risk mitigation exercise. For example, as well as providing a calendar schedule, it would be good practice to reappraise your data privacy compliance whenever there is a major hardware, software, or program change or when there is a data breach. In other words, events that have either revealed or could lead to new risks.

Finally, from data collection to data deletion, instances of the data asset under review are going to be captured and stored in multiple software and hardware platforms and transferred across a variety of network configurations, all of which will—or at least should—undergo regular maintenance and receive regular updates. If that were not difficult enough, consider what might happen when personal data collected by one company gets shared with another organization, going from one set of privacy and security policies to another: responsibility and oversight become very hard to track and trace. Although you may not consider this an immediate privacy concern, compare it to moving a box of eggs from a fridge in one room to a fridge in another room when you don't know whether the kids are running riot. Drop them, and you have scrambled data assets all over the floor, inedible and in breach of your data protection responsibilities.

As we've seen, the privacy lifecycle is largely determined by both the type and sensitivity of the data involved as well as the consented agreement and expectations of the data owner or consumer. But what ultimately informs and determines the lifecycle of your data is the degree to which your privacy policies and mechanisms are understood, managed, and respected by everyone in your organization. If it were easy, you wouldn't be reading this book!

Data Lifecycle ~ Justine

All living things in the natural world have a beginning, middle, and end life cycle. The seasons cycle through summer, fall, winter, and spring—the moon cycles through new, quarter, half, and full moons. Humans gestate for a nine-month cycle. Once born, we cycle through birth, infancy, childhood, puberty, adolescence, middle age, old age, and death. Although data is not a living thing, it mimics life because we create it. Because data is not a part of the natural world, it could persist in perpetuity if we let it. Given its potential for perpetual existence, we have legal and ethical obligations to create a privacy lifecycle to protect data. Defining that lifecycle is tied to risks and benefits. As I write, I am mindful that data lifecycle and privacy lifecycle may be two separate concepts. But I am drawn back to data's lifecycle because privacy is the impetus for us to create a cycle for data that ends in destruction.

Understanding Benefits or Rewards of Consumer Data

Data is born when it is created and stored. Wearables, for example, collect biometric data from the person wearing the device and store such data on the cloud to be accessed as needed. Who can access and use that data depends mainly on the terms and disclosures in privacy policies. Data elements like heart rate, number of steps, geolocation, fitness, exercise, facial scans, and voice scans belong to an individual human. The data has the most value, benefits, and rewards early in its life. A user may want to see how many steps she took on a particular day to confirm if she reached her 10K-a-day goal. Or perhaps she wants to see highs and lows for her heart rate for the previous week. As data enters its middle age it may continue to have incremental value, but less than it once did. As time wears on, the data becomes less valuable to the user.

Aggregate data measuring a range or period may still have residual value but looking at how far one walked four years ago on a particular day may be less important than how far she walked the day before. In the final stages of a data's lifecycle, the risk likely outweighs the benefits. At this point, data is at the end of its lifecycle. Privacy programs that can articulate the benefits/rewards of data in comparison to the risk will reduce enterprise risk. See Chapter 2, "Risk Treatment—The Big 4," to learn how to weigh data's risk against its benefits/rewards.

Cradle to Grave: Transparency About Data Lifecycle

Until recently, laws did not force businesses to disclose the data lifecycle to individuals. However, regulations and laws like GDPR and CCPA/CPRA require businesses to explain the data lifecycle in detail in their consumer-facing policies. For example, CCPA requires businesses to inform consumers about where and how it collects data, the purpose and use, and any sharing with third parties. CPRA further provides that "[a] business that *controls the collection* of a consumer's personal information shall, at or before the point of collection, inform consumers *of the following*... (3) *the length of time the business intends to retain each category of personal information, including sensitive personal information, or if that is not possible, the criteria used to determine that period...*"[56] For a business to explain its data collection practices and data lifecycle, it must first understand them.

Data Metamorphosis: Transforming and Evolving Personal Information

Data lifecycles can run their natural course from inception to destruction or birth to death. Or data can be transformed—like a caterpillar into a butterfly—from personal information into de-identified data, thereby ending a data lifecycle that has increased risk and regulatory requirements. On the other hand, aggregate data has many benefits, creates less risk, and is not subject to most privacy laws. Businesses can avoid regulatory risks and requirements by de-identifying data so that consumers do not have the right to make requests to access or delete the data. Many privacy laws carve out de-identified data from the definition of personal information.

---

[56] See CPRA Section 1798.100(a)(3) here: https://cpra.gtlaw.com/cpra-full-text/.

Taking the "Personal" Out of "Personal Information:" De-Identifying Data

In most jurisdictions, information is "de-identified" when it does not directly or indirectly identify a particular consumer. California law spells out additional obligations on the business for the data to qualify as de-identified data:

- Has implemented technical safeguards that prohibit reidentification of the consumer to whom the information may pertain.
- Has implemented business processes that specifically prohibit reidentification of the information.
- Has implemented business processes to prevent inadvertent release of de-identified information.
- Makes no attempt to reidentify the information.

The National Institute of Standards and Technology (NIST) comprehensive guide, "De-Identification of Personal Information,"[57] is a helpful resource for "technical safeguards" and "business processes" that prohibit reidentification. HIPAA also has a de-identification standard that requires companies to either: (a) remove any and all of 18 types of identifiers listed in the standard, or (b) engage an expert with appropriate knowledge and experience who can apply technical means to de-identify the information.

Aggregation

Businesses can also move identifiable data out of the scope of privacy laws by aggregating data. Aggregate consumer information is information that:

- Relates to a group or category of consumers;
- Removes individual consumer identities; and,
- That is not linked or reasonably linkable to any consumer or household, including via a device.

---

[57] NISTIR 8053 De-Identification of Personal Information, Simson L. Garfinkel, https://nvlpubs.nist.gov/nistpubs/ir/2015/NIST.IR.8053.pdf.

Generally, the process of aggregating data is an act of summarizing data across a given population to perform analytics or draw statistical information from that data. For example, this could include reporting the number of crimes each month rather than releasing data about individual crimes and victims.

A comparative analogy may be found in the HIPAA Privacy Rule, which describes data aggregation as combining protected health information from multiple covered entities "to permit data analyses that relate to the health care operations," such as quality assurance, case management, care coordination, and outcomes evaluation. In other words, an individual's personal health information is combined to extrapolate general statistical information about health care operations.

Derivative Data Analytics

Data's value can be renewed and transformed by combining it with other data sets. These combined data repositories—sometimes called "data lakes"—create opportunities to analyze behavior and outcomes further. The most critical aspect of aggregated data is removing the individual's identifiable information from the data set so they can no longer be identified. We call this de-identified, aggregated, or anonymized data.

Different laws have different definitions of what it means to de-identify an individual. The more specific data elements that remain, the more likely it is that the individual can be identified. For example, a data set that includes my name, age, address, phone number, and number of kids is considered personal information in many jurisdictions. If you remove only my name, the data is not de-identified because my address and phone number remain, and one can easily use those to look me up. However, if you remove my name, address, and phone number and only include my age and number of kids, that is likely de-identified.

As discussed further in Chapter 8, privacy by design principles must be followed when developing the architecture to pull data from and to create a de-identified data set. Before ingesting data into the data lake, the data is typically de-identified or anonymized—which ends one lifecycle of the data as it relates to the individual and begins a new aggregate lifecycle.

Meaningful de-identification is important to the business because individuals do not have rights to access, modify, or request deletion if the information does not personally identify them. At the point of de-identification, the data's lifecycle ends as it relates to the individual, and their privacy rights cease. The data begins a new cycle as a small component piece of an aggregated data set.

Businesses have more freedom to analyze aggregated or de-identified data because they do not have to obtain additional consent before conducting new analyses. For example, if a California resident bought a puppy on a hypothetical online platform called Pupster, the personal information and data collected about that individual and their transaction are likely subject to privacy rights requests provided under CCPA/CPRA. If Pupster analyzes the consumer's website behavior leading up to the purchase, like how many puppies were viewed, the type of searches run, or other websites visited, that information may also be subject to a rights request. Suppose Pupster decided to combine all transactions into a data lake to understand how users in the aggregate make certain decisions. In that case, there is little benefit or value to keeping the individual's personal information associated with the data. Accordingly, before adding it to the data lake, the individual's name, address, and other information that could identify the person are removed. The metadata and transaction history are ingested into a data lake and then the business may analyze the data at their discretion.

Derivative data analytics can also inform businesses of trends or biases that may be implicit and unidentified. For example, payroll data is regulated personal information. Increasingly, governments require businesses to submit aggregated and de-identified payroll data annually to identify employers that pay women and people of color less than other workers. Frequently, companies are unaware of unequal pay trends if they do not conduct a disparate pay impact analysis. When the business submits data to the government, the individual's name or other identifiable information is not associated with the payroll data.

Data Retention and Destruction Mandates

Data retention policies and schedules often dictate the end of the data lifecycle for structured data. The policies direct the business on how long they must keep the data—these retention periods are often tied to legal and regulatory risks and requirements. For example, payroll data may have to be maintained under the Labor Code for three years from the date of its creation. After that time, the data can be automatically deleted pursuant to a setting in the payroll software. Keeping that data longer than the law requires may create increased costs and risk if the business is sued for wage and hour violations. Recently, major privacy laws began imposing data storage limitations forcing businesses to delete data pursuant to a consumer request and to keep data no longer than is reasonably necessary.

For example, CPRA affirmatively prohibits businesses from "retain[ing] a consumer's personal information or sensitive personal information for each disclosed purpose for which the personal information was collected for longer than is reasonably necessary for that disclosed purpose."

The data that's removed is just as important as the data that's retained. The less personal information that's retained, the easier it will be for companies to fulfill CPRA mandates like individual requests to access, delete, correct, or opt-out of selling or sharing that data. And eliminating obsolete data means the business has less data it must safeguard, thereby reducing cyber risk.

Privacy Lifecycle—A Helpful Construct ~ Matt

Privacy programs do not exist in a vacuum. There is a critical organizational context that informs privacy practices throughout the privacy lifecycle. Like so many other disciplines, however, depending upon your role in the organization, you may miss important context related to how and why the organization collects personal data, how it is used internally, and where or if it is shared, sold, or transferred to other entities or affiliates. Taking a high-level look at each phase, step by step if you will, in the privacy lifecycle offers insights into privacy practices and requisite privacy controls. Recall the privacy lifecycle depicted in Chapter 4.

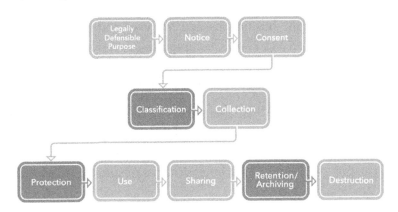

Before we begin, a quick note of caution. Depicting a lifecycle is useful in that it provides a discrete abstraction of *requisite* practices. Few organizations, however, have privacy programs that reflect the unique phases outlined in the diagram above. Organizational dynamics are messy. Politics and internal battles over budgeting and resources frequently generate departmental or functional rivalries at the worst or minimally walled gardens where information and practices are poorly understood by all but a small cadre of senior executives who have a supra view of the organization.

Each phase in the privacy lifecycle has important details to evaluate. Use the privacy lifecycle described below to identify key organizational stakeholders, departments, systems of record, and other context that will facilitate and enhance the maturity of your organization's privacy program. Consider drafting a simple narrative of each phase that you can consult as you assess the broader privacy practices of the overall program. While each phase is important and will be discussed, I want to call attention to three functions that often prove more challenging than others: data classification, data protection, and data retention and archiving practices.

Legally Defensible Purpose

Privacy begins with a legally defensible purpose for the collection and processing of an individual's personal data. Oddly, this simple proposition is frequently overlooked, and collection practices have centered on what is desired by marketing departments or what is feasible based on the various technologies that enable collecting personal data. To avoid being in the crosshairs of regulators, organizations need to take pause and validate whether collecting personal data is, indeed, legally defensible. Recital 39 of the GDPR[58] offers an excellent example and practical guidance on what data processing should encompass to meet this legally defensible threshold. Specifically, Recital 39 states the following:

> Any processing of personal data should be lawful and fair. It should be transparent to natural persons that personal data concerning them are collected, used, consulted or otherwise processed and to what extent the personal data are or will be processed.

Recital 39 goes on to note:

> Natural persons should be made aware of risks, rules, safeguards and rights in relation to the processing of personal data and how to exercise their rights in relation to such processing.

Recital 39 offers guardrails that, when followed, mitigate the risk that an organization employs privacy practices that would be deemed "unfair and deceptive" (i.e., not legally defensible). Section 5 of the Federal Trade Commission Act remains the quintessential standard

---
[58] The text of the GDPR can be found here: https://gdpr-info.eu/recitals/.

of legally defensible practices, at least in a U.S. context. Returning to Recital 39, additional guidance is offered:

> The principle of transparency requires that any information and communication relating to the processing of those personal data be easily accessible and easy to understand, and that clear and plain language be used. That principle concerns, in particular, information to the data subjects on the identity of the controller and the purposes of the processing and further information to ensure fair and transparent processing in respect of the natural persons concerned and their right to obtain confirmation and communication of personal data concerning them which are being processed.

Transparency and trust are integral to the legally defensible standard. Boiled down to the simplest notion, legally defensible privacy practices are those where the data subject is adequately and accurately informed of the processing activities that are contemplated, and that their consent is freely given sans any coercion.

Notice

Legally defensible privacy practices and the programs that underpin them are founded on trust and transparency. Communicating the nature and extent of contemplated processing activities requires unambiguous detail to inform the data subject of what will happen should they provide their personal data to your organization. Privacy notices (aka policies) play a critical role in privacy programs and require well-crafted and legally reviewed content and accurate organizational context. One simple piece of advice is to review "actual" privacy practices in the context of the organization's privacy notice. To the extent they differ materially, that is a red flag. For example, if a privacy notice says that the organization does not sell information to third parties and the actual practice is that personal data is being sold to third parties, that is clearly a potential "unfair and deceptive" practice. Notices must be clear, concise, and accurately reflect the actual privacy practices of the organization.

With the advent of the CCPA, which will become the California Privacy Rights Act (CPRA) in 2023, companies must convey specific requisite detail in the notice. Minimally, under the CCPA, but arguably reflecting ideal transparency regarding processing activities, notices should inform the consumer or data subject of the categories of personal data that is being collected about them. They should also list the sources of this information, how it will be used, whether it will be shared or sold to third parties, and the individual's rights over the contemplated processing activities. This includes the right to access, update, acquire, and transfer personal data from one entity to another (i.e., data portability). Notices must also convey important context regarding if or how personal data is deleted from the organization's environment. Chapter III of the GDPR outlines privacy rights that arguably set the tone globally. Notices should indicate how the data subject can exercise their rights. Notices also need to convey how the data controller or processor will protect that individual's information. In short, notices are about transparency. They provide the context to the data subject, a priori to collection so that the individual can decide whether to provide their personal data to that entity.

Consent

Notice and consent are two sides of the same coin. Consumers cannot freely consent absent accurate and complete notice of the contemplated processing activities. Consent should be unambiguous. An individual's consent must be contextualized to the specific processing activities and time limited. Consent does not last in perpetuity. Avoid attempts to obtain blanket consent covering all potential processing activities. Stated differently, consent is ephemeral and should be re-validated as changes to processing activities occur. As an example, suppose I provide my name, address, and email to an organization to have them send me a package and track the package. Unless I explicitly consent to receive subsequent marketing messages, the consent I offered was only to track and receive the package I ordered, not to have my email used for ongoing marketing messages. Recital 32 of the GDPR notes, "When the processing has multiple purposes, consent should be given for all of them." The example above highlights the critical role of notice in privacy programs. Where the notice does not contemplate future processing activities—adding my email to a marketing campaign—the organization faces potential challenges. Minimally, as a consumer, I'll be frustrated by the unsolicited emails, and my perception of the organization will diminish. Depending upon the circumstances where the consent offered does not relate to the actual processing activities, the organization may find it confronts regulatory action.

Consent should be "freely given," sans any influence undermining that status. What classifies as freely given is the subject of regulatory context and privacy norms. For example, consent from employees in an employee/employer relationship may not be freely given due in part to the asymmetries associated with this relationship. Effectively, the employer has undue influence on the employee/employer relationship. As Recital 42 of the GDPR notes, "Consent should not be regarded as freely given if the data subject has not genuine or free choice or is unable to refuse or withdraw consent without detriment." As a topical extension, the CCPA provides essential protections for consumers when they exercise their rights under the CCPA. The CCPA specifically precludes discrimination against consumers when they exercise their rights. Consumers should not be denied services, pay different prices, or receive lesser quality goods and services when they exercise their rights. The above serves to highlight the nuance related to consent.

In the E.U., consent is so integral to the privacy lifecycle that it becomes a condition precedent to establish the legal basis for the processing of personal data. Article 6 of the GDPR (Lawfulness of processing) notes in Section 1, "Processing shall be lawful only if and to the extent that at least one of the following applies: (a) the data subject has given consent to the processing of his or her personal data…" Article 6 continues with examples of processing activities, but all are predicated upon freely given consent, unambiguous, informed, and evidenced by an affirmative action (i.e., explicit consent).

Grossly exaggerated, privacy practices in the U.S. have frequently been at odds with the consent expectations that we see in Europe. Too often, data is collected from the consumer without their explicit consent and for purposes that differ from the privacy notice, requiring the data subject or consumer to "opt-out" of processing activities. Think about how frequently we "unsubscribe" from marketing emails from organizations that we have never visited online or in person. As we discuss in Chapter 8 on privacy by design principles, take time to think about how your organization manages consent. Is consent explicit, a priori to the initiation of processing activities, and contextualized to the actual processing activities? Is consent re-established when there are changes to the stated processing activities? To the extent the answer is no, there are likely refinements and work to be done to both minimize privacy risks for the organization and improve the consumer's confidence that their data is being used as they had intended.

Classification

In collaboration with their security counterparts, privacy leaders should outline the nature and extent of the specific classes of data the contemplated processing activities will collect. This detail and context become foundational to numerous privacy controls.

I have taken liberties in expanding this privacy lifecycle to include the vital topic of data classification. Classifying the data elements that are part of the processing activities is integral to broader data governance practices, including security, retention, and other potential regulatorily or contractually obligated controls over that data based on its classification. At the risk of overstating the obvious, not all data is created equal. Depending upon the data element's classification there may be distinct obligations, including retention periods. As a case in point, in the U.S. protected health information (PHI) is defined within the Health Insurance and Portability and Accountability Act (HIPAA) and requires a minimum six-year retention period from the date of its last use or creation, whichever is later.

Classifications also inform requisite security controls. Many classes of data elements should be encrypted or pseudonymized. Many data elements warrant these security controls based on either regulatory requirements, contractual obligations, or company policy. You can incorporate the requisite governance controls into the processing activities by bringing classification into the privacy lifecycle and before its collection.

Privacy leaders should collaborate with their organization's counsel to classify data. As a rule, organizationally derived definitions should be avoided. For example, if Article 4 of the GDPR defines "personal data," why should my organization develop a different definition? Similarly, if the CCPA defines "sensitive personal data," use that definition. It is prudent to incorporate these definitions into the organization's data classification schema (obviously assuming applicability of the regulation).

Collection

Collecting data without appropriate notice and consent should be avoided as these practices will likely result in reputational challenges or regulatory action. As we discuss in Chapter 8 on privacy by design, collection practices should reflect data minimization principles. Only collect the minimum data necessary to fulfill the stated purpose of the processing activities. The collection phase introduces important administrative and technical controls to the privacy lifecycle. Administratively, context is added at the point of collection based on the data's classification. The data collected may require specific security controls, specific retention periods, and other actions. Also, collection practices should inform broader data mapping and data flow documentation. Data mapping facilitates documenting how personal data enters the organization, how it is used internally, and where or if it is shared with third parties. Ensuring that this documentation is incorporated as part of the collection process will minimize the challenges of uncontrolled data sprawl. Data mapping also captures context related to the applications used for the processing activities, which departments or roles within the organization will have access to the collected data, where it is stored, and how it's shared externally (if part of the processing activities).

Technical controls, including data validation, which ideally should occur when data is ingested (collected), are critical during the collection phase. Data integrity is also integral to the collection process. Controls should be implemented to validate data classification and protection as it moves from the initial collection point (be it a website, point-of-sale system, or contact center) to its next stage. Well-controlled data collection practices mitigate risk and provide the foundation for broader governance practices.

Data Protections

Large multinational organizations and small businesses alike must implement reasonable security procedures to protect information from accidental misuse or nefarious action. The privacy leader and executive leadership team should monitor the security procedures and evaluate them for efficacy. Where the organization has a board of directors, periodically report status so it may discharge its governance responsibility.

Daily media reports of "yet another" data breach highlight that protecting information is challenging. We discuss reasonable security procedures and the expectations they create for the organization's security program in Chapter 11 in detail. In the interim, as part of the privacy lifecycle, privacy leaders must be engaged with their security counterparts to validate that certain minimum administrative, technical, physical, and operational controls are present.

The "classification" and "collection" phases noted above have important linkages to how personal data and other forms of information are protected. Ideally, specific controls should be implemented based on the information or data element's classification (e.g., encryption, access controls, and basic data protection and governance procedures). Certain data may at times be subject to a litigation or legal hold warranting special protections, treatment, and retention periods. Should there be personal data subject to these preservation requests, it's advisable to consult counsel to understand what would be required should a data subject access request come into the organization for data that is subject to a legal hold.[59] Similarly, by documenting collection procedures and validating how data flows through the organization to its ultimate archival or destruction, privacy and security leaders can evaluate the adequacy of data protection mechanisms throughout the privacy lifecycle.

Various regulations, frequently sector-specific, require that organizations establish security practices that provide "reasonable" security. These same regulations also call organizations to task when they overstate the capabilities of the security programs and the data protections they offer in public-facing notices. The most obvious example is the U.S. Federal Trade Commission and its enforcement of Section 5 of the Federal Trade Commission Act, which protects consumers from "unfair and deceptive trade practices." Privacy leaders need to develop the appropriate technical oversight competencies to ensure that their organization's data protection practices are "reasonable" and consistent with the organization's consumer-facing notices. In addition, privacy leaders need to be engaged with the business and evaluate privacy practices and the security controls protecting data associated with material business processes. Notably, those where sensitive or protected data are collected. Therefore, how organizations use personal data is critical.

Use aka Data Processing

While an analyst, I fielded many inquiries from security and risk management leaders addressing the GDPR. There were certain common themes I would offer as guidance. First and foremost, I would recommend that the individual with whom I was meeting read Recital 39 of the GDPR as a means to evaluate their organization's privacy practices. This recital should be front and center for all

---

[59] These preservation orders may necessitate special controls and isolation for data and information subject to legal proceedings. Data and information subject to legal or litigation hold needs to be proactively identified and controlled accordingly. This is a case where the adage 'inspect what you expect' is in order.

privacy leaders, even when the GDPR is not in scope for their organization. Recital 39 offers clear expectations regarding how organizations should use personal data in processing activities. Specifically, the recital notes, "Any processing [use] of personal data should be lawful and fair. It should be transparent [notice] to natural persons that personal data concerning them are collected, used, consulted or otherwise processed and to what extent the personal data are or will be processed." I added the bracketed terms to highlight an important linkage. The advice that I would offer in these inquiries was that the organization should evaluate whether its data processing activities were consistent with its consumer-facing notices. How an organization uses data collected from individuals must be consistent with the notice it provided to these same individuals before the information was collected. This is the "transparency" expectation noted in Recital 39.

The CCPA requires in-scope organizations to inform the consumer about what data they will collect about them, the sources of this data, how they will use it internally, and if it will be shared with or sold to third parties. This level of concrete detail on processing activities requires direct, hands-on knowledge of the organization. The privacy leader must understand the uses of collected personal data. As part of the review and ongoing monitoring, it is critical to evaluate whether collection practices are consistent with data minimization principles. Effectively, is the organization collecting more personal data than is necessary to fulfill the stated purpose of the contemplated processing activities? This insight requires informed detail on the uses of personal data. Are the data elements used in the processing activities appropriate and necessary for the purpose they are they collected, or are they collected for some future or ancillary use that is inconsistent with the privacy notice? When this is the case, the privacy leader needs to collaborate with line of business colleagues to address this disconnect.

Document the uses of data. Article 30 of the GDPR offers excellent insights into what these "records of processing activities" should encompass. Key topics include the purpose of the processing activities, categories of data collected (this is similar to the expectations established with the CCPA), whether data will be shared or transferred internationally, retention periods, and security controls. Ideally, material business processes that collect personal data should be documented with this context and complemented with data mapping or data flow diagrams that show how the organization ingests the information, uses it internally, or shares it with third parties. These narratives are akin to a network administrator maintaining accurate and complete network diagrams with IP address management as an analog to inventories of data elements collected. Without this detail, it is unlikely that the organization can confidently assert that its privacy practices are indeed consistent with the stated purposes provided in privacy policies and notices.

The information that an organization collects is rarely stagnant. Information and personal data are frequently shared with other departments internally (including access by other staff) or shared with or sold to third parties. This context must be understood and documented. Let's first begin with how data is used internally.

Internal Sharing

Data mapping exercises provide essential context to internal processing activities and can be used to capture how personal data is used and shared internally within the organization. Typically, creating data maps and documenting data flows uncovers external sharing relationships that may not have been originally documented or fully understood. As part of this analysis, some important areas of context should also be captured. Notably, the following should be documented and validated:

- which applications are used for processing activities;
- whether APIs or algorithms are used in the processing of personal data;
- which departments or groups of users have access to these applications and/or the personal data;
- whether the level of access is appropriate and tied to the specified processing activities or indicative of shadow processing activities;

- where the applications are hosted, the IT infrastructure upon which the application is deployed, and the data sinks or storage where personal data resides; and,
- whether security functions tied to the infrastructure noted above are appropriate?

Data mapping exercises offer a treasure trove of context related to processing activities.

There may be disparate privacy and security practices employed within different operating units in larger organizations. The privacy leader must understand this nuance and determine if sharing data internally is consistent with the stated purpose for its collection and whether privacy rights and security controls are adequately addressed. Concerns with unfettered internal data sharing have also surfaced with privacy regulations, including U.S. Commonwealth of Massachusetts' Standards for the Protection of Personal Information of Residents of the Commonwealth (201 CMR 17.00) which defines a breach as "…unauthorized use of unencrypted data…"

> Breach of Security, the unauthorized acquisition or *unauthorized use of unencrypted data* or, encrypted electronic data and the confidential process or key that is capable of compromising the security, confidentiality, or integrity of personal information, maintained by a person or agency that creates a substantial risk of identity theft or fraud against a resident of the commonwealth.

The principles of *least privilege* and *need to know* should guide internal data sharing activities. Similar to external sharing relationships (aka onward transfers), many organizations establish internal operating agreements between departments, subsidiaries, and affiliates (the latter two may actually be classified as external entities in certain jurisdictions) that require that the data be used consistent with its stated purpose and expectations for requisite security controls be validated. These environments are excellent targets for the privacy leader and internal audit reviews.

Marketing and sales departments warrant a double click. The creativity these departments bring to "unauthorized" uses of personal data should not be underestimated. The "transparency" of disclosures of these uses should also be a subject of concern. With the advent of data lakes and marketing tools that leverage metadata and directly collected personal data, do not discount the opportunities for collection practices that fall outside of the privacy leader's purview. Privacy leaders will need to be proactive and spend quality time with their colleagues and counterparts within sales and marketing functions. The use of personal data by these departments is not inherently wrong. However, it is wrong when these uses are not tied to the notice provided to the data subject or consumer and the consent for sales and marketing activities is notably absent. Sales and marketing activities that have explicit consent from the consumer and are consistent with the notice provided can engender trust and build the organization's reputation and brand. Without this, dynamic, unfettered, and unauthorized activities can result in lost trust, damaged reputation, and potential regulatory action. Spend the time necessary to ensure these activities are well understood, documented, and reviewed for risk.

External Data Sharing

How information is shared with third parties remains a hot topic in privacy. When sharing data across borders, the potential scrutiny increases. Privacy leaders need to maintain an accurate and complete inventory of data-sharing relationships with their firm and validate any international data flows. Triage this inventory from multiple perspectives. First and foremost, validate data-sharing relationships vis-à-vis the notice that is provided to the consumer or data subject. If data is sold or exchanged with third parties, has the consumer provided their explicit consent for these data-sharing activities? Have that third-party recipient's privacy and security practices been adequately reviewed? This context is integral to evaluating external data-sharing relationships.

Data classification also plays a critical role in data sharing. In the U.S., when PHI is shared with third parties, certain legal protections need to be established a priori. Notably, a business associate agreement (BAA) must be executed between entities that share PHI. The BAA establishes an important principle that should guide most if not all data-sharing activities. Specifically, the covered entity (effectively the data controller) cannot abdicate its accountability over the personal data (PHI) that the covered entity shared with a third party. This accountability generally requires that the covered entity adequately assess the recipient entity's risk profile and validate that the recipient entity has established appropriate administrative, technical, and physical safeguards over the personal data it receives from the data controller. These assessments and reviews are generally the purviews of the organization's vendor management/procurement team or security team. The privacy leader should work with these stakeholders to ensure assessment activities are sufficient and address the organization's legal obligations and risk management practices.

The privacy leader must document and evaluate other forms of external data-sharing for privacy risk. Technology may obscure or hide data sharing from all but a small number of those developers who have direct, hands-on knowledge of how data flows from one application to another. Of note, there may be APIs used to exchange information from one application or business process to another. Validating these data flows requires diligence and highlights the importance of data mapping exercises. There may also be third-party applications used to support internal business processes that process personal data. For many organizations, payroll processing services serve as an obvious example. As a rule of thumb, privacy practitioners should assume that external data-sharing occurs until corroborated otherwise. With larger organizations having vendor inventories numbering in the thousands, evaluating external data-sharing relationships can quickly subsume the privacy team's day-to-day activities. Without collaboration and support from other departments, notably vendor management/procurement team and security team, potential risks from third-party data processing activities cannot be overstated. This phase of the privacy lifecycle will always be inherently high-risk.

Retention (Archiving)

Many forms of personal data require mandated retention periods. To keep with the healthcare theme above, in the context of HIPAA, PHI has a minimum retention period of six years, though it may be considerably longer (e.g., the patient's life for certain forms of PHI). Financial data, including details related to loans, are typically retained for the life of the financial instrument plus an additional period that varies based on the nature of the financial transaction. The purging of data that has exceeded its retention period also requires programmatic attention and scheduling.

How organizations store, retain, and occasionally archive information is an area that is commonly subject to internal ambiguity, an ambiguity that frequently leads to conflicting actions or internal misunderstandings related to actual practices. Let's unpack this a bit. Corporate IT, generally the infrastructure and operations teams, are responsible for maintaining the storage and backup systems (many of these are now cloud-based). Capacity planning for on-premises storage systems is critical as storage volumes tend to grow significantly year-over-year. The consequence is that storage and backup administrators may make decisions to purge certain data to allocate space for new applications or more current data volumes. These decisions often occur in a vacuum and are driven by operational imperatives (e.g., finding space to provide production storage and backup services).

For many organizations, storage and backup services are underfunded. When the CIO builds the IT budget, one of the largest line items is storage for its data. CFOs, balancing infinite demands on capital, may "axe" some portion of the budget request, requiring the CIO and the storage and backup teams to make do. One result is data that may require a longer retention period may be deleted or removed by storage and backup teams, potentially unaware of mandated retention requirements. The privacy leader is rarely engaged in funding decisions related to storage and backup infrastructure from a privacy perspective. The three stakeholders—IT, finance, and privacy—need to "declare war on ambiguity" and validate operational understandings. Let's make this collective action problem a bit more challenging. Retention and archival periods should not be established randomly nor in a vacuum. How long to retain data reflects regulatory requirements or contractual obligations. The organization's legal team has significant input here.

More than likely, there's consensus between the privacy leader and counsel about these retention periods. While these two principals share a common understanding of the retention period, the organization runs the risk that the finance and IT teams may not be fully informed of these obligations.

This phase of the privacy lifecycle requires proactive validation and organizational consensus. Privacy leaders cannot leave retention and archiving functions to chance.

Hard Deletion and Destruction

Ultimately, data should be erased (hard deleted) or destroyed once its required retention period has expired or there is no legitimate purpose for its retention and there is no preservation order in place. These conditions are relatively self-evident, especially when organizations follow privacy by design principles (which we discuss in Chapter 8). Data deletion and destruction, however, is easier said than done. To truly ensure that privacy rights such as the right to erasure are enforceable, organizations need to validate and document where personal data resides throughout the organization, and with third parties where this information has been shared. This effort is relatively straightforward with structured data where rows and records from databases are permanently deleted (and not simply placed in an inactive state or archive copy), but identifying the location of unstructured data (e.g., image files, emails, Word, Excel, PowerPoint, and third-party file sharing applications such as ShareFile, Dropbox, and Box) makes the deletion or destruction of personal data problematic at best. These challenges highlight the importance of data governance. By conducting data mapping exercises, documenting data flows, validating which data is shared with third parties, enforcing proper data handling, and documenting processing activities, we can reduce the difficulty level of data destruction. There is also a vital role for privacy training for the organization's staff. Ensuring staff is aware of their obligations to limit the collection, storage and use of personal data for legitimate purposes can help mitigate risks that unstructured data survives formal destruction requests.

The privacy lifecycle, similar to privacy by design principles, should be used to inform the privacy program and to ensure that risk considerations are adequately captured and documented across each phase. The insights garnered from reviewing each phase of the privacy lifecycle will drive more risk-informed decisions to the overall privacy program. Investments made in documenting and assessing risk through each phase of the lifecycle are invaluable.

Key Insights and Recommended Next Steps

Key Insights

- Context is key. Obtain informed consent by providing transparent notice about why you want to collect each element of personal data and how long you will retain it.
- Data is not a fine wine; it does not age well. As it ages, it loses value and gains liability. This time-value equation should inform each stage of your privacy lifecycle.
- Data transformation techniques and periodic risk assessments are critical to reducing liability and injecting new value into aging data.
- It is unlikely that the privacy leader will have control over all stages of the privacy lifecycle. Collaboration across functions is essential to successfully govern data privacy.
- Regulatory guidance, time-bound consent, consumer requests, and periodic assessments about the value of data sets should be the primary drivers of data destruction.
- Retention and destruction go hand in glove—a valuable calculus is that if you don't have a solid reason to keep it, destroy it.

Recommended Next Steps

- Build a cross-functional RACI matrix (see Chapter 4, Figure 4.5, Sample RACI matrix) for your privacy program and validate understandings related to each role with the identified stakeholders.
- Create data flow diagrams that show how personal data is ingested, used, processed, and retained or destroyed.
- Work with the functions that ingest, use, process, and retain personal data and map usage, retention, and destruction practices to your privacy notices. Then perform a gap analysis and add the results to your privacy risk register.

Chapter 7

Global Privacy Regulations

Introduction

According to Ethnologue, there are approximately 90 languages with ten million or more first speakers,[60] and Stephen R. Anderson of the American Linguistic Society tells us there are roughly 7,000 different languages.[61] The U.N. recognizes six official languages (English, French, Spanish, Chinese, Russian, and Arabic). We're all familiar with the iconic earpieces that delegates wear during speeches and deliberations.

As we entered the communications age, even those of us without access to diplomatic services and having no multi-lingual friends, have had access to a wide range of translation services, from international phone carriers with armies of multi-lingual operators to Google translator to dozens of apps for our smartphones. Still, translation errors occur all the time, creating misunderstandings, embarrassment, and generally slowing things down.

According to Anderson's paper, languages share much in common, using hierarchical constructs to form words based on symbols representing phonetic sounds which are then independently built into words representing objects, actions, and concepts. The same could be said about global privacy regulations. The specifics might be different and different regulations may prioritize different means to outcomes, but they share common underlying principles.

---

[60] Ethnologue, 2019 Edition.
[61] How Many Languages Are There in the World? Stephen R. Anderson, Linguistic Society of America Brochure Series.
https://www.linguisticsociety.org/sites/default/files/how-many-languages.pdf

Each of us has a slightly different view of the commonalities (principles) informing the international privacy regulatory landscape.

In the first essay, "Global Privacy Regulations," David reviews seven principles that will help you avoid duplication of effort and provide a rationale for setting up your global compliance program. David looks directly at the guiding principles of the GDPR as his foundation.

Justine then walks through the evolution of privacy laws in her essay, "How Global Privacy Regulations Come to Be." She provides fascinating insight into how several key laws came into effect, including a look at the democratic process that produced each regulation. She has drawn her list of principles from the four corners of the globe, but while stated and grouped differently, the boil down to the same concepts.

In his essay, "Clearing Up the Confusion about Global Privacy Regulations," Matt takes a head-on look at the misconceptions about privacy laws, especially those from international partners that seem to arrive in the shadow of concern. Matt then builds on the work done by David and Justine and takes a programmatic look at several of the principles that require cross-department initiatives and awareness.

Global Privacy Regulations ~ David

It's a well-known urban myth: you're waiting at a bus stop for ages, then three (or more) buses come along at once. It's actually more than a myth. Anyone who has waited for a bus knows the routine—you wait far longer than you should. The problem, which has a variety of names, plagues buses, trains, and even elevators.[62] The dilemma is whether to just hop on the first one or skip to the second or third.

Surprisingly, much the same can be said about privacy regulations. We went a long time without any comprehensive set of regulations that had binding authority or recognizable enforcement procedures to back them up. True, in the U.S., HIPAA (Health Insurance Portability and Accountability Act) and GLBA (Gramm-Leach-Bliley Act) were enacted in the nineties, but they were specific to the healthcare and financial sectors, respectively, and COPPA (Children's Online Privacy Protection Act) was also quite narrow. In Europe, the Data Protection Directive (DPD) came into force in 1995 to regulate the processing of personal data within the European Union and the free movement of such data. However, its impact was limited by two overarching factors. Firstly, as the DPD was "only" a directive, it was left up to each Member State to interpret or legislate as they saw fit.

Consequently, approaches to data protection varied considerably across the continent and weakened the effectiveness of the directive. Further, consider that the first version of Netscape Navigator, the original user-friendly web browser, was released in 1994; in other

---

[62] Editor's Note: The inspection paradox and length-biased sampling are two common mathematical names. Essentially, even if buses (or, to a lesser degree trains and elevators) all start at the precise intervals necessary to achieve the published schedule and frequency, variances in traffic patterns, loading and unloading, and other events can speed up or slow down individual vehicles. While smoothing out on average, this phenomenon often causes individual passengers to wait longer than they should have to on average for their conveyance to arrive. Given that only a limited number of riders (those bunched) can enjoy the abundance when it occurs and far more experience the delay, that damn bus is always late.

words, the Data Protection Directive was drafted when scarcely anyone was using the internet either for social or commercial purposes. It's hardly surprising that the legislators didn't grasp the scale of the problems the uptake of the internet would harbor.

Cometh the Hour, Cometh the Regulator

Fast forward twenty years, and the landscape has changed beyond all recognition. The explosion of online usage across all sectors of society and the economy worldwide, and particularly the burgeoning data-driven market economy, has triggered a concomitant awareness of data protection and privacy issues that would have been almost unimaginable back in the nineties. Into this abyss came the European Union's General Data Protection Regulation (GDPR), that not only addressed the essential shortcomings of the Data Protection Directive highlighted above, but also went much further in providing a technology-neutral, comprehensive set of guidelines and principles aimed at protecting the rights of European citizens concerning the use of their data anywhere in the world.

After much anticipation and apprehension from corporates scrambling to get their data management houses in order, the GDPR came into force on May 25, 2018. Since then, a wide range of jurisdictions in over 140 countries across the world have developed privacy regulations that mirror or at least aim to achieve a similar level of coverage as the GDPR, including:

- **California**: California Privacy Rights Act (CPRA), the evolution of the California Consumer Privacy Act (CCPA)
- **Canada**: Digital Charter Implementation Act (DCIA), the evolution of the Personal Information Protection and Electronic Documents Act (PIPEDA)
- **India**: Personal Data Protection Bill (PDPB)
- **Mexico**: Federal Law on Protection of Personal Data Held by Individuals (LFPDPPP)
- **Brazil**: General Personal Data Protection Law (LGPD - Lei General de Proteção de Dados)
- **Israel**: Protection of Privacy Law (PPL) and Privacy Protection (Data Security) Regulations

- **South Africa:** Protection of Personal Information (POPI)
- **Singapore:** Personal Data Protection Act (PDPA)
- **Australia:** Privacy Act 1988 (Privacy Act)
- **Russia:** Federal Law of 27 July 2006 N 152-FZ on Personal Data (152-FZ)
- **China:** Personal Information Protection Law (PIPL)

Over the last twenty years, fifteen Caribbean countries have enacted data privacy laws. In the United States, the lead has been taken with the California Consumer Privacy Act (CCPA) as well as Virginia's Consumer Data Protection Act (CDPA) and Colorado's Privacy Act (CPA). In addition, more than 25 other states have introduced comprehensive data privacy bills, not all of which will successfully progress through their respective state legislatures. All of the above could be overshadowed one day by the proposed federal American Data Privacy and Protection Act. Time will tell.

Suffice it to say, within a few years there will be robust, citizen-centric laws concerning the use, management, and transfer of personal data in most corners of the world. They will all be different, but they will be more or less variations on a similar core set of principles and ideals. For companies working across more than one jurisdiction or, for multinationals, many jurisdictions, the situation can appear daunting, particularly if there are, in addition, vertical sector regulations to consider. If you are a healthcare company based in California with customers in Europe, you must contend with CCPA, CPRA (which goes into effect in 2023), HIPAA, and the GDPR. Where do you even begin to understand where you stand without being completely overwhelmed?

Follow the Principle(s)

The best approach to address this maze of different regulations is to drill down into the underlying principles that are common across most jurisdictions. Understanding and then implementing what the legislators have been seeking to achieve over the last decade goes a long way to ensuring compliance or at least having a justifiable rationale for your actions in implementing your privacy program.

A good place to start is to look at the GDPR with its focus on the collection and processing of personal data. There are seven guiding principles of the GDPR, the purposes of which are reasonably self-evident:

- Lawfulness, fairness, and transparency
- Purpose limitation
- Data minimization
- Accuracy
- Storage limitation
- Integrity and confidentiality (security)
- Accountability

The intention is to empower consumers and citizens by letting them know what information you hold about them and how you plan to use it. Transparency and clear communication are critical to your commitment to your customers, demonstrated by providing a user-friendly way to consent or refuse to agree to your usage of their data unless your business has a clear legitimate purpose. It's also essential to make your customers aware that they can legally challenge your company if your business changes how it uses the personal data you have collected without revised consent or loses it due to lack of care.

The GDPR provides that customers have the right to access the data you hold about them and object to how it is used based on your full disclosure and their full access to their data. Of course, not all legislations are that restrictive, but the overriding principle is sound. Importantly, your customers have the right to demand that you erase their data and, in certain circumstances, be able to take a copy of their data to a competitor. However, it's also important to note that these rights are not absolute: for example, there are times when the right to be forgotten should not be executed.

What to Expect Next

Over the coming years, you can expect to see more jurisdictions adopt privacy regulations where there were none before, notably in many of the states of the United States. Alternatively, as will more often be the case, jurisdictions will review the existing legislation that may have been initially drawn up during the last century or in the pre-digital age and then determine whether to draw up new legislation that is based on the previous legislation and best practices from other domains.

It is also to be expected that any privacy laws written over the last five to ten years will need to be reviewed and recast because of the impact of new technologies and applications. Of course, it's always hard to predict, but at the time of writing it would not be surprising if applications based on AI, virtual reality, quantum computing, the identity of "things," or biometrics could trigger such a review. Nonetheless, the original legislators, who would claim to have assiduously attempted to write technology-neutral laws, would assert that their well-written laws should not bend to the ephemeral trends in technology—rather the other way round. Time will tell!

As an indication of what is brewing, in Europe cracks in the implementation of the GDPR are already apparent in how EU Member States have introduced additional legislation, predominantly in the areas of processing genetic data, using biometric data for identification, and the processing of health data. For example, the use of biometrics for the electronic acquisition of handwritten signatures is allowed in 10 out of 19 countries surveyed. In contrast, only a handful of Member States do not allow biometrics in a work environment.[63] The conclusion is that the GDPR is not really a unifying factor for compliance on personal data protection across the EU, but it is more the core or minimum standard that must be reached in all Member States. In large legislative domains such as, for example, the EU, India, or China, it is to be expected that this trend will be repeated.

One of the other issues that will muddy the good intentions of legislators everywhere is how to manage the cross-border transfer of personal data. This is particularly germane for multi-nationals in cases where data must be transferred between two—or as likely, more

---

[63] Heterogeneity of Data Protection Legislation across the EU, Cyber Security for Europe, 09 September 2021, https://cybersec4europe.eu/heterogeneity-of-data-protection-legislation-in-the-eu/.

than two—disjunct legislative domains. The lawyers will have a field day![64] In fact, as of the time of writing, organizations wishing to transfer data between the EU and a non-EU country must grapple with adequacy decisions embedded in the standard contractual clauses introduced in June 2021 because of the Schrems II verdict in July 2020[65]—that will completely replace the original SCCs by 27 December 2022.

The Trans-Atlantic Data Privacy Framework

For years, the major source of contention when it comes to cross-border data transfer has been between the EU and the US, primarily because of the universal presence of the tech giants and their tendency to push the boundaries of acceptable practice, particularly when it came to US surveillance programs and a lack of grievance mechanisms available to EU citizens. As a result, long-negotiated arrangements, such as Safe Harbor and the EU-US Privacy Shield, were found to be wanting and inadequate in meeting the requirements and expectations of the GDPR.

The good news is that on March 25, 2022, US President Biden and European Commission President Ursula von der Leyen announced that the two parties had agreed to a Trans-Atlantic Data Privacy Framework. However, the small print points out that the agreement was 'in principle,' the details of which had yet to be ironed out. In other words, even though it came two years after Schrems II, solutions had still not been found to the outstanding issues raised,

---

[64] Standard contractual clauses for international transfers, https://ec.europa.eu/info/law/law-topic/data-protection/international-dimension-data-protection/standard-contractual-clauses-scc/standard-contractual-clauses-international-transfers_en.

[65] The 'Schrems II' decision: EU-US data transfers in question, IAPP Privacy Tracker, https://iapp.org/news/a/the-schrems-ii-decision-eu-us-data-transfers-in-question/ and
The Court of Justice invalidates Decision 2016/1250 on the adequacy of the protection provided by the EU-US Data Protection Shield, Court of Justice of the European Union, 16 July 2020
https://curia.europa.eu/jcms/upload/docs/application/pdf/2020-07/cp200091en.pdf.

primarily changes to US surveillance laws. To that point, there has also been a nagging concern that this is a political announcement with no text that can be formally analyzed.

Nevertheless, once there is resolution of the issues highlighted in the CJEU ruling, a process that is likely to take months, it should reimplement a mechanism to facilitate data transfers between the EU and the US which is already long overdue.

Take Responsibility

The overall message from various regulatory domains is to take responsibility for the personal data you collect and hold, and recognize that your customers, employees, and suppliers have inalienable rights to information that directly concerns them. It's really that simple. As ever, the devil is often in the details, and the different nuanced interpretations by each set of lawmakers are not to be overlooked or dismissed. The principal relationship is between you and your data stakeholders; if you look at it as a marriage, the regulatory codes are the prenups. If all parties are satisfied, behave according to the principles of mutual trust and respect, and nothing goes awry, no one will bother delving into the legalese to finger point and identify where it all went wrong. It is also worth bearing in mind that with each regulation come enforcement agencies that will have the power to leverage hefty fines if you are found to have contravened the spirit of the deal, such as is the case with the GDPR's option to impose fines of up to four percent of top line revenue.

In summary, the new legislations are a re-calibration of rights and powers between individuals, data controllers, and data processors. Companies that don't realize that the rules of play have changed significantly over the last five to ten years and do not respond adequately will find themselves left behind by competitors who do or be hit with fines or lawsuits potentially large enough to destroy their business. On the other hand, the new regulations present a great business opportunity to reach out and engage with customers and employees on an ongoing basis, demonstrating your trustworthiness and hopefully earning their loyalty—just as an exemplary marriage should be!

How Global Privacy Regulations Come to Be ~ Justine

The Evolution of Privacy Laws

As the digital age has developed, so too have privacy laws. For reasons discussed more fully in Chapter 1, the rise of the digital age created both benefits for and risks to an individual's personal privacy. Notwithstanding an increase in people's concerns about their privacy rights, individuals continue to engage in online behavior that is wholly inconsistent with those concerns. This "privacy paradox" is likely driven by an increased desire to have unlimited and unfettered access to information, social media connections, and the shift from in-person to online experiences, including benign experiences like grocery shopping. The lack of users evaluating the cost/benefit of their online behavior, coupled with the tremendous advantages businesses gain in analyzing those behaviors, has forced legislatures to pass laws requiring businesses to engage in fair information practices.

Laws and Regulations

Laws can mean many things—from general principles of jurisprudence to codified written statutes. Privacy rules typically come in the form of laws and regulations. Laws are the statutory code or written statutes that legislatures create. Regulations are more detailed and practical guidance on implementing the laws. How laws and regulations are created varies depending on the jurisdiction. The one thing all laws have in common: they are all shaped and implemented by humans. Let's take a quick world tour of how laws are made in a few regions of the world.

The European Union

The EU is made up of two decision-making bodies: the Parliament and the Council of the EU. The European Commission proposes new laws. The Parliament and the Council must agree to pass new laws.

The Parliament. In Europe, member nations of the European Union have members elected to the EU Parliament. The Parliament has 705 members, and the number of members from each country depends on the population of the country—the larger the country's population, the more members it has in the Parliament.

The Council of the EU. The Council of the European Union includes ministers that represent the governments and interests of the EU member countries. The ministers are selected based on particular topics. For example, if privacy is the topic, then privacy ministers from each EU member country will meet. The Council makes decisions by a majority vote and, in some cases, unanimously.

The European Commission. The European Commission is made up of 27 members—one president and 26 commissioners. There is one commissioner from each EU country. Commissioners represent the views and common interests of the EU as a whole. In addition, each member of the Commission is responsible for a specific area, such as privacy, energy, economy, or trade. The European Commission proposes new laws in the general interest of the EU.

After a new law is proposed, it is evaluated by the European Parliament and the Council, which either pass, modify, or reject the law.

GDPR. In March 2014, the European Parliament voted on GDPR with 621 votes in favor, 10 against, and 22 abstentions. Over a year later, in June 2015, the Council agreed to establish the European Data Protection Board (EDPB). This new independent European body would include members of all European data protection authorities. The role of the EDPB was to ensure the consistency of the application of the GDPR throughout the EU through guidelines, opinions, and decisions.[66] By December 2015, the text of the GDPR was finalized, and the Parliament, Council, and Commission all reached agreement. On April 27, 2016, the General Data Protection Regulation was adopted by the Parliament and Council to protect

---

[66] The History of the General Data Protection Regulation
https://edps.europa.eu/data-protection/data-protection/legislation/history general-data-protection-regulation_en.

natural persons regarding the processing of personal data and on the free movement of such data. EU businesses and governments had two years to implement regulations aligned with GDPR. On May 25, 2018, the GDPR went into effect, and businesses are expected to comply.

The United States

In the United States, laws can be federal (passed by Congress), state (passed by voters or state legislatures and signed by the governor), county, or municipal (city). Regulations are implementation standards or processes adopted by federal or state government agencies that further explain how the laws should be followed and how the agency will enforce the laws. Many laws call for agencies to create regulations after the law is passed. Regulations are easier to modify than laws and usually are left to the governing agency (subject to public comment) to draft, revise, and enforce.

In 1998, the Federal Trade Commission published an influential report called "Privacy Online: A Report to Congress" which recognized "core principles of fair information practice, widely accepted as essential to ensuring fair collection, use, and sharing of personal information in a manner consistent with consumer privacy interests."[67] Those core principles drove state consumer privacy laws to require online privacy policies that explained how businesses collected and used consumer data online. At the federal level, privacy statutes emerged, focusing on specific industries like healthcare (HIPAA) and financial institutions (GLBA). However, there are currently no comprehensive federal privacy laws in the U.S. California's passage of CCPA in 2018 created the first comprehensive privacy law of its kind in the U.S., but it only provides rights to California residents.

---

[67] Federal Trade Commission., Privacy Online: A Report to Congress (June 1998) at p. 2.

CCPA/CPRA

In 2018, two critical events gave privacy advocates the momentum needed to pass the most comprehensive privacy law in the United States: (1) on March 17, 2018, the Cambridge Analytica and Facebook scandal broke, followed by FTC investigations, Congressional hearings, and class action lawsuits; and (2) on May 25, 2018, GDPR became fully operative, affording EU residents broad protections. In response to these global headlines, advocates in California led by Alistair McTaggart proposed a comprehensive consumer-privacy ballot measure that would have been voted on by California residents on the November 2018 ballot.[68]

In June 2018, proponents for the ballot measure obtained the requisite 600,000 signatures to be on the November ballot, and it was gaining massive support from California voters. Unfortunately, state legislative processes cannot typically amend ballot initiatives, so state assemblymember Ed Chau and state senator Robert Hertzberg proposed a rushed piece of legislation substantially similar to the ballot initiative (now known as CCPA) to replace the ballot initiative.

A deal was struck that if the state legislature passed CCPA, ballot proponents would withdraw their initiative from the ballot. The deadline to withdraw the ballot was quickly approaching, which forced the state legislature to fast-track CCPA. On June 28, 2018, the California state legislature unanimously passed CCPA, and it was signed by the governor—all within one week from the date it was introduced!

The swift legislative action to pass the privacy rules as legislation (rather than a ballot measure) allowed lawmakers to more easily amend CCPA, which happened multiple times throughout 2018 and 2019. Original proponents of CCPA believed the amendments diluted the consumer protection law's original purpose and intent. Then, in November 2020, ballot initiative Proposition 24, which modified CCPA, was placed on the ballot. A majority of California

---

[68] CA Stats. 2018, ch. 55, § 2(g).

residents voted in favor of Proposition 24, and CPRA was born.[69] CPRA goes into effect on January 1, 2023. At the time this book was published, over a dozen proposed amendments to modify CPRA further were working their way through the legislative process.

People's Republic of China

National People's Congress (NPC). The NPC is the governing body that enacts laws in China. It comprises approximately 3,000 individuals elected from 35 provinces, regions, and government-controlled divisions.[70] The NPC meets once a year, and the Standing Committees perform ongoing work related to lawmaking.

On August 20, 2021, the NPC adopted the Personal Information Protection Law (PIPL)—the first comprehensive data protection law in China. PIPL took effect in November 2021, which united existing data privacy laws in China under one omnibus law. PIPL also added several significant new provisions, including steep fines, extraterritorial applicability, the need for data protection officers, and new rules governing cross-border transfers. Throughout the legislative process, experts and privacy professionals contributed to PIPL based on lessons learned from GDPR.[71]

Core Principles of Privacy Laws

Global privacy laws and regulations generally follow several core privacy principles:

- **Transparency:** giving notice and awareness to consumers, users, and visitors about the business's data collection, sharing, and use practices.

---

[69] Initiative Measure (Prop. 24) approved Nov. 4, 2020, eff. Dec. 16, 2020.
[70] The national People's Congress of the People's Republic of China (English site), http://www.npc.gov.cn/englishnpc/c2846/201903/b149298c33b24f1e8aaa7b8b0e45fa77.shtml.
[71] China's new comprehensive data protection law: context, stated objectives, key provisions, Future of Privacy Forum, https://fpf.org/blog/chinas-new-comprehensive-data-protection-law-context-stated-objectives-key-provisions/.

- **Data Minimization and Localization:** reducing the data collected and stored to the minimum amount necessary to operate and requiring that the data be stored locally.
- **Options and Rights:** providing individuals with choices and options around the use, storage, management, and collection of personal information, including the rights to opt-in and opt-out and make privacy rights requests on the company to access or delete personal information.
- **Integrity and Accuracy:** ensuring data is accurate when captured and protected from inappropriate alteration.
- **Data Security:** ensuring the information is accessed and used by authorized users with appropriate security controls and protocols.
- **Enforcement:** ensuring that the service, site, solution, and platform have an enforcement component to ensure the laws are being followed.

Determining Which Laws and Regulations Apply to Your Business

Privacy laws protect individuals that reside in the jurisdiction where the law is effective. Accordingly, identifying where consumers or customers reside and whether the business is subject to the laws of that jurisdiction will help determine what privacy laws or regulations apply to your business. For example, if your business uses a sales platform, generate a report that identifies all the jurisdictions where the business has done business, manufactured supplies or products, or sold products or services. Similarly, if HR can generate a list of all the jurisdictions where employees reside, that will help develop the privacy program related to employee privacy rights.

An important factor is understanding the jurisdictions where the company "does business." Oftentimes licenses to do business under the laws of a particular jurisdiction will require the business to attest that it will follow the laws of that jurisdiction. Therefore, confer with your corporate counsel to identify where the business may have licenses to do business.

Another natural set of laws to include in your privacy program is the laws of the jurisdiction where your business has its corporate headquarters.

Finally, consider the type of business or industry you are in and identify any industry-specific laws or regulations that may apply. For example, healthcare providers must comply with HIPAA, and financial institutions must comply with GLBA. However, complying with these federal laws provides exemptions under certain state privacy laws.

Proactive Tip: Create a matrix that identifies all jurisdictions where the company does business, has employees, or must generally comply with privacy laws. Add a column that identifies the percentage of business done in each jurisdiction, then link the privacy laws for each jurisdiction.

After identifying the applicable jurisdictions, consult with corporate counsel to identify the laws that apply to your business. Laws often have exceptions and exemptions and may not apply. For example, if you are a non-profit educational institution or a bank, CCPA/CPRA does not apply to non-profits and has limited exceptions for financial institutions regulated by GLBA and FCRA data. CCPA/CPRA also has exceptions for covered entities and business associates.

Harmonizing and Simplifying Multiple Laws and Regulations

Most large enterprises operate in multiple jurisdictions and will be subject to many different privacy laws. In addition to geographic location, publicly traded businesses must comply with SEC regulations and disclosures. Additionally, certain types of data have specific regulatory requirements like PHI (regulated by HIPAA) and non-public information collected by financial institutions (regulated by GLBA). Having separate privacy frameworks for each jurisdiction and data type is inefficient, expensive, and time-consuming to manage and update. To the extent possible, most businesses want a simplified approach or strategy to privacy. If you do business in the

EU or California and those laws apply, they will likely set the general framework for the privacy program.

Getting Pragmatic: Identify the Nice-to-Haves vs. Need-to-Haves

Not all privacy laws carry the same amount of compliance risk. Identify the laws that are key to success and quantify the risk of not complying. For example, statutory fines, penalties, or class action risk may be higher in California than in other states. A cost-benefit analysis can identify the cost vs. the benefit of compliance. The benefit can be measured by the liability you avoid by complying. For example, violating China's PIPL could risk up to five percent of a company's annual revenue and impose personal liability on individuals running the privacy program. Alternatively, the Chinese government could block your business from doing business in China for failing to comply with PIPL. If sales to China are a significant part of your revenue stream or business operations, devoting time and money to PIPL compliance makes sense. If it would not be a significant impact if you could not operate or do business in China, then perhaps the company will want to assume the risk of non-compliance.

GDPR: Don't Let the Tail Wag the Dog

For U.S. businesses without prior experience with the 1995 Data Protection Directive, the GDPR can be one of the most difficult, time-consuming, and expensive laws to achieve substantial compliance under. GDPR uses unique terms, requires time-consuming DPIAs, ROPAs, and other supporting documentation, and has prescriptive articles, regulations, and requirements. There are less burdensome laws upon which to model your compliance program that may be a better fit and utilize universal or global terms. It depends on several factors, such as where the business is headquartered, where it does business, and potential regulatory considerations. For example, a business that does 98% of its business in the U.S. and only 2% of its business in the EU should build a privacy program that substantially complies with U.S. laws. There may be specific privacy elements tailored to GDPR, like data protection authorities (DPAs) with EU businesses, but there is no good reason to apply GDPR to all data. Instead, adopt a practical and defensible approach to comply with laws and regulations that best serves your business and the consumers your business serves. Focusing on the fundamental privacy principles will put the program on the right path.

Clearing Up the Confusion about Global Privacy Regulations ~ Matt

Everyone loves regulation, right? My first exposure to regulatory requirements came early in my career with the "Public Company Accounting Reform and Investor Protection Act," as it was known in the U.S. Senate, and the "Corporate and Auditing Accountability, Responsibility, and Transparency Act," as it was known in the U.S. House of Representatives; ultimately, it became the Sarbanes-Oxley Act of 2002 (aka "SOX"). SOX was controversial from the beginning and created havoc across public companies during the first few years of its implementation. For CFOs and their teams, it was as though armies of auditors swarmed their departments, assessing and opining on the status of internal controls related to seemingly every corporate activity.[72] However, despite the initial tumult created by SOX, public companies eventually improved how they documented their internal controls over financial reporting and institutionalized best practices for financial governance and disclosure.

Years later, SOX has become ingrained into public companies' finance and accounting functions, and what was once a distracting burden has become relatively routine. Corporate finance and accounting functions have improved business process documentation, analyzed financial disclosure risks and obligations, implemented a more rigorous separation of duties for key accounting functions, and strengthened controls related to the accuracy and quality of financial reporting. While compliance with SOX will never be "fun," it did not, as its critics initially suggested, result in an exodus of public company listings to overseas and foreign exchanges.

---

[72] The whole of enterprise over-the-top assessment of internal controls with process narratives, risk and control matrices, and control testing that interrupted day-to-day operations generated widescale disdain and corporate pushback. Indeed, the Public Company Accounting Oversight Board (PCAOB), overseen by the Securities and Exchange Commission (SEC), ultimately updated Audit Standard 2 (which took a bottom-up approach to assessing internal controls over financial reporting) to Audit Standard 5 (which was a top-down, risk-based view of financial reporting and disclosure controls–those that were deemed material). Years later, SOX has become ingrained into corporate financial governance.

In part, U.S. capital markets remain strong because of the confidence the investment community has in the quality of financial reporting for U.S.-regulated equities.

Today, as an analog to the initial fears related to Sarbanes-Oxley, there is widespread commentary about the perceived damaging effects on organizations confronting a multitude of privacy regulations. Today's perception is that privacy regulations are so onerous that they undermine competitiveness. The GDPR and the CCPA/CPRA are two regulations that draw such attention and ire. The EU did not collapse on May 25th of 2018, nor did California fall into the Pacific Ocean on January 1, 2020. The hype and bluster about the negative impacts of privacy regulations will, over time, diminish. As with SOX, there is a lot that is ascribed to privacy regulations that is just fundamentally wrong, creating confusion and unnecessary angst for organizations that must comply with these and other state, federal, sector, and international privacy regulations, including Canada's PIPEDA (this may change to the Consumer Privacy Protection Act (CPPA) and its accompanying Person Information and Data Protection Tribunal Act (PIDPTA)),[73] India's PDPB, Japan's APPI, Mexico's LFPDPPP, and China's PIPL,[74] among many others. Indeed, the draft of the American Data Privacy and Protection Act (ADPPA), will undoubtedly provoke similar commentary. The proposed ADPPA shares many attributes of other global privacy regulations including placing emphasis on data minimization (Section 101), privacy by design (Section 103), codifying core privacy rights (Title II inclusive), along with expectations for reasonable security. Similar to SOX, one year after the proposed regulation goes into force, the chief executive officer along with the appointed privacy and security officers would be

---

[73] There is proposed regulation that would change PIPEDA to two new regulations: The Consumer Privacy Protection Act (CPPA) as well as the accompanying Personal Information and Data Protection Tribunal Act (PIDPTA). Both originate from Bill C-11, the Digital Charter Implication Act. As of the date of publication, the CPPA has not gone into force.

[74] China's Personal Information Protection Law (PIPL) has important nuance, as is frequently the case with Chinese regulations, that warrants a more substantive deep dive given the complementary Data Security Law that calls out certain classes of information as being tied to China's national interests.

required to certify the status of internal controls related to the privacy program.[75]

I think it's valuable to re-cast how we look at privacy regulations and view good privacy practices as integral to corporate governance, engendering trust with consumers. Ultimately, they are a means to enhance our understanding of how our organizations operate, notably for those functions that collect, process, and store personal data. Moreover, this understanding facilitates enhanced security controls over personal data. Like the process narratives used for Sarbanes-Oxley compliance, documenting processing activities to comply with requirements in Article 30 of the GDPR provides vital context for stakeholders to better understand the nature and extent of personal data that the organization uses. Examples include which applications and systems are integral to the processing of personal data, how personal data is shared with third-party entities (aka processors), data security protection programs, and retention periods. This corporate knowledge is invaluable. It helps the organization understand the various impacts and risks associated with its processing activities and informs the controls that may be required to mitigate these risks. In this context, the time and effort needed to document privacy practices is not an unnecessary burden but an opportunity to foment institutional knowledge and deepen organizational understanding.

While privacy regulations vary from jurisdiction to jurisdiction, there are enough common threads that privacy leaders would benefit from focusing on these common elements as they evaluate their organization's specific privacy program and its ability to comply with multiple, potentially overlapping, and conflicting privacy regulations. Before turning to these similar objectives, I'd like to offer a quick perspective on the regulations themselves. If your organization is an in-scope entity for a given regulation, I suggest you

---

[75] At the time this book was written, the U.S. is one of a relatively small number of countries that does not have a national privacy law. The fact that ADPPA has initial bi-partisan and bi-cameral support suggests that the framework offered in the discussion draft may become the basis of U.S. national privacy regulation.

take the time to read the regulation yourself. Go to the source before widening your perspective with input from attorneys, consultants and service providers. The direct, first-hand insights derived from reading the regulation will allow you to validate the suggestions and guidance you get from auditors, vendors, counsel, regulators, and customers.

The goal of your privacy program is to ensure that your organization can address and comply with regulatory requirements in a manner that aligns with the organization's goals rather than disrupting strategy, initiatives, and operations. This "just right" approach requires that the privacy leader understands the organization and how it derives enterprise value, and that data processing activities are executed in a way that builds trust with consumers and employees alike. As you look at your privacy program, revisit Recital 39 from the GDPR and validate that the principles conveyed in this recital are consistent with your organization's existing privacy practices. If they are not, investigate why not and how privacy practices can be updated to be transparent and trust enhancing. Consistent with Section 5 of the Federal Trade Commission Act, validate that the processing activities conveyed in your privacy notices and policies reflect actual practices. If they differ, again, find out why and address this proactively. The alignment between privacy notices and actual processing activities is foundational and common with most privacy regulations and requisite privacy governance practices.

As noted, there are common threads that permeate global privacy regulations. Chief among these is the importance of informed consent.[76] Whether it's Japan's APPI, India's PDPB, the GDPR in the EU, or the CCPA/CPRA in California, privacy regulations

---

[76] I had the opportunity to assist a company that had an application that provided for verification of income and employment status that was being rolled out globally. As part of the due diligence for this expansion, we evaluated country-specific privacy practices in Canada, India, China, Mexico, Taiwan, the UK, Ireland, Japan, Korea, and Singapore. Despite the geo-political differences among these countries, expectations related to privacy were broadly consistent and founded upon good privacy practices throughout the privacy lifecycle. The importance of informed consent cannot be overstated as it relates to privacy regulatory compliance.

generally call for informed consent, predicated on transparent notice for the use of the data subject's or consumer's personal data. For example, the CCPA requires that consumers be notified about the classes of information collected about them, the sources of that information, and the consumer's right to opt-out of having their data shared with or sold to third parties without risk of discrimination. The ADPPA would build upon the non-discriminatory principles established by the CCPA in Section 104, precluding the denial of services or charging different prices when an individual exercises their privacy rights. Notice and consent requirements also impact data transfers and whether the data subject or consumer has been informed whether their data is processed in a distinct jurisdiction. Spend the time necessary to ensure that your organization manages notice and consent aligned with regulatory requirements. If your organization operates internationally, it would be advisable to have in-country counsel draft privacy policies that are specific to that jurisdiction not just from a regulatory perspective but also consistent with that country's business customs and privacy norms.

Cross-border data transfers is one topic where the value of reading the actual regulation becomes clear. Like the misinformation regarding data retention requirements with SOX, the topic of international data transfers is replete with factual inaccuracies. Most global privacy regulations allow for international data transfers. However, these transfers must be governed appropriately, ensure the data subject's rights over their personal data are not materially changed and remain protected, and adequately disclosed prior to the transfer. If your organization transfers data internationally or across different jurisdictional boundaries, validate the requirements with the specific in-scope regulations. Statements like "the GDPR prohibits personal data from the EU from being transferred to the U.S." are generally inaccurate and omit the nuance as to how international data transfers are permitted.[77] There are conditions required before international data transfers can occur. Know these

---

[77] In March of 2022, the European Commission and U.S. introduced the "Trans-Atlantic Data Privacy Framework" to address the concerns with data transfers to the U.S. that culminated in the invalidation of the U.S. Privacy Shield, effectively the *Schrems II* decision.

explicitly and validate your understanding with counsel. Take a principled approach to cross-border data transfers that ensures that consumer or data subject rights are front-and-center and consistent with the principles established in standard contractual clauses (SCCs) as outlined in Article 46 of the GDPR. Organizations that operate in complex, multi-jurisdictional environments with overlapping controller and processor relationships should consider the use of intra-group data transfer agreements (IGDTAs), consistent with SCCs.

Data retention requirements are also frequently misunderstood as it relates to privacy regulations. Here too, consult with counsel to ensure that retention periods are consistent with the firm's regulatory requirements or other obligations. As a general rule, privacy regulations emphasize the "minimum necessary" concept both for collecting data (collecting only those data elements required for the contemplated processing activities) and retaining it (retaining data only for the necessary period to support the contemplated processing activities).

Collecting more data than is required and retaining it for longer than necessary can potentially create an unfunded liability for the organization if that data is breached and notification and identity protection services are needed. Work to ensure that data collection and retention policies are aligned to in-scope regulatory requirements and consistent with the organization's actual practices. Too frequently, the notice or policy does not reflect the practice of the organization—exposing the organization to potential enforcement action. Validate retention practices with the IT, infrastructure, and operations teams and similarly validate collection practices with those departments that collect and process personal data, notably marketing and sales teams.

The analysis of data collection practices will also help address another common thread found throughout privacy regulations. Not all personal data is created equal. There are subsets of personal data that require special treatment, notably health information in all its guises, personal preferences (ranging from sexual to political party and trade union affiliation), and other forms of sensitive personal information.

Ensure that your understanding of the organization's collection of these special classes of data elements is accurate if applicable. This is where documenting and verifying processing activities and performing privacy impact analyses becomes integral to privacy governance. Validate whether your organization processes sensitive forms of personal data and any requisite controls over that data (e.g., access controls and logging, defined retention periods, data pseudonymization, encryption, or tokenization).

Most privacy regulations call for "reasonable" security protections over the data collected, processed, and stored by the organization and specific disclosures and notifications should there be a data breach. As part of your collaboration with the organization's security leader, typically the CISO, ensure that incident and breach response procedures are well documented and that key stakeholders understand and agree on explicit disclosure requirements. Spend the time necessary to validate security protections over personal data.

Breach disclosure requirements are varied and frequently have provisions related to the number and type of records impacted, whether this data was encrypted or otherwise protected, and risk analyses to determine the level of harm to the individuals affected. In certain jurisdictions, notably in the U.S., the engagement of federal law enforcement may also put a proverbial pause on the disclosure countdown. Many prominent law firms maintain a relatively up-to-date summary of data breach disclosure requirements. Ensure that you and your team are aware of these obligations should a data breach occur.

Most privacy regulations also allow the consumer or data subject to access and review the data collected about them. We address these data subject requests in Chapter 13. At a minimum, again as part of documenting processing activities, work with those departments that field these requests to ensure that these requests are managed in a manner consistent with regulatory obligations and company policy. The right to access information is generally tied to the right to correct or update inaccurate information. How these requests are verified and validated should be reviewed carefully.

Similar to the inaccurate or incomplete information associated with international data transfers, another common attribute of many privacy regulations is the right of the data subject or consumer to request that their data be deleted from the controlling entity's systems (and by extension any data processors the data controller also uses). GDPR's Article 17 contains the most famous example of this, the Right to erasure ('right to be forgotten'). Article 17 wins the prize for the most misunderstood article within the GDPR. The right to be forgotten is not an absolute right. It is subject to the context of the processing activities at hand and potentially competing regulations that may require the retention of personal data even when the data subject has formally requested that their data be deleted. Again, as discussed in Chapter 13 on data subject access requests and other interactions with data subjects and consumers, these scenarios and their nuances should be documented and validated carefully.

Regardless of whether the GDPR is applicable to their organization, privacy leaders would be well served to read Chapter III, Rights of the Data Subject. This chapter and the privacy rights that it outlines have similar pronouncements in many other privacy regulations. Indeed, the GDPR is frequently noted as the point of comparison for other national privacy regulations. Organizations that choose to model their privacy programs and the controls and practices it envisions on the GDPR will not likely be surprised by future privacy regulations that may come into scope for their entity. The comprehensive nature of the GDPR is such that the regulation offers a defensible baseline of privacy activities, including the protection of privacy rights for data subjects and Article 25's call for "data protection by design and by default."

While compliance with privacy regulations is nuanced and detailed, these regulations are not an existential threat to the organization and its business practices. Rather, privacy regulations allow the organization to know the business and its practices in more detail. It encourages the firm to create mechanisms to improve the relationship and trust with consumers by respecting and validating their privacy rights and reducing risks that organizational activities will result in regulatory actions. Moreover, by understanding data flows and associated trust boundaries, we can implement reasonable security practices that reduce the risk of a data breach. By reading the regulations at hand, reviewing key requirements with counsel and other stakeholders, and validating the ground truth of current practices, the privacy leader will help ensure that regulatory compliance becomes a competitive differentiator for their firm versus those firms that take a minimalist approach to data security, data governance, and respecting the privacy rights of their consumers and employees.

Key Insights and Recommended Next Steps

Key Insights

- After a dearth of privacy-related regulatory guidance for most of the digital age, the last five years have seen a plethora of regulation focused on the privacy rights of the individual and the obligations of the data controller.
- Though these regulations are coming from every part of the world, following a set of principals will provide a justifiable rationale for your actions in implementing a privacy program. These principals include lawfulness, fairness, and transparency; consent, purpose limitation, data minimization, accuracy and integrity, storage limitation, and accountability.
- There are many misconceptions about privacy regulations and it's important to read the text of the regulations that apply to your company so you can have an informed discussion with stakeholders and third-party providers.

Recommended Next Steps

- For companies that fall under multiple jurisdictions it is imperative to create a full inventory of the laws you are subject to.
- Read the text of each of the regulations you are subject to so that you can dispel any misunderstandings of requirements.
- When faced with competing obligations or mounting burden, determine where the risk is greatest before spinning up a compliance function. Be risk informed.

Chapter 8

Privacy by Design

Introduction

Even though most of us don't know the details, we all recognize the names of many of these quality programs: Total Quality Management, the Malcolm Baldrige National Quality Program, Six Sigma, ISO-9000, and Lean Manufacturing. Many of us have also heard the Ford Motor Company slogan from the 1980s, Quality is Job #1. Why do they matter? Taken as a whole, they elevated product quality to be a fundamental product feature, at least coequal to other essential product features.

Privacy by Design (PbD) is a concept first developed by Ann Cavoukian, Ph.D., the former Information and Privacy Commissioner for the Canadian province of Ontario. Her seminal paper, "Privacy by Design: The 7 Foundational Principles," was originally published in May 2010 and is widely quoted by public and private institutions.[78] According to the paper, "Privacy by Design advances the view that the future of privacy cannot be assured solely by compliance with regulatory frameworks; rather, privacy assurance must ideally become an organization's default mode of operation."[79]

Essentially, privacy must be a fundamental feature of products and services that collect, use, process, or store personal information, at

---

[78] Privacy by Design: The 7 Foundational Principles, Cavoukian, Ann, Ph.D., https://iapp.org/media/pdf/resource_center/pbd_implement_7found_principles.pdf.
[79] Ibid.

least coequal to other product or service features. By fundamental, we mean you cannot have the product or service without PbD.

We are taking a different editorial approach in Chapter 8, "Privacy by Design." We each hold Dr. Cavoukian's contribution in high regard and present here a single essay that conveys our collective thoughts about the Privacy by Design concept.

Privacy by Design ~ David, Justine, and Matt

Origins of Privacy by Design

Dr. Ann Cavoukian introduced the concept of Privacy by Design in a white paper about privacy-enabling technologies (PETs). She was the Information and Privacy Commissioner in Ontario at the time. Dr. Cavoukian based the paper on ideas that had been brewing over the previous 20 years from observing the systemic effects of ICT (Information and Communication Technology) and large-scale networked data systems.

The overarching principle behind this seminal and foundational work is that consideration of privacy matters should be first and foremost in the minds of software developers and not left as an afterthought. Hence the expression you often come across, "privacy by default," alongside "security by design" and "security by default." It should go without saying that embedding good privacy practices in development is vitally important, so that your processes and software products are 100% aligned with your company's privacy policies. It's unlikely that anyone would ever suggest writing code that did not consider transparency and respecting user privacy. But unfortunately, there are many organizations that don't make privacy job #1 and do collect personal data without notification.

So, it's worth looking at the seven foundational principles listed by Dr. Cavoukian:

1. Proactive not reactive; preventative not remedial
2. Privacy as the default setting
3. Privacy embedded into design
4. Full functionality—positive-sum, not zero-sum
5. End-to-end security—full lifecycle protection
6. Visibility and transparency—keep it open
7. Respect for user privacy—keep it user-centric

In 2010 the International Assembly of Privacy Commissioners and Data Protection Authorities unanimously passed a resolution recognizing privacy by design as an international standard and resolving to promote privacy by design as widely as possible and foster the incorporation of the principle into policy and legislation. It has since been adopted by several standards bodies, both national and worldwide.

Privacy by Design in U.S. Laws

Although privacy by design was incorporated into the GDPR, U.S. state laws have so far resisted using the words "privacy by design."[80] California's Internet of Things law comes close by requiring a manufacturer of a connected device to "equip the device with a reasonable security feature or features that are...designed to protect the device and any information contained therein from unauthorized access, destruction, use, modification, or disclosure."[81] This is more of a Security by Design (SbD) requirement than PbD, but it signals that the legislature is thinking about design principles as a requirement to demonstrate reasonableness. PbD has been popularized, as evidenced by Microsoft CPO Brendon Lynch's article "Privacy by Design at Microsoft,"[82] but neither CCPA nor CPRA includes the language "privacy by design." Surprisingly, this is also true in Canada, where the idea originated and remains influential. Operationalizing PbD is a supreme opportunity to show that your organization and privacy program goes above and beyond what the law requires.

In 2013, there was a resource published by then-Attorney General of California, Kamala Harris, called "Privacy on the Go: Recommendations for the Mobile Ecosystem."[83] Under Ms. Harris'

---

[80] The American Data Privacy and Protection Act (ADPPA), under consideration by the U.S. Congress as of the date of publication, does include preliminary language in Sec. 103. Privacy by Design. The language at this point is principle based and provides commission guidance to define a standard for reasonableness within a year of passage should the act become law.

[81] California Civil Code section 1798.91.04.

[82] Privacy by Design at Microsoft, Brandon Lynch, November 2010, https://blogs.microsoft.com/on-the-issues/2010/11/30/privacy-by-design-at-microsoft/.

[83] Privacy on the Go: Recommendations for the Mobile Ecosystem, Kamala D. Harris, Attorney General California Department of Justice, (January 2013), https://oag.ca.gov/sites/all/files/agweb/pdfs/privacy/privacy_on_the_go.pdf.

leadership, an intentional group of privacy professionals within the Office of Attorney General created several helpful guides and resources for businesses to comply with new laws in a fast-paced tech environment.[84] "Privacy on the Go" outlined simple recommendations to assist app developers and others in considering privacy early in the development process. Although the phrase "privacy by design" was never used, it was the first publication that addressed the need for engineers and developers to prioritize privacy (and security) rather than address them as an afterthought. Many innovative technologies placed convenience and marketability above privacy or data minimization. In many cases they could co-exist if some thought went into the design. "Privacy on the Go" showed the importance of privacy professionals, legal, and compliance getting in the same room to discuss privacy by design.

These principles are philosophical ideals that set a high bar for organizations and offer valuable benchmarks. For example, by their nature responses to privacy breaches are reactive endeavors, but companies can undertake many preventative and proactive efforts long before a breach occurs.

Privacy Design Strategies

There are plenty of ways of approaching a strategy for privacy design. One well-regarded strategy is to look at two different approaches. The first is more technical and focuses on the data itself, while the other addresses the organizational aspects, processes, and procedures associated with the person or entity handling the data.

The data-oriented considerations are to (as much as possible):

- **Minimize** the processing of personal data
- **Separate** the processing of personal data from other processes
- **Abstract** by limiting the detail in which personal data is processed

---

[84] State of California Business Privacy Resources: https://oag.ca.gov/privacy/business-privacy.

- **Hide** by making personal data unlinkable or unobservable, ensuring it does not become public or known

And the process-oriented considerations are to:

- **Inform** data subjects about how and why their personal data is being processed, preferably before they ask you
- Provide data subjects an appropriate level of **control** over the processing of their personal data.
- Commit to **enforcing** the processing of personal data in a privacy-friendly way
- Be prepared to **demonstrate** personal data is being processed in a privacy-friendly way: that is, with respect for a data subject's privacy rights, giving them control over their personal data while at the same time delivering insights for data-driven decisions.

Let's look in detail at each of the seven Privacy by Design principles with some context on how your organization can expand upon them internally.

1. Proactive not reactive; preventive not remedial

This principle emphasizes that privacy risks should be anticipated and addressed proactively throughout all areas of the organization, be it standard business processes (including the use of third parties), application development, or the technologies that underpin both. In security, there is a notion that you cannot protect what you do not know exists. Therefore, implicit in this principle is an intimate knowledge of those functions within the organization that use personal data (broadly defined).

Being proactive requires that the privacy leader develops and maintains a high-fidelity understanding of the organization's inner workings and that this understanding couples both regulatory requirements and contractual obligations with the applications and technologies employed. This understanding will allow the privacy leader to effectively know where privacy concerns may surface and to ensure that these concerns are addressed a priori to risks being realized. Accordingly, fulfilling the spirit of this first principle requires a combination of technical knowledge (to wit the growth of technically focused privacy certifications such as ISACA's Certified Data Privacy Solutions Engineer (CDPSE) or the IAPP's Certified Information Privacy Technologist (CIPT)), complemented and extended by a deep knowledge of business operations. Notably, this includes processes that use personal data as part of their core function and assumes a requisite knowledge of in-scope regulations. Assessing privacy risk is integral to your privacy program's proactive and preventive approach.

One approach to validate whether there is sufficient understanding of processing activities would be to benchmark current privacy documentation and understanding vis-à-vis Articles 30 (Records of processing activities) and 35 (Data protection impact assessment) of the GDPR. Collectively, these two articles help define a minimum, requisite level of documentation to ensure that privacy risks are proactively identified and mitigated. Even organizations that are not subject to the GDPR would be well-served to be familiar with approaches to documenting processing activities and how to evaluate risks to the same. Both Article 30 and Article 35 provide a solid baseline of what to document and assess.

2. **Privacy as the default setting**

There is an elegance to this principle that many organizations fail to grasp. The consumer or data subject should not have to take any action to ensure that their privacy is adequately addressed based on their interests and not the organization's. As an oversimplification, if the consumer has not consented to the collection of their personal data and has to "opt-out," then you have not established privacy as the default setting. Dr. Cavoukian also tied this principle to those of the core elements of Fair Information Practice Principles (FIPPs), including:

- **purpose specification** – effectively the notice provided to the data subject or consumer

- **collection and data minimization** - only collecting those data elements that are specifically required to fulfill the stated purpose of the processing activity
- **use, retention, and disclosure limitations** – personal data should not be used for derivative purposes, retained longer than required to fulfill the contemplated processing activity, or shared unless required to fulfill the processing activities (and then, only if the consumer is informed of these data sharing relationships and has provided their consent and that the processor or sub-processor maintains requisite privacy and security controls)

The consent orders issued by the U.S. Federal Trade Commission (FTC), as well as fines levied by European data protection authorities for GDPR violations, serve as a testament that there is significant work to be done in establishing privacy as the default setting across business processes and within the applications that our organizations use to run our operations. This highlights why conducting data protection impact assessments and creating narratives to describe processing activities are integral to our privacy programs. Taking the time to evaluate whether privacy settings are configured and established to protect the data subject or consumer upfront will ideally mitigate risks of regulatory action after the fact. As Dr. Cavoukian notes, the bar for this principle is clear cut: "No action is required on the part of the individual to protect their privacy—it is built into the system, by default." While the guidance is clear, validating actual practices will require diligence and ongoing monitoring.

3. Privacy embedded into design

Recognizing that privacy and security are separate disciplines, certain best practices benefit both. Notably, establishing security and privacy objectives early in the development process is more effective, less costly, and produces more effective privacy and security outcomes than implementing controls after the fact. These "bolt-on" approaches are error prone and introduce operational, functional, and regulatory risk that could have been avoided if the requisite privacy (and security) considerations were anticipated, established, and integrated into the design.

The above is a "blinding flash of the obvious." Every organizational function benefits from careful planning, risk analysis, and sufficient documentation to inform strategy and risk management decisions. Similarly, we all know that we should "exercise more" and "eat less" to lose weight and live healthier lives. However, there are structural reasons why privacy (and security) is too infrequently embedded into the design of new business processes or applications. We would like to think that there is perfect organizational knowledge in every firm, and all departments or functions have the information they need from other departments to mitigate risks, implement initiatives and strategies effectively, and drive enterprise value. The reality, however, is that departments often operate in a siloed fashion with imperfect and incomplete information on other organizational functions. The result is that processing activities may blindside privacy leaders because they were unaware of or lacked detailed knowledge of the activities at hand.

Embedding privacy into design requires that privacy has a seat at the table. Similar to the business analyst role, we need to develop a privacy analyst role (individuals or departments with both technical and operational insights into privacy practices) to be alongside their colleagues in application development, business operations, and even organizational strategy development. Gartner analysts Joanna Huisman and Mark Horvath wrote extensively of the value of creating "security champions" to liaise with departments across the organization and advocate security best practices.[85] This concept should be extended to privacy for departments with significant privacy impacts. Without privacy analysts working proactively and collaboratively with their colleagues across the organization, there's a risk that privacy by design principles may be overlooked, or worse, ignored, exposing the organization to subsequent remediation and

---

[85] To learn more about security champions, we recommend reading their research on this topic. Details can be found here: https://www.gartner.com/smarterwithgartner/build-a-network-of-champions-to-increase-security-awareness/.

increased risk. Privacy leaders must spend quality time with colleagues from other areas of the organization to review where privacy impacts may come into scope and ensure that privacy practices are incorporated appropriately.

4. Full functionality—positive-sum, not zero-sum

The advent of privacy-enhancing technologies (PETs) should be embraced and expanded upon. Personal data is not always required to support business activities. More so, PII is generally not required. Using privacy-enhancing technologies has essential benefits, including data breach risks mitigation. For example, data protection authorities (DPAs) and U.S. state attorneys general are likely to be less concerned if a data breach exposes pseudonyms rather than actual PII. Similarly, there are generally safe harbor provisions when sensitive personal data has been encrypted.

Beyond the risk mitigations associated with privacy-enhancing technologies, there is value in determining if specification requirements for a given technology or business process can offer complete functionality without practices that could impinge upon the data subject's interests. Essentially, privacy leaders and privacy analysts must ask, "how can privacy rights be maintained while ensuring full functionality of the contemplated activity?" There is clearly some creativity required and an openness to explore different options to the same end.

5. End-to-end security—full lifecycle protection

The adage is, "you can have security without privacy, but you cannot have privacy without security." We discuss reasonable security in a separate chapter, but we would like to highlight here that "by design" principles are required for data protection throughout the lifecycle of data processing activities. Article 25 of the GDPR calls for data protection by design and default. Article 32, considering the operational context of the processing activities, recommends using encryption and/or pseudonyms as part of the broader data protection strategy of the organization. In Chapter 6, we noted the key phases of the privacy lifecycle. Privacy leaders should ask if there are adequate protections implemented at each phase and whether there is sufficient monitoring in place to detect risks to the confidentiality, integrity, or availability of these processing activities. Like principle 3, which requires embedding privacy best practices into the design phase, full lifecycle protection requires that the privacy leader has visibility into this lifecycle and understands when, where, and how protections should be accorded to personal data.

There are also vital technical considerations related to security, notably in today's application-centric business. Privacy and security risks tend to coalesce with technology. Application interfaces, data validation practices, and security controls related to application programming interfaces (APIs) warrant technical due diligence. The privacy leader should validate if personal data elements are conveyed via APIs in clear text or in a manner inconsistent with the application's stated purpose and processing activities. This level of assurance may require direct engagement with security and application development colleagues. Many data breaches have occurred where nefarious actors (or overly zealous marketing teams) have exploited (literally and figuratively) API functionality. Like privacy, security requires a systemic review.

While beyond the scope of this book, the concept of zero trust should be explored with the security leader, typically the organization's chief information security officer (CISO). John Kindervag, at the time a principal analyst at Forrester Research, is credited with developing the concept that "trust" is effectively a vulnerability and that trust should be continually validated and assessed through security applications and the processes they support. Gartner's Continuous Adaptive Risk and Trust Assessment (CARTA) also emphasizes the importance of continuous evaluation of security risks across the organization, including with the organization's business partners (be they clients, suppliers, or third-party vendors), the organization's business applications, the transactions processed by the organization, and, of course, the users of these systems. In short, do not trust; continuously verify. The complexity of keeping systems safe, let alone configured for privacy by default, should not be underestimated and should be a front-and-center topic for privacy leaders. This requires ongoing collaboration with the organization's security, compliance, and risk management teams. Using privacy by design principles as guidance is a step in the right direction.

6. Visibility and transparency—keep it open

Trust is integral to an open, democratic society. As we noted in Chapter 1, economist Stephen Knack's work on trust economics offers a strong theory of why per capita incomes vary globally. High trust societies, even those that do not have abundant natural resources such as Japan, have notably higher per capita incomes when compared to societies where trust principles are fleeting. The Federal Trade Commission Act in the U.S. encapsulates the importance of protecting trust. Section 5 of the FTCA notes that "unfair or deceptive acts or practices in or affecting commerce . . . are . . . declared unlawful."[86] Transparency begins with the notice provided to the data subject or consumer outlining how their information will be used. The CCPA, which will become the California Privacy Rights Act (CPRA) in 2023, requires that in-scope entities inform the consumer as to the nature and sources of information that will be collected, how it will be used, and whether this information will be shared with or sold to third parties. In addition, the CCPA allows the consumer to opt-out (recognizing the privacy by default challenges here) of these activities without facing any discrimination or reduction in the quality of the services the consumer receives when those individuals exercise their privacy rights.

As we discussed in Chapter 6 on the privacy lifecycle, we cannot overstate the role of privacy notices. Transparency is predicated on clear, unambiguous detail and context related to the privacy practices contemplated. We recommend that privacy leaders review their

---

[86] To learn more about the FTC's important role in consumer protections, please visit https://www.ftc.gov/about-ftc/what-we-do/enforcement-authority. Like many government agencies, the FTC is under-resourced but has nevertheless set important precedents for consumer protections vis-à-vis the FTC's consent orders that seek to remediate the "unfair and deceptive" trade practices employed by sanctioned U.S. companies. Consent orders may last up to 20 years and require bi-annual audits of the affected organization's privacy and security practices.

privacy policies and notices against the organization's actual privacy practices. To the extent that actual practices differ from what has been conveyed in the privacy notice, that is a red flag that requires the privacy leader's attention. Again, going back to the often-cited Recital 39 of the GDPR, "Natural persons should be made aware of risks, rules, safeguards and rights in relation to the processing of personal data and how to exercise their rights in relation to such processing. In particular, the specific purposes for which personal data are processed should be explicit and legitimate and determined at the time of the collection of the personal data."

7. Respect for user privacy—keep it user-centric

The last of the privacy by design principles should, by now, be self-evident. If our organizations want to engender trust and build enterprise value, they should aim to do so by taking a privacy-first approach, one where that data subject's or consumer's rights are at the forefront of business processes, data collection, and processing activities. Organizations that choose not to respect the wishes of their customers and how they treat their personal data will see negative impacts on the organization's reputation. These same organizations also run the risk of regulatory enforcement actions. In our opinion, the respect for user privacy principle becomes binary in nature. There are two types of organizations, those that seek to develop transparent, thoughtful, and open relationships with data subjects and consumers and those that employ "unfair and deceptive" practices. It's clear where most people prefer to take their business.

Like the previous chapter's guidance on the privacy lifecycle, privacy by design principles should inform privacy strategy for the organization and can be used as a reliable benchmark for privacy practices that mitigate regulatory risk, engender trust, and drive enterprise value.

Is There a Downside?

But as ever, the devil is in the details, and one of the recurring criticisms of the privacy by design concept is that, although very well-meaning, it is not practical enough, leaving many open questions facing software engineers seeking to apply the principles when developing software systems.

One misconception is that privacy by design covers only software and systems engineering. Indeed, it also includes aspects of administration, business matters, and operations. The mix of legal, ethical, policy, and software design disciplines makes sense but is too high level to parse meaningfully. The overarching principle is to protect the privacy of online users' personally identifiable information (PII) provided to (and handled by) services or applications. In other words, this is not just an exercise in coding and testing. Instead, it should underpin a comprehensive approach to administering your whole privacy program.

One of the other criticisms was that privacy by design came across as a voluntary, nice-to-have concept that individual companies could adapt differently, rather than an effective well-defined standard or piece of legislation. However, all that changed in 2018 with the GDPR, which significantly changed the European privacy landscape. Among those changes was introducing privacy by design and privacy by default as new legal requirements. The message that privacy considerations must be taken on board from the start of any software development process as essential to adequate data protection was finally an enforceable legal obligation in Europe.

Privacy by Design as a Service (PbDaaS)

Some consultants offer privacy by design as a service if you seek third-party validation of your PbD efforts or have limited bandwidth. PbDaaS includes reviewing the privacy infrastructure and business practices and issuing a gap analysis for improvement or a "privacy by design certification" attesting to the organization's proactive efforts to protect the privacy of their customers. See Deloitte's "Privacy by

Design: Setting a new standard for privacy certification."[87] See also KPMG's "Privacy by Design: assessment and certification."[88]

At the end of the day, there is no litmus test for whether PbD principles are adequate, sufficient, or reasonable. PbD is a concept or feeling that cannot be reduced to a binary code. Documenting PbD practices helps the business demonstrate the defensible steps, time, and energy it has taken to incorporate privacy-centric principles enterprise-wide. PbD can be operationalized throughout the data lifecycle by using checklists and written procedures. PbD can be implemented in the early design stage by requiring mandatory training for the engineers responsible for building products and services that host data. PbD can also be incorporated into how businesses use, collect, share, and store data. Finally, PbD principles can be adopted in data destruction and retention policies and schedules. There is a creative process to operationalizing PbD within the organization, and the privacy officer must remain committed to looking at the issues from multiple perspectives to be successful.

The Marketing Department—The Very Hungry Caterpillar

When Justine's kids were young, she read a book with them written by Eric Carle called *The Very Hungry Caterpillar* that tells the story of a small caterpillar with an insatiable appetite.[89] Within the enterprise, the marketing department is the hungry caterpillar—it has an insatiable appetite for consuming as much data as the privacy leader will allow. On Monday, the marketing department wants to launch a digital marketing campaign to capitalize on a social media trend by the end of the week. On Tuesday, the marketing department wants to send all customers a survey to solicit feedback for more customized marketing in promoting a new line of business.

---

[87] https://www2.deloitte.com/content/dam/Deloitte/ca/Documents/risk/ca-eners-privacy-by-design-brochure.PDF.
[88] https://home.kpmg/ca/en/home/insights/2020/06/privacy-by-design-assessment-and-certification.html.
[89] *The Very Hungry Caterpillar*, Carle, Eric, World of Eric Carle; 1st edition (March 23, 1994).

On Wednesday, the marketing department wants to update the website to allow a new vendor to collect data to analyze user behavior. On Thursday, the marketing department wants to create an API with an existing vendor to share additional data elements for analytic purposes. On Friday, the marketing department wants to expand its marketing efforts to Canada. How do you incorporate PbD into the marketing department's workflow?

The goal for privacy is to create a cocoon around marketing so it can become a beautiful butterfly. The cocoon is a welcome and nourishing addition to the privacy garden and ecosystem. Implement clear processes for marketing to follow that include alerting the privacy team before projects commence. Implement a policy that requires marketing to evidence how PbD was considered in their proposed endeavor. For example, was survey data anonymized or aggregated, so that no personal information is collected? Require the marketing department to submit a PbD form with their request to document the measures considered and implemented. Use technology or a simple process to make it easy for marketing to explain the project, articulate any privacy considerations, explain the business need, and incorporate PbD into their project plan. A PbD-centric question to ask the business is whether they can reduce the amount of data or de-identify it while still reaching their goals.

Marketing teams increasingly want to know about privacy practices that directly impact their business. Many of the new laws specifically threaten targeted marketing activities. Train the marketing department and explain new and emerging laws that curtail direct marketing activities and insist on PbD at the forefront. For example, marketing teams should understand consent models like opt-in and opt-out and how that may impact the technology and marketing platforms commonly used for marketing campaigns. Provide simple resources to the marketing team that explain which jurisdictions are opt-in (GDPR) and opt-out (California), which require cookie banners and preference centers (GDPR), which require a posting that states "Do Not Sell My Personal Information" (California), and which restrict data transfers (GDPR). If marketing teams understand these privacy guardrails, they can craft marketing projects that achieve business goals without running afoul of the law.

Collaborating with your marketing teams about privacy's multiplicity of roles can be helpful. For example, many consumers exercise consumer rights (DSARs) in response to some marketing activity they do not want. Creating clear ways for consumers to opt-out of receiving marketing materials will ease the burden of managing unintended consumer requests. Marketing teams do not want to market to consumers who do not want to buy products. Collaborate with marketing to understand the natural lifecycle of marketing data—where/when it has value and the need to destroy data that no longer has value. Marketing sometimes wants to hold onto data "just in case" it one day becomes useful. Data is not a fine wine—it does not get better with age.

How to Operationalize PbD

PbD principles are holistic by nature and require an interactive and fluid process from proof of concept through end of device/data lifecycle. Below are some first steps to inject PbD into your privacy program:

- Consider incorporating PbD into your cyber mantra.
- Create a risk register to identify the data elements collected, stored, shared, or used, the cost of technology to reduce or mitigate privacy risk, user experience, purpose for collecting data, and risk of likelihood and harm to consumer rights.
- Train engineers and software developers in PbD principles so they understand the laws and how devices and data are regulated.
- Consider adding a privacy review to existing software and product development tollgates.
- Adopt internal policies and protocols that call out privacy by design principles and require PbD considerations for all departments and business units.
- Documenting the PbD process and protocols creates a document for defensive use to demonstrate the design principles and intention built into the privacy program. Some examples of PbD in action include the following common best practices in privacy-forward organizations:

- De-identify or anonymize data.
- Implement short retention periods or use ephemeral data.
- Use data minimization (limiting collection to only necessary data elements).
- Invoke access minimization (limiting who can access data).
- Implement privileged access management.
- Empower consumers with control to modify, access, and delete their personal information.
- Require vendors to explain how they have integrated PbD into their organization.
- Update existing products, practices, and SOPs to include new or updated PbD features and language.
- Use well-known privacy-centric technologies to help track and automate PbD features.

Section 3

Risk Assessments

Shining a Light on Risk

Now that you have a strong foundation, it's time to transition to direct assessment. In the following three chapters, we explain how to look at your organization's current state of inherited risk based on the data it collects, holds, and processes, its relationships with various third parties, and how it secures the information in its care.

Chapter 9, "Data Classification and Discovery," will look at identifying the data elements that privacy leaders are most concerned with and how to manage and reduce the associated risk. In Chapter 10, "Vendor Risk Management," we continue the assessment and risk reduction theme by first identifying the types of third-party relationships that bring elevated risk and then reviewing processes and tools that can be helpful in reducing that risk. Finally, in Chapter 11, "Reasonable Security," we provide guidance you can use to get the most out of your partnership with the security team.

In each chapter, we strive to make you aware of the risks that lurk in the shadows of your data protection obligations and to equip and empower you to help your company make meaningful reductions in those risks. But, of course, these are not static risks. As the business grows and changes, as your customers and markets change, and as regulations change, you will need to continue to put time and attention into these risk management activities. With this section as a foundation, you will be well-equipped to do that.

Chapter 9

Data Classification and Discovery

Introduction

We all know what a galaxy is. Astronomers classify galaxies as spiral, elliptical, and irregular. Spiral galaxies have younger stars and more gas and dust than elliptical galaxies. We all know what a gene is. Geneticists classify 17 different types of genes. There are constitutive genes, non-constitutive genes, cistrons, pseudogenes, transposons, and 12 others. Non-constitutive genes have sub-types inducible and repressible. Oncologists are concerned with deleteriously mutated genes.

When we don't know much about a topic, this becomes jargon to us. Jargon-heavy conversations can be hard to follow for the uninitiated. So why do we do this? Other than to confuse non-experts? We classify things so we know how to discuss them instead of something else. For example, an oncologist is far more interested in discussing deleteriously mutated genes than normal genes when discussing potential cancer treatments. Sequencing the human genome, classifying genes by their type, understanding what each gene is responsible for, and recognizing normal versus mutated genes has advanced health sciences in innumerable ways.

It's tempting to equate classifying all your data with sequencing the human genome. But as you will see in Chapter 9, "Data Classification and Discovery," all data are not created equal. Therefore, it's not hard to quickly identify the data that needs specialists' attention. Like our oncologist friends, how you classify data determines how you treat it. Some data need protection, and some don't. Some data types, including personal data, intellectual property, material non-public information, and cryptographic keys, have special handling requirements and would be classified accordingly. It's a waste of time and money to classify public information. Failing to classify protected health information is a liability.

In "Data Classification and Discovery—Essential to Data Governance," David describes key considerations for classifying data along the vectors of sensitivity and type. He also speaks to the value of well-trained individuals calibrating and overseeing the automated tools that become more necessary as the size of our data sets explodes and for detecting and avoiding inherent bias in data classification programs.

Justine defines a deeper granularity of classification so she can tie data classifications to specific regulations and then show you how to relieve some of the burdens by transforming the data to a format with less onerous compliance obligations. In her essay, "Data Classification—Name It to Tame It," she also looks at how classification fits into other essential processes, including incident response, governance of unstructured data, and data retention.

Matt's essay, "Data Classification," studies the full organizational impact of developing a data governance program, emphasizing accountability, process, follow-through, and validation. His emphasis on the RACI matrix, data flow diagrams, and policy provides a strong foundation that will allow even the largest companies to build a data governance program that delivers value and protects the organization from unseen liability.

Data Classification and Discovery—Essential to Data Governance ~ David

At some point in a book about data privacy, you'd expect to come across the statement "the devil is in the details." Well, here it is.

So far, we have looked at some of the overarching principles and concepts around a privacy program and even broad-brush techniques for data management. Here, however, we want to take you on a journey that explores the data elements themselves, looking at how you should approach the classification of both structured and unstructured data in order to discover what data assets you are holding and responsible for. If you can't find what you're looking for or, worse still, you don't know what you've got, protecting your data crown jewels becomes an awful lot harder. Not the least of the challenges is that the data we're referring to will be associated with a wide range of applications. Some will be on-premises, others in the cloud, some more or less secure than others. As a result, you can expect to find them in a wide range of different and probably incompatible formats with varying degrees of verifiable accuracy and correctness. And if that were not enough, data assets will be both digital and hard copy.

Companies adopt data governance processes and procedures to manage, utilize, and protect their data, with accompanying strategies to define how it is named, stored, processed, and shared, with responsibilities and accountability assigned to designated employees or roles. The ultimate goal is to achieve efficiency and consistency in how data is managed to mitigate risk and manage privacy and other data governance policies.

Data Sensitivity

There are varying degrees of sensitivity associated with the data. Most of it is of little interest or value, whereas there will be nuggets of pure gold that are highly sensitive, requiring extra layers of protection.

Although the United States government has seven levels of classification, from restricted data and formerly restricted data to controlled unclassified information, a rule of three works fine for most enterprises. Having more than three classification levels adds undue complexity and is difficult to maintain, and fewer than three are not granular enough to meet compliance expectations.

- The most sensitive data is that which, if stolen or lost, would have the most significant impact and consequently demands the highest level of protection in terms of, for example, encryption and access controls. It includes any data that, if compromised, could result in severe financial harm, from fraud to fines due to regulatory non-compliance to loss of sales revenue because of deprecated brand recognition, or expose your customers to risk. This category also covers legal contracts, trade secrets, patents pending, or personally identifiable information (PII). Think Fort Knox.

- Data of medium sensitivity refers to information that is confidential or intended only for internal use. This level includes non-identifiable human resources data and any data that would, for example, benefit a competitor but wouldn't have any immediate tangible impact. A loss would be embarrassing but not a disaster.

- Information of low or negligible sensitivity is probably already in the public domain, which has its own set of concerns relating more to content and context.

Data Classification

There are several benefits to organizing and analyzing structured or unstructured data into categories based on file type, content, and other metadata. These include mitigating risk, managing privacy and other company data governance policies, achieving efficiency and consistency in how data is managed, discovered, and eliminated, and providing analytics to optimize business performance.

Several fundamental considerations apply to ensuring good governance and compliance with data protection regulations that mitigate risk. For example:

- Identifying a data asset by type and provenance will help determine the sensitivity labeling, who gets access and for what purpose, and whether metadata tags should be applied. The type could be anything from personally identifiable information (PII) to intellectual property (IP). In the case of PII, these data sets must be easy to track and trace, either by indexing or tagging, in case it becomes necessary to demonstrate to privacy auditors how they are being governed.

- A data item may be classified by keyword or concept, depending on its content and context. This will determine whether it is more appropriate to index or tag the data.

- Most current privacy regulations—and future ones probably will as well—include a data subject's right to be forgotten and to make access requests (DSARs), policies which your company should already have incorporated. All of which requires being able to access that data easily and efficiently based on type and usage through optimized tagging.

- As mentioned in a previous chapter, it is vital for efficiency and compliance purposes to delete data that is, for one reason or another, "past its use by (or best by) date."

- It may seem a trivial observation, but you also have to inform your organization's employees where data is stored. While you're considering that, it's also good housekeeping to make the most used data sets easiest and fastest to access from any geographical location.

Whose Job Is It?

The data classification itself can be carried out either manually or by using some form of file parser and string analyzer that would automate the process—or with a combination of both approaches. Well-trained employees should ideally be the best placed to assess, both rationally and instinctively, the sensitivity of the data they are handling, particularly when it comes to determining what should be considered most sensitive. On the other hand, human beings are notoriously fallible, liable to make errors or simply forget to carry out tedious, repetitive chores. Likewise, training machine learning systems must be extremely precise and consistently reviewed to ensure outliers do not disrupt the filtering process. However, machines can handle vast quantities of data much faster than your employees can without ever getting bored or restless. So ideally, you should look for a solution that marries the two to, at the very least, ensure consistency and ultimately eliminate bias as far as possible from either approach. Bias elimination by design!

Bias generally occurs when an algorithm produces erroneous or misleading results due to incorrect assumptions made initially in the machine learning setup. Several approaches can be taken that will not entirely remove unwanted bias in the data classification process but can go a long way towards substantially avoiding it.

- **Content and context.** The chances are that you have an awful lot of data that will need to be classified and, irrespective of whether the approach taken is manual, machine learned, or both, it makes sense to process the information in batches. One advantage is being able to assess the results of the classification as it proceeds step by step. There is another potential benefit. If the characteristics of one batch, its content and context, are not the same as the others, there is the opportunity to reassess and adjust the classification criteria accordingly.

- **Exclusion.** In reviewing a dataset, there may be a temptation to clean the data by excluding some features or attributes, in the belief that they're irrelevant or unrepresentative. Before doing so, it's essential to analyze the rationale behind the exclusion carefully and systematically to ensure that it's really justified.

- **Observer.** Again, whether the approach is manual or programmed, conscious or unconscious prejudices or simply predetermined ideas can creep into how data classification criteria are formulated. This is where training and experience pay dividends. If in any doubt, there's no shame in having a second set of eyes or a review procedure in place.

- **Measurement.** Despite the wondrousness of the devices there are to carry out this task, there must be humans available to check their output to ensure it has not suffered from systemic value distortion. For example, if the training material in a particular dataset is unstructured data and, for whatever reason, it is no longer representative, the algorithm will need to be recalibrated.

Another important aspect of getting the job done is determining what to prioritize and how often, which will be a factor in how the data and the classification process are relevant to your organization's objectives and the associated privacy legislation. Governance of the data classification activity should target managing the data to ensure that sensitive information is handled in accordance with the threat it poses to your company. It should also consider how the data is being used, structured, and stored to allow only authorized personnel access information at an appropriate time.

Getting To Where You Want to Be

A classification program goes a long way to achieving the critical objectives of usability, efficiency, and compliance, consistent with governance of the data you and your organization are responsible for. But it is only the beginning of a journey that will involve taking steps to provide appropriate access rights and security measures where they are deemed necessary.

Data Classification—Name It to Tame It ~ Justine

Classification derives from the word class, which means "category" and comes from the Latin term *classis*. *Classis* referred to an army or group called to arms which eventually came to mean "a group," and thus classify means "to group." It seems appropriate that classification emanates from an army called to arms, because it takes a small army within the enterprise to classify data—and will require lieutenants from each business unit to help with data classification.

Be Mindful of Bias and Increase Diversity

Classification is rooted in dividing things into groups with similar characteristics. Humans have a primal instinct to classify things, grouping similar ideas or objects together by unifying traits like function, color, or shape. But when humans are responsible for deciding what objects belong in particular groups, internal or implicit biases can arise. Bias in data classification, when left unchecked by others, could result in risk. For example, if the person deciding the characteristics of "consumer data" has a background in e-commerce, they might not recognize the need to include employee data or shareholder data. The best way to overcome implicit bias is to have a system of checks and balances with multiple and diverse stakeholders engaged from throughout the enterprise.

What Does It Really Mean?

There are many compelling reasons to classify data, including regulatory and legal compliance, securing data appropriately, legal or contractual requirements about who the data can or cannot be shared with, business operations, and data retention and deletion. Yet, if you ask four people what data classification means, you will likely get four different answers. So, here is a brief overview of common yet fundamentally different types of data classification:

- **Format of Data.** Paper, electronic, hybrid.

- **Level of Sensitivity.** Data classification in government organizations commonly includes five levels: Top Secret, Secret, Confidential, Sensitive, and Unclassified. Sensitive data classifications in the private sector often include the following levels: Restricted, Confidential, Internal, Public.

- **Simple Classification.** Dividing data or elements (facts) into groups according to their qualities.

- **Statistics.** Qualitative or quantitative.

Distinguishing Between Types and Classifications

The difference between *type* and *classification* is essential. *Type* is a grouping based on shared characteristics that often relate to the origin—think of data types as verticals of data in the enterprise. *Classification* is forming data into a class or classes according to common relations, data elements, or attributes and treating the class in a standard manner. Commonly, data classifications have a legal structure. Let's work through an example. Employee data is a *type* of data because it originates from the employee. Within employee data there are several different *classifications,* like "payroll data," "tax data," and "personally identifiable information." These data classes might also apply to other data types, like financial data or consumer data.

The data types and classifications help inform and guide essential elements of a privacy program, like privileged access management, data retention, security safeguards, privacy rights requests, application of certain types of policies, and regulatory or legal requirements. For example, here is a common list of data types in an organization (this is by no means exhaustive and depends on the type of business):

Categories of Personal Information	Examples of Specific Pieces of Personal Information	
Biometric Data	• Biological or behavioral characteristics • DNA • Iris image or retina scan • Finger, hand or palm print • Voice recordings	• Keystroke patterns or rhythms • Sleep • Health • Exercise data • Gait patterns or rhythms • Facial recognition • Vein patterns
Commercial Information	• Records of personal property	• Product or service purchase, review, consideration history
Characteristics of a protected classification under California or Federal law	• Race • National origin • Ancestry • Religion	• Marital status • Sex • Age • Sexual orientation • Physical or mental disability or other medical condition
Geolocation data	• Latitude • Longitude • Altitude • Direction • Time and location	• Country • Region • Continent • State • City
Health Insurance Data	• Health insurance policy number • Subscriber identification number	• Any unique identifier used by a health insurer
Medical Information	• Patient's name, address, email address, telephone number, or social security number	• Other information that reveals the individual's identity
Internet or Network Activity Information (cookie data)	• Browsing and search history	• Advertisement interaction • Information about a consumer's interaction with a website or application
Personal Information	• Real name • Alias • Postal address • Telephone number • Unique personal identifier • Online identifier • IP address • Email address • Social security number	• Driver's license, identification, passport number • Signature • Education • Professional or employment history • Bank, credit, or other financial account number • Account name

Figure 9.1 Common List of Data Types

Data classification also varies depending on the industry or business. Even among data classification professionals, there are different understandings about what classification means depending on the state, business, and type of industry. Here is a typical list of data classification groups:

Classification of Data Elements

- Personally Identifiable Information is a term of art defined by various state breach laws and includes specific data elements and circumstances that trigger notice obligations to individuals and regulators. For a comprehensive list of data breach laws and how states define personally identifiable information, see *Information Security and Privacy: A Guide to Federal and State Law and Compliance*, 2020-2021 ed.

- Personal Information (defined by laws like California Consumer Privacy Act, see Cal. Civ. Code § 1798.140(o), and California Privacy Rights Act, see Cal. Civ. Code § 1798.140(v)).

- Confidential Information

    o Public vs. Nonpublic
    o Sensitive vs. Non-sensitive
    o Confidential
    o Trade secret or intellectual property or business information

Classes of data under specific laws and regulations create other types of data classes like:

- PHI under HIPAA. See 45 C.F.R § 160.103.
- Personal Information under FCRA. See 15 U.S.C. § 6809(4).
- Financial data under PCI DSS. (Although PCI DSS is not required by federal law, some states have enacted similar provisions. See, e.g., Minn. Stat. § 325E.64; Nev. Rev. Stat. § 603A.215.)
- Medical Information under the Confidentiality of Medical Information Act (CMIA). See Cal. Civ. Code § 56.10(j).

Other classes of data offer safe harbors under various laws or remove it from the scope of being personal information including:

- De-identified
- Anonymized
- Pseudonymized
- Encrypted
- Aggregated

Data classification requires time and attention from the enterprise. Often classification is assigned during data mapping, data retention, and privacy projects. Privacy professionals are often leaders of these projects as their subject matter expertise is required to engage and ask stakeholders questions to understand and assign appropriate data types and classifications. Therefore, it is crucial to identify the proper stakeholders and persons most knowledgeable (PMKs) about data and assets.

Rallying the Troops: Who Are the Right People to Engage?

You don't want to start a war when you propose to enterprise leaders that all data must be mapped and classified, but it can sometimes feel like you are in hostile lands. Classifying data allows us to safeguard it appropriately, retain it for the right amount of time, understand legal requirements if or when we share the data, and comply with other applicable laws. Data classification is not a solo venture—it is an opportunity to rally key stakeholders in the organization that have a vested interest in the outcome. Appoint a privacy champion or advocate for each type of data classification. For example, the HR leader will support (or delegate somebody from their team to support) employee data. The CFO will oversee financial data. General Counsel may be the privacy champion for corporate or regulatory data. The role of the privacy professional is to lead your champions to compliance victory.

When Is the Right Time to Classify Data? Now!

On a going-forward basis, an excellent time to classify data is when evaluating new technology and negotiating the contract with the vendor. As part of the contracting process, provide the vendor with a questionnaire or assessment as a means to explain how the new technology collects, uses, stores, shares, and safeguards certain data elements. You can easily classify the data based on those responses. For example, suppose your business creates data or devices that collect, store, or transmit data. In that case, the business unit responsible for that development can complete a similar assessment during a privacy by design review. These assessments are sometimes called Data Privacy Impact Assessments under GDPR or Privacy Impact Assessments under emerging U.S. privacy laws.

Legacy data presents more complex issues because of the time and energy required to map and classify the data. For businesses that can afford it, consider using an automation tool (like BigID, I.B.M., Boomi, or Altova) to scan your systems for data to find, inventory, and classify structured and unstructured data. Many businesses use tools like OneTrust and Exterro to automate the process of data mapping using assessments. This process still requires a good amount of leadership to prepare the assessments, distribute them, hold others accountable for returning the completed assessments, then effectively classify the data once the responses are received. If the answers to the assessments are incomplete, then the results of the mapping and classification will also be incomplete. Finally, some mapping and classification is done the good old-fashioned way through custodial interviews and documenting responses in an Excel spreadsheet or a Word document. This approach is effective but time-consuming.

Reasonable Minds May Disagree: Keeping Data as Long as "Reasonably Necessary"

New laws like CPRA require businesses to tell consumers the length of time the data will be kept and impose "reasonably necessary" storage limitation requirements. CPRA states, "[a] business that controls the collection of a consumer's personal information shall, at or before the point of collection, inform consumers as to . . . the length of time the business intends to retain each category of personal information, or if that is not possible, the criteria used to determine such period." The law also expressly prohibits businesses from "retain[ing] a consumer's personal information or sensitive personal information for each disclosed purpose for which the personal information was collected for longer than is *reasonably necessary* for that disclosed purpose." (See Cal. Civ. Code § 1798.100(c).)

Although CPRA is the first law in the United States to impose a broad storage limitation requirement, it will not be the last. Businesses often decide data retention schedules after collecting data based on a cost/benefit analysis. When the risk associated with the data outweighs the benefits, then it is reasonable to destroy the data. CPRA will require that analysis occur before data is collected and require the business to disclose the length of time it intends to retain the data.

Goldilocks on Data Retention and Destruction

When it comes to data retention, organizations have to strike the right balance: not too short, not too long, just right. Companies traditionally developed data retention policies and schedules because certain laws or regulations required businesses to maintain data for a certain period. As a result, most organizations set a floor to retain data at least as long as various laws require it. New laws, however, are imposing restrictions on how long businesses may retain personal information. These new laws force companies to re-evaluate data retention and destruction policies and conduct a risk/benefit analysis on data types and classes.

Moreover, organizations that have been through a data breach or litigation understand the importance of deleting data that is no longer useful or of any value. If the floor is how long the law requires data to be maintained, then the ceiling should be measured by the data's usefulness to the consumer and business. For example, the California Labor Code requires companies to retain certain payroll records for at least three years. If the employer maintains ten years of payroll records, then that data has little business value and a tremendous amount of risk of compromise and cost to safeguard. On balance, the risk of retaining the data greatly exceeds the benefit or usefulness. A data retention policy can also be used proactively in litigation by the defense if the plaintiff requests data that was deleted pursuant to typical retention requirements.

Data in the Wild—Classifying Unstructured Data

Humans love to put things in a nice, neat little box—but unstructured data is neither nice nor neat to classify. Unstructured data is precisely what it sounds like—data that is not indexed and does not have a clear and defined box. For example, unstructured data may include email, social media conversations, customer feedback, webpages, business documents saved in random places, source code, documents, images, video, and audio.

Classifying structured data is less complex and time-consuming than classifying unstructured data. Data living in the wild is difficult to search, map, and categorize without using AI tools that can sift through, analyze, and categorize. If the data is unstructured, it is also challenging to create retention periods, which often makes organizations retain the data much longer than reasonably necessary. For example, when an organization is the victim of a data breach, email accounts are often targeted because they include treasure troves of data that span years. The cost of collecting those email accounts, processing the data into a review platform like Relativity, then running targeted searches is driven by the size of the email account. The fewer emails contained in the account, the less costly to investigate. One of the least expensive email breaches I worked on had a rule enabled on the Microsoft Office 365 account that deleted emails older than 90 days. If a user wanted access to the emails for a longer period, they had to move the email into a folder. Enabling rules that automate the deletion of unstructured data is one way to manage data retention and destruction of data in the wild.

Getting users involved to help manage their unstructured data requires education and sometimes consequences. Think about your precious email inbox and the number of emails you receive each day. Do you save emails in a pst (personal storage table) or folder by client or topic to give them structure? How long does your business allow users to save emails in their inboxes? If your inbox is anything like mine, you are lucky to get through all your emails in a day, let alone organize them. Sometimes the only compelling reason to organize and sort through emails is if I am at risk of losing access to the data. Many businesses have email providers that allow rules or settings that can help automate data classification and destruction. For example, all emails from a particular domain may be automatically saved and diverted to a folder for that client. All other emails that are not archived are automatically deleted after a set time.

Let's stay with the email example. Our emails contain many data types and classifications with different retention periods. For example, tax documents may be retained for seven years; payroll records may be retained for three years; customer files may be retained for ten years after the end of the relationship pursuant to contractual obligations. This means the IT department can't implement a universal end life rule for the data in my email because it has different values, benefits, and legally required retention periods. From a security perspective, it would be helpful to archive or move the email into a pst or vault with MFA enabled to retain it in a general structure (e.g., emails by year). Then it would not be sitting in an active email account lumped together with all other incoming emails.

Classification Drives Action and Incident Response

Data classification can also help businesses determine how to react before, during, and after data is lost or breached. For example, assume a threat actor accesses a *nonpublic* database that contains the names, social security numbers, and financial data of all your employees or customers. If the database is not classified or mapped, then it may take weeks before realizing that PII was accessed during this event. Now suppose the databases were mapped and classified as personally identifiable information. <u>Before</u> the event occurred, Information Security could have applied reasonable security measures like encryption and MFA to those databases. Access management restrictions to limit access to the database to only individuals with a role or project-based need to access the database could also have been implemented. During the event, the investigation team would have quickly identified critical assets, servers, and databases on which to focus their attention and investigation. After discovering that an unauthorized user potentially accessed PII, a legal analysis regarding notice obligations would have been prioritized so the business could meet time-sensitive deadlines for individual and regulatory notice obligations.

Data Classification ~ Matt

When I started working as a research director and analyst in Gartner's security and risk management practice, like all new analysts I was assigned a mentor and shadowed their inquiries. My mentor was Jeffrey Wheatman, then Research Vice President. During one of my first shadowed inquiries, a client posited a broad question, namely, "how should organizations think about risk?" Jeffrey's answer combined elegance and pragmatism. To paraphrase, "Grab a blank piece of paper and draw a line down the middle. On one side are the things you care about, and on the other are the things you don't."

There is no doubt that data classification is integral to privacy and security programs. Yet, despite the critical role of classification in both disciplines, data classification is commonly misunderstood or left to the vagaries of departmental boundaries versus formally managed and governed across the organization. Privacy leaders must bring order to this chaos and ensure that their organization's data classification practices are legally defensible, support privacy by design principles, and help the organization with its broader data governance practices.

Data classification, like risk management, can be considered a particularly complicated and challenging affair. However, as Jeffrey's guidance notes, it does not need to be. The binary guidance he offered has an analog in privacy. Certain data elements need to be classified and treated according to this classification, and others don't. Part of the challenges we see with data classification is not with the actual practice of identifying, categorizing, classifying, and treating data accordingly, but rather from organizational ambiguity and missing governance.

If you were to ask individuals within an organization who is responsible for data classification, the responses you would hear would likely include the CIO, the CISO, the CPO, or the DPO. Each role should be part of the broader data governance process. However, from a legal definition perspective, data classification is primarily the responsibility of the organization's counsel when data classifications are based on regulations or contractual definitions.

Too frequently, however, there's ambiguity within the organization about how information should be classified and who is accountable for these classifications. This ambiguity is easily clarified. Counsel owns this functional responsibility and is accountable for data classification activities for regulatorily or contractually in-scope data. Moreover, counsel is also aware of data, regardless of classification, that may be subject to a litigation hold or other proceedings that may mandate special treatment and retention. If different from counsel, the privacy leader should ensure that agreed-to classifications and requisite treatments are documented and that these understandings are disseminated throughout the organization. Other key stakeholders, including the CIO, CISO, CPO, or DPO, should ensure appropriate treatment of information based on its classification. Collectively, these stakeholders should establish an appropriate governance model to ensure that data classification activities mitigate risk and support the privacy and other programs for the organization. We will delve into some of the governance and mechanics of data classification.

Accountability. The organization's counsel is ultimately accountable for guiding data classification activities. This does present a rather obvious challenge. Attorneys do not hold a functional role within organizations—they are not marketing, infrastructure and operations, customer care, sales, security, vendor management, operations, or other line-of-business functions. Instead, attorneys advise on regulatory requirements, contractual obligations, and legal risks to mitigate. Just because counsel defines how data should be classified does not necessarily mean that actual data classification practices accurately reflect that understanding. There are real risks that data may be misclassified and mishandled without counsel's knowledge—obviously exposing the organization to risk. To alleviate these risks, the organization's counsel must collaborate and partner with these stakeholders to ensure that the organization's data is classified and governed appropriately. A simple tool can help clarify responsibilities and key functions for the data classification process, namely a RACI matrix. Draft a RACI matrix that outlines key functions within the data classification and data governance process, indicate who is responsible for each function, who is accountable as well as who should be consulted and informed. Key functions on the RACI will likely include the following:

- **Data Classifications.** The classifications will be based on the regulations in scope for the organization or specific contractual definitions that the organization has established. Certain data classes may not be subject to regulatory or contractual context, including how the organization addresses intellectual property, financial data, encryption keys, and operational data. These may be captured in organizationally defined confidential, proprietary, and public classifications. In addition, organizations that are subject to defense regulations will have distinct classifications. A master schedule that defines all applicable data classes should be created, and key stakeholders should be invited to validate these understandings.

- **Data Inventories.** Data inventories are foundational. Privacy leaders and other key stakeholders must know where various forms of information reside and how it has been shared within the organization or with third parties. Take an expansive view when looking at data inventories to ensure that all material sources are captured, cataloged, and governed accordingly. I cannot overstate the value of getting to know the business. There may be data sources discovered during "walkabouts" that add to data inventories.

- **Data Access.** Many privacy regulations allow data subjects to request access to their data. These classes of data (e.g., protected health information, personal data, credit histories, and the like) should be identified and contextualized. The RACI matrix will likely need to include distinct functions for the specific data elements at hand. It is critical to recognize and capture input from departments that are typically front-and-center for interfacing with consumers and data subjects, notably customer care, sales staff, contact centers, reception areas, and the like.

- **Data Locations.** Data flow diagrams, data mapping exercises, and other context-specific functions will help privacy leaders understand where data, in this case, personal data, resides within the organization. Knowing the organization's core functions and lines of business is critical to this effort. Data maps should capture which departments collect, use, share, or retain in-scope information. These maps should clearly indicate the department and the department's applications, where these applications are hosted, and relevant storage and backup detail for these applications and systems. Bluntly, there should be no ambiguity about where personal data resides within the organization. Drafting the initial data flow diagrams and data maps will take time, so plan accordingly. Depending upon the operational complexity and the availability of resources, these core documents could take several weeks to several months to draft. These maps, narratives, and diagrams should be kept current and reviewed at least annually for accuracy and completeness.

- **Data Security.** Not all data warrants administrative, technical, or physical security controls. The data's classification should inform which security controls should be implemented. These controls can include methods like pseudonymization, tokenization, encryption of specific data elements, and access controls. Data classification should drive and contextualize how to protect this information. We address reasonable security practices in Chapter 11.

- **Data Retention.** When data is not classified correctly, multiple risks arise. One of the most salient is that the company deletes or destroys data that is subject to specific retention periods before its expiry date or while it is subject to a litigation hold. Equally challenging, data may be retained past its expiry date, creating both increased storage expenses and an unfunded liability if that data is breached. Similar to data classification, data retention periods for regulated or contractual data sets should be initially defined by the organization's counsel and reviewed by key stakeholders for other organizational considerations. As a reminder, privacy by design principles suggest that companies retain data for the minimum period necessary to fulfill its stated purpose. Unfortunately, for too many organizations, data becomes digital detritus. Spend the time needed to clarify which data classes should be retained and for how long. Then, take the necessary steps to ensure that the appropriate stakeholders understand these requirements.

- **Data Destruction.** Once data has served its stated purpose, and consistent with the organization's policies, regulatory requirements, and contractual obligations, data should be deleted or destroyed. The complexity of fulfilling deletion requests will vary based on the systems at hand. While deleting a record from a database is relatively straightforward, deleting unstructured data (including its metadata) is not for the faint of heart. This is where the investments in data flow diagrams and data mapping exercises are critical. Be mindful of the nature and extent of end-user access to various forms of data. The systems, locations, applications, and third-party entities where data resides must be fully known to ensure that data is destroyed.

  The privacy leader will need to understand the ground truth of what can be done technically to effect deletion requests. Spend time with your organization's IT leaders and the practitioners that administer storage and backup environments. You will also need to understand the practices for data deletion with business partners, including those providing outsourced services such as payroll and marketing and cloud services, including popular cloud storage services. Ideally, the service agreements with these providers have clear instructions for data security while the data is in use and for its return or destruction when the contract expires, or circumstances require these actions. These practices should be validated as part of the vendor onboarding process (see Chapter 10) and during the ongoing stewardship of the relationship with the vendor during the term of the services agreement. Where oversight over deletion and destruction activities is not viable, consider having the service provider certify that they indeed did delete or destroy the data as required.

As you review your organization's specific data processing activities, you will likely find other items to include in the RACI matrix. The RACI matrix should be a living document, validated from time to time to ensure that it is accurate and complete. Don't overlook the consulted and informed stakeholders in the process. By drafting even a somewhat abstract and high-level RACI matrix for data classification activities, key risks can be identified and mitigated. Add these risks to your privacy risk register.

Policy. Formalize data classification activities and incorporate them into an organizational policy that is distributed and acknowledged by appropriate stakeholders. The policy should identify the classes of information that the organization processes, establish expectations for treating specific data classes, including requisite security and privacy controls, and codify the responsibilities and accountabilities established in the RACI matrix. The RACI matrix should form part of the policy. Like all policies, the policy should evidence managerial reviews and approvals, the effective date, the next scheduled review date, the policy's version, as well as the overall scope. Depending upon the regulatory context of the organization, data classification policies may also benefit from the inclusion of a sanction policy—the obligatory "failure to comply with this policy may include disciplinary actions up to and including termination."

Policies play an integral role in establishing the right tone at the top for the organization while also establishing and codifying governance expectations. Policies should not be shelfware and should accurately reflect organizational expectations. When policies are created in a vacuum, material risks occur. When a policy does not accurately reflect the organization's practices and is aspirational in nature, the executive leadership team may operate with the understanding that the contemplated activities are indeed occurring and provide disclosures and assurances to external stakeholders and regulators indicating the same. Effectively, there is a risk that the organization is falsely disclosing the status of its practices.

For consumer-oriented organizations in the U.S., this could be interpreted as "unfair and deceptive" trade practices by the FTC. Similarly, when policies are aspirational but assumed to reflect ground truth by the executive leadership team, they may assume that required resources have been provisioned. When the reality of the disconnect between the policy and the practice is made clear, additional resources will likely be needed. In conjunction with other stakeholders, the privacy leader needs to understand the organization's actual capabilities—notably around the classification of unstructured data—and, again, ensure that this detail is captured in a risk register where material gaps are evident.

Depending upon organizational preference, the procedures required to fulfill the stated objectives of the policy may be captured in the policy itself or in separate procedure documents and checklists. Given that procedures tend to be more dynamic, my personal preference is that the procedural documentation should be outside of the policy itself. The policy may include high-level, abstracted procedures to provide context for those that are acknowledging the policy.

Procedure. The details derived from the data mapping exercise where data flow diagrams and inventories of specific data classes are captured should inform procedures. The procedures will vary notably from one class of data to another in addition to the distinct operating context of the data processing activities (e.g., the business process, the applications or services providers that underpin or support those processes, as well as the IT infrastructure including the storage and backups). Likewise, how data is classified can range from system-specific labels (e.g., all data processed by this application is considered personal data), to tagging data with its classification, to the footers commonly found in documents. Regardless of the mechanism for labeling and classifying data, the procedures should be clear and concise for the stakeholders who access, share, or process this data.

Provide training to these identified stakeholders to ensure that organizational expectations are fully understood and agreed to. Never underestimate the value of training—be it formal or informal "water cooler" discussions. Leverage this training to validate understandings and determine if the original data mapping and data flow analyses failed to capture any sources of specifically classified data. To the extent possible, look for means to automate procedures. For example, if all documents and files that contain personal data are expected to be labeled in a specific way, but this labeling is handled at the discretion of the end-user, you can bet that there will be errors and deficiencies in the process.

Validation and Audit. Whether through the efforts of the privacy leader or a separate internal audit function, how data is classified in practice within the organization should be validated. Do not assume, for example, that because the policy says that all protected health information should be labeled a specific way that it has been labeled as the policies and procedures dictate. This requires verification and control review. Privacy leaders should be actively engaged with the other stakeholders throughout the organization to ensure that requisite privacy controls, including those associated with data classification, are designed appropriately and operating effectively. Use these validations and audits to enhance your understanding of the organization, its business processes, data processing activities, material vendors, and other critical organizational contexts. The value of these insights cannot be overstated.

Data classification is foundational to privacy. The classification of data elements will inform requisite privacy controls, including the right to access, rectify, request deletion, or limit processing activities. The classification also informs security practices including access controls, encryption, tokenization, and pseudonymization of specific data elements. How data is classified informs multiple obligations and controls, including data loss prevention controls, when and where to use watermarks, breach notification requirements, least privilege and need to know objectives, and retention periods. In short, data classification requires thoughtful, proactive engagement across the organization. The invaluable context provided by accurate classification of data elements should not be left to chance and should be a linchpin of the overall privacy program.

Key Insights and Recommended Next Steps

Key Insights

- All data are not created equal. It is a waste of time and money to classify public information and a potential liability to fail to identify data that is subject to regulation or contract obligations.
- Most organizations require three to four data classification levels; more than that are unnecessary and introduce confusion.
- Validation is essential as oversight and to guard against inherent bias.
- The best time to classify data is when it is initially created or acquired. Data that is not classified at that point adds to governance debt.
- Privacy-enhancing technologies such as de-identification, anonymization, encryption, and aggregation can remove data from compliance scope.
- Legal counsel must be involved in classifying regulated data and data covered by contractual obligations.
- It is essential to validate that data is handled according to how your company has classified it and how you publicly state you are treating that data. Disconnects in this regard create regulatory and contractual liability.

Recommended Next Steps

- Work with departmental leadership to create a RACI matrix for data classification, ensure legal counsel is accountable for classification involving data subject to regulation or contractual obligations.
- Work with legal counsel to validate or develop your data classification policy.
- Partner with the appropriate individuals identified in your RACI matrix to conduct an assessment of data that is classified and data that is not. Validate that data subject to regulation or contractual obligations is treated per policy and develop an action plan to close any identified gaps.

Chapter 10

Vendor Risk Management

Introduction

In 2005, a "housing bubble" that had been inflating in the U.S. for several years started to deflate. This led, in part, to a large re-evaluation of mortgage-backed securities that took place between 2007 and 2008. At the peak of this re-valuation, there was significant volatility in securities markets. The primary cause of the volatility was a lack of visibility into the extent of third-party liability for financial instruments related to these mortgage-backed securities and a lack of certainty about how far governments would go to backstop losses and guarantee the solvency of the banking system.

Before the cyberattacks on the technical supply chains that started spilling into the news in 2020 and the disruptions to physical supply chains brought on by the worldwide repositioning of manufacturing to combat the COVID-19 pandemic, the "great recession" demonstrated what could happen when we are ill-informed about the risk that lurks in our ecosystem. As David, Justine, and Matt will explain in Chapter 10, "Vendor Risk Management," you are ultimately responsible for the data placed in your custody, and there are ways of managing and minimizing the risk.

In "Vendor Risk Management—Protect Your Reputation," David puts into focus the risks you take when you use third parties, in whole or in part, to manage processes that involve caring for the data you hold in trust for your customers. He then widens the aperture and shows how the problems of managing your vendors grow as you add scale and how automation and upfront diligence are essential to protecting your reputation from future harm.

Justine does a deep dive into the different types of third-party relationships you'll need to deal with, why it's critical to identify and catalog them correctly, and the value of focusing on the contract language that defines your relationship with your critical third parties. Her essay, "Vendor Risk Management—Shared Risk, Shared Accountability," provides some practical tools to assist with both the cataloging and contract requirements to hold your vendors accountable when necessary.

Matt's essay, "Managing Vendor Risk," provides a roadmap of the definitions, sources, and impacts of third-party risk pertaining to material third parties. Recognizing that we rely on third parties for critical functionality and this reliance has a material impact on core business processes allows us to put third-party risk into perspective and prepares the organization to assign appropriate importance to the task.

Vendor Risk Management—Protect Your Reputation ~ David

Suppose your organization is really remarkable in that you have an in-house team of hardware and software designers and developers so good that you don't have to rely on products or services from external vendors or, for whatever other reason, you do not rely on any third-party services. In that case, this chapter may not be for you, although we can always learn something from the lessons others are having to absorb. For everyone else, please read on.

Letting third-party products and services into your company should, in the first place, be an expedient and efficient way of getting a particular task done better than you could do it. But it also assumes that you trust the vendors in question with a concomitant leap of faith that the products and services the vendors provide are 100% trustworthy and will remain so, causing you no harm. Needless to say, even if you trust the vendors and their offerings justify your trust, bad things can happen. Even if your trust is based on previous personal or company experience or widespread adoption by organizations large and small, there is no guarantee that the vendor or its product will not be subject to a cyberattack in the future. That could have a deleterious impact on your business—and that of your partners and customers.

Consequently, vendor risk management is intended to ensure that introducing third-party suppliers, irrespective of their brand reputation, will not disrupt your business processes—or worse. Hence, to manage any unfortunate outcomes, it is vitally important that you regularly assess and monitor the risks you might be exposed to from externally sourced products and services that are part of operational systems or have access to company information.

House Party

Imagine throwing a house party in the time of COVID-19. You leave the front door of your home wide open and let as many families, friends, and professional colleagues as possible—people you like and trust—come over the threshold and wander through the house without socially distancing or wearing face masks. The chances are nothing will go wrong, no one will get infected, and, given that you are selective about who you invite in, nothing goes missing. On the other hand, it's equally possible that one of the invitees is already infected, or, worse still, a super spreader who could ruin the health of everyone at the party—it's a considerable risk with foreseeable potential consequences.

From a privacy perspective, consider how many personal assets there are in your home that your guests could deliberately or inadvertently stumble upon. In the privacy of your own home, you tend not to be aware of what the pictures on your walls, the clothes in your wardrobe, the notes on the kitchen family notice board, or the contents of your fridge tell others about you. Your guests could innocently remark on them to others or leave the party, remember what they've heard or seen, and casually share it with someone you don't know and never met. With the best intentions in the world, you cannot be entirely sure who or what you're letting over your threshold, past your real-world personal perimeter or firewall. Under normal circumstances, you cannot fully anticipate what happens next when a disparate group of people comes together.

Coming back to the reason for the house party digression: as much as you trust your regular suppliers and however well you carry out due diligence on new vendors, there is always a risk when you bring third parties into your shop. The best you can do is to deep dive into identifying the potential technical and contractual risks and provide mitigating strategies to prevent collateral damage. Just like in our imagined house party, you have to be concerned about letting in hardware and software elements that could have bugs that could infect other elements, either when they are brought in or when they're in place and receive an unstable upgrade. Likewise, you have a mountain of data either in deep storage or traversing your networks, and your brought-in hardware and software could be responsible for collecting, storing, managing, or sharing some or all of that data.

In essence, you could conceive of a vendor risk management program as if you were expecting any number of cyberattacks to occur and were putting in place a set of damage limitation steps to protect your vital company assets from data breaches or data leaks by, among other things, protecting sensitive data and ensuring the continuity of the business.

Ideally, you should integrate this risk management process with other risk management processes already in place. As well as assessing the impact of technical systems and solutions, it's equally important to consider the contractual arrangements, the license agreements, and the terms of usage you are entering into and the potential legal consequences if anything were to go awry. For example, if there is a data breach resulting in direct or indirect financial losses to your company or your customers that can be traced to an imperfect software upgrade or a malfunctioning hardware component, are you covered by standard contract clauses or the master service agreement?

Roll Your Own?

The next question to address is whether to develop a vendor risk management program internally or seek the assistance of one of the growing number of third-party risk management software solutions that will focus on your vendor management program. At first sight, it would seem that the task is not especially complex—how difficult can it be to design and send a form-based questionnaire to your vendors and then collect and validate their responses? However, although you may consider it a task that could be undertaken internally with reasonable ease, inevitably it will turn out to be more challenging than it at first appears. Consequently, my advice is that you seek help from someone who has the skills and, as important, extensive experience in carrying out such an exercise. Not least, the results and conclusions of the analysis will be viewed by senior company stakeholders and will be referred back to you if and when a problem arises.

Probing the risks associated with engaging a supplier doesn't appear to be a great way to initiate what will hopefully be a fruitful long-term relationship. But, just as having a prenup in place before getting married gets around some of the horrors of a future divorce settlement, so the same applies to carrying out a vendor risk assessment—it's an insurance policy that neither party ever wants to refer back to. Additionally, there will be those who question the value of carrying out the exercise, particularly if it creates unpopular delays in deploying new or upgraded products and services. And it will be hard to respond to push back when asked to quantify or qualify the extent of the privacy protection you anticipate.

Realistically, you cannot make any 100% guarantees, and despite best efforts, something will slip through unforeseen cracks. One of the significant imponderables will be gauging how all the imported elements will work together, what impact systems will have on each other, from the outset and after each set of upgrades and fixes, not only peer-to-peer but also end-to-end. But perhaps we're getting ahead of ourselves, and this worry belongs in the next chapter.

Overall, as with any comprehensive insurance policy, the more consideration you give to what may go wrong, the greater the relief if the policy has to be called in. Every opportunity to be circumspect will one day be repaid in spades.

Vendor Risk Management—Shared Risk, Shared Accountability ~ Justine

Vendor describes those who sell any goods or services, especially a specialized product. Technology vendors are a necessary component of every business' ecosystem and should be considered an integral part of a company's critical infrastructure. Software as a Service ("SaaS") is a term that describes increased risk because it means a vendor is providing some service related to data collected. Management of this risk requires time, information, diligence, organization, and a solid contractual agreement.

Head In the Sand

A 2020 survey by BlueVoyant[90] shared the views and experiences of 1,505 CIOs, CISOs, and Chief Procurement Officers in organizations with more than 1,000 employees across a range of sectors, including business and professional services, financial services, healthcare and pharmaceutical, manufacturing, utilities, and energy. It covered five countries: USA, UK, Mexico, Switzerland, and Singapore. Results indicate the fundamental lack of understanding of the danger that third-party vendors create:

- 77% have limited visibility around their third-party vendors.
- 2.7 is the average number of breaches experienced in the past 12 months.
- 80% have suffered a third party–related breach in the past 12 months.
- 29% of respondents say they have no way of knowing if cyber risk emerges in a third-party vendor.
- Fewer than one-quarter (22.5%) monitor their entire supply chain.
- 32% only re-assess and report their vendor's cyber risk position either semi-annually or less frequently.
- The average headcount in internal and external cyber risk management teams is 12.

---

[90] Managing Cyber Risk Across the Extended Vendor Ecosystem, October 2021 (https://www.bluevoyant.com/resources/ciso-report-download-form/).

- 81% say that budget for third-party cyber risk management is increasing by an average figure of 40%.

What Is Vendor Risk Management?

Vendor risk management ("VRM") is a process that deals with the management and planning of third-party products and services. The business must first identify and evaluate the potential risks of working with a vendor during this process. Second, the company must decide whether the benefits of the partnership outweigh the risks. Finally, the business must mitigate, reduce, or transfer the risk once the vendor is engaged. Not conducting vendor risk management can result in reputational damage, lost business, legal fees, and fines.

Resolving Vendor Risk

As more fully discussed in Chapter 2 on enterprise risk, there are generally four ways to handle or treat vendor risk: (1) avoidance; (2) acceptance; (3) mitigation; or (4) transference.

Avoidance can be *complete or partial*. For complete avoidance, you avoid engaging the vendor altogether because the risk of doing business outweighs the benefits. For partial avoidance, you may accept in part and avoid in part. For example, partial avoidance engages a vendor to license their software and place it within your firewall. However, you declined the SaaS services, which would allow the vendor to host and analyze the data collected.

Acceptance means you understand the vendor risk and choose to accept it. Vendor risk is often accepted, although far too often businesses do not fully appreciate or understand the risk they are accepting. It is imperative to conduct a comprehensive review of the risks and benefits the vendor's services create before agreeing to accept the risk.

Mitigation is the act of reducing vendor risk in either severity or frequency. For example, encrypting data in transit between the business and the vendor, then requiring the data be de-identified of all personal information once stored by the vendor (to the extent possible). Another imperative way to reduce risk is multi-factor authentication to access the database where the data resides. MFA should be required of both the vendor's employees and any users accessing the database where the data is stored. Encryption or multi-factor authentication mitigate or reduce privacy risk because they offer safe harbors under laws and can thwart threat actors from accessing protected data.

Risk transference is shifting or sharing risk with the vendor. The classic examples of risk transference are (1) the purchase of cyber insurance that provides coverage if there is data loss and (2) the inclusion of indemnity provisions in vendor contracts. If your business has enough bargaining power with the vendor, you may be able to ask to be added as an additional insured to the vendor's cyber insurance policy. Risk should be transferred and owned by the party that is best able to control that risk—and perhaps equally as important is confirming that the vendor is capable of accepting the risk transference and itself has adequately insured against loss. If there is a breach, then the party responsible for preventing that breach from occurring carries the risk of indemnifying impacted businesses. Frequently, indemnity is limited by terms in the contract that limit liability. For example, indemnity might be limited to the amount paid for services in the last 12 months.

Would a "Vendor" By Any Other Name Smell as Sweet?

Privacy laws like CCPA and CPRA create new and critically important categories for vendors and entities. Here is an overview of why it is crucial to identify what type of vendor you manage.

It All Starts with Your Business

Even though not all businesses in the United States must comply with laws like CPRA or GDPR, all businesses should manage and govern vendor risk. Identifying the primary laws or regulations that apply to your business (or your customer's businesses) will drive the steps required for vendor management. For example, companies that do not collect data on EU data subjects or do business in the EU may not have to comply with GDPR or conduct ROPAs, DPIAs, or

DTIAs. Similarly, not all "businesses" must comply with CCPA/CPRA.

The CCPA broadly defines a "Business" as an entity that determines the purposes and means of processing consumers' personal information, either directly or jointly with others. The CCPA applies to any "Business" which operates for profit, collects California residents' personal information, and meets one or more of the following criteria:

- Annual gross revenue over $25 million;
- Buys, sells, shares, or receives for commercial purposes the personal information of more than 50,000[91] consumers; or
- Derives more than 50% of annual revenue from selling consumers' personal information.
- A "Business" also includes any entity that controls or is controlled by a Business and shares common branding with the business.

What Is a Service Provider?

A Service Provider is a vendor that collects, stores, or processes personal information on behalf of the Business. Most Businesses want vendors to qualify as a Service Provider because if they don't, then they are de facto third parties. Under CCPA/CPRA, a consumer has the right to opt-out of the selling or sharing of personal information with third parties. However, consumers do not have the right to opt-out of sharing personal information with Service Providers. The links that state "Do Not Sell My Personal Information" give consumers an opportunity to opt-out of sharing their information with third parties. With the exception of marketing, Businesses prefer to share data with Service Providers. However, if the entity does not meet the service-provider definition under CCPA/CPRA, they are de facto third parties.

Under CCPA/CPRA, an entity is a service provider if the entity:

---

[91] Effective January 1, 2023, the threshold will change to 100,000 as the CPRA supersedes the CCPA.

- operates for profit;
- processes information on behalf of a Business or organization; and
- processes consumer's personal information on behalf of a Business for a business purpose, pursuant to a written contract.

To qualify as a service provider, the vendor must agree in writing to specific language. The written contract must prohibit the vendor from:

- selling the personal information;
- retaining, using, or disclosing the personal information for any purpose other than for the specific purpose of performing the services specified in the contract, including retaining, using, or disclosing the personal information for a commercial purpose other than providing the services specified in the contract; or
- retaining, using, or disclosing the information outside of the direct business relationship between the person and the business.

A Service Provider's use of personal information received from one Business to provide services to another Business is not a "necessary and proportionate" use of personal information. This is because such use illustrates a "commercial purpose" of the Service Provider rather than a "business purpose" of the Business. However, there is an exception if the Service Provider comingles personal information from another Business for security or anti-fraud purposes. Additionally, entities that meet the definition of a Service Provider and collect personal information directly from a consumer rather than from the Business are also considered Service Providers.

What Is a Third Party?

Under the CCPA, a Third Party is everything left over. Third Party is a catch-all category that includes any person or entity that does not meet the definition of a "Business" and is not a "Service Provider."

Third Parties do not include entities that receive data pursuant to a contract, even if that entity does not process the information for a "business purpose." Therefore, an entity that receives personal information from a Business can be excluded from Third Party classification and not qualify as a Service Provider.

What Is a Contractor Under CPRA?

A Contractor is defined as a "person to whom the business makes available a consumer's personal information for a business purpose, pursuant to a written contract." CCPA requires that contracts with Service Providers prohibit the retention, use, or disclosure of personal information for purposes other than performing the services specified. CPRA makes one adjustment to this requirement—limiting processing to a specified "business purpose," defined in the Act, and subject to future regulations.

The Mountain of Vendor Contracts

One of the most time-consuming and important tasks a privacy professional will undertake is vendor management. Getting started can feel like planning to summit Mt. Everest. However, with some strategy and planning, vendor management is well worth the climb. First, gather all vendor contracts from procurement, IT, Legal, and other business units. Next, identify APIs shared with third parties that may uncover additional vendors that share enterprise data and find those agreements. If your enterprise has hundreds of contracts or agreements with vendors, consider using a contract review platform or vendor management application to maintain and manage vendors. The contractual provisions will help determine the type or class of vendor.

Where Do Vendors Fall Under the CCPA?

The CCPA states that Businesses and Service Providers exist in a relationship when there is a written contract where the Business determines the purpose and means for the processing of consumers' personal information and discloses that information to the Service Provider, who then processes that information for the Business, pursuant to the contract. In contrast, the relationship between a Business and a Third Party is one in which consumers' personal information is disclosed and there is no contract, or the contract does not provide specific protections for the consumers' personal information, or the disclosure is not made for a business purpose.

Businesses must contract carefully as there are several circumstances in which a vendor may not satisfy the requirements to be considered a "Service Provider" under the CCPA, resulting in differing business obligations. A vendor is not a Service Provider in situations where:

- the parties have no written contract governing the relationship;
- the contract permits the vendor to retain consumers' personal information beyond the direct relationship with the business;
- the contract permits the vendor to use consumers' personal information for a purpose other than the business's purpose as defined by the contract; or
- the contract permits the vendor to make independent decisions about the processing of consumers' personal information.

Illustrative Examples of Classification

An Email Marketing Provider sends promotional emails to subscribers then shares the personal information collected with an Analytics Firm. No money is exchanged. The Analytics Firm adds this new personal information to their more extensive database to provide aggregated demographic information back to the sender. The Email Marketing Provider determined the purpose of processing the data by asking the analytics firm to provide demographic information. Provided the Email Marketing Provider meets the CCPA thresholds, it is considered the "Business" under CCPA. The Analytics Firm in this scenario is considered a "Third Party" because it processed the information then added the personal information from the sender to its database. Therefore, the Analytics Firm retains personal information from the Email Marketing Provider for purposes other than for the specific purpose of performing the service, i.e., generating demographic statistics.

Supply Chain Attacks Erode Trust

In addition to helping businesses meet their privacy obligations, privacy technology can also create vulnerabilities in our supply chain. Several similar high-profile breaches recently occurred that heightened our awareness and understanding of the fragility of our trust in third-party software. Our consciousness of the potential of these risks was solidified by March 2021, when Microsoft Exchange also experienced such an event—a patch included malware that created a backdoor that threat actors could exploit. When we download trusted software, we do not expect it will include malicious code. One way to mitigate the impact of malicious code is to ensure the contract or terms of use include adequate notice requirements if vulnerabilities exist in the software or products and proper risk shifting provisions. SaaS agreements are more likely to have indemnity provisions, whereas licensing or software agreements may limit liability. However, vendor management and diligence cannot be reserved only for SaaS-type agreements because software can also create vulnerabilities.

Shifting/Sharing Risk: Vendor Agreements

Managing, governing, transferring, and mitigating vendor risk is almost exclusively accomplished in contracts. Most in-house legal teams spend hours and hours revising vendor agreements to shift and share risk.

Many in-house legal teams are strained to redline thousands of vendor agreements each year. There are ways to simplify the process by creating standardized addendums or Data Privacy Agreements that articulate the key provisions for service providers under various laws and shift/share risk to the vendor.

Managing Vendor Risk ~ Matt

Few areas of our privacy program can present more risk and be more challenging than vendor risk management and oversight over third-party functions, effectively the data processors in various guises that may process personal data on behalf of our organizations. And as we saw with data classification, vendor management is a whole-of-enterprise function that requires collaboration and insights from key stakeholders, including line-of-business executives and the legal, security, finance, and privacy teams. A key challenge with vendor and third-party risk management is blurry accountability over this function. This ambiguity accentuates the risks associated with vendors and other third parties and should be clarified. Even procurement departments of large organizations confront this ambiguity. Here is another high-impact use case for RACI matrices that can help explain who is accountable for vendor decisions, who should be consulted, and who should be informed of the risk factors associated with using specific third parties. While the topic of vendor management warrants a stand-alone book, let's look at vendor risk through the lens of privacy and highlight those areas where the privacy leader can help inform risk decisions.

First and foremost, we must recognize just how dependent most organizations are on the services and applications provided by third parties. I cannot overstate the dependencies on third parties for (SaaS) applications, payroll processing, advisory services (including finance, tax, legal, and accounting), and even independent contractors who complement internal staff on projects. Large organizations will frequently have vendor master files with thousands of identified third parties. Even small organizations may have a significant number of material service providers. In addition, regulations such as the GDPR, GLBA, and HIPAA-HITECH require organizations to evaluate the risks associated with the data elements shared with these third parties (be it personal data, financial data, or protected health information). Conducting vendor assessments at this scale requires prioritization and a definition of materiality that can separate non-material services from those that have regulatory and privacy risk.

The foundation of any vendor management program is a clear definition of materiality. While more expansive than the topic of privacy alone, the definition of a material vendor could be as basic as "those vendors with whom the organization shares or discloses regulated information, notably personal data" to an amalgam of risk factors that include weightings for the following:

- **Privacy.** This risk factor centers on how expansive the privacy impacts are associated with the contemplated services. Vendors that process regulated information, be they data elements that are considered personal data, financial, or health-related, are, by definition, material. For example, suppose a controller sends personal data to a processor outside of the Europe Union operating in a country where there is no adequacy decision, or protected health information is shared or disclosed by a covered entity to a service provider in the U.S. healthcare sector. In both cases, there must be requisite contracts established, be they standard contractual clauses (SCCs) or business associate agreements (BAAs) respectively. Marketing services and those focused on human resources warrant your attention, given the nature of the data they process. Effectively, depending on the type of data that may be processed by the vendor, or third party, distinct contracting arrangements and obligations may be at hand. Article 28 of the GDPR outlines in detail the obligations that the data controller must establish over the services provided by the data processor.

- **Security.** As discussed in Chapter 11, "Reasonable Security," vendors should be triaged based on their potential or inherent security risk to the contracting organization. The assessment should determine the nature and extent of the impact should the vendor suffer a security incident or data breach. The impact could range from service interruptions to a personal data breach requiring disclosures to affected parties and regulators. Members of the CISO's team may serve as the primary technical points of contact to help evaluate the vendor's security and data protection capabilities. However, the privacy leader will need to evaluate these assessments and determine if the assurances offered by the vendor to protect and control the use of personal data are commensurate with the organization's risk tolerances and regulatory and contractual obligations. In the context of a controller and data processor relationship, it's incumbent upon the controller to explicitly, and in requisite detail, define permitted processing activities. I cannot overstate the importance of collaboration between the privacy and security teams.

- **Reputation.** Definitions of materiality can also be extended to capture whether a vendor's services enhance or degrade the contracting organization's reputation with its stakeholders. This is a nuanced risk factor but should not be overlooked and should anticipate the downstream consequences of selecting a vendor without appropriate diligence. Corporate social responsibility initiatives are intertwined with reputation impact reviews.

- **Regulatory.** Vendors who provide services that are regulated or process regulated information (e.g., personal data, financial data, material, non-public information, and protected health information) are by definition material. This becomes a binary assessment for the privacy leader that can be as simple as "do we share personal data or sensitive personal information with this service provider or vendor?" If the answer is yes, the vendor is material and should be assessed further.

- **Operations.** Certain classes of vendors are material to the organization's operations. As a simple case in point, network service providers are generally material as few organizations can maintain operations within defined service level targets absent internet access. Other vendors, including those in the supply chain, may also be material if their products or services are required for the organization to deliver its products and services to the market. While not directly tied to privacy, operational impacts carry significant weight in evaluating vendors. The privacy leader should anticipate potential disagreement where vendors with high impact on operations also have privacy and security practices assessed as suboptimal. As an example from the bio-tech industry, lab equipment that processes and stores PHI is frequently procured sans privacy and security reviews. Effectively, high-priority vendors, given their role in operations, may be onboarded even when their security and privacy practices are not ideal.

- **Enterprise Value and Revenue.** Assess prospective vendors if they play a role in the organization's ability to drive enterprise value and grow revenue. Some vendors effectively underpin the procuring organization's strategy. Like the operational impacts noted above, vendors who are materially significant from an enterprise value perspective are likely to be onboarded even when concerns vis-à-vis privacy and security practices are identified. Stakeholders must agree to how these variables, and conflicts between them, are ultimately weighted.

- **Financial Viability (Vendor Orientation).** Evaluate vendors based on their financial health and viability. There are some basic indicators that the vendor management team should evaluate, namely, is the prospective vendor profitable or how does the vendor fund their operations and services?

- **Service Capability (Vendor Orientation).** The vendor management, security, and privacy teams should evaluate if the prospective vendor has the operational wherewithal to deliver services as contemplated. In addition, the individuals who assess vendors should be aware of critical and frequent asymmetries between procuring entities and their prospective vendors. For example, large vendors with strong balance sheets and diverse customer bases may not adjust their privacy and security practices to accommodate a smaller customer. Small vendors, conversely, may acquiesce to requested changes from larger customers on paper, knowing that their ability to fulfill the requested changes may be suboptimal concerning actual operations and governance practices. Regardless of where the asymmetries may surface, they should be evaluated.

In the aggregate, the risk factors and considerations described above can help inform which vendors and suppliers are material to the privacy program, as well as security and operations when evaluated from a variety of perspectives. However, manually conducting these reviews is costly, time-consuming, and does not scale for organizations with material vendors numbering in the hundreds if not thousands. Unless the vendor management or procurement teams are sufficiently large and tooled to carry out these evaluations, the privacy leader will need to work diligently to identify those vendors that process personal and sensitive data provided by your organization.

If you are not part of the organization's legal team, spend time with the organization's counsel to determine which vendors have been subject to data protection addendums, standard contractual clauses, business associate agreements (where applicable), and other legal obligations. Take time to meet with colleagues throughout the organization, notably those in departments or functions with a higher proclivity to process personal data.

Cases in point would include sales and marketing, human resources, and accounting—notably in consumer-oriented businesses. Spend time with these and other departments to determine if personal data are in scope with their departmental functions and if there are third parties used to support their operations, aka processors. Validate if requisite privacy controls have been put in place with these vendors. Explicitly validate the contractual relationship between the firms. For example, verify that the agreement limits processing activities explicitly to those authorized by the controller, that instructions for handling DSARs are outlined, that data security and data retention provisions are addressed, and that fundamental confidentiality and code of conduct expectations are codified. If not, coordinate with vendor management and counsel to remediate privacy gaps and collaborate with the department to ensure that future contracting efforts account for required privacy controls.

Effective vendor risk management establishes clear accountability for the process with no ambiguity about who is responsible for triaging key functions and who should be consulted and informed. Too frequently, however, the accountability for vendor management activities is placed on a back-office accounting function, and the line-of-business departments that request third-party services exit the process after identifying their required services. The risk factors noted above may go unidentified in these circumstances, presenting various risks to the organization. Good vendor management requires collaboration, open communication, and tactical excellence to identify, categorize, appropriately onboard, and manage third-party relationships.

While most of the attention related to vendor management occurs during the onboarding process, that is only where the real work begins. Establish a stewardship program for those vendors that are especially germane to your privacy program. Meet with your counterparts with these vendors and evaluate their privacy and data governance activities. Find ways to look for collaboration, enhanced monitoring, and mutual identification of privacy risks that could surface during the engagement. Collaborate on DPIAs or PIAs as the case may warrant. Don't adopt an adversarial posture with vendors. Vendor bashing is counter-productive and only engenders distrust and conflict. Instead, where appropriate, spend time to have open, honest, and standardized reviews of services with both parties focused on improving services over the term of the engagement. As part of these stewardship reviews, evaluate the nature and extent of the service provider's service providers. These subservice relationships can be fraught with risk and should be evaluated appropriately. Given that these activities require commitment and time, the privacy leader will need to focus on the most material relationships. To help scale these stewardship reviews with other vendors and data processors, create a basic stewardship review checklist and establish training related to the same with other members of your extended team.

As part of the stewardship reviews, validate disclosure and notification requirements. Ensure that points of contact between and among the organizations, akin to an "authorized personnel and emergency contact" (APEC) list, are accurate and complete. You and the vendor's counterpart should know who will be contacted should issues arise. There may be escalation matrices for sensitive issues such as data breaches or service interruptions for certain services. Validate these for the cadence of communications and the recipients of these escalations.

There may also be legal requirements for certain disclosures, notably with security incidents and data breaches. These legal requirements should be captured in the service agreement between the two entities (effectively, incident and breach notification clauses). These obligations should be thought of expansively to include independent contractors, third parties and data processors, as well as cloud service providers, notably IaaS and SaaS providers. Vendor disclosure requirements (inclusive of their contractors) should be consistent with the contracting entity's regulatory requirements or contractual obligations. Stated differently, if the contracting entity has an obligation to notify the data protection authority within 72 hours (think Article 33 of the GDPR), its vendors (data processors) should not have disclosure requirements in their service agreements (data processing agreements) that extend beyond that period. Disclosure requirements should be inventoried, verified, and reviewed procedurally as part of the stewardship activities mentioned above.

For particularly sensitive services, the privacy leader should engage the security team to draft data flow diagrams that show how personal data moves from one entity to the other—and, where possible, capture detail as to how that vendor uses that data and its specific data flows. The data flow diagram should indicate trust boundaries, system interfaces, data sinks (storage), and the locations for the same. These locations may cross international borders or jurisdictional boundaries. Data mapping exercises that capture detail in data flow diagrams can be reviewed with your counterpart at the service provider to validate your understanding. The security team should also evaluate if application programming interfaces (APIs) are used to move information from one system to another. APIs that are not appropriately reviewed and evaluated for privacy risks can represent a source of risk that is commonly overlooked.

Ultimately, vendor risk management is a whole-of-enterprise effort. Effective vendor management requires collaboration not only internally with stakeholders across departments and functions within the organization but also with your counterparts for those vendors that are material to your privacy program. Vendor evaluation and vendor stewardship should be a top priority for all privacy leaders. The time spent with these activities will ultimately underpin your privacy program.

Key Insights and Recommended Next Steps

Key Insights

- Every organization, large or small, relies on various third parties that have special expertise or can simply relieve them of operational burden.
- Where those third parties assist in collecting, processing, using, and storing personal information, companies must exercise additional diligence in the selection and management of these third parties.
- Various regulations impose different requirements depending on the nature of the third-party relationship and the type of data. Therefore, it is imperative to classify these third-party relationships correctly.
- Given the number of third-party relationships large firms must manage, well-defined governance processes are essential, and automation is desirable.
- To properly share accountability with the third parties you employ, you must validate the contract language and perform your due diligence before the relationship begins.

Recommended Next Steps

- Work with your stakeholders to identify the third parties that are material to fulfilling your privacy obligations. Knowing the business and the vendors used by different departments and stakeholders will help discover material service providers who process personal data.
- Review the types of data, the contract language, and the data protections that are in place for that third party. Rate any deficiencies in your privacy risk register and ensure you have adequate corporate visibility of the associated risks.
- Create a gap assessment and action plan to close the gaps you recorded. Collaborate with material providers to establish a governance model that ensures that requisite privacy controls are reliably delivered.

Chapter 11

Reasonable Security

Introduction

Uncertainty is unsettling. To validate that the Apollo lunar modules could execute a soft landing on the moon's surface, NASA, the U.S. space agency, launched seven Surveyor missions between 1966 and 1968. Five succeeded, two failed. Based on the results, NASA knew it could be done, but it was by no means certain.

Soft landings on the lunar surface were not the only tests conducted. Among others, NASA did several flybys to validate that the landing site's surface was relatively free of RADAR obstructions and scheduled ten Apollo launches before Apollo 11 to eliminate as much uncertainty as possible before sending humans to walk on the moon.

"Reasonable security" is a subjective term. Without clear guidance, we may be uncertain what reasonable security looks like. And that, too, is unsettling. Failing to provide reasonable data protections opens the company to potential findings of negligence in the case of a data breach. Beyond the potential monetary impact of fines and plaintiff awards, the independent judgment of a court or regulatory body that the company failed to provide reasonable security could cause customers and potential customers to make other choices. Absent that, you still failed to protect their data from a breach.

In Chapter 11, "Reasonable Security," we will provide some of that guidance. In "Reasonable Security—Not Just the Minimum Required," David points out that regulatory bodies have struggled to define exactly what reasonable security means as well. He makes the case that whatever the minimum per any specific regulation, the objective is to protect the customer's personal data. To do that, work with your security team to ensure that the security standard they chose as best suited to your firm extends to protect the data covered by your privacy program.

Justine unpacks decades of precedent and provides insights into various courts' thinking regarding what would be considered reasonable. Her essay, "Reasonable Security—What the Courts and Regulators Say," grounds us in case law and shows how regulators have begun to clear up the uncertainties around the expectation of reasonable security.

In Matt's essay, "A Holistic Approach to Reasonable Security," he looks at the key elements of the security function and breaks down the requirements for each layer in the technology stack. While privacy leaders are not expected to be security experts, his essay provides a roadmap for those faced with assessing an immature program or helping to shore up a program that has recently been under fire. In addition, he provides checklists for each layer that you can use to drive a thorough review of the security program.

Reasonable Security—Not Just the Minimum Required ~ David

Following the conclusions in the last chapter, let's consider what might happen if something were to go wrong—there is a severe data leak or breach, and sensitive personal data is compromised. The worst-case scenario is that your company is deemed to be at fault. Then, when you or one of your senior executives appear in court or before a tribunal, you are going to be asked, "Please explain what reasonable security measures you took to protect your data sources."

If you are unfamiliar with the regulation (or before reading this chapter), you might scratch your head and ponder about what constitutes reasonable or appropriate security. You may as well be asked, "How long is a piece of string?" You can make it as long as you can possibly imagine, but to be a reasonable length at some point it needs to be cut.

As we have observed before, it is virtually impossible to guarantee full protection against a cyberattack. And it's just as improbable that you will be able to successfully prevent data breaches from occurring due to leakages resulting from human error. Human beings are fallible, and mistakes happen. So what can you realistically expect to do?

Most of the well-known data protection regulations refer to reasonable security without clarifying what they mean, leaving it to cybersecurity and privacy professionals to come to a broad agreement on what it should encompass. And the good news is that the key elements of what constitutes "reasonable" or "appropriate" security are reasonably well understood and agreed upon, at least as far as meeting your legal responsibilities are concerned.

Further good news is that if you have followed the thread from the preceding chapters, you will at least know what you're expected to secure, where personal data is located and how it's classified. So that's a great start.

Appropriate Security

For example, Article 32 states:

> Taking into account the state of the art, the costs of implementation and the nature, scope, context and purposes of processing as well as the risk of varying likelihood and severity for the rights and freedoms of natural persons, the controller and the processor shall implement appropriate technical and organisational measures to ensure a level of security appropriate to the risk, ...

Despite the vagaries of this statement, the recital tries to help us understand what to do by continuing:

> ... including inter alia as **appropriate**:

And proceeds to enumerate four different approaches that could be taken. However, none of the tips provided are straightforward and it's not 100% clear how to execute them in most organizational environments. The article goes on to explain further:

> In assessing the **appropriate** level of security account shall be taken in particular of the risks that are presented by processing, in particular from accidental or unlawful destruction, loss, alteration, unauthorised disclosure of, or access to personal data transmitted, stored or otherwise processed.

The word **appropriate** is used judiciously four times, suggesting that it is up to your privacy and security leads to figure out what it might mean in any particular context.

Hence, it could be said that appropriate security, to use the language of the GDPR, is subjective but nevertheless has to be dealt with objectively in order to get the right balance between corporate security and privacy to ensure the rights of individuals, with the priority clearly being the latter. Hence, despite the possible temptation, appropriate security should not just be interpreted as 'minimum security' – the objective is to protect individuals' personal data that you are responsible for. The crunch comes when there is a data breach and having to justify your processes and preparations in court.

In addition, the growth in the number of intelligent and Internet-connected devices together with the emergence of 5G are introducing new data-driven and increasingly autonomous scenarios. For enterprises, that includes surveillance cameras as well as personal objects and devices that hackers could attack to gain further access into your network, systems and other vital resources.

In Europe, guidance and insights beyond the GDPR itself are offered by ENISA[92] and the UK's National Cyber Security Centre (NCSC),[93] but at the confluence of privacy and security we are looking at a moving target.

Reasonableness

Consequently, privacy professionals the world over have sought to dot the 'i's and cross the 't's to provide a level of detail about security measures their organization can realistically implement. Given the plethora of optional routes to take, ultimately your security experts should be best placed to ascertain which measures are ideally suited to manage your company's identified risks and ensure you uphold the rights enshrined in the legislation pertaining to your location and vertical sector. From a non-technical perspective, the best way to get to grips with the nitty-gritty is to take a deep breath and seek to interpret the spirit of the legislation you're trying to comply with, irrespective of whether it's the GDPR, CCPA, HIPAA, GLBA, or any other.

It is also reasonable to be realistic about how far any security expert's recommendations will impress a CIO or CISO who may well have a competing set of priorities, and what impact that will have on what is ultimately implemented. Overcoming significant differences of opinion, particularly when they are probably well-founded and based

---

[92] Despite being aimed at SMEs, the most useful of ENISA's publications on this topic is its 'Handbook on Security of Personal Data Processing' (https://www.enisa.europa.eu/publications/handbook-on-security-of-personal-data-processing).

[93] GDPR security outcomes (https://www.ncsc.gov.uk/guidance/gdpr-security-outcomes) as well as more general advice on cybersecurity essentials (https://www.ncsc.gov.uk/information/GDPR).

on other expert findings, adds a whole new dimension to the challenge.

Finding Motivation

But regulatory compliance should not necessarily be your only motivation for implementing good privacy-preserving security. For example, it may turn out in the case of a data breach that you actually satisfy a court that you met the legal requirements on the grounds of reasonable security. Nevertheless, the loss of your customers' data would have a severely detrimental impact on your company's reputation and the consumer-perceived safety of associating with your much treasured and protected brand. By understanding the bigger set of problems you're trying to solve, you'll get a decent measure of what is and what isn't important.

For example, it clearly makes sense to encrypt and redact all personal data to limit the exposure of sensitive data in applications. However, the procedures required are often inconvenient, cumbersome, and difficult to implement, particularly email encryption in a busy work environment where response speed and agility are demanded or simply part of company culture. Nevertheless, malware or phishing attacks cause most data breaches. At the very least, you should have an active enforceable password management program that ensures that passwords are changed frequently and are strength-based, and that separate passwords are used for different systems. Imposing lockouts after a set number of unsuccessful login attempts or notifying users of suspicious activity may not be popular, but frankly it is necessary.

Although we're primarily concerned with digital assets, most companies still maintain a hoard of physical documentation, which also needs to be properly secured, preferably in a locked room with limited and closely monitored access. Any sensitive personal information in hard copy sitting anywhere in an open office, from the mail room to the CEO's suite, is a potential liability.

For both physical and digital information, it is good housekeeping and a requirement of the GDPR to delete data that is no longer required. Once data has been collected, classified, and stored, the tendency is to forget what you've got and, most probably, why it's there. Retaining out-of-date data is a potential liability because it costs money to store, increases your risk exposure, and the information itself becomes unreliable, which can be challenged by the individual or individuals about whom it relates. On the other hand, there are situations where information does need to be retained for a long time—for example, if it is required by law or ongoing litigation. In addition, the GDPR provides individuals with the "right to be forgotten," in which case you will have no choice.

Another area that needs attention is your network, the front door to all that you hold precious. Most large- or medium-size businesses should already have in place a firewall, a web application firewall, some means of segregating access to most database systems, and a prompt and thorough process of patching all software (and hardware) system updates. For employees, suppliers, and customers—in other words, anyone who is entitled to access the network—it is vital to insist on having at least two-factor authentication and the installation of the best version of anti-virus software available. This is particularly important if they are using their own devices or connecting to the network off-campus.

This is going to be an increasingly prevalent occurrence in the post–COVID-19 era. Having a well-maintained, up-to-the-minute record of who has access entitlements across the network, applications, and databases is another major priority, along with a strict onboarding and, even more importantly, off-boarding regimen for employees. Role-based access systems have a lot of merit in determining the type of person who should have access to a set of assets. Still, they do have to be rigorously watched, such as when people change jobs or leave the company and the role assigned to them passes to someone else.

Listen

For large organizations, the risk assessments available in the ISO 27000 series or from NIST will provide suitable guidance on what a minimum level of network cybersecurity should be for your business. However, this may be a bridge too far for SMEs. But all is not lost—

there is plenty of help out there if you are prepared to seek it out. In all cases, what you are getting at best is guidance and a direction of travel.

If you experience a cyberattack, irrespective of whether it's from a so-called rogue nation, a criminal gang, a well-directed bot, or a nerdy teenager, there is likely to be a well-considered purpose behind the malevolence. The chances are that, in most cases, there will be the expectation of either financial reward or a desire to cause chaos and disruption.

Picture yourself as an insurance broker, looking to assess the damage an attacker could create to price a premium against a cyberattack. Or better still, imagine yourself as the bad actor, with inside knowledge of what could be and what probably wouldn't be valuable if they fell into the wrong hands. Or if your IT infrastructure was threatened with demolition, what would you pull from the impending crash site if you were given, say, half an hour's notice? These questions should not be addressed in the half-hour or so after an actual cyberattack. Why not start now? Confronting these potential eventualities and addressing them head-on while you're taking a shower or having a quiet coffee break is far better than leaving them to when you are also frantically searching for stress-relief medication. Prevention is better than cure.

If that seems too intimidating a prospect, you could do worse than seek out a "white hat" or ethical computer hacker who is a computer security expert specializing in addressing the security of information systems more or less from the perspective of a would-be hacker.

Finally, after a data breach, the last thing you would want to face are the administrators of your company's many data fiefdoms complaining that they could have warned you that "something like this" was bound to happen because the company hadn't listened to them and carried out X, Y, or Z set of reasonable security measures. Even though they may have line responsibilities to the CISO or DPO, their ground-level opinions may not always get expressed in the right meetings. These voices of experience often go unheard. So, go listen to what they might have to say. At worst, you may not learn anything you didn't already know. At best, you could be saving your company a fortune. That would be reasonable.

Reasonable Security—What the Courts and Regulators Say ~ Justine

How Cases Define "Reasonable" and "Negligence"

"Reasonableness" first appeared in case law in 1837. The "reasonable person" concept was a standard instruction to the jury to help decide whether the defendant in the case acted negligently. Negligence is the cause of action that gives rise to liability and damages.

Vaughan v. Menlove (1837) 132 ER 490 (CP)[94] is an English case that first introduced the concept of the reasonable person standard to determine whether a defendant was negligent for starting a fire. In *Menlove*, the defendant had stacked his hay in a way that was likely to catch on fire. His neighbors repeatedly warned him about the danger, and he said he would "chance it." Five weeks later, the hay ignited and burned the defendant's barns and then spread to the plaintiff's property, burning down the cottages. *Menlove's* attorney admitted his client did not have "the highest order of intelligence" and argued that negligence exists only if the jury decided *Menlove* had not acted "to the best of his [own] judgment." The court rejected the defendants' argument and held that the standard for negligence is objective. One behaves negligently if they act in a way contrary to how a *reasonably prudent person* would have acted under similar circumstances. The standard holds that each person owes a duty to behave as a reasonable person would under the same or similar circumstances—even if they weren't born with the highest order of intelligence. The *Menlove* court explained why it was necessary to apply the reasonable standard objectively:

> The care taken by a prudent man has always been the rule laid down; and as to the supposed difficulty of applying it, a jury has always been able to say, whether, taking that rule as their guide, there has been negligence on the occasion in question. . . [T]herefore, saying that the liability for negligence should be co-extensive with the judgment of each individual, would be as

---

[94] Vaughn v. Menlove— "The unreasonable Hay Stacker," Harvard Law School (Innovation Lab), https://h2o.law.harvard.edu/collages/4855.

variable as the length of the foot of each individual, we ought rather to adhere to the rule which requires in all cases a regard to caution such as a man of ordinary prudence would observe.

This case rejects the argument that a defendant's particular sensibilities or weaknesses should be considered when evaluating negligence claims. Instead, one must look only to whether the person was reasonable under similar circumstances of an ordinary person. This early case illustrates the difficulty of deploying reasonable security that a court of law will deem sufficient.

Twenty years later, in *Blyth v. Company Proprietors of the Birmingham Water Works,* English courts once again discussed reasonableness juxtaposed to negligence:

> Negligence is the omission to do something which a reasonable man, guided upon those considerations which ordinarily regulate the conduct of human affairs, would do, or doing something which a prudent and reasonable man would not do.

Data breach laws require companies to protect consumer data by implementing "reasonable" security measures. However, determining what is *reasonable* is a moving target due to many factors, including complex attacks deployed by nation-state actors, evolving technologies, and the inherent insecurity in our supply chain. In other words, if the hay in *Menlove* were actually a server, and the FBI and news article had repeatedly told the CISO that the server was vulnerable, and the CISO said "I will take my chances," the result would be clear: the business did not act reasonably and was therefore liable for the damage caused by the attack. In addition, the amount of information readily available about threats and vulnerabilities (whether read by InfoSec professionals or not) creates both actual and imputed knowledge to the enterprise.

So can a business that suffers a breach prove that it did employ reasonable security practices and acted as a reasonably prudent business? I think the answer is yes, so long as the business documents its "reasonableness" in a defensible manner. For example, conducting vendor assessments and diligence to ensure the third parties and businesses that host your data are also secure. Or having an independent third party conduct an annual security audit. Or implementing reasonable security assessments to justify action (or, more importantly, inaction) to implement a particular safeguard. Finally, improving vulnerabilities discovered during the audit, or at least documenting why the expense associated with the improvement is too tremendous and working it into a longer-term plan.

FTC Enforces Reasonable Security

The Federal Trade Commission is a federal agency responsible for protecting consumers. The FTC focuses on deceptive and unfair business practices through law enforcement. The FTC is a complaint-driven agency and responds to consumer complaints, such as if a business breached a consumer's data or failed to secure data reasonably. The FTC is not an auditor and is not the type of regulator that requires reporting obligations or notice of a data breach.

The FTC's enforcement actions contain helpful guidance about what the FTC considers *is* and *is not* reasonable security. Until recently, "reasonableness" was the heart of FTC enforcement actions. However, in 2019, the FTC's data security orders quietly stopped including the word "reasonable." Although the FTC has given no reason, it may have something to do with improving specificity in FTC guidance.

The Basics According to the FTC

Although the FTC does not clearly define "reasonable security," it provides guidance (and a Guide with lessons learned from FTC enforcement actions on its website[95]) regarding cybersecurity basics to secure business data. Failure to adhere to the basics could result in an adverse enforcement action from the FTC if PII is compromised:

- Control access to data sensibly.
- Require secure passwords and authentication.

---

[95] Start with Security: A Guide for Business, Federal Trade commission, https://www.ftc.gov/business-guidance/resources/start-security-guide-business

- Store sensitive personal information securely and protect it during transmission.
- Segment your network and monitor who's trying to get in and out.
- Secure remote access to your network.
- Apply sound security practices when developing new products.
- Make sure your service providers implement reasonable security measures.
- Put procedures in place to keep your security current and address vulnerabilities that may arise.
- Secure paper, physical media, and devices.[96]

The FTC Security Guide provides additional guidance and details about how to reasonably secure data according to the FTC. Unreasonable security measures can subject a company to millions of dollars in FTC fines and legal fees.

True Happiness Is When What You Think, Say, and Do Are in Harmony

The FTC takes the position that affirmatively stating in your privacy policy that a business has "reasonable" security measures can form the basis for a claim of deceptive practices under the FTC Act if the data was not actually secure. *See Federal Trade Commission v. Wyndham Worldwide Corporation*, et al. 2:13-cv-01887, D.N.J. (2012).[97] In other words, if a company is the victim of a data breach *and* their privacy policy states they implement reasonable security measures, then they could face an enforcement action from the FTC for unfair or deceptive business practices.

The FTC sued Wyndham, alleging that data security failures led to three data breaches in less than two years at Wyndham hotels.

---

[96] "Start with Security: A Guide for business. Lessons learned from FTC cases." https://www.ftc.gov/system/files/documents/plain-language/pdf0205-startwithsecurity.pdf.

[97] https://www.ftc.gov/system/files/documents/cases/140407wyndhamopinion.pdf.

According to the complaint, those failures resulted in millions of dollars of fraudulent charges on consumers' credit and debit cards. In 2015, the Third Circuit Court of Appeals agreed that the FTC could pursue Wyndham for failing to secure data under the deceptive practices rule—which created regulatory risk for businesses that made statements in their privacy policy about reasonable security that businesses practices or documentation may not support.

Demonstrable evidence must support any representation a company makes to consumers concerning a product's security. Under the FTC Act, companies will be responsible for any express or implied representation made to consumers. Consequently, companies should consider whether any statement or depiction included in any marketing materials, packaging, social media posts, privacy policies, or in any other company content would be understood by a consumer, acting reasonably under the circumstance, to constitute a promise or representation regarding the product's security. If so, such statements or depictions must meet truth-in-advertising standards.

So why include any statements at all in your privacy policy about reasonable security practices? In the absence of an express legal requirement, a business should not make affirmative statements about the reasonableness of the safeguards taken to secure consumer data. However, certain laws do require affirmative statements to consumers about security and in those cases, include a statement. For example, GLBA requires disclosure to consumers of policies and procedures regarding protecting the confidentiality and security of non-public information in privacy notices. 12 C.F.R. § 1016.6.

Life Is Short: Learn from Ashley Madison

The case of Life Inc. ("Ruby Corp.," owner of the AshleyMadison.com website), which settled in December 2016, involved a data breach that exposed the profile information of 36 million of the site's users. Ashley Madison was an online cheating site breached by a group of hacktivists named the Impact Team. Ashley Madison charged customers that no longer wanted to be associated with the site **$35 per person** to delete their profile information. However, the Impact Team discovered that rather than deleting these profiles, Ashley Madison moved the profile data from their active site into an unsecured database that was easy to exploit. The Impact Team claimed to have stolen more than 300 GB of data and warned the company to shut down their site or else they would post the data. In August 2015, the Impact Team leaked millions of Ashley Madison's users' email addresses and damaging emails from the CEO's account. The FTC's complaint stated that, despite claims that the website was "100% secure," "risk-free," and "completely anonymous," the company "engaged in several practices that, taken together, failed to provide reasonable security to prevent unauthorized access to personal information on their network." The complaint concluded that "[i]n truth and in fact ... [Ruby] did not take reasonable steps to ensure that AshleyMadison.com was secure."

The Stakes Are High: Private Right of Action for Failing to Reasonably Secure Data

"Reasonable security" is a legal requirement born in California in 2003 that has since grown globally. California was the first state in the United States to pass a law that imposed obligations on a business to "reasonably secure" Personally Identifiable Information ("PII"). If PII was breached, the business must comply with certain notice and reporting obligations. Initially, there were no statutory damages or civil penalties for failure to reasonably secure PII. Therefore, courts often dismissed class action lawsuits for data breaches because of failure to prove damages, which was an essential element of the negligence cause of action.

With the passage of CCPA and CPRA, individuals now have a statutory right to bring claims against businesses for the failure to "reasonably secure" data. California uniquely allows a consumer to sue a business if certain data is compromised. A private right of action in California Civil Code Section 1798.150 is based on a business violating its "duty to implement and maintain reasonable security procedures and practices." Failure to implement reasonable security procedures and practices puts businesses at risk of statutory damages ranging from $100 to $750 per person per incident and penalties ranging from $2,500 to $7,500 per violation.

Moreover, CCPA and CPRA vastly expand the scope of data that must be "reasonably secure." For example, Section 1798.100(e) directs any business that collects a consumer's personal information to "implement reasonable security procedures and practices appropriate to the nature of the personal information to protect the personal information from unauthorized or illegal access, destruction, use, modification, or disclosure." Previously, only PII was subject to reasonable security requirements under California law. These new provisions significantly expand the need to implement reasonable security across previously unregulated data. For example, data collected by a business about a consumer when interacting with its website is now arguably subject to a reasonable security requirement. Notwithstanding the expansion of the data types that must be reasonably secured, statutory damages only apply to traditional PII that includes more sensitive data elements like SSN, government-issued ID, health information, and insurance information.

State Attorney General Regulatory Risk

In 2012 and 2016, the California Attorney General's office published a "Data Breach Report," which analyzed the historical data it collected about data breaches impacting California residents.[98] The California Attorney General had access to this data because the laws require notice to the California Attorney General if a data breach impacts more than 500 Californians. The 2016 breach report listed safeguards that were "reasonable security practices," at that time emphasizing a set of twenty data security controls published by the Center for Internet Security as the universal baseline for any information security program. The Breach Report is clear: Failure to implement all 20 controls from the Center for Internet Security's Critical Security Controls (formerly the "SANS Top 20") that apply to an organization's environment "constitutes a lack of reasonable security."[99] The Breach Report goes on to recommend multi-factor

---

[98] California Data Breach Report, February 2016, Kamala D. Harris, Attorney General, California Department of Justice, https://oag.ca.gov/sites/all/files/agweb/pdfs/dbr/2016-data-breach-report.pdf.

[99] CIS Critical Security controls: https://www.cisecurity.org/controls.

authentication, data minimization, and encryption as "reasonable security measures."

California IoT Laws

Privacy laws are not the only laws that require "reasonable security." California's Internet of Things law[100] requires manufacturers of devices that connect to the internet to equip the devices with "reasonable security features" that deter unauthorized access and protect user privacy. The law does not clearly define that term but gives some safe harbors and examples.

Future of Reasonable Security

The velocity at which we are collecting data and evolving technology in combination with the exploitation of our supply chain makes "reasonable security" a moving target precariously positioned on a slippery slope. Reasonable security practices will depend on the circumstances and whether a business's decisions were sound in hindsight. Documentation of a reasoned decision will give evidence to the trier of fact that shows the business considered the risk and options and, for legitimate business reasons, may not have implemented a solution.

The law is like the slow-moving tortoise, and the technology and adversaries are the hares. Laws are hesitant to clearly define what it means to act reasonably because (1) the legislators are not cybersecurity experts, and (2) by the time the law is published, the technology has changed so dramatically the law is outdated. However, some states have recognized that being too vague also does not serve security interests. At least two states have tried to articulate how to create a reasonable security program.

---

[100] Civil code section 1798.91.04, https://leginfo.legislature.ca.gov/faces/billTextClient.xhtml?bill_id=201720180SB327.

Massachusetts' Written Comprehensive Information Security Program

Massachusetts was the first state in the United States to require a written information security program. In 2010, Massachusetts required every business that owns or licenses personal information about one or more of its residents to develop and implement a written information security program that includes administrative, technical, and physical safeguards.[101] Massachusetts law describes the bare minimum for the comprehensive information security program as follows:

- Designating one or more employees to maintain the comprehensive information security program.

- Identifying and assessing reasonably foreseeable internal and external risks to the security, confidentiality, and/or integrity of any electronic, paper or other records containing personal information, and evaluating and improving, where necessary, the effectiveness of the current safeguards for limiting such risks, including but not limited to:

    o ongoing employee (including temporary and contract employee) training;
    o employee compliance with policies and procedures; and
    o means for detecting and preventing security system failures.

- Developing security policies for employees relating to the storage, access and transportation of records containing personal information outside of business premises.

- Imposing disciplinary measures for violations of the comprehensive information security program rules.

---

[101] Standards For the Protection of Personal Information of Residents of the Commonwealth, https://www.mass.gov/doc/201-cmr-17-standards-for-the-protection-of-personal-information-of-residents-of-the/download.

- Preventing terminated employees from accessing records containing personal information.

- Oversee service providers, by:

    o Taking reasonable steps to select and retain third-party service providers that are capable of maintaining appropriate security measures to protect such personal information consistent with these regulations and any applicable federal regulations; and

    o Requiring such third-party service providers by contract to implement and maintain such appropriate security measures for personal information; provided, however, that until March 1, 2012, a contract a person has entered into with a third party service provider to perform services for said person or functions on said person's behalf satisfies the provisions of 17.03(2)(f)(2) even if the contract does not include a requirement that the third party service provider maintain such appropriate safeguards, as long as said person entered into the contract no later than March 1, 2010.

- Reasonable restrictions upon physical access to records containing personal information, and storage of such records and data in locked facilities, storage areas or containers.

- Regular monitoring to ensure that the comprehensive information security program is operating in a manner reasonably calculated to prevent unauthorized access to or unauthorized use of personal information; and upgrading information safeguards as necessary to limit risks.

- Reviewing the scope of the security measures at least annually or whenever there is a material change in business practices that may reasonably implicate the security or integrity of records containing personal information.

- Documenting responsive actions taken in connection with any incident involving a breach of security, and mandatory post-incident review of events and actions taken, if any, to make changes in business practices relating to protection of personal information.

Massachusetts also includes technical requirements for the program:

- Secure user authentication protocols including:

  o control of user I.D.s and other identifiers;
  o a reasonably secure method of assigning and selecting passwords, or use of unique identifier technologies, such as biometrics or token devices;
  o control of data security passwords to ensure that such passwords are kept in a location and/or format that does not compromise the security of the data they protect;
  o restricting access to active users and active user accounts only; and
  o blocking access to user identification after multiple unsuccessful attempts to gain access or the limitation placed on access for the particular system;

- Secure access control measures that:

  o restrict access to records and files containing personal information to those who need such information to perform their job duties; and
  o assign unique identifications plus passwords, which are not vendor supplied default passwords, to each person with computer access, that are reasonably designed to maintain the integrity of the security of the access controls;

- Encryption of all transmitted records and files containing personal information that will travel across public networks, and encryption of all data containing personal information to be transmitted wirelessly.

- Reasonable monitoring of systems, for unauthorized use of or access to personal information.

- Encryption of all personal information stored on laptops or other portable devices.

- For files containing personal information on a system that is connected to the internet, there must be reasonably up-to-date firewall protection and operating system security patches, reasonably designed to maintain the integrity of the personal information.

- Reasonably up-to-date versions of system security agent software which must include malware protection and reasonably up-to-date patches and virus definitions, or a version of such software that can still be supported with up-to-date patches and virus definitions and is set to receive the most current security updates on a regular basis.

- Education and training of employees on the proper use of the computer security system and the importance of personal information security.

Yielding the Sword Under New York's SHIELD Act

Nearly ten years after Massachusetts' law took effect, New York created a set of reasonable security requirements. To provide incentive for action, if a business implements the provisions, then it is deemed to comply with the reasonable security requirements under the SHIELD Act.

On March 21, 2020, the data security provisions of New York's Stop Hacks and Improve Electronic Data Security Act ("SHIELD Act") went into effect. The SHIELD Act requires any person or business owning or licensing computerized data that includes the private information of a resident of New York ("covered business") to implement and maintain reasonable safeguards to protect the security, confidentiality, and integrity of the private information.

A covered business is deemed to comply with the SHIELD Act's data security requirement if the business implements a data security program that includes reasonable administrative, technical, and physical safeguards, such as:

- Reasonable administrative safeguards: (1) designating one or more employees to coordinate the security program; (2) identifying reasonably foreseeable internal and external risks; (3) assessing the sufficiency of safeguards in place to control the identified risks; (4) training and managing employees in the security program practices and procedures; (5) selecting service providers capable of maintaining appropriate safeguards, and requiring those safeguards by contract; and (6) adjusting the security program in light of business changes or new circumstances.

- Reasonable technical safeguards: (1) assessing risks in network and software design; (2) assessing risks in information processing, transmission and storage; (3) detecting, preventing and responding to attacks or system failures; and (4) regularly testing and monitoring the effectiveness of key controls, systems and procedures.

- Reasonable physical safeguards: (1) assessing risks of information storage and disposal; (2) detecting, preventing and responding to intrusions; (3) protecting against unauthorized access to or use of private information during or after the collection, transportation and destruction or disposal of the information; and (4) disposing of private information within a reasonable amount of time after it is no longer needed for business purposes by erasing electronic media so that the information cannot be read or reconstructed.

Clients often ask what law or regulation is the most important to comply with to be considered "reasonable." As their legal counsel, I usually identify the law that is core to their business operations and creates the most financial, regulatory, or litigation risk. For example, a healthcare entity must comply with HIPAA's Security Rule, or else it risks its ability to submit claims to insurance companies. An e-commerce site must follow PCI DSS regulations, or else it risks its ability to process credit card transactions. Additionally, reputational risk is important, particularly if you are a business that sells security either in the form of goods or services.

While it is important to identify and articulate the most salient risk to the business, many reasonable security practices have common threads that can defend against any law. My recommendation is to follow the New York SHIELD Act. The SHIELD Act is currently the most prescriptive law in the country, and most businesses have some information on New York residents. There is the added bonus that New York will deem your business in compliance with its reasonable security requirements—so in at least one jurisdiction, your security practices are arguably considered "reasonable." This reasonableness argument can transcend jurisdictions by making persuasive arguments that the business was following the most prescriptive laws in the United States.

A Holistic Approach to Reasonable Security ~ Matt

Just what is *reasonable* security? If you are a privacy leader trying to evaluate the reasonableness of your organization's security practices, having reasonable assurance that security practices are appropriate can be a daunting task. The term "reasonable" has implications from a legal as well as from a fiduciary perspective. Many regulations globally are replete with references to required security programs and calls for "reasonable" security practices.

How do we move from regulatory references to concrete validations that the security program is appropriate to the organization's operating environment and its obligations to protect personal data and other forms of valuable information? While it is easy to say that an organization should have reasonable security practices, what this implies and requires is nuanced and detailed.

Let's begin with a definition of reasonable security. Here is the definition I gave while presenting at a *Wall Street Journal* event where my co-author, Justine, and I spoke on this topic:[102]

> Reasonable security is that level of security capability that meets the organization's agreed-to risk tolerances while fulfilling regulatory requirements and the contractual obligations of the organization.

While this definition works at a conceptual level, it does not adequately inform some of the requisite elements of the organization's security program. The devil is in the details. It also doesn't address the detailed administrative and technical controls that should be implemented across the organization's IT infrastructure, applications, and systems. As the reference above notes, there is also the critical role of contextualizing the security program to its operating environment and risk tolerances. Figure 11.1 below provides a model to help contextualize the numerous factors that, in the aggregate, influence how an organization's

---

[102] The presentation that Justine and I gave on reasonable security can be seen here: https://vimeo.com/416462336.

security program will be related to the organization's operating environment.

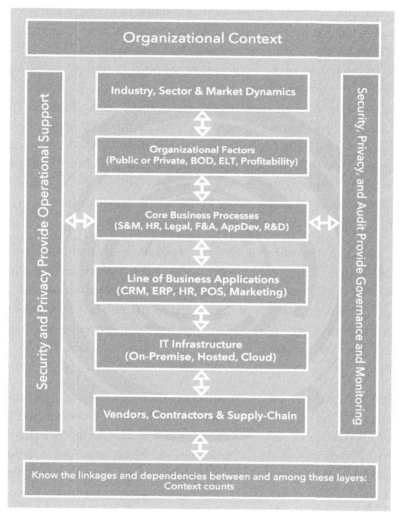

Figure 11.1 Organizational Context

Knowing an organization's operational context is critical to reasonable security. As shown in Figure 11.1, the sector, industry, and market in which an organization operates will inform which regulations are in scope, the type of customers the organization will serve, and other important dynamics. Businesses focused on selling their goods and services to other businesses will have notably different privacy and security programs than those focused on consumers.

Beyond these external market factors, internal to the organization are its corporate culture and other internal dynamics, including whether the organization has an independent board of directors, the qualities and competencies of the C-suite, how the organization is funded, and whether the organization is growing or contracting. Core business functions, including operations, marketing, sales, finance and accounting, and human resources, may have nuanced requirements related to security and privacy. It's critical to understand the unique attributes of different organizational functions and departments, including their unique applications. These line-of-business applications and the underlying IT infrastructure that supports them are integral reference points to reasonable security.

As noted in the previous chapter, vendors and other third-party relationships will profoundly impact security and privacy activities. None of these layers exist in a vacuum. Each layer is influenced by the dynamics and factors of the others. As the pillars on the left and right—monitoring, governance, privacy, and security—illustrate, their roles are pervasive. For each topic, there is a critical role for security.

Let's unpack some of the constituent parts of a reasonable security program. First and foremost, there are higher-level security activities that must occur to pass the "red face" test and avoid the "we should have thought about that" moment when issues arise. We'll group these functions into core security administrative activities. Separately, I want to highlight more nuanced security requirements based on the technology stack or layers associated with a particular environment, service, process, or application.

The Socratic method offers a simple yet elegant approach to addressing reasonable security requirements and can be summed up in the following questions: "What is it that we don't know that we should know about our organization's security practices and capabilities, and how could this impact our organization's security and privacy obligations?" Questions are at the heart of security.

Another seminal question to keep top of mind is "What is it that we don't see that we should see, and how does that influence the levels of assurance we have over our security practices?" Keep these basic questions in mind as we look at core security functions. For those of us who have worked in security, there is a strong tendency to be paranoid that culminates in "What questions didn't I ask that I should have asked, and what are going to be the consequences for not digging in deeper?" As a privacy leader, you must invest the time to be security-conversant and knowledgeable about these requisite elements of a reasonable security program. The items below should be front-and-center as you evaluate your organization's security program.

Risk Analysis

Risk management is at the heart of organizational governance and is the cornerstone of security program development. Organizations confront infinite risk with finite resources. Not all risks are material, nor do all risks have a high probability of occurring. Reasonable security should anticipate which risks the organization will likely confront and document the organization's risk treatment strategy (risks can be mitigated, insured against (transferred), accepted, avoided, or a combination of these strategies, but risks should never be ignored). A simple risk register is a powerful tool to track risks, risk ownership within the organization (i.e., the department or function accountable for keeping the risk within organizationally defined thresholds), and the agreed-to risk treatment strategy culminating in how risks will be accepted. A great question to ask when thinking about risk management is "Which material risks have we not identified, why, and how do we document and manage these risks accordingly?"

Various privacy regulations also require risk assessments to be performed to evaluate reasonably anticipated risks to personal data in various guises. Key regulations include HIPAA-HITECH, GLBA, and clearly the GDPR. Data protection impact assessments (DPIAs) as outlined in Article 35 of the GDPR, require a structured review of processing activities including an assessment to the risks of the 'rights and freedoms' of the data subject. DPIAs are required when the nature and extent of the processing activities are likely to result in a high risk to the privacy rights and freedoms of the data subject. In short, conducting risk assessments is integral to your privacy program.

Access, Credential, and Entitlement Management (Collectively, Access Management)

A foundational element to any reasonable security program is to understand how access to business processes, applications, and IT systems is governed and managed throughout the organization. Three fundamental principles should inform this effort: "need to know," "least privilege," and "separation of duties." Access to systems should be predicated on a documented and legitimate business requirement, and the entitlements provided should be the minimum necessary to support the documented function. Knowing what level of access (e.g., root, admin, local, or basic user) and what that access level entitles the account to do within the system is a key control.

Reasonable security requires that access rights be documented, reviewed (at least annually but ideally quarterly), and adjusted based on common circumstances, such as onboarding a new employee or contractor, the departure of an employee or contractor, or an employee or contractor changing their role within the organization. Access and credential management are where security and corporate governance intersect. Internal controls over financial reporting are founded on key controls, including separation of duties, monitoring changes to entitlements, including privilege escalation within systems, and appropriate audit trails to support attribution (non-repudiation) for material changes to the operating environment. Identity and access management controls have a pervasive impact on security and governance, and the time and resources required to address general access management should not be underestimated.

This domain also encompasses more technical controls, including the use of multi-factor authentication (MFA), the use of secure authentication protocols such as security assertion markup language (SAML) to support single sign-on (SSO), password and password-less approaches to accessing systems, credential monitoring, and insider threat reviews. In short, access management is a specialized and detailed domain. An important question to ask in this regard is the following: "Are our access management activities, resources, and practices sufficient to detect credential compromises, the unauthorized elevation of privileges, the creation of rogue accounts, and the attribution and non-repudiation of material changes to our environment?"

Security Awareness and Training

Most security incidents occur not because of a failure of a technical control, but rather due to an employee or contractor falling victim to a phishing or spear-phishing email that allows the perpetrator to gain access to a system and bypass typical security controls. Generally speaking, employees and contractors want to help when asked. This tendency to respond to inquiries and questions is readily exploited. Be they emails asking employees to update their passwords or complete a questionnaire or phone calls from the "help desk" or other departments, unsuspecting employees inherently trust the legitimacy of these requests, and their willingness to entertain and respond to these requests presents risks.

Security awareness training is vital to reasonable security. Security awareness training is also frequently required in regulations. Good security awareness programs convert susceptible employees and contractors into the first line of defense and an early warning system (forgive the military analogy) to detect and report suspicious and anomalous activity. Given how important security awareness is to minimizing risks, numerous training applications have come to the market that simulate phishing emails, track click-through rates, and provide instructional videos to help employees recognize the telltale signs of nefarious solicitations. Security awareness training goes beyond these elements to also address regulatory and contractual obligations of the firm, including practices to authenticate individuals exercising their privacy rights. Those departments that interact with consumers should be prioritized to ensure that they understand how privacy regulations, notably the privacy rights of their consumer clients, should be addressed. Do not leave these interactions to chance. Ensure that staff is informed and trained on what is appropriate behavior.

Incident Response

Reasonable security requires that organizations document and test incident response plans and procedures. The topic of incident response is addressed in more detail in Chapter 12 and will address data breach requirements. Preparing for a security incident requires a whole-of-enterprise perspective, and incident response should not be viewed as strictly an IT or security matter. Security incidents impact all corners of an organization and can damage an organization's reputation and finances, impact operations, result in regulatory sanctions, and a host of other consequences if security incidents are not anticipated and their risks mitigated proactively. The National Institute of Standards and Technology's (NIST) Special Publication 800-61r2, "Computer Security Incident Handling Guide,"[103] emphasizes the critical role of incident response preparation.

Preparing requires knowing the context of systems, processes, and applications (see Figure 11.1 above), the data these systems process, and the privacy and security obligations associated with these data elements. Dependencies on staff, technology, vendors, and forensic support should be anticipated. Security incidents are enormously distracting and can effectively place the organization's strategy and initiatives on hold as leaders attend to the myriad consequences of the incident. Privacy leaders need to know if their organization's incident response program is adequately documented and tested. Ideally, tabletop exercises to address common security incidents, including compromised credentials, lost or stolen devices, data breaches, ransomware, and other common scenarios, should be prioritized and evaluated at least annually.

---

[103] Consult this reference for more information: https://nvlpubs.nist.gov/nistpubs/specialpublications/nist.sp.800-61r2.pdf.

If key stakeholders across the organization, including members of the executive leadership team, have not reviewed the organization's incident response plan, that is a red flag. The privacy leader should ask, "how prepared is our organization to address a security incident?" If there is any ambiguity regarding the capabilities and response to that basic question, take pause and ensure that incident response practices are prioritized. A quick note of caution related to incident response. Traditionally, business continuity management and disaster recovery preparedness disciplines were separate from security incident response. These disciplines are highly interrelated. We'll touch upon this in Chapter 12.

Patching and Vulnerability Management

IT systems and the applications they support change over time, requiring patches and maintenance. Beyond operating system patches, the firmware of the underlying infrastructure should also be evaluated to determine if it is current and configured correctly. Patching can be laborious and require that critical systems be brought offline to facilitate maintenance. For many organizations that have not designed their systems to be fault-tolerant, operational imperatives tend to trump security hygiene. Patches that do not get deployed timely ultimately become technical debt and put the organization at risk. Reasonable security practices require that patches be implemented as close to their availability as practicable and that the organization scans its applications, operating systems, and other IT infrastructure for vulnerabilities.

The Common Vulnerability Scoring System (CVSS) rates the potential impact, ranging from a score of 0 (no risk) to 9-10 (critical). Patches labeled as "critical" or "security" are labeled as such to highlight their importance. That being said, vulnerabilities that are scored as low or moderate can be "daisy-chained" (effectively combined) to launch successful attacks, so a strategy of ignoring or delaying patches that are labeled low to moderate in terms of their impact is not advisable.

Patching and vulnerability management are foundational to reasonable security practices. The privacy leader should ask "Are there applications or systems that are not being patched frequently, and what would be the implications if these systems were to be compromised?" Not patching all material environments in a timely and complete manner is akin to a CFO or Corporate Controller not reconciling all material financial accounts before completing their financial close.

The activities noted above are requisite components of any reasonable security program. These activities, however, are just the tip of the iceberg as it relates to comprehensive security practices and represent some of the administrative areas of focus that should be evaluated by the privacy leader. Effectively, the privacy leader must understand their organization's competencies and capabilities related to each of those disciplines. Ultimately, what's deemed reasonable will be predicated on the organization's unique operating environment, risk tolerances, regulatory requirements, and contractual obligations.

Let's turn now to the considerations of reasonable security at each layer in the technology stack of a given application or system. Essentially, "what are reasonable security practices in the context of the given technology layer?" The items below are high-level and each area has detailed security practices that the Chief Information Security Officer (CISO) and members of the CISO's team should evaluate both in the design and the operating effectiveness of the controls.

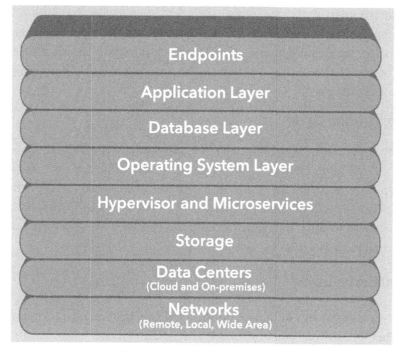

Figure 11.2 Technology Layer Stack

Endpoints and Mobile Devices

Endpoints, including smartphones, are ubiquitous in organizations. Workstations have frequently been replaced with laptops. Employees and contractors use their own mobile devices to access organizational email and other applications containing personal and other forms of sensitive information. Endpoints are frequently lost or stolen and depending upon the security controls associated with the endpoint, the resultant incident may become a data breach (e.g., where a non-encrypted endpoint containing personal data, protected health information, or sensitive personal information is lost). The privacy leader should review the basic endpoint protection capabilities of their organization and ask follow-up questions to help evaluate if reasonable security protections are in place.

Laptops and mobile phones are lost all the time. The organization needs to ensure that its incident response practices consider how these scenarios are addressed. Ideally, where mobile device management tools are employed and the device has full-disk encryption, the impact of a stolen device can be minimized. Least privilege and need to know principles are also critical. Employees and contractors should not be granted more access than is required to conduct their work.

Application Layer

The application layer is arguably the most inherently high-risk layer of a technology stack. Applications contain business logic. Applications also integrate and share information with other applications via manual processes (e.g., downloads, uploads, batch processing), and increasingly through APIs that automate the exchange of information between two or more applications.

Database Layer

Organizations run on data, and we live in an information economy. Whether stored and processed in relational or non-relational databases such as key-value pairs, document-based, column-based, or graph-based, each needs to be adequately secured. Of special note are the communication strings that link or connect an application to its underlying database. Since databases have the proverbial crown jewels—information—for an organization, database security should be a top priority.

Operating System Layer

Applications and databases are installed on operating systems (typically, variants of Windows or Linux). Operating systems should be hardened to remove superfluous systems, processes, and access rights that do not apply to the operating environment at hand. Like endpoints and mobile devices, server operating systems should have rigorous access controls and be patched and updated on a frequent and controlled basis. Operating systems, be they for servers, endpoints, or mobile devices, should have endpoint protection (EPP) and endpoint detection and response (EDR) applications installed (EPP and EDR tools have effectively replaced legacy anti-virus or anti-malware applications).

The point above regarding access rights and privileges associated with the user's role on the operating system cannot be overstated. Significant data breaches generally benefit from overly promiscuous access to systems. While a more specialized area of review, the security leader should validate if there are PowerShell or similar scripts used to access operating system functions and how these are controlled and validated.

Hypervisors and Microservices

As we move further down the stack, operating systems are rarely deployed in a one-to-one relation to the underlying physical server. The advent of virtualization technologies has allowed a single physical server to support multiple "guest" operating systems. The use of hypervisors is pervasive and has been an integral component of the broader development of modern cloud architectures. As a logical extension to hypervisors, container services and other microservices allow for further decoupling of the application from its underlying physical infrastructures. Containers can be readily disposed of, and like hosts in a cluster, support portability of operating systems (and components to the same). End-users generally do not have access to these components, but system administrators and the tools they use do, so these permissions should be evaluated. Although privacy leaders may not have deep technical understanding of these technologies, they should be prepared with specific questions if they sense a lack of thoroughness during initial discussions.

Privacy leaders also need to understand how modern cloud architecture's function, using continuous integration and continuous deployment (CI/CD) methodologies, and ensure the microservices that they consume to deliver applications are secured appropriately. As noted above, application programming interfaces (APIs) at the application layer and web services all have security implications if they are not managed and secured appropriately.

Networks (Remote, Local, and Wide Area)

Historically, the topic of security dealt primarily with network security, notably the use of firewalls to determine who has access to the network and which protocols or services are permitted. While network security remains a critical security function, the focus on end-users and the applications that they use and the data they have access to has resulted in a far more expansive view of security services. Nevertheless, reasonable security must consider how the organization protects and monitors its networks.

Network security remains an integral component of reasonable security practices. Still, with so many organizations using SaaS applications that only require direct internet access, network security and its criticality is changing for many smaller organizations that do not have traditional local area networks (LANs). Users are now more frequently segmented based on their roles or permissions within the application versus the virtual LANS (vLANS) that they have access to. Separately, regardless of whether the application or service is on-premises or delivered via the cloud, how data moves should be documented in data flow diagrams that document trust boundaries between systems and, importantly, how data exfiltrates or exits systems. Egress, notably for systems that contain sensitive information, should be monitored, logged, and analyzed for reasonableness. Large data transfers, access to networks at times of day that are not consistent with normal operations and from improbable locations should be alerted upon, gated, and reviewed. The privacy leader should spend some time with their security counterpart to review core network security practices.

Data Protection and Backups

The data lifecycle—its creation, storage, use, sharing, archiving, and ultimate destruction—should inform requisite security controls at each phase. Where and how data is stored and backed up is essential to know at more than just a high level. This detail should be front-and-center to any reasonable security review. The location of data storage and processing activities (i.e., "use") has jurisdictional implications, as does with whom the organization shares this information. This is why data flow diagrams are necessary. They help us understand where and how information is created or ingested by the organization, identify the business processes, applications, and systems that are used internally, and whether the organization makes data available to third parties. To be complete, they must include data sinks or storage and backup environments.

How data is shared also has critical implications. Include in your review the interfaces between applications or systems and the contracts that may be required (e.g., binding corporate rules, standard contractual clauses, business associates agreements (should PHI be in scope), data protection addendums, and the like). Review data validation controls. Evaluate manual processes such as batch transfers and contact centers that assist individuals who call in to request information. Examine how such manual interactions are authenticated for the legitimacy of the request.

The data lifecycle and the protections and backups that it contemplates should also inform the use of cryptographic services to either encrypt data in transit or at rest. The media upon which data is stored should also be a consideration for the reasonable security review. Media can include devices, endpoints such as mobile phones and laptops, external hard drives (e.g., thumb drives), storage arrays (e.g., network-attached storage (NAS) or storage area network (SAN)), and backup devices that could be either disks or tape and either on-premises or remote. The location of and access to these environments should be well-governed and controlled.

The time that the privacy leader invests in evaluating data protection, storage, and backup environments will be time well spent. Declare war on ambiguity and validate data classification, data protections (e.g., cryptographic services, tokenization, and pseudonymization controls), data labeling, data retention, and configuration details, including capacity information. The adage "inspect what you expect" could not be more germane.

Data Centers

Security is generally considered an amalgam of three key attributes: confidentiality, integrity, and availability (CIA). These core attributes have been extended to include the notions of privacy and safety. As part of a general reasonable security review for the organization, to the extent that it uses internal data centers you should review the availability of data center services. Data centers, notably third-party colocation facilities, may be rated based on their "tier" designation. Tier IV data centers are designed for the highest availability and uptime. Tier III data centers are those that are designed for concurrent maintainability of their heating, ventilation, and air conditioning (HVAC) and power supply systems. Tier II and tier I centers have less redundant capabilities and may have single points of failure regarding their power and HVAC infrastructure. Ideally, the data center's design should reflect the criticality and obligations of the workloads and applications deployed in the data center.

This context should inform the evaluation of reasonable security controls for the organization. Ensuring that risk assessments, security training, patching and vulnerability management, access control reviews, and incident management practices are appropriate requires collaboration between key organizational stakeholders, including the privacy leader, the CISO, the CIO, and counsel. When these stakeholders take proactive measures to evaluate security practices and affect appropriate remediations, reasonable security is attainable. A note of caution: never stop questioning and evaluating the status of your organization's security program. Continue to ask probing and open-ended questions throughout the organization to identify and treat risks. Look for interdependencies between and among layers, examine the role of third parties and service providers, and leverage data flow diagrams to validate these relationships. Never stop asking questions.

Key Insights and Recommended Next Steps

Key Insights

- All companies that hold personal data in trust are expected to implement reasonable data protections to secure that data.
- There is no one-size-fits-all definition of reasonable security, but regulators, including those for Massachusetts and California, are providing some guidance.
- At the end of the day, reasonable is what the courts or regulators decide it is, depending on the facts at hand for the case before them.
- Regardless of precedent or regulator-defined minimum reasonable security, what is reasonable is ultimately what your customers expect.
- The privacy leader's role is to work with the security leader to determine the right approach for the company and work with them to uncover deficiencies and advocate for improvements where needed.

Recommended Next Steps

- Work with your security partners to ensure that the security program meets the requirements for the jurisdictions that apply to your privacy program.
- Create a gap assessment and action plan to close the gaps you recorded. Ensure that these gaps are captured in your risk register.
- Spend extra time to evaluate key security disciplines including the organization's incident response program and how credentials and entitlements are reviewed for appropriateness.

Appendix to Chapter 11 – Security Question Checklists

Application Layer

The application layer is arguably the most inherently high-risk layer of a technology stack. Applications contain the business logic. Applications also integrate and share information with other applications via manual processes (e.g., downloads, uploads, batch processing), and increasingly through application programming interfaces (APIs) that automate the exchange of information between two or more applications. Privacy leaders also need to understand how modern cloud architectures use continuous integration and continuous deployment (CI/CD) methodologies and ensure that the microservices they use to deliver applications are secured. APIs at the application layer and web services all have security implications if they are not managed and secured appropriately. Questions that should be evaluated by the privacy and security leaders include:

- Which business processes does the application support?
- What type of data does the application process?
- Is the application patched and maintained appropriately?
- If this is a SaaS application, does the provider have a SOC 2 Type II audit (or similar) that addresses privacy and security controls?
- How has the application's security been evaluated (e.g., penetration tests, static and dynamic code reviews)?
- How are inputs into the application validated?
- Have the privacy and security considerations of the applications been evaluated recently?
- How are role-based access controls (RBAC) and credential management addressed by the application?
- Where is the application hosted and are there jurisdictional considerations based on that venue?
- Is access to the application logged and reviewed for appropriateness?
- How are secrets, passwords, and cryptographic services handled by the application?

Database Layer

Organizations run on data, and we live in an information economy. Whether stored and processed in relational or non-relational databases such as key-value pairs, document-based, column-based, or graph-based, each needs to be adequately secured. Of special note are the communication strings that link or connect an application to its underlying database. Since databases have the proverbial crown jewels, information for an organization, database security should be a top priority. Some questions that should be posited include the following:

- ☐ How is access and activity to the database monitored and controlled?
- ☐ Is the database actively patched, maintained, and hardened (e.g., the removal of unnecessary processes)?
- ☐ Is access and activity, including transactions, logged and how long are these logs maintained and how are they reviewed?
- ☐ Who and what has system or elevated privilege access to the database and do these individuals or systems employ multi-factor authentication or other controls to access the database?
- ☐ How are cryptographic services used with the database?
- ☐ Are certain data elements, tables, or columns encrypted, pseudonymized, or tokenized?
- ☐ What controls are in place to prevent data loss or unsanctioned access to the database and its information?

Operating System Layer

Applications and databases are installed on operating systems (typically, variants of Windows or Linux). Operating systems should be hardened to remove superfluous systems, processes, and access rights that do not apply to the operating environment at hand. Like endpoints and mobile devices, server operating systems should have rigorous access controls and be patched and updated on a frequent and controlled basis. Operating systems, be they for servers, endpoints, or mobile devices, should have endpoint protection (EPP) and endpoint detection and response (EDR) applications installed (EPP and EDR tools have effectively replaced legacy anti-virus or anti-malware applications). Questions that should be considered to determine the reasonableness of OS security controls include:

- ☐ What practices are in place to harden the OS?
- ☐ How frequently is the OS patched and reviewed for vulnerabilities?
- ☐ Are access rights limited and controlled on the OS or do users have rights that are not commensurate with their role and function?
- ☐ Are changes to the OS logged and monitored?
- ☐ Are applications and services that are deployed on the OS governed by organizational policy or deployed without oversight by the organization?

The point above regarding access rights and privileges associated with the user's role on the operating system cannot be overstated. Significant data breaches generally benefit from overly promiscuous access to systems. While a more specialized area of review, the security leader should validate if there are PowerShell or similar scripts used to access operating system functions and how these are controlled and validated.

Endpoints and Mobile Devices

Endpoints, including smartphones, are ubiquitous in organizations. Workstations have frequently been replaced with laptops. Employees and contractors use their own mobile devices to access organizational email and other applications containing personal and other forms of sensitive information. Endpoints are frequently lost or stolen and depending upon the security controls associated with the endpoint, the resultant incident may become a data breach (e.g., where a non-encrypted endpoint containing personal data, protected health information, or sensitive personal information is lost). The privacy leader should review basic endpoint protection capabilities of their organization and ask the following questions to help evaluate if reasonable security protections are in place:

- ☐ Do endpoints and other devices have mobile device management software installed that can enforce security controls and remotely wipe the device should it be lost or stolen?
- ☐ What level of access is afforded to end users on their endpoints and mobile devices and are these access rights commensurate to the user's role within the organization?
- ☐ Is the endpoint or mobile device encrypted?
- ☐ How does the organization govern and control access to organizational data from endpoints that are brought by employees and contractors (e.g., bring your own device)?
- ☐ Are endpoints and similar devices inventoried and tracked by the organization?
- ☐ Do the EPP and EDR tools help contextualize access to the device and its services in the context of the user's role, their location, and standard time-of-day considerations?

Laptops and mobile phones are lost all the time. The organization needs to ensure that its incident response practices consider how these scenarios are addressed. Ideally, where mobile device management tools are employed and device have full-disk encryption, the impact of a stolen device can be minimized.

Hypervisors and Micro Services

As we move further down the stack, operating systems are rarely deployed in a one-to-one relation to the underlying physical server. The advent of virtualization technologies has allowed a single physical server to support multiple 'guest' operating systems. The use of hypervisors is pervasive and has been an integral component of the broader development of modern cloud architectures. As a logical extension to hypervisors, container services—and other microservices—allow for further decoupling of the application from its underlying physical infrastructures. Containers can be readily disposed of, and like hosts in a cluster, support portability of operating systems (and components to the same). End users generally do not have access to these components, but system administrators and the tools they use do, so these permissions should be evaluated. Privacy leaders will be unlikely to evaluate these environments in detail, but some questions that can be posited include:

☐ How have hypervisors and micro services been hardened and controlled?
☐ How is access to these systems governed and controlled?
☐ Are these systems publicly accessible (e.g., are the ports and processes for access to these systems accessible via the internet)?
☐ How are secrets and credentials for these systems governed and controlled?
☐ Are credentials shared?
☐ Is access to the systems logged and monitored for appropriateness?
☐ Is the underlying IT infrastructure (the physical servers and the networks they connect to) reasonably fault tolerant?
☐ How are these systems patched and maintained current, notably the firmware and protocols used by these systems?

Networks (Remote, Local, and Wide Area)

Network security remains an integral component to reasonable security practices. Still, with so many organizations using SaaS applications that only require direct internet access, network security and its criticality is changing for many smaller organizations that do not have traditional local area networks (LANs). Users are now more frequently segmented based on their roles or permissions within the application versus the virtual LANS (vLANS) that they have access to. Separately, regardless of whether the application or service is on-premises or delivered via the cloud, how data moves should be documented in data flow diagrams that document trust boundaries between systems and, importantly, how data exfiltrates or exits systems. Egress, notably for systems that contain sensitive information, should be monitored, logged, and analyzed for reasonableness. Large data transfers, access to networks at times of day that are not consistent with normal operations, and from improbable locations should be alerted upon, gated, and reviewed. The privacy leader should spend some time with their security counterpart to review core network security practices and consider the following questions:

- ☐ How is the network segmented?
- ☐ How is this segmentation governed and controlled?
- ☐ How are firewalls implemented and managed including the use of advanced firewall settings that review applications, users, and data access permissions?
- ☐ How are anomalies within the network identified and triaged?
- ☐ Have insecure protocols such as SSL v2, SSL v3, TLS 1.0, and TLS 1.1 been deprecated?
- ☐ Where remote access to internally hosted applications is required (e.g., non-SaaS applications), how is this governed and controlled?
- ☐ How are changes to the network managed, monitored, and governed?

Data Protection and Backups

The data lifecycle— from its creation, storage, use, sharing, archiving, and ultimate destruction—should inform requisite security controls at each phase. It is essential to know where and how data is stored and backed up. This detail should be front-and-center to any reasonable security review. The location of data storage and processing activities (aka 'use') has jurisdictional implications, as does with whom the organization shares this information. Here are some questions the privacy leader should consider and evaluate with the organization's chief information officer (CIO), director of IT, or similar role within the organization:

- ☐ Are there systems and applications that have personal data that are not presently being backed up? If so, why?
- ☐ Is the data encrypted as it moves through its lifecycle?
- ☐ Is the data encrypted in storage arrays and backup systems?
- ☐ Who has access to these systems and how is this access monitored, logged, and controlled?
- ☐ What type of data validation occurs to ensure the integrity of the data (e.g., input validation controls)?
- ☐ Are backups maintained on-site or off-site?
- ☐ Are there jurisdictional implications related to where data is stored and backed up?
- ☐ Are third-party vendors supporting backup processes and how have they been vetted?
- ☐ Is the data labeled consistent with the organization's data classification scheme?
- ☐ Have retention terms been verified by counsel to validate regulatory and/or contractual retention periods?
- ☐ Do storage and backups systems configurations meet availability and service management requirements?
- ☐ Do storage and backup systems have the appropriate capacity to meet backup windows and the required retention periods?

Data Centers

Data centers, notably third-party colocation facilities, may be rated based on their tier, whereas tier IV data centers are designed for the highest availability and uptime. Tier III data centers are designed for concurrent maintainability of their heating ventilation and air conditioning (HVAC) and power supply systems. Tier II and tier I centers have less redundant capabilities and may have single points of failure for their power and HVAC infrastructure. Ideally, the data center's design should reflect the criticality and obligations of the workloads and applications deployed in the data center. While not likely the purview of a privacy leader's analysis of reasonable security controls, the organization should evaluate important data center controls including:

- ☐ Physical access procedures and logging of data center access
- ☐ Service level agreements and uptime metrics
- ☐ The nature and extent of network service providers to the facility
- ☐ The data center's power infrastructure and its configuration (e.g., 2N, N+1, N, etc.)
- ☐ The data center's battery backup and UPS capabilities
- ☐ Onsite security and monitoring services

Data center services are nuanced and the level of review for data centers again should be tied to the inherent risks associated with the applications and services that run in the data center.

Section 4

Making It Happen

Prepare to Respond

You tell the host you're checking in for your 6:00 reservation and spell your name, and the host looks you up in the system, sees your name, smiles, checks you off, and says, "All set." Then you ask: "May we sit inside instead tonight?" The host frowns, says, "It's my first day on the job," and motions for the supervising host. We've all had a variation of that happen more often than we can count. Employees are often not trained in every task their job requires until they encounter the need to perform it.

Now imagine that you've called an ambulance because you need urgent help. When the ambulance arrives, you tell the emergency responder you have chest pain and trouble breathing. You want to hear something like, "You're going to be OK. We're here to help you. But first, I need to take your blood pressure and pulse." You don't really want to hear, "It's my first day on the job."

The processes you will train your team to execute live somewhere between restaurant host and emergency responder. While certainly not life and death, as David points out in his essay on data subject access requests (DSARs), turning a consumer's request to exercise their privacy rights into a data breach is the privacy equivalate to an own goal.

Of course, there is more to data breach response and handling data subject access requests than training. As we discuss in Chapters 12 and 13, we must have the business processes in place to activate the appropriate response when triggered. Though these are new disciplines, they build upon processes we have years of experience with.

Chapter 12

Data Breach Response

Introduction

It is helpful to think of the privacy leader's role in data breach response in three distinct stages. The first stage is preparation—working with stakeholders to do the necessary upfront work described in Section 2, "Preparing the Program," and Section 3, "Risk Assessments." This ensures that the organization has an inventory of its custodial data and understands how the data flows into and out of the organization. By working with stakeholders to assess each corporate function and each related business process, you'll reduce the likelihood of a data breach and increase the effectiveness of the response when the inevitable happens.

The second stage begins when a security breach or inappropriate disclosure triggers the incident response team. Your role in this stage is to help the team respond appropriately, ensuring that regulatory compliance obligations are fulfilled (e.g., notifying regulators and affected consumers) and that responders don't inadvertently make matters worse.

The final stage begins when the incident is declared closed. In this stage, you assess what business processes need improvement to decrease the likelihood of future data breaches. All three stages are essential to maintain good standing with regulators and protect your company's reputation as a trustworthy brand they can rely on.

In David's essay, "Breach Response," he draws parallels with examples in the physical world to show the different phases in a way that requires no specialized training. It is essential that we use non-technical teaching examples when explaining our approach to broader audiences.

Justine reminds us that sometimes a leader's most important role is to help the team under fire stay calm and carry on. In her essay, "Preparing for Breach Response," Justine highlights the value of planning and provides several practical aids. She then walks us through essential concepts for asserting and protecting attorney-client privilege, which is vital to conducting thorough post-mortem analysis without subjecting the company to undue legal or regulatory risk.

In "Mitigating the Risks of Data Breaches," Matt then shows how to use post-mortem techniques pre-incident to help the organization reduce the likelihood of data breaches and strengthen the responses when breaches occur. Using root cause analysis and the 5 Whys allow the breach response team to game out preventive measures and anticipate necessary responses.

Breach Response ~ David

According to the ITRC 2021 Annual Data Breach Report, there were more data compromises reported in the United States in 2021 than in the previous 20 years, and a 68% year-on-year increase compared with 2020.[104]

The report identified three primary causes:

- **Cyberattacks:** data exposed or stolen through phishing/smishing, malware and weak or stolen credentials.
- **Human error:** when an employee mislays one of their devices, sends sensitive information to the wrong recipient, leaves an unattended computer during a lunch break—in the UK, human error accounted for 22% of security breaches in 2020, exacerbated by home working because of the pandemic.
- **Opportunistic physical attacks:** for example, a fraudster looking over your shoulder at an ATM or at a retail outlet to steal payment card data.

Over a third (38%) of data breaches did not reveal the root cause of a compromise, a 190% increase in 2021 over 2020.

As ransomware-related data breaches doubled in each of the previous two years, it is predicted that soon ransomware attacks will pass phishing/smishing as the primary cause of data compromises.

So, it wouldn't be surprising, if despite everything we've talked about, all the security measures and vendor risk management precautions you and your colleagues have undertaken, you're awakened one morning with a phone call informing you that there was an overnight data breach that could result in the compromise of potentially thousands or even millions of customer records. Your company will now be judged based on its responses to this incident,

---

[104] 2021 in review Data Breach, Annual Report, https://www.idtheftcenter.org/wp-content/uploads/2022/04/ITRC_2021_Data_Breach_Report.pdf.

however promising, considered, and well-intentioned the privacy program that was put in place.

So, what to do?

When Constantinople fell to the Ottomans in 1493, the city was besieged for weeks. With waves of successive attacks, the invaders sought to find a weak spot to breach its walls, with only occasional but limited successes.

The fall of Constantinople in 1453 to Ottoman Turks under the leadership of Mehmed II, the last day of the siege is depicted here in a diorama in the Istanbul Military Museum (Askerî Müze), Turkey

After the final assault, the Ottomans and their allies fanned out across the city, predominantly interested in looting and pillaging. The Byzantines had a very limited response strategy, suffered horribly as a consequence, and, in modern parlance, went out of business.

Burning Down the House

The good news is that modern businesses are far better equipped than the hapless medieval cities ever were, both to prepare for breach incidents and to carry out quick and effective post-incident responses. And it's got to be a coordinated team effort—when you see a house on fire, you don't just call the fire department, you make sure the police and ambulance services are also on the scene as soon as possible:

- the fire department to get the fire under control and to put it out,
- the police to investigate causes, to control the growing crowd of onlookers, and to detect if there was any malfeasance; and finally,
- the medics to support the victims.

In other words, you have an emergency situation, and you are responsible for notifying everyone who may be impacted and everyone who can help with the recovery. And in doing so, you must provide them with clear and concise up-to-the-moment information, the accuracy of which will inevitably fluctuate as the details of the breach become clearer.

What needs to happen falls into two categories—firefighting and damage limitation through targeted communication.

Firefighting:

- An **emergency response team** comprising network and security experts who can discover where and how the breach occurred and provide an initial estimate on the scale of the damage (the fire service). The initial probe will be focused on the evidence provided from where a suspected breach was reported or detected. These could be one or a series of unusual events or activities, observed either by a single individual or collectively, such as the appearance of suspicious emails or files, compromised user credentials or access rights to systems or accounts and any other forms of abnormal administrative activity. Given that one of the main motivators for carrying out a cyberattack is for monetary gain, a key indicator is to look out for any indications of unusual or suspicious financial activity.

Damage limitation:

- The relevant **data protection regulators**, which for large, and particularly for multinational enterprises, could span different geographic or industry-specific jurisdictions (the police).

- An all-hands internal notice informing **everyone** in the company of the situation, emphasizing the importance of not spreading news of the incident or responding to external snoopers. Depending on the damage created by the attackers, caution may have to be applied in choosing a secure communication channel.

- As soon as there is a reliable indication of the breach's impact, you should communicate an indicative notice to all your **stakeholders**—employees, customers, partners, and suppliers—whose personal data may have been compromised.

By the time the fire-fighting team has come up with its assessment of the source of the breach, the scale of the damage, and an initial remediation plan, it'll be time to cycle through the damage limitation process over the following days, weeks, or even months.

Bad news is contagious. After the initial round of hopefully discrete communications, news of the breach will inevitably go viral and start appearing across social media. But before that happens, it will be vital to be ready with timely Twitter messages and press releases and interviews to satisfy the news outlets baying at your door.

Once the breach in your data walls have been rebuilt, and all those individuals whose data was compromised or put at risk have received the appropriate advice or guidance (or even compensation), the process of analyzing why the breach occurred must take place and plans put in place to prevent (as far as possible) the incident from happening again. Unfortunately, the damage done to your brand and business as usual could take much longer to assess.

A European Perspective

The GDPR introduced two articles that specifically indicate a data controller's communication responsibilities in case of a personal data breach.

Article 33 looks at the regulatory requirement to the appropriate supervisory authority:

In the case of a personal data breach, the controller shall without undue delay and, where feasible, not later than 72 hours after having become aware of it, notify the personal data breach to the supervisory authority competent in accordance with Article 55, unless the personal data breach is unlikely to result in a risk to the rights and freedoms of natural persons. Where the notification to the supervisory authority is not made within 72 hours, it shall be accompanied by reasons for the delay.

Whereas Article 34 addresses how to communicate a personal data breach to the data subject:

When the personal data breach is likely to result in a high risk to the rights and freedoms of natural persons, the controller shall communicate the personal data breach to the data subject without undue delay.

The article goes on to specify that the communication should be in 'clear and plain language' – in other words, not shrouded in technical gobbledygook that the average person wouldn't understand. The get-out for the controller is if, due to the appropriate measures taken before or after the breach, the personal data is rendered unintelligible or not presenting a risk to the data subject. In the case of a major breach impacting a large number of individuals, it is considered acceptable to make a public, rather than a private, announcement.

In October 2017, eight months prior to the introduction of the GDPR, the Article 29 Working Party produced a general guidance on data breach notification, analyzing the relevant sections of the regulation.[105] However, due to its nature and timing, this document could not adequately address all the known—and unknown—practical issues that have emerged since GDPR's introduction. Consequently, in 2021 the EDPB adopted a practice-oriented, case-based guidance, that utilizes the post-GDPR experiences as observed by the various supervisory authorities in the EEA. All in all, the

---

[105] Guidelines on Personal data breach notification under Regulation 2016/679, WP 250, https://ec.europa.eu/newsroom/article29/redirection/document/49827.

EDPB report highlights eighteen different use cases in a number of clearly identifiable categories that provide far greater depth and insights than the basic statements in the GDPR. These include:

- Ransomware (with and without proper backup, with and without exfiltration)
- Data exfiltration attacks (e.g., a job application or a hashed password from a website)
- Internal human risk source (exfiltration of business data by an employee, accidental transmission of data to a trusted third party)
- Lost or stolen devices and paper documents
- Mispostal (postal mail mistakes)
- Other cases (social engineering, identity theft)

Given the propensity for attackers to keep ahead of the game and invent new strategies, it would not be surprising if the EDPB in conjunction with supervisory authorities worldwide were to approve a further update to these best practice guidelines in the coming years.

Figuring Out What to Do Better

You thought you'd done all the right things—and hopefully, you find that to be the case. Assuming that you have, it's vitally important to communicate back to the correct stakeholders, even if they are only internal, the final results and lessons learned and changes to be made. The incident is not over until all corrective actions have been taken.

Needless to say, it is vital not to be complacent about keeping your detection systems up to date. Ensure that breaches are flagged as soon as possible, and that alerts do not emerge from external sources, such as customers, social media, or journalists: the consequences of public shaming are considerable in terms of financial penalties and loss of trust.

In terms of preparing for the type of incident and response we've been describing, one of the most effective approaches is via a simulation exercise. These can be carried out on cyber ranges, which are increasingly being used for enterprise educational purposes. They provide an excellent opportunity to live through a real incident scenario and offer a range of individuals from your company first-hand experience of what it's like, minute-by-minute, to deal with the firefighting and damage limitation dimensions of a data breach. This can be as scary as the "real thing" when done well.

Despite all the preparations and precautions, it is almost inevitable that somebody, somewhere, is trying to breach your walls. Like the Ottomans of old, they will find a way in if they are persistent enough. On the other hand, if you've buttressed your fortress well, hopefully they will not be able to get their hands on anything that could be considered valuable or ransomable.

But whether they do or not, the bottom line is that you have to manage the fire and be as transparent as possible in communicating what has happened. Unfortunately, there is no getting away from the inevitable pain and disruption, but it can be managed with the right preparation.

Preparing for Breach Response ~ Justine

Breach response, by definition, is reactive. Nevertheless, there are many proactive steps you can take to prepare your breach response. I have identified these throughout this chapter as Proactive Tips.

Keep Calm and Carry On

One of the most important qualities to retain during incident response is being fully present in each moment—forget the past and future and be here now. There is a strong temptation to think about the past, like what went wrong, who is to blame, and what could have been done differently. The fear-based part of your brain controls that inclination. The urge to think about the future, like litigation, enforcement regulations, insurance battles, and damage to reputation, is also strong. Dwelling in the future or past is extraordinarily unproductive and wastes valuable time with worry about something that already occurred or may never happen. The most effective state of mind to respond to a breach is to be fully present with the facts as they currently exist in each moment and not what they could have been in the past or might be in the future.

Begin at the Beginning

In a perfect world, breach response begins long before a data breach occurs by creating policies, playbooks and protocols (collectively the "IR Plan" or IRP) that have been exercised, tested, and rehearsed by the Incident Response Team.

Incident Response Team ("IR Team")

The Incident Response Team ("IR Team" or IRT) is a small team of key stakeholders that work together to prepare the IR Plan and respond to and resolve security events. The IR Team may be comprised of internal personnel and external counsel or experts. The IR Plan should identify each member of the IR Team, their role, and contact information (including personal email and mobile device). When an event occurs, the IR Team may elect a coordinator who is responsible for managing the response, maintaining reports on the status of response efforts and measures taken, consulting with the IR Team or other relevant stakeholders when additional resources are needed, and ensuring the response complies with the IR Plan. Frequently, in-house legal or the VP of IT will be appointed as the IR coordinator.

Incident Response Plan ("IR Plan")

An IR Plan memorializes the proactive steps to plan for a cyber event. Below are the fundamentals typically found in an IR Plan:

- Identifies key members of the incident response team and their respective roles and responsibilities
- Defines key terms to create a common language that all members of the team can use
- Provides a threat level matrix to color code or classify cyber events (see sample chart below)
- The steps required when responding to a particular type of cyber event (e.g., ransomware, business email compromise, insider threat, data breach). See the sample chart below that identifies tasks from a ransomware playbook, the accountable member(s) of the IR team, and the timeframes in which the tasks should be completed.
- Escalation considerations—who and when to notify, both internal and external stakeholders
- Playbooks for particular types of events
- Templates for incident reports, logs, and chronology
- Legal considerations like notice obligations pursuant to laws or contracts

#	Tasks	Accountable Parties	Timeframe
1	Contain Incident	CIO (IT Security), Outside Counsel	Immediately
2	Convene Incident Response Team	CISO/CIO	Immediately
3	Engage Forensic Team through Outside Counsel	Legal, CIO, Outside Counsel	24 hours of discovery
4	When to Inform & Involve Executive Officers (Escalation)	CIO	24 hours of discovery
5	Identify & Comply with Cyber Insurance Requirements	Legal	48 hours of discovery
6	Conduct Initial Severity Assessment	CIO, CISO	48 hours of discovery
7	Engage Ransomware Negotiation Consultant	CIO, CISO, Legal, Outside Counsel	48 hours of discovery
8	Fulfill Client, Data Subject, and Regulator Notification Obligations	Compliance, Legal, Outside Counsel Communications	1 week of discovery (Potentially some notifications within 72-hours)
9	If/When to Contact Law Enforcement	Legal, CISO, Outside Counsel	1 week of discovery
10	Determine Statutory and Contractual Notice Obligations	Legal, Compliance, Outside Counsel	1 week of discovery
11	Determine Identity & Risk Profile of Attackers	CIO, IT Security, CISO, Outside Counsel, Forensic Team	1 week of discovery
12	Alert and Engage Communications	Legal, Compliance, Finance, Outside Counsel	>1 week of discovery
13	Decide Whether to Pay Ransom	CEO	>1 week of discovery
14	Conduct Post-Incident Remediation	CIO, CISO	After remediation

Figure 12.1 Sample Response Steps

Proactive Tip: Print a copy of the IR Plan and prepare a brightly colored binder for yourself and each of the members of the IR Team. When systems go down, electronic copies may not be available. You can also have an alternative communications platform and store the IR Plan there.

Technical and Legal Response Tracks

There are two teams and response tracks that activate when a cyber event occurs: technical and legal. This chapter focuses on the legal response. It is imperative that both teams understand their respective roles, communicate freely and frequently, and coordinate their individual responses.

Proactive Tip: Before a cyber event occurs, conduct tabletop exercises and breach simulations that allow the respective teams to test the plans and understand how their roles and responsibilities are distinct and overlap. During a breach, it is disruptive and time-consuming if the technical and legal teams are duplicating efforts or in conflict.

Steps to a Successful Response

- **Preparation.** Implement administrative and technical measures to reduce the likelihood of a security event. Collaborate with key stakeholders to ensure the incident response is effective and efficient. Train personnel on their responsibilities and expectations for their contributions to a security program.

- **Detection and Analysis.** When suspicious activity or a security event is detected, analyze and identify the type of threat based on available information. Determine whether it is an actionable security event that warrants escalation. Determine whether impacted data includes any personal information that may trigger notice obligations.

- **Containment and Eradication.** Contain the security event through strategies designed to eradicate the threat, eliminate the potential for damage or further compromise, and preserve evidence. Gather and preserve evidence that may be needed to comply with legal obligations.

- **Recovery and Remediation.** Restore systems to normal operations, including backups or system rebuilds. Remediate vulnerabilities to prevent similar incidents.

- **Investigation.** To the extent a business must disclose the event to consumers, regulators, insurance carriers, or other third parties, a privileged investigation overseen by outside counsel and third-party forensic consultants will commence.

- **Post-Incident Activity/Post-Mortem.** Review actions and stages to ensure adherence to this Plan. Make sure to finalize the incident response report and supporting documentation, including relevant attachments or supporting documents. Key stakeholders should review the investigation response process and update the IRP based on the lessons learned and root cause(s) to prevent risks of similar security incidents in the future.

Technical Investigation to Contain/Identify/Remediate Active Threats

The immediate technical response to a cyber event is to identify, contain, and remediate any active threats. Fact gathering and preserving raw data is typically not privileged. Sometimes the technical teams engage vendors that augment the technical team or have specific subject matter expertise. The evidence and facts gathered by the technical teams can be used later in a privileged forensic investigation, so long as the data is collected in a forensically sound manner. Once the IRT determines that data may be impacted, then a separate, privileged investigation directed by outside legal counsel commences.

Proactive Tip: The technical team <u>should not</u> render any legal conclusions, e.g., "there was a data breach." The technical team should gather facts, preserve and collect evidence, and keep legal informed if they believe the impacted systems contained personal information.

Why Attorneys Get Invited to the Breach Party: Privileged Cyber Investigation

After the technical team reviews the threat activity and determines that personal information may have been impacted, the business will want to conduct a privileged forensic investigation so it can: (1) receive legal advice about potential legal consequences and any reporting obligations and (2) conduct a thorough investigation about the cyberattack in anticipation of litigation or regulatory proceedings. Although some limited privilege exists if in-house counsel is included in cyber investigations, the investigation is often directed/controlled by outside legal counsel to reinforce privilege. As discussed further below, cases in the last decade have held that in-house counsel's role during a cyber investigation is often for a business purpose and therefore the attorney-client privilege does not attach. To keep the investigation privileged and protected from discovery, outside legal counsel must retain the forensic investigator and direct/control the investigation, conclusions, and reports. The forensic investigation relies on two distinct legal principles to maintain privilege: the attorney-client privilege and the work product doctrine.

The privilege is not absolute, and businesses must take care to preserve the privilege and not waive the privilege. For example, sharing a privileged forensic report with law enforcement, auditors, or non-essential members of your business may waive the privilege.

Work Product Doctrine and Attorney-Client Privilege

Recent cases have eroded both the attorney-client privilege and work product doctrine in breach investigations. These cases describe conduct that can destroy the confidentiality of the investigation and reports when responding to a data breach. Often the two principles are conflated, which can undermine the application of both. Understanding the difference between the attorney-client privilege and work product doctrine is key to upholding the confidentiality and privileged nature of the investigation.

Work Product Doctrine. The work product doctrine (WPD) protects an attorney's thoughts, impressions, conclusions, opinions, and legal research or theories that are provided in anticipation of litigation, including any investigation conducted. WPD does not require confidential communication with the client to be privileged, but it must be in anticipation of litigation. If an investigation is conducted at the direction of counsel, communications and notes about the investigation are privileged. The WPD is often used in forensic investigations because of the likelihood of class action lawsuits and regulatory enforcement proceedings.

Attorney-Client Privilege. Attorney-client privilege (ACP) is a legal privilege that protects communications between an attorney and their client. The purpose is to encourage frank and direct communication. Communications are for the purpose of giving or obtaining legal advice and should be marked "Privileged and Confidential" or "ACP." The ACP is used during a forensic investigation to protect communications between the attorney and client.

The following three cases illustrate the difficulties and nuances of when and how to invoke the attorney-client privilege and work product doctrine.

In re Capital One Data Sec. Breach Litig., ED VA (May 26, 2020)

In March 2019, Capital One experienced a data breach followed by numerous lawsuits. Plaintiffs sought to compel the production of a forensic report on the incident. Before the breach, Capital One had retained the cyber security firm Mandiant to support incident response if they were breached. After the breach, Capital One hired outside counsel. The law firm then signed an agreement with Mandiant providing that the payment terms and services were to be the same as those between Capital One and Mandiant; however, the work would be done at the direction of counsel with the deliverables provided to counsel instead of Capital One. Capital One argued that the report was protected by the attorney work product doctrine because it was requested by a law firm and prepared in anticipation of litigation. The court rejected this argument for the following reasons:

The court held that Capital One failed to prove the work product doctrine applied because Mandiant was already retained before the event occurred and therefore the investigation was not in anticipation of litigation.

Capital One had an existing SOW and MSA with Mandiant at the time of the data breach that was effectively transferred to outside counsel. As set out in the SOW and Letter Agreement, the work to be performed by Mandiant was the same, the terms were the same, but the work was to be performed at the direction of outside counsel and the final report delivered to outside counsel. The retention of outside counsel does not, by itself, turn a document into work product. [Capital One at p. 3].[106]

Because the court ruled on the work product issues based on the "but for" standard, it was unnecessary to address waiver. However, in a footnote, the court remarked that "the waiver argument may have some merit given the lack of evidence presented . . . concerning the distribution of the Mandiant Report and what protections were taken to avoid having the Mandiant Report or the information contained therein disclosed to a person or entity in an adversarial relationship." [*Id.* at p. 7]. Capital One shared the report with at least some IT personnel and it was used "for various business and regulatory purposes." [*Id.* at p. 10].

Wengui v. Clark Hill PLC, DDC (January 12, 2021)

Clark Hill was a law firm that was breached. One of their former clients sued Clark Hill and sought to compel production of the forensic investigation report. Clark Hill argued the report was privileged because it had initiated a "two-track" investigation: one track using Clark Hill's normal cybersecurity vendor that was not privileged; and the second track using a forensic vendor retained by outside counsel that was privileged. Clark Hill claimed the materials prepared on the privileged track were not subject to discovery and the court should not order Clark Hill to turn over the privileged report. The court disagreed, finding Clark Hill carried the burden to demonstrate privilege and failed to meet its burden. The court held Clark Hill did not provide testimony or evidence showing a separate privileged investigation directed by outside counsel. The forensic report at issue included business continuity issues which were not deemed to be privileged legal issues. The court also found Clark Hill waived the attorney-client privilege because the forensic report was shared widely with leadership, the IT team, and the FBI for non-legal purposes. Accordingly, the court found that Clark Hill failed to establish that the alleged privileged forensic report would not have

---

[106] [Capital 3] and subsequent similar notations refer to the page number in the court's order.

been prepared in the absence of litigation. In other words, the court believed regardless of whether litigation did or did not occur, the report would have been prepared.

In re Rutters Data Sec. Breach Litig. (July 22, 2021)

Following a breach, Rutter's hired outside counsel, which hired Kroll Cyber Security to investigate the incident. Kroll provided Rutter's with a written forensic report. Class action plaintiffs from subsequent litigation sought to compel the production of the report and related communications between Rutter's and Kroll. Rutter's argued that the Kroll report was protected from disclosure by both the attorney-client privilege and work product doctrine. The court rejected both arguments.

For the Kroll report to be considered attorney work product, the court stated the "primary motivating purpose" behind the report's creation must have been a "unilateral belief" that litigation would result from the data security incident. Kroll's statement of work for the matter had stated that the purpose of the forensic investigation was to determine "whether unauthorized activity within the Rutter's system environment resulted in the compromise of sensitive data" and "the scope of such compromise if it occurred." Moreover, "Kroll provided its report to Defendant when it was completed, and there is no evidence that it was provided first to [outside counsel]." [Rutter's p. 3].

The attorney-client privilege did not protect the forensic report because its contents were factual and did not involve legal opinion or tactics. Further, the report was shared with Kroll and Rutter's IT personnel, who were not legal professionals, "and this service involves those two entities working alongside each other with no mention of attorney involvement."

Determine Whether There Is a Data Breach

The first step for the privacy professional in breach response is to conduct a preliminary review to determine the scope and impact on data and personal information. Cyber events can be actual or attempted compromises to an IT asset or system that disrupts how it operates. The cause of a cyber event can be malicious, negligent, or a combination of both.

Identifying Data Types Impacted

Not all types of data trigger state breach laws. If the breach does not impact personal information, then state breach laws may not apply. Similarly, not all formats of data (like paper) are protected. Many state breach laws only apply to digital or electronically stored information. Only four states impose reporting obligations if paper records are breached.[107]

When a Cyber Event Becomes a Potential Data Breach

Any time there is a cyber intrusion, the response should include an analysis of the impact on data and personal information potentially accessed by unauthorized users. However, not all cyber events are data breaches. Data breaches are ultimately a legal conclusion based on the laws that apply.

Is There a Privacy Risk? Or Indicators Personal Information Is Compromised (IPIC)

Privacy risk is not always present in a security event. For example, network vulnerabilities can create security risk that never implicates privacy. There are dual investigations that unfold during a cyber event. Privacy professionals get involved in security events when there are indicators that personal information is compromised (let's call this an "IPIC"). For example, a documented risk assessment may be necessary if an unauthorized party accessed consumer data. The forensic investigation to identify the evidence and artifacts will provide helpful information for the IPIC analysis, such as when the access occurred, whether the individual was authorized, what files or data was accessed, and whether data exfiltration occurred. Quickly identifying the data elements that may have been accessible is the key to understanding which laws and regulations to follow. These data elements are often included in detailed data maps or data impact

---

[107] Hawaii; North Carolina; Alaska; Iowa.

assessments (if/where available). If no protected personal information was accessed, document the analysis and conclude there is no privacy risk.

What Is the Legal Definition of a Data Breach?

Most state laws define data breaches narrowly. A data breach occurs when a certain type of consumer data commonly referred to as PII has been accessed and/or acquired by an unauthorized actor. Depending on the state, access to data may be sufficient, while acquisition is required to trigger reporting obligations in other states. For example, in Florida, "breach of security" or "breach" means <u>unauthorized access</u> of data in electronic form containing personal information. (Fla. Stat. § 501.171.) In California, "breach of the system's security" means <u>unauthorized acquisition</u> of computerized data that compromises the security, confidentiality, or integrity of personal information maintained by the person or business. (Cal. Civ. Code § 1798.82 et seq.) In Connecticut, "breach of security" means <u>unauthorized access to or unauthorized acquisition</u> of electronic files, media, databases, or computerized data, containing personal information when access to the personal information has not been secured by encryption or by any other method or technology that renders the personal information unreadable or unusable. (Conn. Gen. Stat. § 36a-701b.)

Example. VicTim Co.'s servers and files are encrypted after malware traverses across its network. It is unclear whether an unauthorized actor accessed personal information before encryption. All log files and artifacts that could show access to the personal information are also encrypted or have been deleted. Some partial data captured from log files show that the unauthorized actor had access to the network and explored the files but does not indicate acquisition or exfiltration. The threat actor leaves a ransom note claiming they have stolen all your data before encrypting your files. Under Florida and Connecticut law, a breach has occurred because the threat actor had access to the data. Under California law, although there is no evidence the data was acquired, there is a reasonable belief the data was acquired because the threat actor claimed to have the data, and also many post-2020 ransom attacks had data exfiltration associated with the encryption.

Contractual Obligations

Even if state breach laws do not apply, there may be contractual obligations to notify or take specific actions. For example, suppose the data breach impacts a customer's confidential information, but the data does not contain personal information. In that case, state breach laws will not require notice, but the contract may require you to give your customers notice that their confidential information was impacted. In addition, as privacy laws require greater oversight of vendors, contractual obligations are also increasing. See Chapter 10 on vendor management for a detailed discussed about contractual notice obligations.

Proactive Tip: Track contracts that impose obligations if data or systems are compromised. Then incorporate contractual reporting obligations into your Incident Response Plan. Many contracts include very short deadlines for reporting, like 24 to 72 hours after discovering a cyber event.

Mitigating the Risks of Data Breaches ~ Matt

Few challenges test an organization's resilience more than a widescale data breach. Of note, organizational strategy and agreed-to initiatives are effectively put on hold as the organization enters a highly reactive incident and data breach response mode. Depending upon the organization's resilience and capabilities, several months may be lost to ongoing distractions (be they regulatory, media, or partner inquiries) and the commensurate effort to address the breach technically and operationally. The challenges of a data breach are pervasive, impacting the organization's operations, finances, reputation, and sales and marketing efforts. Data breaches result in increased regulatory oversight and breach notification obligations. Responding to a data breach can be a make-or-break moment for both the organization and its security and privacy leaders. Technically speaking, data breaches suck.

These impacts are not limited to the organization alone. Essential staff who are part of either the cybersecurity incident response team (CIRT) or the broader data breach response team (consisting of counsel, executive leadership, corporate communications, HR, and other critical functional department leaders) will have their lives kicked off the proverbial rails. It's not uncommon for security teams to work two or three days straight, triaging and remediating impacted systems during the initial period following the discovery of a data breach, and then weeks if not months on end of twelve-to-sixteen-hour days addressing and remediating security control failures systemically. Staff who may have been on family vacations or attending special events will receive "that call" and be asked to drop whatever they are doing, regardless of the personal impact, to support the response effort. Stress and tension are omnipresent as these key members are expected to put their jobs ahead of personal and family obligations during the response. Too frequently, relationships, marriages, or careers are damaged. Regrettably, for many, the damage lasts well beyond the data breach.

Beyond the organization, and most importantly, are the individuals—the data subjects or consumers—who have had their personal information stolen from an entity they had trusted with their personal data. These individuals confront account takeover risks and identity theft. The time required to restore credit and address fraudulent activity can be all-consuming. Calls from collection agencies and mounting invoices and bills for purchases that were not legitimately made will be ever-present until the individual's identity has been restored and protected from these risks. The FTC and other consumer-oriented agencies typically have important guidance to help victims navigate the plethora of challenges that result from identity theft.[108] Privacy leaders would be well served to review these materials proactively.

Sadly, data breaches are common, and it appears that unsuspecting organizations and consumers alike have become indifferent to the near-daily reports of yet another organization having its security and privacy controls fail, resulting in the exfiltration of personal data. The number of personal data records that have been compromised and now widely traded in nefarious circles is stunning, numbering in the hundreds of millions of individuals and their impacted data. Privacy Rights Clearinghouse maintains a database of U.S. data breaches by industry, cause, and the number of records compromised.[109] While the numbers are staggering, they are also likely understated as many data breaches go unreported. Despite efforts to establish reasonable security over personal data, the frequency of data breaches suggests that there's important work to be done. Our security and data protection efforts must keep pace with adversaries who are increasingly using sophisticated techniques, including the exploitation of APIs of consumer-oriented applications. These adversaries, however, are ultimately pragmatic. Complicated attack techniques are generally not required when individuals succumb to basic social engineering attacks and open attachments or click on URL links that allow their devices to be compromised. Timely and frequent security awareness training is integral to reducing the

---

[108] The Federal Trade Commission's guidance to address identity theft can be found here: https://www.identitytheft.gov/#/.
[109] To learn more about the important work of Privacy Rights Clearinghouse and their work, see https://privacyrights.org/data-breaches.

efficacy of these attacks, as discussed in Chapter 11 on reasonable security.

Breach response obligations are almost perfunctory these days. As privacy and security leaders, we must not become numb to data breaches and accept security incidents as part of the status quo. Reasonable security practices dramatically reduce the likelihood of a data breach. We don't allow public companies to disclose inaccurate financial statements. We don't tolerate airlines with histories of maintenance issues and accidents, nor do we allow manufacturers to sell products that catch fire or have safety issues. Other industries and professions simply don't experience the level of failures that we've witnessed with our security programs. We should not accept the status quo and strongly advocate security and privacy by design principles that reduce the risks of data breaches and other security incidents.

U.S. federal departments such as the Department of Health and Human Services and its Office of Civil Rights have created websites to streamline obligatory disclosures to the Department when breaches occur.[110] States' Attorneys General are also required to be notified under certain circumstances, as is the FTC. Disclosure obligations vary based on jurisdiction (be it international, federal, state, or sector), the number and type of records impacted, and the time allocated to report the breach to the appropriate authority and impacted individuals. A key responsibility for privacy and security leaders is to inventory and document their organization's respective disclosure obligations. This function requires direct input from the organization's counsel if the privacy leader is not an attorney.

These agencies, and their counterparts across the globe, frequently provide guidance covering requirements for organizations that have had the personal data under their control breached.[111] In the U.S., all 50 states now have data breach disclosure laws. These laws vary in

---

[110] The OCR's submission form is found here: https://ocrportal.hhs.gov/ocr/breach/wizard_breach.jsf.
[111] The FTC's data breach response guidance can be found here: https://www.ftc.gov/tips-advice/business-center/guidance/data-breach-response-guide-business.

how they address safe harbor provisions where personal data may have been encrypted or similarly protected (e.g., tokenized or pseudonymized) and the potential to delay public disclosure and victim notification if law enforcement engages in response efforts.[112] In Europe, Article 33 of the GDPR describes the obligations of in-scope entities to notify data protection authorities (DPAs) within 72 hours, absent a justifiable reason for delay. Responding to data breaches has become so common that data breach disclosure software is now available.[113] The large credit reporting agencies have also produced well-documented guidance for addressing data breaches.[114] In short, data breaches have become commonplace, and our responses have started to become almost routine. *Take pause.* We must avoid ambivalence to the risks of a data breach and the impacts that ensue. Incident response and preparedness to address data breaches in a timely and effective manner must become a top organizational priority.

As professionals working in privacy and data security, we should also reflect on why our track record of protecting the personal data entrusted to our respective organizations is frankly so poor. Data breaches do not happen in a vacuum and generally reflect systemic control failures of the organization. Data breaches are rarely the result of a technical failure, even though inadequate security protections or inappropriate technical configurations are clearly at the heart of the breach. Stated differently, even when a security failure is identified, it's rarely the primary cause of the data breach. Instead, broader underlying organizational issues allowed the security issue to exist. If these systemic challenges can be identified proactively and addressed

---

[112] The National Conference of State Legislatures maintains a reasonably current list of U.S. state disclosure laws. It's advisable to go to the direct legislation for specific guidance but this site offers an excellent summary and can be found here: https://www.ncsl.org/research/telecommunications-and-information-technology/security-breach-notification-laws.aspx.

[113] This class of application will indicate disclosure obligations based on the domicile of impacted individuals, the number and type of records impacted, as well as whether safe harbor provisions minimize disclosures.

[114] Experian's *Data Breach Response Guide* is a good example of the type of prescriptive guidance provided by the credit bureaus. Details can be found here: https://www.experian.com/assets/data-breach/brochures/response-guide.pdf.

in a timely and appropriate manner, we can make the likelihood of a widescale data breach far less commonplace. To do this requires proactive organizational commitment. There are some simple but effective methodologies to start the process. Three that tend to be effective include the premortem, a root cause analysis (RCA), and the 5 Whys approach. There is important overlap with each approach, and they are not mutually exclusive. However, the investment in time and organizational commitment to explore this process will certainly yield important insights that will ideally help reduce the likelihood of a widescale data breach. Let's explore each methodology at a high level.

- **Premortem:** The oddly named premortem methodology asks the organization to assume that a future data breach has occurred and brings key stakeholders together to specifically address how the data breach happened. Effectively, what should have been known that was not known that resulted in the data breach. This methodology focuses intently on what could go wrong and result in the negative outcome—in this case a widescale data breach. By proactively anticipating issues (for example, missing resources, insecure vendors, gaps in security technology, inadequate procedures, or lacking organizational oversight over privacy), the organization can implement strategies that anticipate these privacy and security control failures and take proactive measures to remediate *a priori* versus post breach.

- **RCA:** Root cause analyses are traditionally used to address technical failures but may also be employed to address procedural lapses that result in data breaches. With the RCA methodology, gather members of the broader governance, privacy, and security teams and evaluate well-publicized breaches and explore the actual causes that resulted in that specific data breach. As we'll see with the 5 Whys approach, the first several explanations are rarely the actual root cause of the data breach. Another useful variant of this approach is to evaluate the previously reported security incidents and data breaches from various industries to determine if your organization and your team are prepared to address a similar attack on your environment. These tabletop exercises keep your team proactively focused on preparedness. With so many widescale data breaches, there is no shortage of scenarios to evaluate. As the team works through the RCA process, distill the observations and recommendations that result and ensure that these enhancements are translated back to your specific privacy and security programs. Validate the status of procedures required to ensure that remediation is lasting.

- **5 Whys**: The 5 Whys approach has its origins in lean manufacturing and was specifically developed by Toyota to address manufacturing defects and other concerns.[115] The premise of 5 Whys is that during the analysis of a system failure, in this case, a data breach, the first explanation is usually not the real issue. Nor, as it turns out, are the next several explanations that are offered. With each response as to why the data breach occurred, ask "why." As you continue to delve deeper into the analysis, the notion is that by the time the fifth why has been identified, that response and explanation is more likely the actual cause. Validate, however, that there is not a need for a sixth or seventh "why" to be asked. Ideally, the final why reflects consensus by the stakeholders performing the analysis. Frequently, this methodology is used to help conduct RCAs. As noted above, these approaches are not mutually exclusive.

Beyond these analyses, the privacy leader should work collaboratively to review and validate incident response planning and security practices with the organization's security leader. Incident response planning is integral to mitigating data breaches, and organizations should make the efficacy of their incident response programs a top priority.

---

[115] To learn more about 5 Whys, see: https://kanbanize.com/lean-management/improvement/5-whys-analysis-tool.

There are common themes found with successful incident response programs, and these should inform your evaluation of your organization's own efforts.[116] Specifically, take some time to review your organization's incident response capabilities and assess the status of the following:

- **Incident Response Team.** Are the members of the incident response team representative of the organization at large or just the security and IT teams? Incident response is a multi-disciplinary process that requires input from stakeholders throughout the organization including legal, HR, lines-of-business, executive leadership, corporate communications, operations, *and* security and IT teams. Validate that the incident response team understands their respective roles or functions within the incident response program and that there is a well-defined RACI matrix that highlights roles throughout the incident response lifecycle (from preparation to identifying and triaging incidents, containment, eradication, remediation, and after-action analyses and disclosures).[117] Too frequently, individuals identified as being members of an incident response team are completely unaware of the program and the requirements associated with their participation and function in the program. The contact details of the response team should be up-to-date and include both office and after-hours contact information. Incidents rarely occur Monday through Friday during standard business hours. The functional representatives

---

[116] Throughout my career, I've had the opportunity to read hundreds of incident response plans, conduct tabletop exercises simulating multiple security incidents and data breaches, and speak with security leaders globally about incident response programs. Incident response is a topic warranting its own book and there are some excellent references available from the National Institute of Standards and Technology (NIST), specifically NIST Special Publication 800-61r2: Computer Security Incident Handling Guide which can be found here:
https://nvlpubs.nist.gov/nistpubs/specialpublications/nist.sp.800-61r2.pdf.

[117] The incident response lifecycle is nuanced. The phases noted are for illustrative purposes and each phase has multiple functions and activities required to be successfully executed.

should be empowered to affect actions on behalf of their department or area within the organization. These authorizations should be documented and agreed to well in advance.

- **Incident Response Plan and Scenario Runbooks.** The organization's incident response plan should be considered a living document and frequently updated and reviewed by stakeholders. Response plans should be maintained in several media formats to ensure that they are readily available when incidents occur (e.g., online, hard copy, password-protected USB drives). The incident response plan should include, minimally, detail, guidance, and instructions on the following:

    o Definitions of incident types and guidance on how to distinguish between events, alerts, and incidents
    o Identification of systems of record for addressing incident response activities (e.g., ticketing, logging, forensics, communications (in-band and out-of-band))
    o Criticality or priority weightings based on the system or records impacted
    o Escalation matrices that indicate who to contact based on the fact pattern of the incident and how frequently these identified stakeholders should be updated
    o Guidance on resources required and key functions performed for each stage of the incident response process
    o Contact details for the incident response team including extended members of the team
    o Contact and account details for vendors who may be engaged during an incident, including validations of the authorized personnel and emergency contact (APEC) details for those staff who can engage outside vendor support[118]

---

[118] During an incident is precisely the wrong time to find out that individuals on the incident response team are not recognized by the vendor as an authorized contact from the organization. Every minute that is lost during the initial

- Guidance on when and by whom law enforcement should be engaged
- Guidance on who is authorized to speak with outside entities such as media, regulators, and law enforcement
- Details on regulatory and contractual obligations that impact the incident response and breach disclosure functions of the organization
- Expectations for conducting an after-action review or lessons learned exercise once the incident has been formally closed
- Guidance on declaring and formally closing a security incident

The list of topics within the incident response plan will be expansive. It's important, however, to keep the overall size of the plan manageable. Incident response plans that are long—generally over 40 pages—will rarely be read by stakeholders. Instead, use appendices for information that is not required for the live response and ensure that there is explicit guidance on where analysts and incident response teams should go within the plan to address critical issues. Make the plan detailed but simple to follow and easy to read. Runbooks to address common security issues should be drafted and referenced with the plan. Some basic scenarios to cover include the following:

- Lost or stolen devices
- Compromised credentials
- Malware
- Ransomware
- Phishing or spear-phishing
- Suspected data breach[119]
- Third-party vendor compromise
- Distributed or other forms of denial of service

---

response is to the benefit of the adversary. Ensure that these APECs are fully validated and kept up-to-date, notably when there are changes in personnel.

[119] Validate who within the organization is authorized to declare a data breach. Given the legal implications of the term, this should likely be left to the organization's counsel.

- Your organization will likely have other scenarios to contemplate in the runbook. Runbooks should provide high-level guidance and basic steps to address an identified security scenario. For organizations with larger security teams and more mature security programs, runbooks may be complemented with playbooks that provide explicit instructions on how to address specific issues (e.g., how to run commands on specific systems and applications, how to create hashes of files that are suspected to be malware, how to investigate email headers). Frequently, playbooks are becoming more automated through the use of security orchestration automation and response (SOAR) tools. As with the incident response plan, validate runbooks at least annually to ensure that they reflect the operational environment of the firm.

- **Actively Test Incident Response.** You should exercise your organization's incident response capabilities on a frequent basis—certainly no less than once per year. There are a variety of means to evaluate incident response preparation, including workshops to review the incident response plan and program with key stakeholders, tabletop exercises for common scenarios as noted above, along with premortems, RCAs, and the 5 Why exercises for other widely known data breaches. Informally broaching the topic of incident response to specific scenarios with key members of your team and stakeholders who are part of the extended incident response team will raise security and privacy awareness. Posit some basic questions to the team at the proverbial water cooler and walk away to leave them questioning how prepared the organization or department is for that issue. Ensure that incident and data breach responses are standing agenda items on the privacy and security teams' meetings. Incident response is about muscle memory. In the spirit of "shifting left," ensure that the teams declare war on ambiguity and proactively question, validate understandings, and ensure that the broader teams are well prepared for what will likely be the inevitable "this is not a drill" response.

While data breaches have become commonplace, we should not accept this status quo. Instead, invest time and prioritize your organization's capabilities to address a data breach and, most importantly, preclude it from happening based on organizational commitment to reasonable security practices, notably those practices related to data governance and data protection.

Key Insights and Recommended Next Steps

Key Insights

- Humans make mistakes and technology fails. Breaches are inevitable.
- Effective breach response requires extensive preparation and organizational dedication to minimize the impact of breaches.
- During the early stages of a security breach people are reacting and attempting to gain control of the situation. It is essential to have runbooks and templates available that provide guidance for the team's response.
- Not all security breaches are data breaches. It is imperative that technicians responding to a security breach do not label the incident a data breach; that is a legal determination.
- Attorney-client privilege is a misunderstood concept. To assert and maintain the protections afforded to privileged communications, strict rules must be followed.
- A critical skill to develop is the ability to learn the lessons from previous breaches so we can improve. This includes high-profile breaches as well as our own.

Recommended Next Steps

- Work with stakeholders to create a RACI matrix that spells out escalation points for incident response, communications, working with law enforcement, and assessing the impact on data subject to regulatory oversight.
- Conduct tabletop exercises to simulate incident response frequently, ideally quarterly, to validate organizational preparedness. Exercises do not need to be formal to be effective, watercooler discussions, lunch and learn sessions, and standing agenda topics related to incident response help build organizational muscle memory.
- Prepare runbooks for responding to common types of security incidents and include decision points that allow the incident response team to escalate to privacy leadership to determine if a data breach has occurred and trigger the data breach response plan if needed.

Chapter 13

Handling Data Subject Requests

Introduction

The topic covered in Chapter 12, "Data Breach Response," is tied directly to the incident response process with the important distinction that not all security breaches are data breaches. The topic we cover in Chapter 13, "Handling Data Subject Requests," is closely related to customer service requests. The distinguishing factors, in this case, are that DSARs come with a time limit and must be handled in compliance with the governing regulation.

As with data breach response, leveraging the customer service request process requires training for every staff member that might encounter a request and it's essential that staff are trained to recognize the request regardless of how it arrives. As with data breach response, training alone is not enough.

David starts his essay, "Handling Data Subject Requests," by explaining the principal attributes of a compliant request handling process. Note that in addition to the timeframe for complying with a request, it is imperative that you validate the identity of the requestor and the right of that individual to make a request if it is not about them (e.g., for a child or someone else with whom they have a custodial relationship).

Matt's essay, "Data Subject Access Requests," comes next. Matt reminds us that even the much-discussed "right to be forgotten" is not an absolute right. He reviews the major provisions of the regulations covering DSARs to separate fact from myth. Matt points out that DSARs are far-reaching and provides detailed descriptions of the assessment and required modification to business processes that might result.

Finally, Justine provides a thorough review of the impact of the regulations in her essay, "Privacy Rights Requests." In addition to detailing the types and components of privacy rights requests (PRRs) she provides several practical tools based on lessons learned in her practice, including the data taxonomy California uses and helpful flowcharts for how to respond to PRRs.

Handling Data Subject Requests ~ David

After all you've gone through in putting together a comprehensive privacy program and ensuring that it is secure and regulatory-compliant, one of the crucial road tests is going to be responding to requests from customers. They will ask you questions that will demonstrate how well you are managing their data and how effectively you can respond to their legal entitlements.

Data subject access requests, simply referred to as DSARs, are four words that have the potential to strike fear into the hearts of the most prepared and regulatory-compliant businesses. But as with most fears, which truly do exist beyond the privacy world, understanding the worst that individuals, whether irate or simply mildly concerned, can reasonably expect of you will go a long way to allaying those fears.

The basic principle is that data subjects today have more rights than ever before to understand what you're doing with their data and, in some cases, demand changes. And in most jurisdictions, you are legally bound, if not to agree with all their requests, then at the very least to offer a considered response.

So, let's look at what may be involved, using Chapter 3 of the GDPR, the grandparent of the recent slew of global data protection and privacy regulations, for guidance.

- "Without undue delay"[120]

    Companies are expected to respond to an access request as quickly as possible, which practically speaking translates to within one month from receiving the request or verifying the requestor's identity. However, if it looks like it would take longer to respond to the request, a company can extend the

---

[120] GDPR Article 33:0 "*In the case of a personal data breach, the controller shall without undue delay and, where feasible, not later than 72 hours after having become aware of it, notify the personal data breach to the supervisory authority competent in accordance with Article 55, unless the personal data breach is unlikely to result in a risk to the rights and freedoms of natural persons. Where the notification to the supervisory authority is not made within 72 hours, it shall be accompanied by reasons for the delay.*"

period by two months, provided the data subject is notified within the first month with a full explanation for the delay.

- "Manifestly unfounded or excessive"[121]

If a request is unfounded or excessive, it may be justifiable to reject it. If an individual's intentions appear to be malicious or disruptive rather than genuinely wanting to exercise their rights, it may be considered "manifestly unfounded." A request may be excessive if it repeats the substance of previous requests and a reasonable interval has not elapsed, or if it overlaps with other requests. With both scenarios, decisions should be context-based. Don't forget: the burden of responsibility is with you!

- "Concise, transparent, intelligible and easily accessible"[122]

Data subjects are entitled to submit their request in any written form, either paper-based or electronically. They can expect to receive a clear, transparent response electronically or as otherwise requested by the data subject, including orally.

- "Adversely affect the rights and freedoms of others"

Besides the manifestly unfounded or excessive case mentioned above, a DSAR can be rejected if it is shown to

---

[121] GDPR Article 57:"*Where requests are manifestly unfounded or excessive, in particular because of their repetitive character, the supervisory authority may charge a reasonable fee based on administrative costs or refuse to act on the request. The supervisory authority shall bear the burden of demonstrating the manifestly unfounded or excessive character of the request.*"

[122] GDPR Article 12:"*The controller shall take appropriate measures to provide any information referred to in Articles 13 and 14 and any communication under Articles 15 to 22 and 34 relating to processing to the data subject in a concise, transparent, intelligible and easily accessible form, using clear and plain language, in particular for any information addressed specifically to a child. The information shall be provided in writing, or by other means, including, where appropriate, by electronic means. When requested by the data subject, the information may be provided orally, provided that the identity of the data subject is proven by other means.*"

negatively affect others, including, for example, the misuse of trade secrets, intellectual property, or software copyright. In addition, a DSAR can be turned down or at least suspended if the information requested forms part of an ongoing legal process.

- "Fair and transparent processing"

  Businesses are expected to provide data subjects with a clear and well-defined set of contact details and information concerning the purpose of the intended data processing and the period for which the data will be stored, or at least the criteria for determining what that period will be. In addition, you, as a data controller, are expected to make the data subjects aware of their right to request:

  o access to and rectification or erasure of personal data[123]
  o restriction of processing, or to simply object to processing[124]
  o data portability[125]

- "The right to withdraw consent"[126]

  In most cases, data subjects can also choose to withdraw or modify their consent to any processing they previously had agreed to, "without affecting the lawfulness of processing based on consent before its withdrawal."

In addition to being mindful of the rights of data subjects in terms of access to information and the limits to what they are entitled to, it's just as important to have a rigorous, auditable process in place that all the relevant stakeholders in your company are aware of. A

---

[123] GDPR Articles 15 and 17 respectively.
[124] GDPR Article 18.
[125] GDPR Article 20.
[126] GDPR Article 7: *"The data subject shall have the right to withdraw his or her consent at any time. The withdrawal of consent shall not affect the lawfulness of processing based on consent before its withdrawal. Prior to giving consent, the data subject shall be informed thereof. It shall be as easy to withdraw as to give consent."*

data subject also has the right to lodge a complaint with the appropriate supervisory body about your handling of their data and their DSAR.

Processes, Policies, and Procedures

Perhaps the most important thing to consider is ensuring that efficient and transparent processes, policies, and procedures are in place to handle incoming DSARs. As you already have a robust privacy program, it would be lamentable if this did not carry through to your handling of DSARs. On a day-to-day basis, the process should typically be under the aegis of your DPO, who should be responsible for communicating to all your employees including CxOs how to recognize a DSAR and what to do next.

Receiving DSARs

DSARs made verbally, by letter, email, online chat, and even social media posts are all equally valid, and data subjects don't need to justify why they are making the request. However, ideally, you should appoint a specific person or mailbox to receive DSARs, which should be recorded in a DSAR log to keep track of the details of the request, the action taken, and the length of time taken to respond.

Although promoting a single point to receive DSARs will cover many incoming requests, in reality, everyone in the company may be in a position where they have to recognize and respond to a DSAR—for which they'll need explicit training. Specific departments—those that are the most customer-facing—are more likely to field requests than others and you should provide them with robust training.

Know Who You're Dealing With

Although many DSARs are straightforward to deal with, some may have an ultimately mischievous purpose that could even be harmful to your business. So, before you start processing the request, you should make sure the data subject is the person they claim to be using a KYC[127] approach. Having done that, you must go the extra mile to ensure they have a right to access the information, which in most cases will be about themselves. However, if they are acting on behalf of a third party, it becomes particularly sensitive. For example, in the case of parents or guardians seeking access to children's data, it should be someone with power of attorney or an appropriately sanctioned law enforcement agency. Basically, the process must be really careful that the requestor has the legal right to receive someone else's personal information.

Unfortunately, although DSARs usually relate to the personal information you process about the individual requesting the information, there are cases when they are used to access information for purposes that are not legitimate. The process should be black and white—and in most cases it will be—but there will be instances where discretionary caution needs to be applied. Releasing sensitive personal information to the wrong individual is effectively a data breach, with all the consequences derived from it—the equivalent to an "own goal" in soccer or hockey.

Putting It All Together

Once you've acknowledged the DSAR and clarified the required response, you must collate the information. This could be in emails, social media logs, telephone calls, on paper, in electronic format, or even data held by third-party data processors. Given the potentially widespread distribution of the data, pulling it all together is likely to be an onerous and time-consuming task. Acting as quickly as possible is really important, particularly given the time-constrained imperative to respond to the DSAR formally. However, this task will be immeasurably simplified if you have followed all the advice provided so far and know where all the data subject's personal information is stored and how to access it!

---

[127] Know Your Customer.

Reviewing and Sharing

Before sharing the information that you have carefully pulled together you need to assign the task of carrying out thorough due diligence on your proposed response to a specific individual, someone other than the person responsible for compiling the information in the first place. This separation of duties may not be required for simple requests but is highly advisable where the data warrants the review, such as in the case of sensitive personal information and health records. The job of the reviewer is to check that what you will send back to the requestor is complete and comprehensive. They will also ensure that there are no references to any other individuals, which would be a breach of that other person's personal data.

It's time to share your response with the requestor referencing the original request and keeping a record of all the information sent and updating your DSAR log accordingly.

Summary

Although receiving any number of DSARs is no adverse reflection on your company, in some sense, it demonstrates how effective you have been in making the process transparent to the individuals whose data you process. However, the mishandling of a DSAR could have serious negative knock-on effects, not the least of which would be an erosion of trust and loyalty amongst your employees and customers. Therefore, it's worth making any amount of effort to avoid that!

Data Subject Access Requests ~ Matt

With the advent of codified privacy rights for consumers and data subjects, a new organizational function has been created: the appropriate and timely response to data subject access rights (DSARs).[128] DSARs result in privacy-specific interactions and obligations with consumers and, in some instances, employees of an organization. Focus on DSARs and the obligations that they create is not new. For example, in the U.S. the Fair Credit Reporting Act (FCRA), originally enacted in 1970, was amended in 2003 with the Fair and Accurate Transactions Act (FACTA) that allows U.S. consumers to obtain a copy of their credit report from each credit bureau. The HIPAA privacy rule, also enacted in 2003, affords individuals the right to access their health records with certain exceptions.

While FACTA and HIPAA created scenarios where individuals could request access to their data, the GDPR highlighted the organizational impacts of fulfilling one DSAR in particular, Article 17 *Right to Erasure ("right to be forgotten")*, that fundamentally changed how we look at DSARs. During my work as an analyst covering the GDPR, how to address the right to be forgotten was front and center on the majority of my GDPR inquiries.[129] Like other access rights requests, including those established by the CCPA/CPRA, my guidance during these discussions was to keep the regulation's text handy to inform how these DSARs should be addressed. So, let's delve into the constituent parts of DSARs and how the organization should be prepared to manage access rights respectfully.

---

[128] DSARs are also frequently referred to as data subject access *requests*. Given the importance of privacy rights, I think it's valuable to emphasize the consumer's or data subject's *rights* with respect to their data.

[129] An inquiry allows an organization to speak with an analyst in depth on a scenario that is particularly germane to that organization. The high volume of inquiries that analysts typically field allow them to quickly distill insights and best practices on the topics at hand and get a pulse of how organizations across the globe are thinking about and confronting privacy, security, and other governance topics.

The right to be forgotten, which is now surfacing in other privacy regulations globally, has important context that should inform how we manage DSARs. Specifically, certain conditions must be met for a data subject to be forgotten. First, there is a misconception that DSARs are absolute rights. This is not necessarily the case. As noted in the GDPR's Article 17 (1)(b), the personal data in question may be subject to "other legal ground[s] for processing." There are also potential issues with regulatory precedence based on the data elements at hand. For example, retention requirements, notably for protected health information, may trump an individual's request to have their information forgotten. And undoubtedly, if, as an example, I have a multi-year agreement with an organization—say for the lease of a vehicle—I cannot simply ask to be forgotten to avoid these obligations. From the obvious to more subtly nuanced scenarios, DSARs are replete with idiosyncrasies requiring context and planning.

First, the organization should know what type of data was collected about the individual, whether this data is subject to organizational or regulatory context that may impact the DSAR, and where this data resides (be it in organizationally managed applications and IT systems or with third parties with whom the organization has outsourced certain data processing functions). Most importantly, the identity of the requestor must be verified—we'll touch upon that below.

Do not underestimate the regulatory context of DSARs. In conjunction with other identified stakeholders, the organization's privacy leader, customer care, Human Resources, and IT should document and maintain an inventory of the regulations that could necessitate this form of interaction with consumers, customers, or employees. These obligations should be validated by counsel for areas of overlap (e.g., where one regulatory response may conflict with another) and the order of precedence (e.g., which regulatory environment has priority in the context of the DSAR at hand). Declare war on ambiguity here. Document all the potential access rights scenarios that the organization may encounter and highlight how to address each of these obligations, including verifications of identities, timeliness of responses, and logging and tracking of these actions. Document these expectations and ensure that staff members who interact with consumers are well-versed on how to process DSARs.

DSARs are about rights. They encompass multiple privacy rights that the organization should be aware of. These include an individual's right to access their information, rectify inaccurate or incomplete information, and opt-out of certain processing activities, including having their data sold or otherwise transferred from the data controller to another entity. DSARs and privacy notices go hand in hand. Before the information is collected, the consumer or data subject should be explicitly informed of their rights over how the company uses their information and how to exercise their rights. They must also be told which regulatory agency is available to adjudicate differences between the data subject or consumer and the data controller if there are disputes.

Processing DSARs should not be a random, reactive, or ambiguous function. There are critical elements to the DSAR process that organizations should validate, document, and train staff on how specific DSAR scenarios are addressed in both the spirit and the letter of the regulation. In the pages that follow, I'll review the essential functions and context necessary to operationalize handling DSARs.

Inventory DSAR Scenarios for the Organization

In collaboration with other stakeholders, the privacy leader should identify the scenarios where DSARs may come into scope. Then, create a knowledge base of these scenarios and highlight fundamental rights and obligations created by each scenario. As part of this effort, capture details related to timing (more on this below), which department will field the request, authentication requirements (more on this below), and other relevant details. As you compile this information, pause to validate your understanding with appropriate stakeholders.

Validate the Obligations for Each DSAR Scenario

The knowledge base should clearly describe how to address each DSAR scenario. As an example, if an individual is legitimately asking to be forgotten, determine and validate how to expunge that individual's personal data from the various systems where their specific personal data resides. This validation would also ensure that the response to the DSAR is addressed within mandated timeframes. Think expansively about these obligations and any dependencies that may apply to the scenario. Then, ensure that these dependencies are captured accurately and fully within the knowledge base.

Determine the Inherent Risk Associated with the DSAR Scenario

The processing of DSARs should not be perfunctory. Specific scenarios may have risk factors that require special consideration and analysis. While not required for each DSAR scenario, consider a conducting a quick threat model of high-risk scenarios with a simple STRIDE analysis.[130] Specific scenarios, including removing an individual's records from a system, will require context and validation of the individual's identity. Spoofing risks, where an individual assumes the identity of another individual for potentially nefarious purposes, should be addressed proactively. Effectively, validate how the right to access, rectify, or be forgotten could be invoked and used in inappropriate or nefarious ways. Imagine, as a case in point, that an individual's identity is spoofed and their personal data, including health records, are disclosed to a domestic violence perpetrator or someone who is subject to a restraining

---

[130] STRIDE represents a series of undesirable risks including Spoofing, Tampering, Repudiation, Information Disclosure, Denial of Service, and Elevation of privilege. Each risk has an associated control. To conduct a threat model using STRIDE, stakeholders should evaluate the appropriate controls to address each of the risk factors associated with STRIDE. Where control gaps are noted, ensure that these risk factors are captured in a risk register for appropriate treatment.

order.[131] In addition, DSARs face social engineering risks. Ensure that as your team documents the various DSAR scenarios, they capture risks and mitigation strategies related to each scenario. Think expansively about risk considerations.

Document How the Data Subject or Consumer's Identity Will Be Verified

Not all DSARs are created equal. Specific scenarios, as noted above, have inherently higher risk considerations than others. How the organization validates the individual's identity should be commensurate to the risk considerations associated with the request. Individuals who live in the U.S. have the right to access and review their credit history and affect changes to information determined to be incomplete or inaccurate. Getting access to one's credit history requires a higher level of authentication and corroboration of one's identity. There are inherently high risks associated with inadvertent or illegal access to credit histories that could facilitate identity theft and other risks. Accordingly, the credit bureaus require multiple validations of an individual's identity before disclosing credit-related data. Based on their risk profile, scenarios should capture how to authenticate the data subject's or individual's identity. Ideally, these authentication controls are automated. Where the DSAR involves interaction with staff, they must be trained on how to authenticate identities. These teams should also be aware that specific regulations, notably the California Privacy Rights Act, allow individuals to designate organizations to act on their behalf to process DSARs. How these designated entities should be verified and validated should be incorporated into the process where designated entities make requests on behalf of data subjects or consumers. The privacy leader may want to spend some time with the organization's security

---

[131] The scourge that is domestic violence has critical implications with respect to DSARs and privacy practices in general. Individuals who are fleeing abusive relationships need to maintain their privacy and have the details related to their address and the services they receive kept in the strictest of confidence. Too frequently perpetrators, who excel at manipulation, find ways to get an unknowing service provider to disclose an address or other details that allow the victim's location to be identified.

leadership to evaluate approaches to identity authentication and the risks and controls for various authentication methods.

Document, Log, and Track the Status of DSARs

Privacy regulations that outline scenarios for responding to DSARs provide expectations related to how these requests are logged and tracked for compliance purposes. Ideally, the organization should use an application that can help automate essential governance activities related to the processing of DSARs. Document which requests may be legitimately denied based on regulatory or organizational context, and how these activities are logged, time-stamped, and tracked through their fulfillment or denial lifecycle. Multiple purpose-built applications can assist with these obligations. As part of the core inventory of DSAR scenarios, ensure that the timing and logging of these requests are captured accurately. Many regulations require that responses to DSARs are handled within a given timeline. These obligations should be known, validated, and incorporated into training. This context should be incorporated into the knowledge base that provides context for the contemplated DSARs.

Identify the System of Record for the Processing of DSARs

As we have noted throughout this book, personal data can permeate all corners of an organization. This data can reside in multiple applications or be processed by third parties on behalf of the organization. In all their guises, these systems must be identified to address DSARs related to providing the individual with access to their data, the ability to update or correct that data where changes are in order, and to have their data removed from the organization and its systems. This context should be incorporated into the organization's knowledge base. In the context of good change management practices, it's important that changes to records, including record deletion, be maintained in the context of the underlying regulation.

Beyond the systems where personal data may be processed or stored, identify which system of record to use to process DSARs and other privacy-related matters. Link the DSAR management systems to the knowledge base, wiki, or intranet site where you maintain the requirements for authentication, the timelines for the response, and exclusions. The system should be intuitive for the users, and the application(s) should track the timing of responses from the moment the individual submitted the DSAR through its completion (even when the request is denied).

Train Staff, Notably Those that Interact with Data Subjects and Consumers

As part of the core documentation related to DSARs, it is critical to identify staff interacting with consumers, individuals, data subjects, and employees. As noted above, there are inherent risks with DSAR processing. For example, a bad actor could spoof the individual's identity, records that warrant longer retention periods per other regulations could be deleted, or inappropriate information could be disclosed. Inform staff who interact with DSAR processing about these risks, train them on the process, and ensure they know to escalate concerns when the current level of documentation is inadequate.

To avoid falling prey to social engineering schemes and processing DSARs inappropriately, pay special attention to call centers, customer contact centers, sales and marketing staff, and receptionists. Include everyone who fields direct inquiries from consumers or data subjects. The privacy leader should not assume that the organization follows even well-documented procedures. Validate that the ground truth is consistent with organizational policy and regulatory obligations. The privacy leader should spend time with staff who interact with the DSAR process to confirm their understanding and validate risk factors and organizational obligations related to DSAR processing. Invite stakeholders to question the process and validate their understanding. "I was not aware" is never an appropriate response should a DSAR be handled in an inappropriate or untimely fashion.

Processing DSARs, depending upon the organization's industry and sector, should be a defined business function with clear guidance and training for the teams that interact with the process, whether through direct interaction with consumers or back-office functions where personal data is processed and stored. In addition, procedures related to verification and the explicit documentation of DSAR obligations should be front and center and free of ambiguity. Beyond these "well-managed" attributes to the DSAR function, the privacy leader should spend time with other key executives to ensure that the tone at the top of the organization engenders trust with the consumer by respecting the privacy rights of individuals and making the exercise of these rights simple and straightforward to enact. I believe organizations that respect the privacy rights of individuals will ultimately be those whose brands and enterprise values shine. Respect and trust matter.

Privacy Rights Requests ~ Justine

Privacy Rights Request ("PRR") is a term[132] that is intentionally broad and all-inclusive to describe the process when an individual exercises their rights under a particular law by asking a business to respond to their requests. PRRs are also referred to as Data Subject Access Requests (DSARs) under GDPR and Consumer Rights Requests (CRRs) under CCPA/CPRA. When building a global privacy program, PRRs are a neutral term that can help describe the general process and protocol for responding to these requests.

California Love

Broad privacy laws (and regulations interpreting those laws) typically provide detailed requirements about what a business must do to comply with the individual's requests. Most organizations want to have a simplified and universal way to process PRRs. Unfortunately, the laws are nuanced enough to make it impossible to design a one-size-fits-all approach to comply with all laws globally. However, the common principles are pretty standard across the laws. For purposes of this section, I will focus on CCPA/CPRA and creating a workflow to process requests from a California resident. If the enterprise primarily operates in the United States, then using CCPA/CPRA as the baseline will cover most jurisdictions throughout the United States. If the enterprise has headquarters in Europe with some presence in the U.S., then it may make sense to have a GDPR-centric privacy program with some California and U.S.-specific disclosures. The workflows in this section adhere to the laws outlined in the California Civil Code and the regulations adopted by the California Attorney General and leverage some technology to streamline the PRR response process.

---

[132] My colleague Kieran de Terra developed this term of art to help our clients and team create a common language around privacy that was not beholden to any particular statute.

The Types of PRRs

The types of PRRs vary by jurisdiction but generally include the following rights to request:

- additional information from the company about the data collected, the purpose, how it was used, and who it was shared with
- access to the data collected
- deletion (aka the "Right to Be Forgotten")
- modification
- opt-out of selling or sharing personal information
- opt-out of cookies and other tracking technologies

The foregoing list does not include all the rights granted by CCPA/CPRA or other privacy laws; rather, it includes the type of privacy rights that gives consumers a legal entitlement to make *requests* of the business.

The Laws

Rights emerge from laws. As discussed in Chapter 12, the laws and the rights they bestow apply to those residing in a particular jurisdiction. Privacy and consumer protection laws provide individuals with rights to make privacy requests. The purpose and intent of these laws and rights are to give individuals meaningful access to and control over their personal information. Therefore, it is imperative to identify the laws that provide privacy rights requests to individuals whose data the business collects so you can develop workflows to allow individuals to assert those rights.

Complying with privacy rights requests is one of the more complicated compliance areas and requires thoughtful leadership and a deeper understanding of the data flows and data elements. Below are two examples of how laws grant individuals the right to assert privacy rights requests from businesses.

- **GDPR.** "A data subject should have the right of access to personal data which have been collected concerning him or

Handling Data Subject Requests

her, and to exercise that right easily and at reasonable intervals, to be aware of, and verify, the lawfulness of the processing." Recital 63 of the GDPR.

- **CCPA.** "[...] It is the intent of the Legislature to further Californians' right to privacy by giving consumers an effective way to control their personal information, by ensuring the following rights: [...] Section 2 of the CCPA.

Pro Tip: During data mapping, add a column or field that identifies the jurisdictions where consumers or data subjects reside to understand which privacy laws apply to them. Also identify how many individuals reside in the various jurisdictions. Laws like CCPA/CPRA have thresholds that trigger application. One of the thresholds is if the business collects data from California residents or households (CCPA = 50,000 and CPRA = 100,000), then the law applies. Record the jurisdictions and number of individuals within each jurisdiction from the data map to create a matrix of those jurisdictions. Then layer in the laws within those jurisdictions to identify whether there is a broad privacy law that allows individuals to assert privacy rights requests. This will help develop workflows that can be geographically limited to individuals that reside in those jurisdictions or customized to comply with the laws of those jurisdictions.

Methods for Asserting Privacy Rights and Receiving Requests

Laws and regulations may specify the required methods to submit PRRs. Under CCPA's regulations published by the Attorney General, all businesses (except those who operate exclusively online) must provide a toll-free telephone number so consumers can assert PRRs. Businesses that operate solely online may provide an email address instead. Additionally, businesses that operate websites or mobile apps must also provide an online webform. The regulations go on to clarify that businesses must provide at least one method that reflects the way "the business primarily interacts with the consumer, even if that requires a business to offer three methods[.]"[133]

Pro Tip. Develop workflows that ensure individuals can submit PRRs in a standardized, uniform way. To the extent feasible, use webforms to allow consumers (or personnel receiving the request from the consumer) to enter information related to the request into the webform. Standardized intake also increases efficiency in managing requests, ensuring that businesses request the information that is necessary to comply with the CCPA. Utilizing technology to support or automate PRRs also creates a digital trail of the PRR which can be helpful in meeting deadlines and reporting.

Whatever the method the business creates, they must "[e]nsure that all individuals responsible for handling consumer inquiries . . . are informed of all the requirements [related to consumer rights] and how to direct consumers to exercise those rights[.]"[134] This usually means that any individuals that are involved in the PRRs process must receive some training that is customized to that particular law.

Pro Tip. For businesses subject to CCPA/CPRA, consider offering CCPA/CPRA training that explains the laws and privacy rights, workflows, and how to respond to those workflows in compliance with the law. Award certificates of completion of the training and maintain those to demonstrate that all individuals that are part of the process have received this training.

Be Mindful of Deadlines

The laws also provide specific deadlines to acknowledge receipt of the request and substantively respond to PRRs. These nuances make standardizing a single global process difficult because the deadlines are different under various laws. For example, in California, the business must confirm receipt of the request within ten days and provide basic information about how the business will process the request or what the consumer may expect. Then substantive compliance must be completed within 45 days (absent an extension).

---

[133] Cal. Code Regs tit. 11 § 999.308(c)(6).
[134] Cal. Code Regs tit. 11 § 999.317(a).

Under GDPR, the request must be completed within 30 days from receiving it.

Operationalizing the PRRs

Disclosures about How to Exercise Privacy Rights

Most broad privacy laws require a business to describe in a privacy policy or notice how individuals may exercise their rights under the law—for example, posting a website disclosure that explains the methods for an individual to submit their requests (e.g., toll-free telephone number, email address, online webform, in person or by mail). Certain laws require multiple methods to be available to the individuals. One practical tip is to think about the standard ways the business communicates with the consumer. An e-commerce site will undoubtedly want a web collection form, while a restaurant may offer a disclosure in their window or a QR code on the menu. The disclosure about exercising PRRs is often contained in an online privacy policy (although if the business doesn't communicate with consumers electronically, a paper copy may be required). Another practical tip is to make the disclosure simple to understand. The California Attorney General recommends writing a privacy policy at an eighth-grade reading level.

Pro Tip. Leverage technology to see how your efforts are measuring up. For example, Microsoft Word offers readability statistics as part of their "Authoring and Proofing Tools" features. Or run policies, notices, or disclosures through Grammarly to ensure the sentences are grammatically correct. Finally, on your website, run an open-source cookie scan like Ghostery to confirm that what is happening on your website is consistent with what is posted in your privacy policy. These are the types of tools used by regulators and plaintiffs' attorneys.

Notice at Collection and The Right to Know

Businesses must include a notice at the point information is collected. These notices at collection are intended to provide transparency to individuals about privacy practices before the information is collected. Presumably, these notices will sufficiently inform consumers about practices so that they can decide whether or not to share their information with the business. The notice at collection can be linked to a privacy policy that contains a list of the categories of personal information collected and the business purpose for each category.

What Is a Privacy Policy?

Privacy policy has many different meanings. In legal circles, privacy policy often refers to an online privacy policy that must be conspicuously posted on a website. In 2003, California was the first state in the United States to require businesses to post a privacy policy on their website. Since then, the information required in privacy policies has grown, and these policies are now used to serve purposes well beyond website disclosures. With laws like CCPA and GDPR, privacy policies are the place where most disclosures about privacy practices for both digital and physical data are contained. Privacy policies now include descriptions of privacy practices online, in mobile applications, paper records, offline, and in person.

Pro Tip. When writing your privacy policy, make it simple. As the California Attorney General recommended in the CCPA Regulations, prepare the notice in "plain, straightforward language that avoids technical or legal jargon." After preparing the notice, make sure that it is posted in a clear and conspicuous place when you hand it off to the website development team so consumers can see it. Remember to translate the notice into languages in which the business operates. Finally, don't forget ADA and website accessibility, so the notice is accessible to consumers with disabilities.[135]

One of the requirements in most comprehensive privacy laws is informing individuals about the "right to know" things. California, for example, requires a business to disclose the following rights to create transparency:

---

[135] Web Content Accessibility Guidelines, version 2.1 of June 5, 2018, from the World Wide Web Consortium.

- categories of personal information it has collected about the individual
- categories of sources from which the personal information was collected
- business or commercial purpose for collecting or selling personal information
- categories of third parties with whom the business shares personal information
- specific pieces of personal information it has collected about them

Pro Tip. Spend some time thinking about all the places your business takes in personal information and include them in the privacy policy. Solicit ideas from your colleagues about collection points. For example, are you including website interactions? What data is collected when your customer visits your store or calls the Help Desk or Customer Service? Taking a comprehensive approach to your privacy policy will save time complying with a PRR under the Right to Know.

Processing the PRR and Engaging Service Providers

Complying with a PRR requires the business to notify any service providers of the request and ensure they also comply. As more fully discussed in Chapter 9, "Vendor Management," service providers are vendors that enter into a written agreement with the business and agree they will only retain, use, host, disclose, or share data to perform the contract. Service providers must also agree to comply with a PRR if they receive it. Service providers do not directly need to receive and process requests from consumers, but they need to comply with a request the business receives. On the other hand, a third party does not have to comply with PRRs submitted to the business. Although third parties do not have to comply with PRRs the business receives, the consumer does have the right (1) to know the categories of third parties and (2) to opt-out of the business sharing their data with third parties. This gives the consumers control over how their personal information is shared with others.

Opt-In vs. Opt-Out Models

User-enabled control over data is the trend, which means the right to opt-in and opt-out of certain privacy practices appear in most comprehensive privacy laws.

- **Opt-In.** Opt-in means the business is not permitted to collect, store, share, maintain, or use data unless the individual affirmatively opts-in to the practice. Opt-in methods typically include a disclosure and a box acknowledging consent to allow the company to collect, store, share, maintain, or use the data. In other words, the business can only collect, store, share, maintain, and use data after the individual affirmatively opts-in and consents. Opt-in is primarily the model used in the EU under GDPR but is also used for HIPAA disclosures and COPPA.

- **Opt-Out.** An opt-out model means the business can collect, store, share, maintain, or use data, but with the requirement that the business offers the individual the right to opt-out of the practice. For example, a disclosure may appear that explains the right to opt-out, but the business may collect the data consistent with the notice unless an individual does opt-out. This is the model used primarily in the U.S. under CCPA/CPRA for sharing data with third parties.

Selling/Sharing Personal Information and Rights to Opt-Out under CCPA/CPRA

Under CCPA/CPRA, individuals have a right to opt-out of the sale of their personal information to third parties.[136] Sale is broadly defined as sharing personal information with any third parties for monetary or other valuable consideration. This often includes businesses conducting targeted marketing or advertising like Google Analytics, Facebook, and Instagram. However, if a business uses a service provider to process or host consumer data and fails to meet

---

[136] On January 1, 2023 this right to opt-out will expand to the selling **or sharing** of personal information.

the criteria of a service provider (e.g., having an agreement with a vendor that restricts how they can use the data), then that vendor may be a third party and there is arguably a right to opt-out.

Businesses that sell (or, effective 2023, "share") personal information are required to provide consumers with (a) notice and (b) the ability to opt-out of the sale of personal information to third parties (the "Right to Opt-out"). A business must not sell the personal information it collected when the business did not have a notice explaining the right unless it obtains the affirmative authorization of the consumer. A business that does not sell personal information is not required to disclose or explain the right to opt-out. Instead, businesses that don't sell data to third parties must state that they do not sell personal information in their privacy policies.

Methods for Submitting Requests to Opt-Out

The business must comply with the laws that proscribe specific methods for submitting requests to opt-out. For example, California residents have a right to opt-out of their information being sold or shared with third parties if they click a link on the businesses' website that says: "Do Not Sell My Personal Information." Other methods to opt-out include calling a toll-free phone number, submitted an email form, or sending a request to an email address. In California, the Attorney General also requires businesses to recognize a "Global Privacy Controls" setting by the user as an opt-out request. Global Privacy Controls may include a browser plugin or privacy setting, device setting, or user-enabled privacy control that communicates or signals the consumer's choice to opt-out.

Responding to an Opt-Out Request

It is essential to prepare a policy, disclosure, and workflow that allows users to submit requests. But it is equally important that the technology complies with the opt-out request and the user's information is not shared or sold. Under California law, businesses have 15 days to comply with the opt-out request. However, a business may deny a request if the business thinks the request is fraudulent.

The Right to Access

Complying with a request to access data is the most time-consuming and challenging aspect of PRRs. A consumer may request access to specific pieces of personal information collected. If such a request is received, a business must provide the consumer the data free of charge and in a "portable, technically-feasible, and readily-useable format." A business does not need to provide a copy of the consumer's data more than twice in 12 months.

If it is not technically feasible to produce the data, for example due to high cost or burden, businesses may either decline to produce the data or charge a reasonable fee. The business bears the burden of proving the request is excessive and that any proposed costs are reasonable.

It's likely a team effort with your stakeholders (and service providers) to produce the information. Most data mapping is done anticipating eventual PRRs so the data sources and record owner can be flagged within the intake workflows. Then, when the request comes in, the PRR responder knows whom to ask to pull the data for that individual. Once the data is gathered, you must put it in a format accessible to the consumer.

What Is the Difference Between Categories of Personal Information and Specific Pieces of Personal Information?

CCPA/CPRA specifically reference certain "categories of data" as groups of different types of personal information. "Data elements" are the specific pieces of personal information contained within each category. Recall the chart (below) from Chapter 9, "Data Classification." Categories may have specific characteristics that warrant classification for other purposes like data retention obligations.

Handling Data Subject Requests

Categories of Personal Information	Examples of Specific Pieces of Personal Information	
Biometric Data	• Biological or behavioral characteristics • DNA • Iris image or retina scan • Finger, hand or palm print • Voice recordings	• Keystroke patterns or rhythms • Sleep • Health • Exercise data • Gait patterns or rhythms • Facial recognition • Vein patterns
Commercial Information	• Records of personal property	• Product or service purchase, review, consideration history
Characteristics of a protected classification under California or Federal law	• Race • National origin • Ancestry • Religion	• Marital status • Sex • Age • Sexual orientation • Physical or mental disability or other medical condition
Geolocation data	• Latitude • Longitude • Altitude • Direction • Time and location	• Country • Region • Continent • State • City
Health Insurance Data	• Health insurance policy number • Subscriber identification number	• Any unique identifier used by a health insurer
Medical Information	• Patient's name, address, email address, telephone number, or social security number	• Other information that reveals the individual's identity
Internet or Network Activity Information (cookie data)	• Browsing and search history	• Advertisement interaction • Information about a consumer's interaction with a website or application
Personal Information	• Real name • Alias • Postal address • Telephone number • Unique personal identifier • Online identifier • IP address • Email address • Social security number	• Driver's license, identification, passport number • Signature • Education • Professional or employment history • Bank, credit, or other financial account number • Account name

Recently, the California Attorney General published a seminal legal opinion holding that "specific pieces of personal information" includes internally generated inferences the business holds about the consumer from either internal or external information sources.[137] This opinion has broad implications for inferential or derivative data that may be compiled about California residents.

What NOT to Include in PRRs

A business must not disclose specific pieces of personal information that create risk if the data is not secured. For example, businesses should never disclose in a PRR response: social security numbers, government issued IDs, financial, health or insurance information, or usernames and passwords.

The Right to Deletion

Consumers can request that a business delete any personal information collected from the consumer. If a business receives a request to delete, it must comply with the request and direct any service provider to do the same unless one or more of the enumerated exceptions apply. Businesses must make the same methods available to submit requests to delete as described for other PRRs. Additionally, the business may present the consumer with the choice to delete select portions or all of their personal information. Although consumers have a right to request deletion, many exceptions apply.

Exceptions to the Right to Delete

There are many legitimate reasons and legal exceptions for denying a deletion request. For example, a business is not required to delete personal information if the business or service provider must maintain personal information to:

- Complete the transaction for which the personal information was collected, provide a good or service requested by the consumer, or reasonably anticipated within the context of a business's ongoing business relationship with the consumer, or otherwise perform a contract between the business and the consumer;

---

[137] Office of the Attorney General, State of California, https://oag.ca.gov/system/files/opinions/pdfs/20-303.pdf.

- Detect security incidents, protect against malicious, deceptive, fraudulent, or illegal activity, or prosecute those responsible for that activity;
- Debug to identify and repair errors that impair existing intended functionality;
- Exercise or ensure free speech, or exercise another right provided for by law;
- Comply with the California Electronic Communications Privacy Act;
- Engage in public or peer-reviewed scientific, historical, or statistical research in the public interest;
- To enable solely internal uses that are reasonably aligned with the expectations of the consumer based on the consumer's relationship with the business;
- Comply with a legal obligation; or
- Otherwise use the consumer's personal information internally, in a lawful manner that is compatible with the context in which the consumer provided the information.

Complying with PRRs to Delete by Deletion, De-identification, and Aggregation

Assuming no exception applies, the business must comply with the consumer's request to delete their personal information by (1) permanently and completely deleting the information; (2) de-identifying it; or (3) aggregating it. Whatever the action, the business must describe it in response to the request, including whether it relies on any exceptions to retain data.

Deletion

A business can comply with a request to delete under the CCPA by "permanently and completely erasing the personal information on its existing systems." However, due to the significant costs of deleting information from backup systems, California regulations provide that data may remain on archived or backup systems unless or until the archived or backup system is next accessed. In other words, businesses do not need to delete personal information stored on backup systems unless the data is restored from backups to an active state—then the business would need to apply all of the PRRs they previously received to delete an individual's personal data.

Deleting data is easier said than done. For example, removing files from systems may create technical issues and interfere with functionality. Data may exist in several copies across systems or backup systems. Moreover, since businesses must direct service providers to delete data, those service providers may face similar problems. In some instances, de-identifying the data may be the most technically viable solution to a request for deletion. Whichever method you use, you must provide consumers with clear information on the steps that the business took to eradicate the personal information from their systems.

De-identification

A business may also respond to a request to delete by de-identifying or anonymizing the data. Information is "de-identified" when it does not directly or indirectly identify a particular consumer, and the business has implemented technical safeguards and business processes that prohibit the reidentification of the consumer to whom the information may pertain.

The following are resources that set standards for "technical safeguards" and "business processes" that prohibit reidentification:

- The National Institute of Standards and Technology (NIST) comprehensive guide on the De-identification of Personal Information.[138]
- The HIPAA de-identification standard[139] requires companies to either: (a) remove all of 18 types of identifiers listed in the standard, or (b) engage an expert with appropriate knowledge and experience who can apply technical means to de-identify the information.

---

[138] De-identification of Personal Information, National Institute of Standards and Technology, Simson L. Garfinkel, https://nvlpubs.nist.gov/nistpubs/ir/2015/nist.ir.8053.pdf.
[139] 45 CFR § 164.514(a)-(b).

Aggregation

Aggregate data is information that:

- Relates to a group or category of consumers;
- From which individual consumer identities have been removed; and,
- That is not linked or reasonably linkable to any consumer or household, including via a device.

Generally, aggregating data involves performing analytics or drawing statistical information from that data. For example, this could include reporting the number of crimes each month rather than releasing data about individual incidents. A comparative analogy found in the HIPAA Privacy Rule describes data aggregation as combining PHI from multiple covered entities "to permit data analyses that relate to the health care operations," such as quality assurance, case management, care coordination, and outcomes evaluation. In other words, individuals' PHI is combined to extrapolate general statistical information about health care operations.

Automated Technology to Process PRRs

Many businesses elect to use technology to help automate and streamline the processing of PRRs. Webforms allow you to collect requests in a standardized, uniform way. The business must evaluate the cost/benefit ratio. If the business only receives five PRRs a year, implementing an automated solution may not be the best use of time and money. But five requests a week or month may justify the cost of having a platform to automate the process, particularly if many people are involved in servicing the request. Using webforms created by your business or hosted by a third-party provider allows consumers or personnel to enter information related to the request.[140] This standardized intake increases efficiency in managing requests and ensures the business follows the process steps and meets deadlines.

---

[140] There are many options, two of the more popular are OneTrust and TrustArc.

Manually managing PRRs can be time-consuming, and compliance steps and deadlines can easily get missed.

Be a Good Communicator

An individual that takes time to submit a PRR wants to be heard, and the law requires a response. Being a good communicator can help manage the requestor's expectations. For example, many consumers submit CCPA requests to businesses when all they really want is to opt-out of receiving marketing emails and materials. Under California law, being a good and timely communicator is a legal requirement.

Verifying the Requester Is Authentic

After receiving a PRR, a business must promptly take steps to verify that the request is authentic. Businesses must establish, document, and comply with reasonable procedures to verify or authenticate that the person making a request is, in fact, the consumer or an authorized agent of the consumer. California law requires a certain degree of care depending on the type of request. If the request is general (e.g., what type of information does the business collect), verification should be reasonable (e.g., verify one data element like address, date of birth, or email address). However, if a requester seeks access to specific pieces of personal information collected, a business must verify the consumer's identity with a "reasonably high degree of certainty." Under California law, a reasonably high degree of certainty may include matching at least three pieces of personal information maintained by the business. Depending on the sensitivity of the information involved, the business may even require a signed declaration under penalty of perjury.

Identity Verification Methods

Identity verification methods help the business verify that the requester is the person they purport to be and that the request is authentic. The California Attorney General provided helpful guidance for developing identity verification methods that include matching identifying information the business already maintains, avoiding collecting additional sensitive information like social security number, considering the risk of harm and fraudulent or malicious activity, and utilizing verification technologies.[141]

Verification for Password-Protected Accounts

If a business maintains a password-protected account for consumers, it may verify their identity through the authentication process used in the account (e.g., entering their username and password). However, the business should still consider the risk-mitigating measures discussed in the section above. For example, if the business suspects there is fraudulent or malicious activity on the account, it should reject a request to know until it can further verify that the request is authentic using other verification steps that it would use for non-password protected accounts.

Time Period to Respond to Requests to Know

Laws typically impose deadlines to respond to consumer requests. These timelines require organization and are one of the key reasons businesses use technology to automate the response process. Below is a quick reference chart for timelines to respond to PRRs under CCPA/CPRA.

Rights Request	Initial Request Response Time	Total Response Time Allowed In Case of an Extension
Acknowledgement	10 Days	
Correct	45 Days	90 Days
Delete	45 Days	90 Days
Know (Access)	45 Days	90 Days
Opt Out of Sale	15 Business Days	15 Business Days

Figure 13.1 Timelines for PRRs

Confirming Receipt. In California, the business must confirm receipt of the request within ten days. This confirmation must provide information about how the business will process the request, including a description of the verification process. The business must also describe when the consumer should expect a response. In cases where the business grants or denies a consumer request within ten

---

[141] 11 Cal. Code Regs. Tit. 11 § 999.323(b).

days of receipt, the business does not have to send a receipt confirmation to the consumer.[142]

45-Day Response Deadline. The CCPA/CPRA requires that businesses respond to consumer requests to correct, know (access), or delete data within 45 days from the date of receiving the response. This period begins from the date of receiving the request and includes the time it takes to verify the individual.

Extension of Time to Respond. When it is reasonably necessary under the circumstances, a business may extend the 45-day response deadline once by an additional 45 days, giving the business a total of 90 days to respond. Acceptable reasons to extend may include complicated processes or systems, the data is not readily identifiable, or a service provider maintains the data and is non-responsive or slow to cooperate.

Privacy Rights Requests Templates

Developing sample or template responses before responding to privacy requests is highly recommended. Legal analysis is often required to identify what data qualifies as "personal information," whether exceptions apply, and whether the business is legally required to delete data. It also saves time when the clock is ticking on consumer response deadlines. Although software and tools provide some template language, they still require customization to reflect your particular business and circumstances.

Pro Tip. Use language that captures the essence and tone of how your business communicates with its customers. Make the responses easy to understand and clear about what is being produced in response to the request. Write at an eighth grade reading level. Remove legalese as consumers are not likely to understand it.

---

[142] See Code Regs., tit. 11, § 999.313 (a).
Civ. Code § 1798.130(2).
Code Regs., tit. 11, § 999.313 (b).
Civ. Code § 1798.130(2).

Model Workflows to Respond to The Rights to Know and Access

Whether using software or an application that helps automate the response process, or doing it manually, businesses can benefit from workflows that demonstrate the key steps in managing requests from start to finish. These workflows can then be integrated into the automated tool or can serve as a DIY guide for responding. The Workflow sections at the end of this essay include sample workflows for consumer requests.

Wrapping It All Up with a Bow

Most comprehensive privacy laws require that businesses maintain records related to privacy rights requests. Also, good privacy hygiene requires creating and retaining evidence that the business met its obligations under the law. Additionally, CCPA/CPRA requires businesses to retain records of consumer requests and how the business responded to such requests for at least 24 months. Certain businesses also have compliance reporting obligations to the State. Certain technologies help document and maintain a record of consumer requests and how the business responded.

We dedicate tremendous time and energy to a privacy program, and documents are compelling evidence of those efforts. If nothing ever goes wrong, the reports will never be revisited, and after the retention period, they will be deleted. But in the unfortunate event of an audit, litigation, or regulatory proceeding, the documentation will demonstrate defensible and reasonable efforts you and the business took to create a meaningful privacy program built on principles of trust and in the spirit of upholding privacy laws.

Workflows

Creating a visual workflow like the one below can help streamline compliance with privacy rights requests:

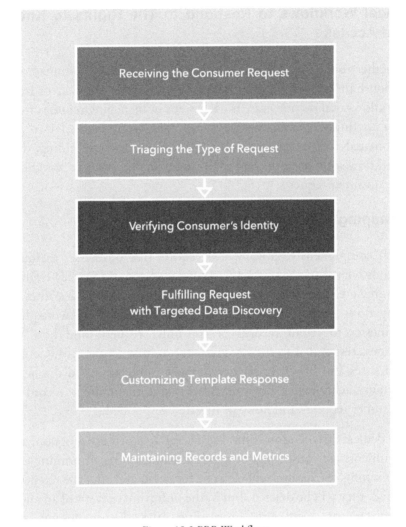

Figure 13.2 PRR Workflows

Key Insights and Recommended Next Steps

Key Insights

- Data subject access requests (DSARs) or privacy rights requests (PRRs) can come into the organization in many ways, not just through traditional customer service and support channels. It is imperative that all customer-facing staff are trained in recognizing and handling these requests.
- DSARs and PRRs are about the assertion of rights that an individual has over their data, but these rights are not absolute. It's important to validate the request before fulfilling it.
- To meet the requirement to honor rights requests, to gather all information on an individual or to delete this data, it is best to tag the data as it is collected, identifying the data subject and the internal owner of that relationship.
- Verifying identity is critical to validating the rights request and to ensuring that the process is not misused or abused.
- Rights requests are time-bound. Have runbooks in place, so you do not lose time figuring out how to respond.
- The rights request requirements on your third-party providers are dictated by the type of third party.

Recommended Next Steps

- Work with stakeholders responsible for data collection to tag all data subject to privacy regulations, identifying the data subject and the record owner.
- Create runbooks for customer-facing staff to identify and respond to rights requests.
- Spend time with the departments and their staff that process DSARs and PRRs to ensure practices are consistent with organizational policy and regulatory requirement. Validate that these staff and departments are well trained on DSAR and PRR processing and that they are aware of the various risks of how these processes can be used in appropriate ways.

Conclusion

Throughout the *Data Privacy Program Guide,* we have shared our perspectives on balancing the rights of the consumer and the business imperatives of the companies that have custodial responsibilities for the data they collect, process, and use. We believe this book is very timely—most of the books that cover privacy are oriented toward consumers who want to reassert their anonymity in the digital age. In this book, we acknowledge that desire, but show privacy leaders how to manage a program to meet those needs while allowing their organization to meet its objectives. Any transaction that provides value to both sides must balance the needs of both.

We've written this book to lay out the fundamental constructs of corporate privacy programs as well as give you actionable steps you can take to assess and enhance your company's privacy program. As we said in the introduction, we've included almost 100 key insights and recommended next steps. We encourage you to review those insights and see how they apply to your company and assess which of the steps we've recommended you could take to improve your current program.

We'd like to leave you with one final thought. Inherent in the role of a privacy professional is the opportunity to elevate your company's relationship with your customers and that requires that you become an advocate for the privacy program as a driver of corporate value. This in turn requires that you learn how to manage the balance between your company's obligations and the rights of the data subjects whose data you have a custodial duty to protect. To succeed, we suggest you adopt a mindset of continued outreach and continual learning. Network with other privacy professionals, including corporate practitioners, consumer advocates, and regulators. Join professional groups. Attend conferences, read books, and contribute to the profession.

We welcome your feedback and invite you to visit our website: http://www.cisodrg.com or our LinkedIn company page:

https://www.linkedin.com/company/ciso-desk-reference-guide.

Appendix to Data Privacy Program Guide

Disambiguation Guide

Not surprisingly, there are several terms and expressions used across the book that appear similar in meaning in certain contexts but different in others. The objective of this section is to, as far as possible, clarify and disambiguate between these terms.

Security

Appropriate security	The GDPR does not explicitly use this term, but it does emphasize the appropriateness of security measures to be taken. For example:

"Taking into account the state of the art, the costs of implementation and the nature, scope, context and purposes of processing as well as the risk of varying likelihood and severity for the rights and freedoms of natural persons, the controller and the processor shall implement appropriate technical and organizational measures to ensure a level of security appropriate to the risk, including inter alia as appropriate"

And further:

"In assessing the appropriate level of security account shall be taken in particular of the risks that are presented by processing, in particular from accidental or unlawful destruction, loss, alteration, unauthorized disclosure of, or access to personal data transmitted, stored or otherwise processed."

(Article 32, Security of processing)

Reasonable security	Reasonable security has a similar meaning to that outlined in the GDPR and is a requirement of the CPRA, which specifically provides that: *"A business that collects a consumer's personal information shall implement reasonable security procedures and practices appropriate to the nature of the personal information to protect the personal information from unauthorized or illegal access, destruction, use, modification, or disclosure in accordance with Section 1798.81.5."*
Necessary security	Essentially, an alternative industry expression for the above.

Roles & Responsibilities

Data Protection Officer (DPO)	A DPO is a role identified by the GDPR and can be appointed in certain conditions specified in Article 37 or voluntarily. The specific, but not necessarily exclusive, tasks assigned to the DPO are listed in Article 39. A CPO could also have DPO responsibilities, although that cannot be an assumption.
Chief Privacy Officer (CPO)	A CPO is a corporate executive charged with developing and implementing policies designed to protect employee and customer data from unauthorized access. This role is a requisite for HIPAA compliance—see also Privacy Official.

Chief Information Security Officer (CISO)	A CISO is the senior-level executive within an organization responsible for establishing and maintaining the enterprise vision, strategy, and program to ensure information assets and technologies are adequately protected. An organization may include the role of CPO within that of the CISO, but it is usually kept separate.
Privacy Advocate	One of the primary roles of the Privacy Leader is to be an organization's Privacy Advocate.
Privacy Leader	Typically, the role of Privacy Leader would be held by the CPO/DPO, but in smaller companies, for example, the responsibility could fall on another member of an organization's senior management team.
Privacy Official	An alternative title to CPO.

Privacy

Privacy-enabled Privacy-enhancing Privacy-preserving	Although these three terms semantically could be interpreted quite distinctly from each other, essentially, they are more or less interchangeable. The most common expression using one of these terms is "privacy-enhancing technologies (PETs)." Ironically, this definition from the Royal Society captures all three: *"What are **Privacy Enhancing** Technologies (PETs)? PETs are a disruptive set of technologies and approaches which, when combined with changes in wider policy and business frameworks, could **enable** the sharing and use of data in a **privacy-preserving** manner."*[143]

---

[143] How can technologies help organizations and individuals protect data in practice and, at the same time, unlock opportunities for data access and use?

Assessment

Data Protection Impact Assessment (DPIA)	A data protection impact assessment must always be conducted when the processing could result in a high risk to the rights and freedoms of natural persons. The assessment must be carried out especially if one of the rule examples set forth in GDPR Article 35(3) is relevant.
Privacy Impact Assessment (PIA)	Both PIA and DPIA are mentioned in GDPR Article 35, but DPIA is assumed to be the 'norm.' A PIA is all about analyzing how an entity collects, uses, shares, and maintains personally identifiable information, related to existing risks and is used prior to the setting up of a privacy program. A DPIA is about identifying and minimizing risks associated with the processing of personal data and is often carried out in the context of the GDPR requirement or voluntarily.

The Royal Society, https://royalsociety.org/topics-policy/projects/privacy-enhancing-technologies/#:~:text=What%20are%20Privacy%20Enhancing%20Technologies,in%20a%20privacy%2Dpreserving%20manner.

Disambiguation Guide **435**

Records Of Processing Activity (ROPA)	The GDPR obligates, according to Article 30, written documentation and overview of procedures by which personal data are processed. ROPAs must include significant information about data processing, including data categories, the group of data subjects, the purpose of the processing, and the data recipients. This must be completely made available to authorities upon request. By necessity, ROPAs should be kept at a long arm's length from the carrying out of a GDPR-required DPIA.

Individual/Person

Citizen	A legally recognized subject or national of a state or commonwealth, either native or naturalized.
Consumer	A person who purchases goods and services for personal use. Some business have both customers (B2B) and consumers (B2C) whereas for others the terms are interchangeable.
Customer	A person who buys goods or services from a shop or business
Data subject	The GDPR term for the identified or identifiable living individual to whom personal data relates.
Individual	A single human being as distinct from a group.
Person	A human being regarded as an individual.
User	A person who uses or operates something.

The GDPR and Its Terminology

The General Data Protection Regulation (GDPR)[144] came into force on May 25, 2018 and became applicable across all Member States of the European Union to harmonize data privacy laws across Europe.

The GDPR replaced the Data Protection Directive, officially Directive 95/46/EC, enacted in October 1995, which was an EU directive which regulated the processing of personal data within the European Union and the free movement of such data. During those intervening 20+ years the world of data protection and privacy changed radically with the growth of the internet and the widespread availability of data. The most notable difference is that the GDPR is, as its name suggests, a regulation, enforceable in law across the EU, whereas the Directive was interpreted independently across Member States without the mandate or budget to effectively enforce.

The GDPR consists of two components: the articles and recitals. The *articles* constitute the legal requirements organizations must follow to demonstrate compliance. The *recitals* provide additional information and supporting context to supplement the articles.

---

[144] REGULATION (EU) 2016/679 OF THE EUROPEAN PARLIAMENT AND OF THE COUNCIL of 27 April 2016 on the protection of natural persons with regard to the processing of personal data and on the free movement of such data, and repealing Directive 95/46/EC (General Data Protection Regulation) – as published in the Official Journal (OJ) or the EU on May 4, 2016.

Articles

Across the book we reference the following key GDPR articles:[145]

Article 4	Definitions
Article 6	Lawfulness of processing
Article 7	Conditions for consent
Article 12	Transparent information, communication, and modalities for the exercise of the rights of the data subject
Article 15	Right of access by the data subject
Article 17	Right to erasure ('right to be forgotten')
Article 18	Right to restriction of processing
Article 20	Right to data portability
Article 25	Data protection by design and by default
Article 30	Records of processing activities
Article 32	Security of processing
Article 33	Notification of a personal data breach to the supervisory authority
Article 35	Data protection impact assessment
Article 37	Designation of the data protection officer
Article 39	Tasks of the data protection officer
Article 55	Competence
Article 57	Tasks

---

[145] General Data Protection Regulation, Intersoft Consulting, https://gdpr-info.eu/

Recitals

Across the book we reference the following key GDPR recitals:[146]

Recital 32	Conditions for consent
Recital 37	Group of undertakings
Recital 39	Principles of Data Processing
Recital 42	Burden of Proof and Requirements for Consent
Recital 63	Tasks

Terminology

The GDPR introduces many new terms, some of which are referenced in the book:

Controller (or data controller)	The natural or legal person, public authority, agency, or other body which, alone or jointly with others, determines the purposes and means of the processing of personal data; where the purposes and means of such processing are determined by Union or Member State law, the controller or the specific criteria for its nomination may be provided for by Union or Member State law. (Article 4, Definitions)
Processor (or data processor)	A natural or legal person, public authority, agency or other body which processes personal data on behalf of the controller. (Article 4, Definitions)
Data protection impact assessment (DPIA)	The data protection impact assessment is enumerated in Article 35. *See also Disambiguation.*
Data protection officer (DPO)	The designation, position and tasks of the data protection officer are described in Articles 37-39.

---

[146] Intersoft Consulting, Recitals, https://gdpr-info.eu/recitals/

Data subject	The identified or identifiable living individual to whom personal data relates. *See also Disambiguation.*
Data subject access rights (DSAR)	DSAR is not an expression mentioned explicitly in the GDPR, although the rights of data subjects are listed in Chapter 3, covering Articles 12-23. In the context in which it is used in the book, Recital 63 states: *"A data subject should have the right of access to personal data which have been collected concerning him or her, and to exercise that right easily and at reasonable intervals, in order to be aware of, and verify, the lawfulness of the processing."* The equivalent in the CCPA is: *"[...] It is the intent of the Legislature to further Californians' right to privacy by giving consumers an effective way to control their personal information, by ensuring the following rights: [...] (4) The right of Californians to access their personal information."*
Group of undertakings	A controlling undertaking and its controlled undertakings. (Article 4, Definitions)
Personal data breach	A breach of security leading to the accidental or unlawful destruction, loss, alteration, unauthorised disclosure of, or access to, personal data transmitted, stored or otherwise processed. (Article 4, Definitions)
Supervisory Authority	An independent public authority which is established by a Member State pursuant to Article 51.

Glossary of Terms and Acronyms

The primary source of definitions for terms and acronyms related to cybersecurity used in this book is from the Computer Security Resource Center. The online version can be found here: https://csrc.nist.gov/glossary.

While some of the following terms or phrases may be defined in other places, for this book they have the meanings and definitions provided below.

Terms

Accountability   Every individual who works with an information system should have specific responsibilities for that information's protection.

Article 29 Working Group

Assessment   See *Security Control Assessment*.

Asset   In information security, computer security, and network security, an asset is any data, device, or another component of the environment that supports information-related activities.

Assurance   The measure of confidence that the security features, practices, procedures, and architecture of an information system accurately mediates and enforces the security policy.

Assurance Case	A structured set of arguments and a body of evidence showing that an information system satisfies specific claims concerning a given quality attribute.
Authentication	Verifying the identity of a user, process, or device, often as a prerequisite to allowing access to resources in an information system.
Authenticity	The property of being genuine and being able to be verified and trusted; confidence in the validity of a transmission, a message, or message originator. See *Authentication*.
Authorization	A concept that directly relates to who has the right or privilege to access the information infrastructure. Access rights are determined by an information security plan that should be approved by the organization's legitimate authority or governing board.
Availability	Ensuring timely and reliable access to and use of information.
Boundary Protection	Monitoring and control of communications at the external boundary of an information system to prevent and detect malicious and other unauthorized communications, through the use of boundary protection devices (e.g., gateways, routers, firewalls, guards, encrypted tunnels).
Business Continuity Planning (BCP)	Business continuity planning is the process of creating systems of prevention and recovery to deal with potential threats to a company. In addition to prevention, the goal is to enable ongoing operations before and during the execution of disaster recovery.

Terms and Acronyms 443

C.I.A.	Confidentiality, Integrity, Availability: This is known as the Triad of Cybersecurity; the ultimate goal of security measures and controls is to protect information assets' *Confidentiality* (only those authorized to access the information can access it), *Integrity* (assurance that the information has not been altered or deleted), and *Availability* (the information is accessible by authorized individuals when it is needed).
Center for Internet Security (CIS)	The Center for Internet Security (CIS) is a 501(c)(3) nonprofit organization formed in October 2000. Its mission is to "identify, develop, validate, promote, and sustain best practice solutions for cyber defense and build and lead communities to enable an environment of trust in cyberspace."
Chief Information Officer (CIO)	Executive responsible for providing advice and assistance to the executive leadership of an organization or other senior management personnel to ensure that information technology is acquired and information resources are managed in a manner that is consistent with laws, directives, policies, regulations, and priorities established by the organization; Developing, maintaining, and facilitating the implementation of a sound and integrated information technology architecture for the organization; and promoting the effective and efficient design and operation of all major information resources management processes for the organization.

Chief Information Security Officer (CISO)	A chief information security officer (CISO) is the senior-level executive within an organization responsible for establishing and maintaining the enterprise vision, strategy, and program to ensure information assets and technologies are adequately protected. The CISO directs staff in identifying, developing, implementing, and maintaining processes across the enterprise to reduce information and information technology (IT) risks. They respond to incidents, establish appropriate standards and controls, manage security technologies, and direct the establishment and implementation of policies and procedures.
Chief Privacy Officer (CPO)	A chief privacy officer (CPO) is a corporate executive charged with developing and implementing policies designed to protect employee and customer data from unauthorized access. Other elements of the CPO job include maintaining a comprehensive and current knowledge of both corporate operations and privacy laws, as well as communicating details of the company's privacy policy to staff and customers alike. The CPO is typically the organization's point person for media and other external inquiries about privacy-related matters.
Cloud Computing	Cloud computing is the on-demand availability of computer system resources, especially data storage and computing power, without direct active management by the user. The term is generally used to describe data centers available to many users over the Internet.
Confidentiality	We are preserving authorized restrictions on information access and disclosure, including means for protecting personal privacy and proprietary information.

Countermeasures	Actions, devices, procedures, techniques, or other measures that reduce the vulnerability of an information system. Synonymous with security controls and safeguards.
Credentials or Electronic Credentials	A credential is an attestation of qualification, competence, or authority issued to an individual by a third party with a relevant or de facto authority or assumed competence to do so.
Critical Security Controls (CSC)	The CIS Critical Security Controls are a recommended set of actions for cyber defense that provide specific and actionable ways to stop today's most pervasive and dangerous attacks. A principal benefit of the Controls is that they prioritize and focus a smaller number of actions with high pay-off results.
Cyber Attack	An attack, via cyberspace, targeting an enterprise's use of cyberspace for the purpose of disrupting, disabling, destroying, or maliciously controlling a computing environment/infrastructure; or destroying the integrity of the data or stealing controlled information.
Cybersecurity	Computer security, cybersecurity, or information technology security is the protection of computer systems from the theft of or damage to their hardware, software, or electronic data, as well as from the disruption or misdirection of the services they provide.
Cyberspace	A global domain within the information environment consisting of the interdependent network of information systems infrastructures, including the Internet, telecommunications networks, computer systems, and embedded processors and controllers.

Data Mining/Harvesting	An analytical process that attempts to find correlations or patterns in large data sets for data or knowledge discovery.
Developer	A general term that includes: (i) developers or manufacturers of information systems, system components, or information system services; (ii) systems integrators; (iii) vendors; and (iv) product resellers. Development of systems, components, or services can occur internally within organizations (i.e., in-house development) or through external entities.
Disaster Recovery (DR)	Disaster recovery involves a set of policies, tools, and procedures to enable the recovery or continuation of vital technology infrastructure and systems following a natural or human-induced disaster.
Domain	An environment or context that includes a set of system resources and a set of system entities that have the right to access the resources as defined by a common security policy, security model, or security architecture. See *Security Domain*.
Enterprise	An organization with a defined mission/goal and a defined boundary, using information systems to execute that mission, and with responsibility for managing its risks and performance. An enterprise may consist of all or some of the following business aspects: acquisition, program management, financial management (e.g., budgets), human resources, security, and information systems, information, and mission management. See *Organization*.

Enterprise Architecture	A strategic information asset base, which defines the mission; the information necessary to perform the mission; the technologies necessary to perform the mission; and the transitional processes for implementing new technologies in response to changing mission needs; and includes a baseline architecture; a target architecture; and a sequencing plan.
Event	Any observable occurrence in an information system.
Exfiltration	The unauthorized transfer of information from an information system.
Fair Information Practice Principles	Principles that are widely accepted in the United States and internationally as a general framework for privacy and that are reflected in various federal and international laws and policies. In some organizations, the principles serve as the basis for analyzing privacy risks and determining appropriate mitigation strategies.
Firmware	Computer programs and data stored in hardware—typically in read-only memory (ROM) or programmable read-only memory (PROM)—such that the programs and data cannot be dynamically written or modified during execution of the programs.
Hardware	The physical components of an information system. See *Software* and *Firmware*.
Identity and Access Management (IAM)	Identity management, also known as identity and access management, is a framework of policies and technologies for ensuring that the proper people in an enterprise have the appropriate access to technology resources.

Impact	The effect on organizational operations, organizational assets, individuals, other organizations, or the Nation (including the national security interests of the United States) of a loss of confidentiality, integrity, or availability of information or an information system.
Incident	An occurrence that actually or potentially jeopardizes the confidentiality, integrity, or availability of an information system or the information the system processes, stores, or transmits or that constitutes a violation or imminent threat of violation of security policies, security procedures, or acceptable use policies.
Incident Response (IR)	Incident response is an organized approach to addressing and managing the aftermath of a security breach or cyberattack, also known as an IT incident, computer incident, or security incident. Incident response is initiated in teams by an organization's security team leadership.
Information	Any communication or representation of knowledge such as facts, data, or opinions in any medium or form, including textual, numerical, graphic, cartographic, narrative, or audiovisual. An instance of an information type.
Information Resources	Information and related resources, such as personnel, equipment, funds, and information technology.
Information Security	The protection of information and information systems from unauthorized access, use, disclosure, disruption, modification, or destruction to provide confidentiality, integrity, and availability.

Information Security Policy	An aggregate of directives, regulations, rules, and practices that prescribes how an organization manages, protects, and distributes information.
Information Security Risk	The risk to organizational operations (including mission, functions, image, reputation), organizational assets, individuals, other organizations, and the Nation due to the potential for unauthorized access, use, disclosure, disruption, modification, or destruction of information or information systems.
Information Steward	An organizational employee with statutory or operational authority for specified information and responsibility for establishing the controls for its generation, collection, processing, dissemination, and disposal.
Information System	A discrete set of information resources organized for the collection, processing, maintenance, use, sharing, dissemination, or disposition of information.
Information System Component	A discrete, identifiable information technology asset (e.g., hardware, software, firmware) that represents a building block of an information system. Information system components include commercial information technology products.
Information System Service	A capability provided by an information system that facilitates information processing, storage, or transmission.

Information Technology (IT)	Any equipment or interconnected system or subsystem of equipment that is used in the automatic acquisition, storage, manipulation, management, movement, control, display, switching, interchange, transmission, or reception of data or information by the organization.
Information Type	A specific category of information (e.g., privacy, medical, proprietary, financial, investigative, contractor-sensitive, security management) defined by an organization or in some instances, by a specific law, directive, policy, or regulation.
Insider	Any person with authorized access to any internal organizational resource, to include personnel, facilities, information, equipment, networks, or systems.
Insider Threat	The threat that an insider will use her/his authorized access, wittingly or unwittingly, to harm the security of their organization. This threat can include damage through industrial espionage, unauthorized disclosure, access or theft of company proprietary information, or through the loss or degradation of departmental resources or capabilities.
Integrity	Guarding against improper information modification or destruction and includes ensuring information non-repudiation and authenticity.
Intrusion Detection System (IDS)	A security service that monitors and analyzes network or system events for finding, and providing real-time or near real-time warning of, attempts to access system resources in an unauthorized manner.
Label	See *Security Label*.

Terms and Acronyms 451

Likelihood of Occurrence	Sometimes measured as the "Frequency of Occurrence," this refers to the probability of a particular vulnerability will be exploited by any particular threat, or how often a vulnerability will be exploited over one year.
Line of Business	The following process areas are common to many organizations: Procurement, Financial Management, Comptroller, Human Resources Management, Information Systems, Information Security, Training, Sales, and Product/Strategy.
Malicious Code	Software or firmware intended to perform an unauthorized process that will harm the confidentiality, integrity, or availability of an information system. A virus, worm, Trojan horse, or other code-based entity that infects a host. Spyware and some forms of adware are also examples of malicious code.
Malware	See *Malicious Code*.
Media	Physical devices or writing surfaces including, but not limited to, magnetic tapes, optical disks, magnetic disks, Large-Scale Integration (LSI) memory chips, and printouts (but not including display media) onto which information is recorded, stored or printed within an information system.
Member State	One of the 27 countries in the European Union.
Metadata	Information describing the characteristics of data including, for example, structural metadata describing data structures (e.g., data format, syntax, and semantics) and descriptive metadata describing data contents (e.g., information security labels).

Mobile Device	A portable computing device that: (i) has a small form factor such that a single individual can easily carry it; (ii) is designed to operate without a physical connection (e.g., wirelessly transmit or receive information); (iii) possesses local, non-removable or removable data storage; and (iv) includes a self-contained power source. Mobile devices may also include voice communication capabilities, on-board sensors that allow the devices to capture information or built-in features for synchronizing local data with remote locations. Examples include smartphones, tablets, and E-readers.
Multifactor Authentication (MFA)	Authentication using two or more different factors to achieve authentication. Factors include: (i) something you know (e.g., password/PIN); (ii) something you have (e.g., cryptographic identification device, token); or (iii) something you are (e.g., biometric). See *Authenticator*.
Network	Information system(s) implemented with a collection of interconnected components. Such components may include routers, hubs, cabling, telecommunications controllers, key distribution centers, and technical control devices.

Terms and Acronyms 453

NIST	National Institute of Standards and Technology (within the U.S. Department of Commerce): This is the federal agency responsible for creating cybersecurity standards and guidelines, which are generally mandatory for all U.S. government agencies, as well as private companies under government contracts. Otherwise, the standards provide private businesses with a common set of security measures, most of which are mapped to other regulatory standards, such as HIPAA (Health Insurance Portability and Accountability Act) and PCI-DSS (Payment Card Industry Data Security Standards).
Non-repudiation	Protection against an individual falsely denying having performed a particular action. It provides the capability to determine whether a given individual took a particular action, such as creating information, sending a message, approving the information, and receiving a message.
Object	Passive information system-related entity (e.g., devices, files, records, tables, processes, programs, domains) containing or receiving information. Access to an object (by a subject) implies access to the information it contains. See *Subject*.
Operational Controls	The security controls (i.e., safeguards or countermeasures) for an information system that are primarily implemented and executed by people (as opposed to systems).
Organization	An entity of any size, complexity, or position within an organizational structure (e.g., a corporation, an agency, or, as appropriate, any of its operational elements).

Personally Identifiable Information (PII)	Information which can be used to distinguish or trace the identity of an individual (e.g., name, social security number, biometric records, etc.) alone, or when combined with other personal or identifying information which is linked or linkable to a specific individual (e.g., date and place of birth, mother's maiden name, etc.).
Potential Impact	The loss of confidentiality, integrity, or availability could be expected to have: (i) a *limited* adverse effect; (ii) a *serious* adverse effect; or (iii) a *severe* or *catastrophic* adverse effect on organizational operations, organizational assets, or individuals.
Privacy Impact Assessment (PIA)	An analysis of how information is handled: (i) to ensure handling conforms to applicable legal, regulatory, and policy requirements regarding privacy; (ii) to determine the risks and effects of collecting, maintaining, and disseminating information in identifiable form in an electronic information system; and (iii) to examine and evaluate protections and alternative processes for handling information to mitigate potential privacy risks.
Provenance	The records are describing the possession of, and changes to, components, component processes, information, systems, organization, and organizational processes. Provenance enables all changes to the baselines of components, component processes, information, systems, organizations, and organizational processes, to be reported to specific actors, functions, locales, or activities.
Purge	Rendering sanitized data unrecoverable by laboratory attack methods.

Records	The recordings (automated or manual) of evidence of activities performed or resulted achieved (e.g., forms, reports, test results), which serve as a basis for verifying that the organization and the information system are performing as intended. Also used to refer to units of related data fields (i.e., groups of data fields that can be accessed by a program and that contain the complete set of information on particular items).
Remote Access	Access to an organizational information system by a user (or a process acting on behalf of a user) communicating through an external network (e.g., the Internet).
Resilience	See *Information System Resilience*.
Risk	A measure of the extent to which a potential circumstance or event threatens an entity, and typically a function of (i) the adverse impacts that would arise if the circumstance or event occurs; and (ii) the likelihood of occurrence. Information system-related security risks are those risks that arise from the loss of confidentiality, integrity, or availability of information or information systems and reflect the potential adverse impacts to organizational operations (including mission, functions, brand image, or reputation), organizational assets, individuals, other organizations, and partners.

Risk Assessment	The process of identifying risks to organizational operations (including mission, functions, image, reputation), organizational assets, individuals, other organizations, and partners, resulting from the operation of an information system. Part of risk management incorporates threat and vulnerability analyses and considers mitigations provided by security controls planned or in place. Synonymous with risk analysis.
Risk Management	The program and supporting processes to manage information security risk to organizational operations (including mission, functions, brand image, reputation), organizational assets, individuals, other organizations, and partners, and includes: (i) establishing the context for risk-related activities; (ii) assessing risk; (iii) responding to risk once determined; and (iv) monitoring risk over time.
Risk Mitigation	Prioritizing, evaluating, and implementing the appropriate risk-reducing controls/countermeasures recommended from the risk management process.
Role-Based Access Control	Access control based on user roles (i.e., a collection of access authorizations a user receives based on an explicit or implicit assumption of a given role). Role permissions may be inherited through a role hierarchy and typically reflect the permissions needed to perform defined functions within an organization. A given role may apply to a single individual or several individuals.

Record of Processing Activity (ROPA)

The GDPR obligates, according to Article 30, written documentation and overview of procedures by which personal data are processed. ROPAs must include significant information about data processing, including data categories, the group of data subjects, the purpose of the processing and the data recipients. This must be completely made available to authorities upon request.

Safeguards

Protective measures prescribed to meet the security requirements (i.e., confidentiality, integrity, and availability) specified for an information system. Safeguards may include security features, management constraints, personnel security, and security of physical structures, areas, and devices. Synonymous with security controls and countermeasures.

Security

A condition that results from the establishment and maintenance of protective measures that enable an enterprise to perform its mission or critical functions despite risks posed by threats to its use of information systems. Protective measures may involve a combination of deterrence, avoidance, prevention, detection, recovery, and correction that should form part of the enterprise's risk management approach.

Security Capability

A combination of mutually-reinforcing security controls (i.e., safeguards and countermeasures) implemented by technical means (i.e., functionality in hardware, software, and firmware), physical means (i.e., physical devices and protective measures), and procedural means (i.e., procedures performed by individuals).

Security Control	A safeguard or countermeasure prescribed for an information system or an organization designed to protect the confidentiality, integrity, and availability of its information and to meet a set of defined security requirements.
Security Domain	A domain that implements a security policy and is administered by a single entity.
Security Functions	The hardware, software, or firmware of the information system responsible for enforcing the system security policy and supporting the isolation of code and data on which the protection is based.
Security Incident	See *Incident*.
Security Label	The means used to associate a set of security attributes with a specific information object as part of the data structure for that object.
Security Plan	A formal document that provides an overview of the security requirements for an information system or an information security program and describes the security controls in place or planned for meeting those requirements.
Security Policy	A set of criteria for the provision of security services.

Security Requirement	A requirement levied on an information system or an organization that is derived from applicable laws, directives, policies, standards, instructions, regulations, procedures, or mission/business needs to ensure the confidentiality, integrity, and availability of information that is being processed, stored, or transmitted. **Note:** Security requirements can be used in a variety of contexts, from high-level policy-related activities to low-level implementation-related activities in system development and engineering disciplines.
Security Service	A capability that supports one, or more, of the security requirements (Confidentiality, Integrity, Availability). Examples of security services are key management, access control, and authentication.
Software	Computer programs and associated data may be dynamically written or modified during execution.
Spam	The abuse of electronic messaging systems to indiscriminately send unsolicited bulk messages.
Spyware	Software that is secretly or surreptitiously installed into an information system to gather information on individuals or organizations without their knowledge; a type of malicious code.
Subject	Generally, an individual, process, or device causing the information to flow among objects or change to the system state. See *Object*.

Subsystem	A major subdivision or component of an information system consisting of information, information technology, and personnel that performs one or more specific functions.
Supervisory Authority	A Supervisory Authority (SA) (a.k.a. Data Protection Authority (DPA)) is an independent public authority that supervises, through investigative and corrective powers, the application of European data protection law.
Supply Chain	Linked set of resources and processes between multiple tiers of developers that begins with the sourcing of products and services and extends through the design, development, manufacturing, processing, handling, and delivery of products and services to the acquirer.
System	See *Information System*.
Threat	Any circumstance or event with the potential to adversely impact organizational operations (including mission, functions, image, or reputation), organizational assets, individuals, other organizations, or partners through an information system via unauthorized access, destruction, disclosure, modification of information, or denial of service.
Threat Source	The intent and method targeted at the intentional exploitation of a vulnerability or a situation and method that may accidentally trigger a vulnerability. Synonymous with threat agent.
Trustworthiness	The attribute of a person or enterprise that provides confidence to others of the qualifications, capabilities, and reliability of that entity to perform specific tasks and fulfill assigned responsibilities.

Trustworthiness (Information System)	The degree to which an information system (including the information technology components that are used to build the system) can be expected to preserve the confidentiality, integrity, and availability of the information being processed, stored, or transmitted by the system across the full range of threats.
User	Individual, or (system) process acting on behalf of an individual, authorized to access an information system.
Virtual Private Network (VPN)	Protected information system links utilizing tunneling, security controls, and endpoint address translation giving the impression of a dedicated line.
Vulnerability	Weakness in an information system, system security procedures, internal controls, or implementation that could be exploited or triggered by a threat source.

Acronyms

ACP	Attorney Client Privilege
ADA	Americans with Disabilities Act
AFTS	Automatic Funds Transfer Services
APEC	Authorized Personnel and Emergency Contact
API	Application Programming Interface
APPI	Act on the Protection of Personal Information (Japan)
AUP	Acceptable Use Policy
AWS	Amazon Web Services
B2B	Business to Business
B2C	Business to Consumer
BAA	Business Associate Agreement
BCE	Before the Common Era (equivalent to BC)
CARTA	Continuous Adaptive Risk and Trust Assessment (Gartner)
CCPA	California Consumer Privacy Act
CDPA	Consumer Data Protection Act (Virginia)
CDPSE	Certified Data Privacy Solutions Engineer
CE	Common Era (equivalent to AD)
CEO	Chief Executive Officer
CFO	Chief Financial Officer
CI/CD	Continuous Integration and Continuous Detection
CIA	Confidentiality, Integrity, and Availability
CIPM	Certified Information Privacy Manager
CIPP	Certified Information Privacy Professional
CIPT	Certified Information Privacy Technologist
CIRT	Cybersecurity Incident Response Team

Terms and Acronyms

CISO	Chief Information Security Officer
CMIA	Confidentiality of Medical Information Act
COPPA	Children's Online Privacy Protection Act (1998)
COPTA	Cigarettes and Other Tobacco Products Act
CPA	Colorado's Privacy Act
CPO	Chief Privacy Officer
CPRA	California Privacy Rights Act
CRR	Consumer Rights Request
CSR	Corporate Social Responsibility
CVSS	Common Vulnerability Scoring System
DCIA	Digital Charter Implementation Act (Canada)
DFD	Data Flow Diagrams
DHS-CISA	Department of Homeland Security – Cybersecurity Infrastructure Agency
DLP	Data Loss Prevention
DMV	Department of Motor Vehicles
DPA	Data Protection Authority
DPD	Data Protection Directive (EU)
DPIA	Data Protection Impact Assessment
DPO	Data Protection Officer
DSAR	Data Subject Access Request
DTIA	Data Transfer Impact Assessment
ECPA	Electronic Communications Privacy Act (1986)
EDPS	European Data Protection Supervisor
EDR	Endpoint Detection and Response
EDR	Endpoint Detection and Response
EEOC	Equal Employment Opportunity Commission
EKG	Electrocardiograms

ELT	Executive Leadership Team
EPDB	European Data Protection Board
EPP	Endpoint Protection
EQ	Emotional Intelligence
ERM	Enterprise Risk Management
EU	European Union
FACTA	Foreign Account Tax Compliance Act
FAIR	Factor Analysis of Information Risk
FBI	Federal Bureau of Investigation
FCRA	Fair Credit Reporting Act
FERPA	Family Educational Rights and Privacy Act
FTC	Federal Trade Commission
FTCA	Federal Trade Commission Act
GDPR	General Data Protection Regulation
GLBA	Gramm-Leach-Bliley Act (1999)
HIPAA	Health Insurance Portability and Accountability Act (1996)
HITECH	Health Information Technology for Economic and Clinical Health Act (2009)
HR	Human Resources
HVAC	Heating Ventilation and Air Conditioning
I&O	Infrastructure & Operations
IA	Internal Audit
IAPP	International Association of Privacy Professionals
ICT	Information Communication Technology
IoT	Internet of Things
IPIC	Indicators Personal Information is Compromised
IQ	Cognitive Intelligence

Terms and Acronyms 465

IR	Incident Response
IRT	Incident Response Team
ISACA	Information Systems Audit and Control Association
ISO	International Organization for Standardization
IT	Information Technology (see also ICT)
KISS	Keep It Super Simple
LAN	Local Area Network
LFPDPPP	Federal Law on Protection of Personal Data Held by Individuals (Mexico)
LGPD	General Personal Data Protection Law (Lei Geral de Proteção de Dados) (Brazil)
MDM	Mobile Device Management
MFA	Multi-Factor Authentication
MNPI	Material Non-Public Information
MSA	Master Services Agreement
NAS	Network Attached Storage
NASA	National Aeronautics and Space Administration
NIST	National Institute of Standards and Technology
NPC	National People's Congress (China)
NPS	Net Promoter Score
OCR-HHS	Department of Health and Human Services' Office of Civil Rights
OS	Operating System
OSINT	Open-Source Intelligence
PbD	Privacy by Design
PbDaaS	Privacy by Design as a Service
PCI	Payment Card Industry
PCI DSS	Payment Card Industry Data Security Standard

PD	Personal Data
PDPA	Personal Data Protection Act (Singapore)
PDPB	Personal Data Protection Bill (India)
PEO	Professional Employer Organization
PET	Privacy-Enabling Technology
PHI	Protected Health Information
PI	Personal Information
PIA	Privacy Impact Assessment
PII	Personally Identifiable Information
PIPEDA	Personal Information Protection and Electronic Documents Act (Canada)
PIPL	Personal Information Protection Law (China)
PMK	Person Most Knowledgeable
POPI	Protection of Personal Information (South Africa)
PPL	Protection of Privacy Law (Israel)
PR	Public Relations
PRR	Privacy Rights Request
RACI	Responsible, Accountable, Consulted and Informed
RADAR	Results, Approaches, Deploy, Assess, Refine (?)
RAM	Random-access memory
RBAC	Role Based Access Control
RCA	Root Cause Analysis
ROPA	Records Of Processing Activity
SaaS	Software as a Service
SAML	Secure Assertion Markup Language
SAN	Storage Area Network
SbD	Security by Design
SEC	Securities and Exchange Commission

SHIELD	Stop Hacks and Improve Electronic Data Security
SLA	Software Licensing Agreement
SME	Small to Medium-sized Enterprise
SOAR	Security Orchestration Automation and Response
SOC 2	Service Organization Control 2
SOP	Standard Operating Procedure
SOW	Statement of Work
SOX	Sarbanes-Oxley Act (2002)
SPI	Sensitive Personal Information
SSL	Secure Socket Layer
SSO	Single Sign-On
STRIDE	Spoofing, Tampering, Repudiation, Information, Disclosure, Denial of Service and Elevation of privilege
TLS	Transport Layer Security
UEBA	User Entry Behavior Analytics
VIN	Vehicle Identification Number
VPPA	Video Privacy Protection Act (1988)
VRM	Vendor Risk Management
WPD	Work Product Doctrine

Security Policy ~ Bill Bonney

The following essay is taken from Bill Bonney's contribution to Chapter 9 of the *CISO Desk Reference Guide* which was created to disambiguate terms such as policy, procedure, standard, and guideline.[147]

Policy Is Foundational

Policies for information security primarily serve a foundational purpose. Except where the requirements are specific, such as with cryptographic standards for PCI-DSS, for example, a policy should be as high-level as it can be while still providing the necessary guidance to the organization.

What do I mean by a foundational purpose? Information security policies provide direction on behavior in the realm of handling sensitive or protected data. This behavior might tell individuals what specific precautions they must take, or inform internal developers about minimum coding requirements, or provide direction for the required level of encryption when programmatically handling data that falls within data handling requirements for regulatory or contractual obligations the organization might have. And while the high-level outcome might be the same (to handle specific data in a particular way), the audience (all employees, application developers, data custodians) and specific guidance could be very different.

It is also worth noting that in certain circumstances, such as data handling for regulatory frameworks such as the Sarbanes-Oxley Act, and contractual obligations, such as complying with PCI-DSS, the policies are often required to meet specific minimum standards. For

---

[147] Chapter 9 of the *CISO Desk Reference Guide*, *Volume 1, 2nd Edition*, CISO DRG Publishing – Bonney, Hayslip & Stamper.

example, in PCI-DSS 3.2 there are specific requirements that institutions that handle payment card data must have information security policies (requirement 12). Further, PCI-DSS 3.2 requirement 9.6 mandates that there is a policy to control the distribution of media.

Also, for multiple PCI requirements, the audit testing procedures specifically instruct the QSA (Qualified Security Assessor) to verify that the organization's information security policies conform to minimum standards in domains such as cryptographic standards, data retention, access controls, firewall rules, and others.

PCI DSS Requirements	Testing Procedures
	3.1.c For a sample of system components that store cardholder data: • Examine the files and system records to verify that the data stored does not exceed the requirements defined in the retention policy • Observe the deletion mechanism to verify data is deleted securely

There are also examples where regulations do not give minimum guidance, but adherence to policy might still be a specific topic of an audit. This condition is especially true for financial institutions, which may have a Statement on Standards for Attestation Engagements (SSAE) 18 in place for specific services they provide for their customers. It is extremely common to audit adherence to an organization's own internal security policy as part of the test of the effectiveness of internal controls. Because of these requirements, some organizations fall into the trap of asking the auditors or the QSA to "just tell us what the policy is supposed to say."

It's important to note that this is always the wrong approach. Abdicating responsibility in this manner separates decision makers in the organization from policy setting, and that has the immediate effect of disconnecting execution from principles. Further, "the auditor told us to do it" does not help anyone understand why a policy is written one way and not another and therefore creates a hesitancy to make needed changes. People become helpless to make necessary changes because they lack the backstory and don't know what other problems, they might cause by doing so.

There are many ways to provide guidance at different levels of detail and in various settings. These include guidelines, best practices, procedures, processes, standards, specifications, and policies.

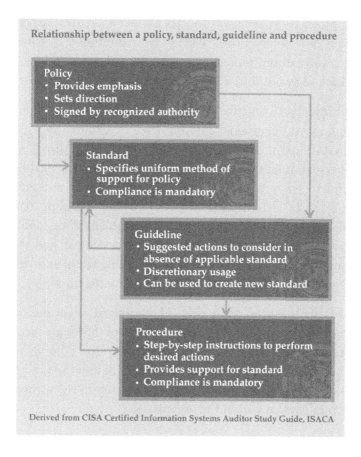

When I say policies are foundational, I mean that if an organization wanted to give direction to its development team, it would want to set its policy first, then work with product architects to choose standards compatible with its environment that will allow it to adhere to its policy, and then let the development organization create specifications derived from those standards. Similarly, if an organization wanted to give direction to an operations team, it would set policy first, then as needed issue guidelines or cite best practices and then allow the operations team to develop procedures that adhere to policy and take into consideration the guidelines and best practices provided.

Unintended Consequences

While information security policies do serve many purposes, it's important not to overload policies by including guidelines, best practices, procedures, processes, standards, and specifications. Doing so can have several unintended negative consequences.

One unintended negative consequence is an overly restrictive development or operational environment. Procedures and standards are by nature more detailed than policy. A policy is directional and constitutional. It lays out high-level parameters such as establishing a requirement for stepped up or more restrictive authentication mechanisms for determining access rights for handling data at a particular sensitivity level to meet a regulatory or contractual obligation. A policy is typically drafted, recommended, and approved according to governance rules that tie publication and adoption directly to senior management or the board of directors.

Standards are measures or models. The standard might indicate that one-time password (OTP) tokens or use of SMS are acceptable provided passwords rotate no less than every sixty seconds or SMS codes are valid for at most 120 seconds. Standards are typically drafted, recommended, and approved according to rules imposed by architectural groups within the organization.

It would be a mistake to build the standard into the policy as the group developing the standard is usually closer to operations and is more intimately familiar with operational goals, problems, and limitations.

Another potential unintended negative consequence is an overburdened policy writing function that is hopelessly behind, producing policy that is out of date and irrelevant. This breakdown can create significant friction for any development or operations team. Let's explore the above example of OTP and SMS options for two-factor authentication. By the time you bake these standards in and publish the policy, authentication apps on mobile phones might have become available that would meet the standard of 60 to 120-second password rotation but would not be usable within the organization because the policy was explicit about using OTP and SMS only and did not mention authentication apps.

While there are indeed examples where the exact type of two-factor authentication might need to be specified, the more significant point is that there are often many ways to solve a problem. Leaving as much flexibility as possible to the teams that are close to the issues is usually a good strategy, and that strategy also applies when writing policy.

A final unintended negative consequence worth mentioning is that, as noted above, auditors often test policies as part of the audit process. Investigators regularly review policies as part of investigations associated with regulatory enforcement, contract enforcement, breach investigation, whistleblower investigation, or for other corporate governance-related reasons. There is often a tendency to interpret findings of failure to follow internal policy as indicative of systemic wrongdoing, lax oversight, or careless behavior.

It bears repeating that except where the requirements are specific, such as with cryptographic standards for PCI-DSS, policy should be as high-level as it can be while still providing the necessary guidance to the organization. That leaves more room for variation in implementation and less likelihood of audit findings for a failure to follow policy given that real-world standards and procedures often change more rapidly than policy can be approved and issued.

Recognize that policy comes with liability at the audit, regulatory, and prosecutorial level when not followed – don't just write it and forget it.

Policy Has a Purpose

One more abstract concept before we turn to the practical. When we think about what we want to get from setting and publishing policy, we should focus on two fundamental things: risk mitigation, and education and awareness.

As we identify risks and obligations, we set policy for the behavior we believe will allow us to manage those risks and obligations. The policy helps us draw a direct line from senior management, with whom the identification and management of these risks and obligations sit, to every line employee who carries out the wishes of management to the customer's or shareholder's benefit. This direct line also serves as an educational vehicle to inform all employees, and state publicly for customers, auditors, and shareholders, how the organization discharges its responsibilities.

Establishing Policies

Now that we have explored information security policy in the abstract, including that policy should be at the foundational level and some of the consequences of failing to acknowledge that, let's talk about how we would establish these policies and for what essential activities we should have information security policies in place.

Principles for establishing information security policy:

- o Understand, document, and communicate the relationship in your organization between policies, standards, specifications, guidelines, best practices, procedures, processes, contractual language, service level agreements, non-disclosure agreements, contract addendums and other ways that you codify and communicate behaviors within your organization and with other organizations with whom you share data handling responsibility.

- o Understand, document, and communicate how to request changes for each of these, including who approves changes. Publish this information and routinely communicate outcomes of requests (accepted, rejected, redirected to a different governing body for consideration, etc.). Establish governing bodies as needed and record requests and results.

Be prepared to provide this documentation as requested by auditors and investigators.

- Write policy to provide foundational guidance. Avoid the temptation to endorse policies that institutionalize activities that drive internal agendas. This concern often applies to customer advocates such as sales or product support teams, who are sometimes tempted to codify customer outcomes (whether for data handling or coding standards or response times, etc.) into internal compliance requirements via policy. When considering a policy change that enforces customer-facing behaviors, ask whether a policy, procedure, or contractual language (such as a service level agreement would best address the concern.

- Fully explore and document how your information security policy should extend outside of your organization, through third-party agreements and contracts. At a minimum, review the regulations you are subject to and the contracts you currently have in place.

- Beyond that, evaluate when policies you have in place for employee behavior should apply to contractors and consultants who might have identical or very similar data handling requirements. Make sure you enforce this through contract review, security addendums, non-disclosure agreements, and periodic audits of compliance. As with policy for internal use, a policy that extends contractually cannot be written (or signed) and then forgotten. You must enforce it.

- Consider using a well-known security authority as a source for templates, wording, and a starter list of policies for your organization. An excellent reference that I recommend is the SANS Institute. They make their policy templates for general, network security, server security, and application security available for free. Suggested sections for the security policy template include:

- Overview
- Purpose
- Scope
- Policy
- Policy Compliance
- Related Standards, Policies, and Processes

Many of the words we use in information security, like "insurance," "risk," "breach," and "control," come with baggage. This reality applies to "policy" more than all the others. The dictionary tells us that policy is "a course or principle of action, adopted or proposed by a government, party, business or individual." The key words here, as I've mentioned above, are principle and action. A policy is deliberate, it guides decisions, and once decisions are made the expectation is that action will be taken to ensure that the policy is implemented. Keep policy at the institutional level and leave the "how" to the people closest to the operations and you can take away some of the baggage.

Index

A

Access Management, 330, 336, 337, 345, 346
  identity, iii, 6, 9, 58, 60, 102, 156, 180, 193, 257, 259, 359, 362, 391, 392, 393, 408, 485
  least privilege, 155, 193, 275, 330
  MFA, 144, 266, 287, 330
  physical, 321, 350
Act on the Protection of Personal Information (APPI), 57
Action
  regulatory, 56, 57, 121, 186, 188, 194, 226, 236
Agencies
  regulatory, 48
Amazon, 10, 38, 145, 159
  Alexa, 25
Apple
  Hey Siri, 25
Application, 57, 239, 336, 343
Attorney General, 19, 47, 232, 318, 405, 407, 409, 410, 413, 415, 416, 420
Authorities
  regulatory, 32, 69, 71, 303
Awareness, 36, 377

B

Bazzell, Michael
  Extreme Privacy, 25, 160
Budgeting
  percentage, 196
Business Continuity, 41, 283, 333, 371
  disruption, 279
  planning and policy, 41
  recovery, 333, 359
Business Impact Assessment, 180

C

California, 14, 16, 17, 18, 19, 20, 21, 24, 46, 47, 48, 50, 52, 57, 104, 111, 145, 149, 164, 178, 180, 185, 204, 205, 212, 213, 217, 220, 222, 232, 233, 240, 244, 261, 264, 317, 318, 319, 341, 374, 401, 405, 407, 408, 409, 410, 413, 415, 416, 417, 420, 421, 486, 487
CCPA, 19, 20, 24, 52, 60, 97, 104, 113, 114, 116, 117, 170, 177, 180, 185, 186, 188, 191, 204, 205, 212, 213, 216, 220, 222, 232, 240, 287, 288, 307, 317, 318, 397, 405, 406, 407, 408, 410, 412, 414, 417, 420, 421, 422, 423, 486, 487
CPRA, 20, 47, 164, 170, 177, 180, 181, 185, 204, 205, 213, 214, 216, 220, 232, 240, 263, 264, 287, 288, 290, 317, 318, 397, 405, 406, 407, 408, 412, 414, 421, 422, 423, 486, 487
  Proposition 7, 16
CCPA
  California Privacy Rights Act, 19, 24, 47, 57, 145, 149, 204, 205, 261, 486
Chief Information Officer, 72, 89, 114
  CIO, 61, 89, 134, 196, 268, 269, 307, 340, 349
Chief Information Security Officer, 71, 73, 89, 334
  CISO, 37, 55, 61, 71, 73, 88, 89, 103, 108, 133, 134, 225, 239, 268, 269, 294, 307, 310, 313, 334, 340, 487
Children's Online Privacy Protection Act
  COPPA, 49, 100, 203, 412
China, 26, 141, 205, 207, 214, 217, 220, 222, 487

Personal Information Protection
 Law (PIPL), 205, 214, 220
Community
 Organizations
  ISACA, 235, 487
 trust relationships, 11
Compliance
 regulations, 80
 regulatory, 222, 227, 308, 355
 requirements, 69, 74
Consent, 185, 186, 240
Controls
 control environment, 189, 413
 preventative, 231, 233
Corporate Culture, 38
Cory, Kenneth, 14, 17, 18
COVID, 21, 82, 102, 150, 279, 281, 309
CPRA
 California Privacy Rights Act, 20, 47, 164, 185, 204, 240, 261, 401
Critical Infrastructure, 285
C-suite, 328
Customer Care, 60, 86
Cyber Insurance, 52, 287

D

Data Accuracy, 206, 215
Data Breach, 35, 318, 355, 357, 372, 373, 374, 379
Data Governance, 87, 116, 121, 124, 132, 158, 162, 163, 169, 187, 197, 227, 254, 268, 269, 298, 386
 Data Classification, 132, 249, 251, 414
 Data Retention, 132, 181, 264, 271
Data Minimization, 117, 215
Data Protection Directive, 203, 204, 217
 DPD, 203
Data Protection Impact Assessment, 51, 101, 134
 DPIA, 101, 131, 165, 166
Data Protection Officer, 72, 73, 79, 80, 84
 CPO, 69, 71, 72, 73, 79, 84, 125

DPO, 37, 61, 69, 72, 73, 74, 75, 77, 78, 84, 92, 99, 102, 103, 154, 268, 269, 310, 394
Data Subject Access Request, 389
 DSAR, 86, 245
Deficiency
 resolve, 46
Department of Motor Vehicles, 50
 DMV, 50
Devices
 Laptop, 59, 163, 323, 335, 339, 346
 mobile, 114, 162, 335, 336, 345, 346, 364
Domain expertise, 487
Doxing, 160

E

Encryption, 52, 287, 322, 323
Enterprise Risk Management, 32, 41
 ERM, 62, 65, 487
Environment
 regulatory, 398
Equal Employment Opportunity Commission, 20, 463
 EEOC, 20, 21
Eric Topol, 158
European Commission, 208, 210, 211, 223
European Union, 6, 23, 57, 160, 203, 204, 208, 209, 210, 211
 Council of the European Union, 211
 EU, 23, 73, 100, 118, 160, 207, 208, 210, 211, 213, 217, 220, 222, 223, 287, 412
Executive Leadership
 ELT, 62, 90

F

Facebook, 23, 38, 56, 147, 148, 213, 412
 Mark Zuckerberg, 7
 Meta, 23, 38, 56
Federal Bureau of Investigation
 FBI, 35, 48, 313, 371, 487

Federal Law on Protection of Personal
 Data Held by Individuals
 (LFPDPPP), 204
Federal Trade Commission, 48, 56,
 183, 190, 212, 222, 236, 240, 314,
 315, 377
FTC, 47, 48, 56, 57, 100, 213, 240,
 274, 314, 315, 316, 317, 377,
 378
Frameworks
 regulatory, 229
FTC
 Consent Orders
  Microsoft, 232, 265, 292, 409

G

Gartner, 237, 239, 268, 487
GDPR
 Article 12, 392
 Article 15, 393
 Article 17, 226, 393, 397, 398
 Article 18, 393
 Article 20, 393
 Article 25, 129, 226, 238
 Article 28, 147, 294
 Article 30, 101, 122, 134, 191, 221, 235
 Article 32, 238
 Article 33, 299, 391
 Article 35, 74, 329
 Article 37, 73, 92
 Article 39, 74, 92
 Article 4, 89, 132, 188
 Article 55, 361, 391
 Article 57, 392
 Article 6, 186
 Article 7, 393
 Chapter 3, 391
 General Data Protection Regulations Act, 23, 57, 204, 211
 Recital 32, 185
 Recital 37, 75
 Recital 39, 183, 190, 222, 241
 Recital 42, 186
 Recital 63, 407

General Personal Data Protection Law
 (LGPD - Lei General de Proteção de
 Dados), 204
Google, 27, 38, 56, 201, 412
 OK Google, 25
Governance, 47, 106, 126, 127, 189,
 257, 413
 compliance obligations, 62, 88, 124,
  132, 188, 196, 234, 252, 266,
  269, 272, 276, 277, 295, 299,
  326, 331, 334, 375, 384
 controls, 189, 413
 due diligence, 222, 239, 282, 301,
  396
 independence, 14, 75
 internal audit, 62, 74, 193, 275
 internal controls, 62, 219, 221
 inventory, 59, 65, 88, 93, 112, 131,
  138, 164, 192, 194, 195, 228,
  263, 270, 274, 355, 378, 398,
  399, 402
 legal mandate, 61, 85, 86, 225, 403
 legal obligations, 61, 85, 86, 225,
  403
 mandate, 6, 61, 73, 95, 117, 129,
  135, 164, 173, 195, 196, 269,
  400
 obligations, 22, 112, 117, 145, 163,
  195, 276, 297, 367
 oversight, 42, 62, 71, 74, 86, 90,
  106, 108, 154, 174, 190, 262,
  272, 276, 293, 321, 345, 375,
  380
 privacy obligations, 121, 123, 144,
  292, 301, 328
 vendor inventory, 88
Gramm-Leach-Bliley Act, 203
 GLBA, 100, 203, 212, 216, 293,
  307, 316, 329

H

HIPAA-HITECH
 administrative safeguards, 324
 business associate agreement, 194,
  297
 HIPAA, 47, 48, 79, 87, 104, 116,
  132, 134, 170, 173, 178, 179,

187, 195, 203, 205, 212, 216,
261, 293, 307, 324, 329, 397,
412, 418, 419, 487
PHI, 132, 133, 134, 164, 187, 194,
195, 216, 261, 296, 339, 419
Human Resources, 54, 86, 107, 115,
116, 398
HR, 36, 54, 55, 86, 97, 113, 125,
135, 162, 165, 215, 262, 376,
382

I

IBM, 6, 142, 485
Incident Response, 41, 118, 266, 332,
364, 365, 375, 382, 383, 385
attorney-client privilege, 238, 356,
369, 370, 371, 372
escalation, 126
Indicators Personal Information Is
Compromised, 373
IPIC, 373
Infrastructure and Operations, 58, 89
Internal Audit, 62
International Association of Privacy
Professionals, ii
IAPP, ii, 208, 235
International Standards Organization
ISO 31000, 43, 44
Internet of Things, 143, 232, 319
ISACA, 235, 487
CDPSE, 235, 487

J

Japan
APPI, 220, 222

K

k-anonymity, 27
Knack, Stephen, 23

L

Laws

breach notification
Massachusetts, 47, 193, 320,
322, 323, 341
Legal Requirements
Contracts
master service agreements, 146,
370
non-disclosure agreement
(NDA), 107
service level agreement (SLA),
146
contractual obligations, 62, 88, 124,
132, 188, 196, 234, 266, 269,
272, 276, 277, 295, 299, 326,
331, 334, 375, 384
federal law, 204, 205, 219
lawsuits & litigation, 36, 46, 82,
148, 209, 213, 317, 369, 370
state laws, 14, 21, 47, 232, 374

M

Milk, Harvey, 16
Moscone, George, 14, 16, 17

O

Obligations
regulatory, 61, 85, 86, 225, 403
Organizational Hierarchy
Chief Executive Officer, 40, 71, 90,
123, 308, 317
Chief Financial Officer, 46, 71, 82,
115, 262, 334
Chief Information Officer, 61, 72,
89, 114, 134, 196, 268, 269,
307, 340, 349
Chief Privacy Officer, 61, 69, 71,
72, 73, 75, 79, 84, 92, 95, 125,
128, 232, 268, 269
Organizational Structure
authorized, 257, 298, 383
centralized / decentralized, 164, 166
embedded, 24, 26, 208, 231, 236,
237

Index

leadership team, 23, 37, 62, 71, 90, 123, 130, 135, 189, 273, 274, 333, 376, 382
personnel, 42, 75, 150, 162, 364, 367, 371, 372, 384, 408, 419
Organizations
  InfraGard, 487
  ISACA, 235, 487
Oversight
  regulatory, 376, 388

P

Passwords, 19, 27, 108, 308, 314, 322, 330, 331, 343, 362, 383, 416, 421
Patch management, 108
Penalties, 47, 48, 49, 75, 76, 77, 217, 317, 362, 420
Personal Data, 57, 204, 205, 307
Personal Data Protection Bill (PDPB), 57, 204
Personal Information Protection and Electronic Documents Act (PIPEDA), 57, 204
Personally Identifiable Information
  PII, 132, 133, 238, 242, 254, 255, 261, 266, 314, 317, 318, 374
Policies
  acceptable use, 59, 108, 118
  privacy, 37, 52, 83, 112, 136, 173, 174, 315, 316, 409, 410, 411
Privacy
  Chief Privacy Officer, 69, 71, 72, 73, 79, 84, 125
  data privacy, 46, 101, 205, 208, 220, 223, 235, 263, 292
  privacy Impact, 101
  privacy regulations, 162
  trust principles, 240
Privacy By Design, 69, 117, 128, 229
Privacy Impact Assessment, 101, 134, 263
  PIA, 101, 102, 122, 131
Privacy Laws, 18, 210, 214
  ADPPA, ii, 101, 220, 223, 232
  CCPA, 19, 20, 24, 52, 60, 97, 104, 113, 114, 116, 117, 170, 177, 180, 185, 186, 188, 191, 204,
  205, 212, 213, 216, 220, 222, 232, 240, 287, 288, 307, 317, 318, 397, 405, 406, 407, 408, 410, 412, 414, 417, 420, 421, 422, 423, 486, 487
  CPRA, 20, 47, 164, 170, 177, 180, 181, 185, 204, 205, 213, 214, 216, 220, 232, 240, 263, 264, 287, 288, 290, 317, 318, 397, 405, 406, 407, 408, 412, 414, 421, 422, 423, 486, 487
  GDPR, 23, 24, 27, 52, 57, 59, 60, 72, 73, 74, 75, 76, 77, 79, 80, 84, 87, 89, 92, 97, 101, 104, 113, 114, 116, 122, 129, 130, 132, 134, 147, 151, 165, 170, 177, 183, 185, 186, 188, 190, 191, 202, 204, 205, 206, 207, 208, 209, 211, 213, 214, 217, 220, 221, 222, 223, 226, 232, 235, 236, 238, 241, 242, 244, 263, 287, 293, 294, 299, 306, 307, 308, 329, 360, 361, 379, 391, 392, 393, 397, 398, 405, 406, 409, 410, 412, 487
Privacy Lifecycle, 115, 129, 130, 169
Privacy Principles, 37, 160
Privacy Shield, 160, 208, 223
Processes
  business, 39, 43, 122, 125, 133, 161, 178, 190, 192, 195, 219, 234, 236, 237, 238, 241, 274, 275, 280, 281, 330, 339, 343, 353, 355, 389, 418
Protected Health Information
  PHI, 132, 133, 134, 164, 187, 194, 195, 216, 261, 296, 339, 419
Protection, 14, 18, 47, 82, 116, 152, 181, 262, 264, 314
Protection of Personal Information, 205
Protection of Privacy Law, 204
Public Company Accounting Oversight Board (PCAOB), 219

R

Regulations, 60, 201, 204, 210, 212, 215, 216, 219, 410

federal, 47, 48, 216, 219, 321
fiduciary, 71, 326
financial
  SOX, 219, 220, 223
  FTC act, 47, 48, 56, 57, 100, 213, 236, 240, 274, 314, 315, 316, 317, 377, 378
  GLBA, 100, 203, 212, 216, 293, 307, 316, 329
  HIPAA-HITECH, 47, 48, 79, 87, 104, 116, 132, 134, 170, 173, 178, 179, 187, 195, 203, 205, 212, 216, 261, 293, 307, 324, 329, 397, 412, 418, 419, 487
  privacy, 10, 20, 23, 28, 29, 34, 39, 50, 52, 57, 58, 60, 61, 64, 69, 73, 76, 84, 100, 116, 159, 160, 164, 165, 170, 174, 193, 195, 201, 204, 205, 206, 208, 212, 216, 220, 221, 222, 223, 224, 225, 226, 228, 238, 255, 262, 270, 285, 287, 293, 294, 307, 316, 319, 324, 329, 331, 378, 379, 384, 391, 398, 426
  SB 6280, 27
  state
    Massachusetts, 47, 193, 320, 322, 323, 341
Regulators
  FTC, 47, 48, 56, 57, 100, 213, 240, 274, 314, 315, 316, 317, 377, 378
Regulatory
  oversight, 112, 222, 269, 409
Reputation, 279, 281, 295
Requirements
  regulatory, 61, 62, 87, 88, 132, 165, 177, 188, 196, 216, 219, 222, 223, 224, 234, 269, 272, 299, 326, 334
Resource
  tools, 59
Risk, 41, 42, 44, 46, 47, 48, 51, 52, 98, 99, 128, 146, 177, 239, 247, 280, 286, 287, 292, 318, 329, 355, 400
  regulatory, 46, 56, 85, 177, 181, 236, 241, 316, 356
Risk Management, 43, 53, 62, 64, 99, 122, 127, 128, 166, 190, 195, 237,
  240, 249, 268, 281, 298, 300, 329, 357, 486, 487
  appetite, 41, 80
  assessment, 9, 43, 51, 65, 88, 99, 102, 134, 174, 199, 309, 329, 340, 373
  financial risk, 48, 51
  Privacy Risk, 44, 51, 373
  remediation, 57, 90, 165, 237, 360, 381, 382
  residual risk, 52
  risk exposure, 61, 309
  risk factors, 128, 165, 293, 294, 295, 297, 298, 400, 403
  risk mitigation, 174, 238
  risk profile, 174, 195, 401
  risk tolerance, 41, 62, 90, 127, 165, 295, 326, 334
  third-party risk, 84, 280
  threat modeling
    actors, 52, 266, 287, 374
  threats, 52, 266, 287, 374
Roe v. Wade, ii, 15, 20
Roles and Responsibilities
  executive, 123, 125, 131, 365, 367
RSA, 16

S

Sales and Marketing, 55, 87
Samsung, 25
Sarbanes Oxley
  SOX, 219, 220, 223
Schneier, Bruce, 28
Schrems II, 160, 208, 223
Scotland, 7
Securities and Exchange Commission, 48, 219
  SEC, 47, 216
Security, 12, 25, 28, 48, 59, 60, 89, 107, 108, 109, 193, 204, 207, 215, 220, 232, 266, 271, 294, 303, 307, 315, 342, 372, 382, 487
  hygiene, 333
  incident, 332, 382
  program, 320
  Reasonable Security, 249, 294, 303
  risks, 239

SOC, 88, 343
Security Frameworks
  CIS, 318
  HIPAA-HITECH, 47, 48, 79, 87, 104, 116, 132, 134, 170, 173, 178, 179, 187, 195, 203, 205, 212, 216, 261, 293, 307, 324, 329, 397, 412, 418, 419, 487
  ISO, 43, 44, 229, 309
  PCI, 47, 261, 324
Security Governance, 252
Security Metrics, 213, 214, 308
Security Policy, 108
Security Procedures, 189, 317, 318
Security Testing
  penetration testing, 343
Security Training
  awareness, 36, 377
  policy, 36, 377
  skills, 355
Sensitive Data, 36, 55, 58, 59, 98, 113, 116, 129, 151, 155, 156, 172, 254, 283, 297, 308, 318, 372
  intellectual property, 114, 116, 251, 255, 261, 270, 393
  personally identifiable information, 132, 133, 238, 242, 254, 255, 266, 314, 317, 318, 374
  protected health information, 132, 133, 134, 164, 187, 194, 195, 216, 261, 296, 339, 419
Service
  provider, 288, 289, 290, 291, 411
SHIELD Act, 323
Social Media, 24, 56
  Instagram, 24, 412
  LinkedIn, 27, 56, 79
  WeChat, 24
  YouTube, 25
Supreme Court, ii, 15, 20, 21

T

Third Party
  business associate agreement, 194, 297
  ecosystem, 92, 95, 96, 109, 145, 244, 279, 285

independent contractors, 116, 293, 299
master services agreement, 283
Risk
  access, 24, 56, 315
  contractors, 116, 293, 299
Training, 331
Transparency, 104, 177, 184, 206, 214, 219, 240
Trust, 4, 8, 9, 11, 12, 14, 23, 24, 28, 29, 32, 34, 35, 36, 37, 38, 39, 40, 47, 64, 72, 77, 84, 85, 87, 92, 96, 97, 110, 115, 121, 123, 125, 133, 137, 147, 165, 184, 194, 209, 221, 222, 226, 239, 240, 241, 279, 281, 282, 292, 299, 331, 338, 341, 348, 362, 396, 404, 423, 485
Stephen Knack, 240

U

U.S. Constitution, 14, 16

V

Vendor Management, 51, 85, 88, 162, 168, 195, 269, 375, 486
Vendor Risk Management, 110, 146, 249, 279, 280
SOC 2, 88, 343
Verizon, 35
  Data Breach Investigations Report, 35
Virtual Private Network
  VPN, 24

Y

Yahoo, 19

Z

Zuboff, Shoshana
  The Age of Surveillance Capitalism, 159

About the Authors

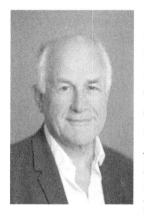

David Goodman is a consultant working in digital transformation, specifically the areas of identity management and security, data protection and privacy regulation as well as emerging technologies. He has worked in senior management positions across a wide range of companies in Europe and North America from start-ups (Soft-Switch, Metamerge) to global brands (Lotus Development, IBM, Nokia Siemens Networks and Ericsson) as well as University College London. David is currently a principal consulting analyst with TechVision Research, chief evangelist with iGrant.io, a senior consultant with Trust in Digital Life association and, until recently, executive director of the Open Identity Exchange (OIX). He is work package leader for dissemination and communication in the CyberSec4Europe and CSI-COP H2020 projects, and task leader for Open Banking roadmapping and demonstrators in CyberSec4Europe. David has a BA from the University of Manchester and a D.Phil. from the Oriental Institute, University of Oxford.

LinkedIn Profile: https://www.linkedin.com/in/david275/
https://identitas.consulting/

Justine Phillips focuses her practice on both proactive and reactive cybersecurity and data privacy services, representing clients in matters related to information governance, diligence in acquisitions and investments, incident preparedness and response, the California Consumer Privacy Act and cyber litigation.

She provides actionable and practical guidance to help businesses manage data, technology, cyber threats, privacy, security and digital assets. As businesses navigate complex and far-reaching laws and regulations, Justine proactively creates compliance programs customized to client needs and budgets, including data mapping, vendor management, privacy and security by design, cyber risk management and mitigation, eWorkforce policies, data retention and destruction policies and implementation, consumer request workflows, cyber-awareness policies and trainings, and CCPA/CPRA readiness audits. She also provides reactive cyber services, including incident response, crisis management, privileged forensic investigations into business email compromises, data breaches and ransomware attacks, compliance with notice obligations to individuals and regulators, regulatory inquiries and investigations, and cyber litigation. Justine also handles employment litigation and counseling, as well as commercial litigation.

LinkedIn Profile: https://www.linkedin.com/in/justinephillips/
justine.phillips@dlapiper.com

About the Authors

Matt Stamper, CISA, CISM, CRISC, CDPSE, CIPP-US. As a senior security leader with both public and early-stage company experience, Matt brings a broad, multi-disciplinary knowledge of privacy and cybersecurity best practices to his clients. His diverse domain expertise spans IT service management (ITSM),  cybersecurity, cloud services, control design and assessment (Sarbanes-Oxley, HIPAA-HITECH), privacy (GDPR, CCPA, CPRA), governance, enterprise risk, and IT risk management (ERM/ITRM). Matt co-authored the *CISO Desk Reference Guide, Volumes 1 and 2* with Gary Hayslip and Bill Bonney.

Matt's diverse experience also includes sales management and individual revenue contribution, new product and service development, and international experience in both Latin America and China. Matt excels at conveying complex privacy, cybersecurity, and IT concepts to boards of directors, executive management, and professional service providers. His executive-level experience with managed services, cybersecurity, data centers, networks services, and ITSM provides a unique perspective on the fast-changing world of enterprise IT, IoT, and cloud services. Matt has served as a Security Analyst and Research Director at Gartner and in multiple CISO roles. Matt is an IT Sector Chief for the FBI InfraGard program and a member of the Board of the San Diego ISACA chapter.

Matt received a Bachelor of Arts from the University of California at San Diego, graduating Cum Laude and with Honors and Distinction in Political Science. He earned a Master of Arts in Pacific International Affairs from the University of California at San Diego and a Master of Science degree in Telecommunications sponsored by AT&T. He is fluent in Spanish and has worked in executive roles in Latin America.

LinkedIn Profile: https://www.linkedin.com/in/stamper

Made in the USA
Las Vegas, NV
25 April 2024